I HAVE CALLED YOU FRIENDS

THE STORY OF QUAKERISM
IN NORTH CAROLINA

Francis C. Anscombe

I HAVE CALLED YOU
FRIENDS

THE STORY OF QUAKERISM
IN NORTH CAROLINA

By

FRANCIS CHARLES ANSCOMBE, M.A., Ph.D., LL.B.

Professor Emeritus Salem College, N.C.
Member of the North Carolina Bar

THE CHRISTOPHER PUBLISHING HOUSE
BOSTON, U.S.A.

PRINTED IN THE UNITED STATES OF AMERICA

A MEMORIAL

TO

ELBERT RUSSELL

As one recalls Elbert Russell the appellation of Scripture necessarily comes to mind. He was "a Man of God." To thousands of students he was more than a beloved teacher — he was to them a seer; to other thousands who were inspired by his preaching he was a prophet and a priest; to multitudes of his fellow workers he was an elder brother.

Elbert Russell was born of a Quaker family in Tennessee in 1871. He made a great record at Earlham College, and received the A.B. degree in 1894, and the Master's degree the next year. He then was appointed Professor of Biblical Literature at his alma mater. Here he merited recognition, and his classes became one of the distinctive features of the college. At the Friends meeting at that institution Elbert was a preacher of eminence. He taught at Earlham 1895-1901 and then took a leave of absence to do graduate work; he returned and resumed his public service 1903-1915. From the University of Chicago he was awarded the Doctorate in 1919. He also did graduate work in the Oriental Seminary at Johns Hopkins University and was an inspiration in the ministry at the Homewood Meeting at Baltimore. In 1926 he was called to the Divinity School at Duke University as Professor of Biblical Literature. Two years later he was appointed Dean of the School of Religion, which post he filled with efficiency till 1941, when he retired and became Dean Emeritus, and continued his teaching four more years.

During much of this time he had the honor of preaching regularly in the cathedral upon the campus, and also attended innumerable college commencements and other gatherings. He was the author of several books, including *The History of Quakerism*, published in 1942. In 1939 the University of Boston conferred upon him the Degree of Doctor of Literature; in 1944 his Alma Mater (Earlham College) acknowledged his scholarship with the Degree of Doctor of Divinity; in 1951 Haverford College, in recognition of his outstanding contributions to Quakerism, awarded the Degree of Doctor of Literature. In 1942 he was the recipient of the *Mayflower Award* for the best book written that year by a North Carolinian.

ELBERT RUSSELL had few superiors in his chosen field. He was a gifted Friend; he travelled extensively both here and abroad in the ministry; he had a knowledge of the German language, and was a welcome visitor there. He was a teacher who could make the Bible understandable; he enabled his students to regard the Hebrew prophets as real persons; his classes were never dull. Perhaps he was at his best when some boy with preconceived notions as to what the Bible ought to be heckled him. Then Elbert would come to the front of his desk and endeavor with love, skill and patience to help the young man to understand. There was never any irritation or attempt to squelch the inquirer.

For his dedication to public service; for his personal interest in his students; for his patience with those who were slow in apprehending new truth; for his clarity in presenting the Gospel; for his genius in interpreting the Hebrew Scriptures; and re-animating the Prophets as they acted out their messages; for his neighborliness, and for his love and consideration in opening personally the door so that I with lesser ability and qualifications might follow in his footsteps as a teacher of Biblical Literature, for these blessings I write this book not only as a Memorial to Elbert Russell but as an evidence of my gratitude for the privilege of association with the saints.

His influence far exceeded his fellowship with the Friends, for hundreds of candidates for the ministry in other denominations, especially the Methodists "learned the way of God more perfectly" from Elbert Russell. He was a benediction to all who came to know him, and nothing finer can be said of any man. He reached four score years of age, and passed away at St. Petersburg, Florida, in 1951.

It is with sincerest love and deepest gratitude that I dedicate this work to his memory. I am only one among thousands who discovered larger implications of Truth through his teaching and ministry. Through him I became in some measure prepared for my life's work, and through him the great privilege and joy of teaching was made possible. Would to God that all the Lord's servants were prophets such as Elbert Russell.

INTRODUCTION

The test of any teacher is: "Has he acquainted his students with the subject taught?" In like manner the criterion by which any organization should be judged is: "What has it done for its adherents?" The writer has now passed the patriarchal age of four-score and has been associated with the Society of Friends all his life. The challenge must be met. What has fellowship with the Quakers accomplished? George Fox said he was not satisfied with being a Seeker he wanted to be a Finder. It is only because I am conscious of having become a Finder that this book has come into being. Fellowship with Friends has brought me into fellowship with the Eternal Christ, and that fellowship has developed for me purpose and accomplishment; it has set an objective and a pattern. My father passed on when I was twelve and circumstances compelled me to quit school and go to work, I was thirty before unexpectedly college doors opened before me. Since then I have been associated with colleges and universities for more than forty years. For this I am gratefully indebted to the Society of Friends. They have indeed been Friends, and I am conscious that the foundation of that Friendship is the "Fellowship of the Spirit."

My direction to this writing was a recommendation of Raymond Binford, the then President of Guilford College. I first examined the work of the Baltimore Association, and for that received the Master's Degree. I then wrote the record of the Friends' Freedmen's Association, and the two works together were styled: "*The Contribution of the Quakers to the Reconstruction of the Southern States*". This was presented to the University of North Carolina in part fulfilment of the requirements for the degree of Doctor of Philosophy.

I have been unusually fortunate in having among my teachers that great scholar, mystic, saint, humorist and interpreter, Dr. J. Rendel Harris, the President of the group of Quaker colleges at Woodbrooke, England. Rendel Harris was among the world's famous Oriental scholars and without question the most learned Quaker of his generation. Only those who were privileged to come into close association with him can appreciate the benediction, inspiration, and enlightenment that such a fellowship afforded.

7

At Earlham College, Indiana, I had the privilege of sitting at
the feet of Elbert Russell for five years. I shall ever regard this as
the most wonderful and blessed of experiences, and the dedication
of this work to his memory is but a poor and insignificant acknowledgement of my indebtedness to him and to Earlham. I must acknowledge also the invaluable contribution to my enlightenment
rendered by the learned and beloved Dr. Allen D. Hole, Sr., with
whom I studied Geology. His guidance was indispensable in clearing away immature and false concepts and in enabling me to be
informed of some of the processes of Nature. Without hesitation
I affirm that some such studies are necessary for a preacher if he
really desires to know the truth. Were not this work limited to
North Carolina I would name all the distinguished teachers who
helped prepare me for my life's work, for without them I could not
have made intelligent contribution to the Kingdom of God.

Then I had the great privilege of being a student of that distinguished Biblical scholar, Dr. Paul Haupt, of Johns Hopkins University. This was but one of the many doors that Elbert Russell
opened for me. Haupt was essentially an Oriental philologist, and
he knew what too few preachers realize that to expound the Hebrew Scriptures with veracity one should know something of the
life and language of the people who produced those writings. Owing to the kindness and practical interpretation of the Gospel by
the Quakers it has been my privilege to teach Biblical literature
and other subjects in several colleges and also in the University
from which I received my advanced degrees.

And now there has come into fulfilment one of the Queries
periodically read in my home town meeting: "Are Friends careful
to provide for old age, and then to retire and devote the rest of
their lives to public service?" A kind Providence has afforded me
leisure so that I might have the joy of exploring the record of the
Quakers in this State. It has been inspiring to examine the accomplishments of the many Heroes of the Faith who have labored to
establish the Kingdom of God on Earth in this fellowship. The
record, as here set forth, is incomplete, and one might use without
irreverence the words of the sacred record: If all the things were
written that the Quakers did in North Carolina I suppose that the
Guilford College Library could not contain the books that should
be written.

This then, is a slight expression of my love for the Society
of Friends and an acknowledgement of indebtedness. The book

is intended to be not merely a record of past accomplishments, but also a beacon light to show the pathway ahead.

As I have had the privilege of studying and teaching History in College and University I am under necessity to distinguish between eulogy and history. To understand any people it is necessary to view them in their historical setting. This the writer has endeavored to do.

Winston-Salem, N.C., 1958.

TABLE OF CONTENTS

LIST OF ILLUSTRATIONS

ACKNOWLEDGEMENT

In addition to the many friends who assisted me in the preparation of my former work *The Contribution of the Quakers to the Reconstruction of the Southern States,* and whom I acknowledged in that book, I am indebted to the clerks of the several monthly, quarterly and yearly meetings, to the Executive Secretary and to many pastors for information. I am greatly indebted to Dr. Clyde A. Milner, the President of Guilford College and especially to Dorothy Gilbert Thorne, the custodian of the Quaker records, without whose cooperation this work could not have been produced. My thanks are sincere to the Yearly Meeting Committee which examined the draft of this work, especially to Robert H. Frazier.

ILLUSTRATIONS

The Jacket is a reproduction of Drawings made from life by John Collins, of New Jersey, at the N.C.Y.M. of 1869. See text page 234.

The photo of the Faculty of Guilford College in Academic costume was made especially for this work by courtesy of Clyde A. Milner.

The portrait of Nathan Hunt was painted by David Clark and is in the possession of Harriett Tomlinson.

The portrait of Lewis Lyndon Hobbs was painted by Lloyd Freeman and presented by the class of 1914.

The portrait of Mary Mendenhall Hobbs was done by Louis Freeman and presented by friends and alumni in 1929.

Some of the other cuts were used by Dorothy Gilbert Thorne in her work *Guilford, a Quaker College.*

A CHRONOLOGICAL OUTLINE OF QUAKERISM IN NORTH CAROLINA

1665 Henry Phillips and wife settle in Eastern North Carolina
1672 William Edmondson's first visit to North Carolina
1672 George Fox visits North Carolina for 18 days
1676 William Edmondson's second visit
1678-1701 Quakerism the only organized religion in the colony
1680 First known Quaker record in North Carolina
    Perquimans Monthly Meeting
    Eastern Quarterly Meeting
    "General Meeting" in Perquimans Quarter
1681 Fox advised the setting up of a General Meeting
1694-97 John Archdale a Quaker Governor of North Carolina
1698 North Carolina Yearly Meeting established;
    Quarterly Meeting records were made at the home of Henry White, April 4, 1698;
    Yearly Meeting held at the home of Francis Toms, the elder.
1672-1725 Golden Age of Quakerism in North Carolina; the council, Assembly, Public officials, general public in sympathy with Friends
1701 The First Vestry Act — beginning of official opposition
1695-1759 Eastern Quarterly Meeting the only one in North Carolina
1708 Quarterly Meeting held at Little River
1708 Perquimans Monthly Meeting — Thomas Pearce, clerk
1708 First Yearly Meeting of which records exist
1708 Yearly Meeting decided that too many Friends attended; thought only twelve should attend, and they named the twelve.*

---

* This evidently refers to business meetings. The minute reads "Whereas this meeting find it all ill-convenience in having too many Friends in our yearly meeting of business it is our judgment that our yearly meeting consist of twelve men sole chosen, whose names are underwritten, beside the Inspector belonging to our meeting, with the Friends of the ministry, viz., Francis Toms, William Newby, Thomas Pearce, John Barrow, Timothy Clare, Samuel Nichols, Emanuel Low, James Davis, John Hawkins, Henry Keeton, Edward Maye, Augustine Scarsborough. Signed: Wm. Everegin, clerk." This is believed to have been a committee to deal with accusations. The parties were reconciled, and nothing is mentionel concerning the matter in later minutes, *Friends Review*, 1860-61.

1709   Yearly Meeting "of much discord"
1709   Quakers were about one tenth of the population of Eastern Carolina.
         Eastern Quarter had two monthly meetings — Little River (including Pasquotank) and Perquimans.
1740-76   Great Quaker invasion of the Piedmont of North Carolina by families of Friends from Pennsylvania, Virginia, Rhode Island, Maryland, Nantucket Island and Eastern North Carolina.
1751   Cane Creek Monthly Meeting established
1751   New Garden Meeting for Worship allowed
1753   Deep River Meeting allowed
1754   New Garden Monthly Meeting set up by Cane Creek, with forty families attending
1754   Rich Square Monthly Meeting set up by Cane Creek Meeting
1754   Rocky River Meeting for Worship established
1755   Discipline of 1704 revised
1756   Center Meeting for Worship
1759   Western Quarterly Meeting established
1759   Western Quarterly Meeting held alternately at Cane Creek and New Garden
1771-75   Many Friends from Nantucket moved to New Garden
1773   Center Monthly Meeting allowed
1773   Springfield Meeting allowed
1776   Yearly Meeting concerned over freeing of slaves
1781   New Garden Friends participate in the funerals at the local graveyard of the burial of British and Revolutionary troops who died after the Battle of Guilford Court House, March 15th, 1781
1776-83   Revolutionary War.   Friends torn between loyalty to America and their peace testimony.   Many references in Yearly Meeting minutes to oaths of allegiance, tithes and taxes
1778   Deep River Monthly Meeting set up
1783   Y. M. objects to Friends operating and frequenting saloons
1783   Springfield Friends build log meeting house
1784   Lost Creek Settlement in Tennessee commenced
1787   New Garden Quarterly Meeting established
         Many references in N.C. Y.M. Minutes of this period in regard to oaths of allegiance, payment of tithes and taxes.
1790   Springfield Monthly Meeting set up

1791   First Y. M. at New Garden
1794   Piney Woods Meeting
1760-1800   Beginning of a vast migration of Friends from North Carolina into South Carolina, Georgia, Western North Carolina, Tennessee, Ohio, Indiana, Illinois, Iowa. The movements southward did not long continue.
1800-60   Almost continuous and extensive mass movement of Friends and others from the Slave States to Free Territory north of the Ohio River. Dozens of Friends communities stripped and meetings laid down.
1791   Bush River Quarterly Meeting at Newbury, S. C. set up
1812   Above meeting laid down as members moved to Ohio
1791-1883   Yearly Meeting held alternately at New Garden or in Eastern Quarter
1802   Lost Creek Q. M. in Tennessee; 10 local meetings
1803   Above Meeting "laid down because of strife."
1818   Deep River Quarterly Meeting established
1819   Southern Quarterly Meeting established
1830-60   N.C. Y.M. concerned about slavery
1830-37   Y.M. considers establishment of New Garden Boarding School
1837   New Garden Boarding School established
1837-38   Joseph John Gurney, of England, visits N.C. Y.M. encouraged Friends to read Scriptures and to become evangelistic. Very great influence.
1850-66   Addison Coffin active in persuading Friends to go West
1860-63   N.C.Y.M. had 1,030 members over 18 years of age.
1860-65   Civil War. Friends suffered as Conscientious Objectors, many families impoverished; marauders wrecked estates; bare subsistence for war survivors; Friends shared in the universal ruin; meeting houses and school buildings damaged and defiled; school bonds converted into Confederate currency which became worthless; families divided; Quakers ostracized.
1870   About 1,000 adult members of Friends left in North Carolina
1860-70   New Garden Boarding School continued operations virtually upon a subsistence basis
1864-91   Francis T. King and the Baltimore Association did much to restore the Yearly Meeting, the Boarding School; Meeting Houses were rebuilt; monthly meeting schools restored; training schools for teachers; a model farm; libraries restored; financial help rendered

1860-80   Joseph Moore and Allen Jay from Indiana rendered much assistance

1865   Philadelphia Friends Freedmens Association active in N. C.

1870   Friendsville Meeting in Tennessee transferred to Wilmington Yearly Meeting

1874   The Great Revival among Quakers in North Carolina commences.   Allen Jay and Nereus Mendenhall very active

1881   N.C. Y.M. gives its Meeting House to New Garden Boarding School

1881-92   Friends conduct a Boarding School for Cherokee Indian children in western North Carolina.

1883   N.C. Friends conducting 42 schools with 1,300 non-Friend children attending — aided by Baltimore Association

1883   Springfield Monthly Meeting requests Deep River Quarterly Meeting to establish a meeting at High Point.

1883   High Point Meeting set up.

1883-1904   N.C. Y.M. meets at High Point.

1885   High Point Preparative Meeting

1888   New Garden Boarding School becomes Guilford College

1889   Yadkin Valley Quarterly Meeting established

1892   High Point Monthly Meeting — J. Robert Parker, clerk

1898   Surry Quarterly Meeting established

1902   Five Years Meeting organized

1904   N.C. Y.M. adopts Uniform Discipline

1904   Conservative Friends withdraw from Y.M. at New Garden; form separate congregation attached to the Ohio Conservative Yearly Meeting

1904   N.C. Y.M. informally adopts the pastoral system

1917   American Friends Service Committee receives cooperation from N.C. Y.M.

1920   First World Friends Conference in London; N.C. Y.M. had 16 official delegates

1937   Second World Friends Conference at Haverford and Swarthmore Colleges; N.C. Y.M. had 62 official delegates

1952   Third World Friends Conference, Oxford, England; N.C. Y.M. had 49 representatives

1949   Quaker Lake (20 miles from High Point) purchased by the Yearly Meeting

1953   International Young Friends Conference at Guilford College

1955   Philadelphia Friends (Orthodox and Hicksite) reunite after 128 years separation

1955   New York Friends also re-united.

1955 Canadian Friends (Orthodox, Hicksite and Conservative) unite

1955 High Point Friends build new meeting house near site of the old Yearly Meeting House

1957 Asheboro Street (Greensboro) Friends build a new meeting house on the Friendly Road.

Winston Salem Friends and New Garden Friends prepare to add educational buildings to their existing premises.

NOTE

Dates based largely upon a Booklet "*The Society of Friends in North Carolina, 1672-1953* (some important *Dates and Events*) published by Guilford College; also *MSS* by Alpheus Briggs; also information from works by Stephen B. Weeks; also Thorne, D. G. *First Friends at New Garden.* Discrepancies in old sources are inevitable.

PREFACE

This is the story of a Protestant denomination which developed out of the religious experience of a man of very limited education who lived in England in the seventeenth century. With the exception of pious parents he had no early advantages. For several years in his teens he was disconsolate, seeking wherever he could for an adequate meaning and purpose in life. He gave himself to prayer and Bible study and at length, in common with many Mystics, an Inward Voice assured him that "Christ could speak to his condition." Immediately he was transformed, and he said "he was brought into that condition in which Adam was before his fall." He became the most powerful preacher of his generation, and everywhere he went "multitudes were convinced," and the Society of Friends (commonly called Quakers) was born.

George Fox, for that was his name, came to North Carolina in 1672 and remained but eighteen days, yet lighted a fire which burns till this day. His interpretation of the Gospel was that one could find peace, power and purpose by following the Christ (the Inward Light, or the Inward Voice).

A mighty revival occurred and thousands in Eastern Carolina became members of the Society. For nearly fifty years the Quakers were the dominant religious body in the colony. Then opposition set in and gradually the character of the body was changed, their missionary and proselytizing zeal was lost; they became Quietists, and through supposing they had abandoned all forms in religion they became extreme formalists, and so fundamentally different from the rest of the people, that the Society almost passed out of existence in this State. Then came a spirit of Revival "like a hurricane" and "the dry bones" came to life again.

They "shook off the grave clothes which had bound them" and the visible habiliments of the historic Quaker, and adopted gradually some of the practices of other Protestant bodies. It was the beginning of a complete metamorphosis, and the process of rejuvenation is still proceeding.

The Quakers interpret the Gospel not in terms of theology, ritual and creeds, but in a sensible, practical, natural belief that

27

the Kingdom of Heaven can be established on earth. They have a distinct and vital message for mankind.

Throughout the Quaker world there is now the manifestation of new spiritual power. The Quaker colleges are responding to the necessity of preparing adequately the future ministers and leaders of the Society.

This, then is an attempt to tell the story of a religious body in North Carolina, which in spite of many peculiarities produced citizens of the highest order, and which presents a unique interpretation of the mission and message of Jesus Christ.

NOTE

Asterisks in the text refer to footnotes at the bottom of the page.
Superior figures 1, 2, 3, etc. in the text refer to notes at the back of the book and are numbered by chapter.

GEORGE FOX

I Have Called You Friends

CHAPTER ONE

ON THIS ROCK I WILL BUILD MY CHURCH

THE ENGLISH BACKGROUND. As there can be no fruit apart from a root and as American Quakerism was rooted in English soil it is necessary to explain briefly the circumstances which produced George Fox and the early Quakers. Fully to comprehend the situation one should have a knowledge of European conditions at that time such for instance as may be obtained in reading Draper's *History of the Intellectual Development of Europe.* All that is necessary to refer to here is the religious background. During the Middle Ages the Catholic Church was the only ecclesiastical system permitted. John Wycliffe became "the morning star of the Protestant Reformation" in the XIVth century, and gave England the first Bible in the native tongue. A century later William Tyndale produced the first Scriptures printed in English. This was followed by several other translations, and people crowded into the churches to listen to a person who was able to read. In the XVIth century Henry VIII broke from the Roman Church for personal and political reasons and became the Head of the Church in England, although little if any change was made officially in the belief and practice of the Established Church.

During the brief reign of Edward VI the Reformation began to take form, but Mary Tudor (1553-58) restored Catholicism and hundreds of Protestants were burned at the stake, including such great churchmen and scholars as Bonner, Cranmer, Latimer and Ridley. Elizabeth, who succeeded her half-sister, adroitly avoided siding with either the Catholics or the Protestants. Her successor, James I, precipitated a religious war between England and Scotland, but the most important event of his period was the Hampton Court Conference, which in 1611 authorized an English translation of the Holy Scriptures, which may rightly be regarded as one of the outstanding events in human history.

By this time the Renaissance and the Protestant Reformation

had taken root and Parliament was objecting to the Absolutism of
the Stuarts. The land was ready for the throwing off the shackles
which had held most of the people in poverty, superstition and
ignorance. The so-called Age of Faith (in reality the Age of Credulity) was about to pass and the possibility of having a printed
Bible in the vernacular led thousands to acquire the ability to read,
and to think for themselves.

Erasmus had revived the knowledge of the Greek Testament;
John Knox had introduced Calvinism into Scotland; Presbyterianism spread into England; the Baptists became numerous; but of
greater significance was the development of Puritanism. This had
many phases, but it may be simplified as a protest against the dog-
mas of ecclesiasticism and emphasis upon ritual as the essence of
religion. That Puritanism went to the extremes in requiring simplicity in dress, speech and deportment none can deny, but most
historians will agree that the Puritan Revolt in England was constructive while the Revolution in France was destructive.

At the time of the birth of George Fox England was in a state
of religious ferment, and the political situation can not be discussed
without reference to religious parties. During Fox's life he saw the
government at various times under the influence of Episcopalians,
Puritans, Presbyterians, and Catholics. He was contemporary with
the Bishops' Wars, 1640; the first Civil War, 1642-46; the second
Civil War, 1648; the execution of Charles I, 1649; the Commonwealth under Cromwell, 1649-1658; the deposition of James II,
1688.

To understand Fox the disturbed conditions must be kept in
mind. Practically none of what we call "the instrumentalities of
civilization" existed at that time. There were no public elementary
schools, no libraries, no sanitation, no hospitals, no machine made
goods, no hard surface roads; few newspapers. The scientific spirit
had not yet arrived, so the common notions of the masses were
not dictated by reason.

GEORGE FOX, born in 1624 at Fenny Drayton, England, the founder
of the Society of Friends (commonly called Quakers), was an extraordinary man, one of whom it was said "he was of God's own
making, and like none other." His father, a weaver and a devout
Puritan, was known as "Righteous Christer" and his mother, Mary
Lago, "came of the stock of the martyrs." George was pious and
serious from childhood, and would not stay in the company of
youths who planned mischief. He received but little schooling
and in early life was apprenticed to a shoemaker and wool merchant.

Much of his time was spent on the hills as a shepherd and he became robust and strong. It became noticed that he frequently used the word "verily", and if he committed himself in that way "there was no changing him."

At his time there was a group of people known as "The Seekers." Fox associated with them, for he was conscious that he was seeking something which "would make him adequate for all circumstances and occasions." He was not satisfied to be a Seeker; he wanted to be a Finder. In his search he went long distances to listen to preachers whom he heard presented the truth. He often found them to be "empty casks" or "lumps of earth." He learned to study the Scriptures, and in some almost unaccountable way perceived spiritual truths in the Bible that were not generally recognized at that time. In fact, one may affirm that in general George Fox by reason of "the openings" he received had a somewhat similar manner of interpreting the Holy Scriptures that learned scholars who are versed in the literary-historical-critical method exercise today. In this respect he was over two centuries ahead of the theologians. So well did he know the Scriptures, that it was said "If the Bible were lost it could be made up again out of George's head."

When about nineteen Fox became so uneasy in spirit that like Abraham of old "he went out not knowing whither he went" but he knew why he went, as also did the ancient Hebrew patriarch. He went to find God and truth and inward peace and constant fortitude. He despaired of learning it from the teaching of men. He wrote in his *Journal:*

> When all my hopes of men were gone, so that I had nothing outward to help me, nor could I tell what to do, then I heard a voice which said 'There is One, even Jesus Christ, that can speak to thy condition' . . . And when I heard it my heart did leap for joy . . . and all Nature gave forth a new smell . . . and I was in that condition in which Adam was before his fall."[1]

He became a man full of fire and grace. No longer was he filled with gloom. The Seeker had become a Finder. He no longer needed to listen to preachers — he became the most powerful preacher of his day. Henceforth he placed the utmost importance upon what he called "the Voice Within." Fox had at first no intention of organizing a new sect, for he attended religious services and if not satisfied with what the preacher said he would stand upon a bench and preach the truth as he saw it. This procedure was not then contrary to law or custom, and Fox should not be judged by present canons of behaviour.

There can be but one explanation for the career of Fox, and it is the same as that of the early disciples of the Christ. According to some, Fox "was an unlearned and ignorant man" yet like them "he was filled with the Holy Spirit." He therefore became the possessor of physical endurance, sagacity and spiritual insight far transcending his contemporaries.

He was the product of his age. He remained all his life a Puritan. The Quakers did not adopt any peculiar dress or custom, they simply did not change styles to follow fashion. Friends received their views of music, amusements and general behaviour from the Puritans. Without ordination Fox became a preacher. According to a very ancient custom in England Fox preached at first out-of-doors and only gradually did regular meetings become established.*

It must further be said that the man fitted the age. There was a deep spiritual hunger; the people responded to the message of one who knew that he possessed the peace and power of God within. He was not just a preacher who denounced evil; his marvellous success lay in the fact that he had a Living Message and offered peace in a much troubled world. He stressed the teaching that "one could find God within;" that the Holy Spirit had been poured forth at Pentecost; that the Holy Spirit would lead into Truth; that all might receive the Holy Spirit in fullness; that there was "a Seed of God in everyone which would grow if cultivated;" there was "a Light which lighteth every man coming into the world;" "the Kingdom of God is within." The Christ, for Fox, was not a historic figure to be identified solely with Jesus of Nazareth; the Christ was the Life of God, pure Spirit, eternal, the source of all inspiration and truth and grace. The Christ could be found within. The Christ was the Spirit; the Christ was "that of God" that we might know. "They drank of that Spiritual Rock that followed them, and that Spiritual Rock was Christ."[2]

It was the Christ within that inspired the prophets.

And what followed from the major premise? A whole host of social reforms. Women should no longer be regarded as chattels, for they too were potential children of God, and could receive daily guidance; inhumane punishments and cruel practices were wrong because they made it hard or impossible for such afflicted persons to listen to and obey the Voice within. Any authority

---

* Especially since the rise of Methodism in the next century there have been thousands of "local preachers" who without remuneration walk many miles and preach in a rural church or in the village street.

which interfered with human freedom was contrary to Truth, because men everywhere should be encouraged to follow the Truth as Truth was revealed to them.

It was a new teaching. It divorced religion from "steeple-houses," as Fox dubbed church buildings; it set men free from priestism and ceremonies and creeds. Fox found fertile soil. England was ready for his message. By the hundreds people flocked to him, and without planning Meetings for Worship were established.

Fox did not monopolize the preaching. On occasions when multitudes were gathered he spoke no word. He did not want people to run after him; he encouraged them to worship in silence and allow the "Word Within" to convey the Will of God to each individual. Elbert Russell says: "Fox and his followers set themselves the revolutionary and complex task of revising the whole life of a half-pagan society in conformity with the mind and power of Christ as revealed within — a task vastly more radical than the purifying of the ecclesiastical and moral life proposed by the Puritans."[3]

This is a statement worthy of attention. It reminds one of the word of Jeremiah: "Behold, the days are coming, saith the Lord, when I will make a new covenant . . . not like the covenant that I made with their fathers . . . this is the covenant . . . I will put my law within them, and I will write it upon their hearts, and they shall be my people . . . for they shall all know me, from the least of them to the greatest."[4] It sought to impose no authority over the believer. It was an appeal to conscience, but it was expressed in new terms. It was a much needed message in an age characterized by bigotry and by ecclesiastical authority. It is not the whole of the Gospel, and informed persons today recognize the limitation of the message Fox preached, but who dare say that the Quaker doctrine as conceived by Fox was not an approximation of "the Kingdom of Heaven within". Socrates said that the Spirit within "warned him of evil," and Jesus said "the Spirit will lead into Truth." Here we have a concept of religion which throws upon every individual the obligation to seek the Truth, refrain from evil and do good. Who shall say that such religion is not of more worth to individuals and to society than the most elaborate ceremonies and the most comprehensive creeds.

Fox insisted upon absolute honesty, integrity, truthfulness, sincerity, simplicity and self-control. He was unafraid in denouncing wrong doers, no matter their authority or station. William Penn testified that he had known Fox "under all manner of circumstances; he had known him at home and he had known him abroad; he had known him among friends and among enemies; he had known him when he had his needs well supplied and when he fared ill; he had known him in health and in sickness; but he had never known him when he was not equal to all circumstances and occasions."

As this writing is concerned with Quakerism in North Carolina, and as there are numerous works dealing with Quakerism in England and elsewhere, it is sufficient here to state that Fox travelled extensively throughout England and other places; that he gained converts among the high and the lowly; that he brought into being a religious organization which has profoundly influenced human society for over three centuries.

He took his place among the mystics, among those saints who motivated their lives upon the assumption that God would reveal Truth to them directly without conscious sensory experience. Fox was, however, a practical mystic, though it cannot be denied that he had ecstatic experiences, but such were common to saints at that age. He was in many ways a very practical person. Not only was he a convincing preacher, he was an organizer, reformer, traveller, writer; and he possessed a mind which was receptive to Truth in what we would now call the natural sciences. He was also a great sufferer, for he endured parts of fourteen years in loathsome prisons. He was arrested for refusing to take an oath of loyalty, for not doffing his hat to "superiors," for contradicting the clergy, for meeting for worship in forbidden places, for preaching in the streets and at fairs and markets, for denying the doctrines of the established church. He was accused of "blasphemy, of being a heretic and a seducer," and of treason because he would not bear arms. He was first imprisoned at Nottingham, in 1649; the year after he began his public ministry. He was then imprisoned at Derby, 1650-1651; Carlisle, 1653; Launceston, 1755-56; Lancaster, 1660; Leicester, 1662; Scarborough, 1663-66; Worcester, 1673-75. This last was after his return from America. He was beaten severely in the streets, dragged around and stoned. At times he was alone and others were afraid to aid him, so "that he was often denied lodging . . . and obliged to sleep in the fields."[5] His biographers say that the conditions of English prisons at that time were so filthy that no full description can be published. Fox said "they were nasty, dirty, stinking holes." Little provision was made for food and necessities, and prisoners were dependent upon their friends outside; prison fever was common.

CHAPTER TWO

GREET THE FRIENDS BY NAME

THE BELIEFS OF THE QUAKERS. AS TO GOD. Friends, without question, hold the main tenets of Protestant theology. Concerning faith in God, they hold in common with all monotheists that there is but One Creator, and He is to be regarded as a Personal Spirit, the only source of Creative Energy, including mental and moral attributes. They have carefully refrained from formulating creeds because they believe no language is adequate. They believe that the Presence of God can be a spiritual experience, and that God being Spirit it follows that spiritual realities must be spiritually perceived and experienced.

AS TO CHRIST. Without equivocation they regard Jesus of Nazareth as the promised Messiah, the Son of God, the Saviour of the World, the unique Revealer of the Father. They accept the Scriptures as truly stating that He gave Himself for our sins; that He died and rose again. They refrain from being dogmatic as to the nature of the Resurrection. It is an insoluble mystery.

CONCERNING THE HOLY SPIRIT there is much to say. Friends attach more importance to this doctrine than does any other denomination. It is the essence of Quakerism. It can be simply stated. God is Spirit; God is Holy. The Holy Spirit is the manifestation of the Divine activity. Creation is attributed to the Spirit; "the Spirit of God moved over the face of the waters."[1] Scores of times the messages of the prophets are attributed to the Spirit, in fact the Spirit of God is the central theme of the Holy Scriptures, and the whole would fall to pieces and be meaningless apart from the assumption that human beings could become conscious of the Divine Presence. The Spirit is the source of power of righteous persons. The Christhood of Jesus is attributed to the Holy Spirit. Friends acknowledge that the Christ was conceived of the Spirit, baptized with the Spirit, filled with the Spirit, led of the Spirit, empowered by the Spirit, and that his words were "Spirit and Life."[2] Only in the Spirit can God be truly worshipped.[3] It is further characteristic of Friends that they preached and believed that all men needed to be "born of the Spirit.[4] They emphasized a truth that many denominations ignore that Peter on the Day of Pentecost assured his hearers that "the Spirit was to be poured out upon all flesh"[5] and that all might receive the Holy Spirit. Friends conceived the Holy Spirit as the Eternal Creative Activity of God, and that throughout all time in ever increasing degree those who would could receive this greatest of gifts which the Heavenly Father was anxious to give to those who asked Him.[6] It therefore was a profound conviction of early Friends that the very secret of Christian experience was the consciousness that the Holy Spirit dominated one's personality. God, therefore, was not some Majestic unapproachable Sovereign in the skies but an eternal Source of Vitality within. God was transcendant, but He was also imminent.

THE HOLY SCRIPTURES.   Concerning the Holy Scriptures Friends were perhaps unique.   They were careful to notice that the term "the Word of God" is used in the Scriptures in several senses.   "By the Word of the Lord were the Heavens made."[7]   Scores of times in the Old Testament we read "the Word of the Lord came unto" such and such a prophet.   The Gospel is the Word.[8]   Christ was "the Word made flesh.[9]   Christ's name was "the Word of God."[10] Christ referred frequently to the Old Testament writings as "the Scriptures."[11]   Friends believed that the Word of God is to be found in the Scriptures, but that it was not the writings which were inspired, but the writers, for: "holy men of old wrote as they were moved of the Holy Spirit.[12]   This distinction was of importance, because it implied that God was anxious to speak to his children today; that Revelation was continuous and progressive; that God's Word was not ended when the Canon of the Scriptures was determined at the Council of Jamnia in A.D. 118.   As Pastor John Robinson said to the Puritans when they were leaving Holland for America on the *Speedwell* in 1620: "God has yet more light and truth to break forth from his Holy Word."

Friends valued the Holy Scriptures, yet had perception enough to observe that some statements expressed the common concepts held by past generations concerning cosmology which science has outmoded.   There were also the eternal verities, which should be regarded as revelations of Truth.   They also believed that God had spoken to other peoples in addition to the ancient Hebrews, and that there had been a universal seeking after God. Some truth was to be found in the writings of the Greek and Roman philosophers and the ancient Orientals.

THE HEBREW PROPHETS. Friends were among the first to recognize that the Hebrew prophets were preachers, reformers, revivalists and sometimes poets and princes and that their messages were primarily for their contemporaries. They were forth-tellers rather than fore-tellers; they were men with messages, and they were conscious that they spake in the name of God. If one who loves the Bible will take the pains to learn the circumstances existing at the time of the various writings, one will find that the writings become meaningful as a whole, and the writers will become living characters. It is grossly improper and wrong to tear passages out of their connection. Friends were among the first fearlessly to accept the so-called historical interpretation of the Scriptures.

MEETINGS FOR WORSHIP. Concerning their gatherings. They did not call their assemblies "church services." They met primarily for worship. This was both an individual and a corporate affair. At first the men and women sat upon different sides of the meeting house. There are varying explanations for this custom, but the probability is that the men sat nearer the door to protect the women from molestation if and when soldiers or officers came to arrest the worshippers who were meeting contrary to law.

Worship meant meditation, contemplation, prayer, a review of the past week and the search for Divine assistance for present and future obligations. Friends did not gather to "conduct a service." There was no parson, no ritual, no prescribed order of service, no music and no singing. There was much of silence, but it was not a dead silence, it was a period of vital communion with the Eternal. There was liberty for any "concerned" Friend to deliver a message. It must not be a long sermon, or a display of oratory. The speaker should express himself as briefly as possible, and sit down, and give the Holy Spirit an opportunity to apply the message to the hearers. Usually others would speak briefly along the same line. Women as well as men were at liberty to speak or offer prayer. For many years the men wore their hats except in time of prayer, when the congregation stood. It is said that the origin of this was that the churches in medieval times were unheated and so men kept their hats on for protection. The Quakers did not originate the custom.

CONCERNING THE SACRAMENTS. Church historians are aware that the stormiest and most disruptive movements in the history of Christendom have arisen concerning the proper administration

of the Sacraments.   No one can pretend that any denomination
at this time carries them out as they were in Apostolic times.
Quakers instinctively sensed that ceremonies tend to become
regarded as substitutes for realities.   Friends believed Christ
Himself was "the Bread of Life," and that the saying of Jesus
"he that eateth Me shall live by Me,"[13] was a poetic expression
of a great spiritual reality, and that the periodic partaking of
little bits of bread could be no substitute for a daily experience
of the vitalizing power of the Indwelling Christ.   Similarly with
baptism.   Sprinkling, pouring or immersing were outward per-
formances affecting the body.   Friends held that the true baptism
was that of the Holy Spirit.   It has often been remarked that if
one has been baptized in water it would not be known unless
some one said so, but if a person has really been baptized with
the Holy Spirit there would be no need to say so — it would be
manifest for the rest of that person's life.   It is therefore right
to say that Friends do believe in Baptism and in the Holy Communion, but they desire the reality and not the symbol.

My own view of the Holy Communion is as follows.   Jesus
was a Jew; his disciples were Jews; the Passover was the most
important feast in the Jewish religious calendar; the Scriptures
say Jesus observed the Passover.[14]   The partaking of bread and
wine was an integral part of the feast (and still is with the Jews);
when Jesus passed the bread and wine he knew that the disciples,
as Jews, would continue to celebrate the feast, and he said: "In
future when you do this, do it in remembrance of ME, and not
in remembrance of the Exodus from Egypt."   Ask yourself the
question.   If the Jews had since that fateful night observed the
Passover in memory of Jesus, the Messiah, would it not have
meant far more to the Christian Church throughout the ages and
would not the history of the Jewish people and all mankind have
been different.   Can we imagine a more fitting request for Jesus
to have made to his Jewish disciples and a more appropriate
command to his own nation.

THE MEANING OF SALVATION.   The view of the Quakers was essentially different from that of other denominations.   They believed one needed saving now from everything that would spoil
one's life.   The Christ Within was the guarantee of Salvation.
They did not regard faith in Jesus as a sort of passport to Heaven
after death.   Many regarded the term Eternal Life as implying
a New Life here and now, a Life over which time and circum-

stances had no significance. A good deal of scholarship could be devoted to the real meaning of such terms as "Eternal Life," "Everlasting Life" and the "Kingdom of Heaven." Many Friends, particularly those with advanced education, tend to give to these terms poetic and spiritual implications rather than the assurance of future continuous existence.

THE KINGDOM OF GOD. Friends believe that the Kingdom of God can be established in any life, any home, any business, any political organization and among the nations of men any time that a sufficient number of persons determine it shall be, and follow the leading of the Spirit to accomplish it. Friends do not believe that the Almighty has some time-tables; that the Kingdom of God will ultimately be set up by Divine fiat, and wickedness obliterated by miraculous interposition. All that is needed to correct every wrong and abolish every social injustice is Divine Guidance through the Holy Spirit. Any difference whether in the family or in international affairs can be settled properly, permanently and satisfactorily if the parties concerned would meet together in the Spirit of the Lord Jesus Christ. This is the profound conviction of the Quakers.

THE PRIESTHOOD OF ALL BELIEVERS. Friends believe that the Mosaic priesthood came to an end with Christ. He was the Great High Priest; He also was the One and Only Eternal Sacrifice. All others were mere types. He was the Reality. "He offered Himself as a Lamb without spot or blemish."[15] "On Him was laid the iniquity of us all."[16] The Old Dispensation came to an end in Him. Since then through Faith in Him as the Lamb of God and the Saviour of the World all believers may have boldness to approach the Eternal without any intermediary priest or sacrifice. In Christ all the promises of God are "yea and amen." All believers may be priests,[17] more than that "they are Children of God, and fellow heirs with Christ."[18]

Friends deny the right of priests or parsons to stand between a seeker and the Heavenly Father. Christ is the Only Way. Friends denied the authority of a man to say to a couple "I pronounce you man and wife." They took each other in marriage with the consent of the meeting in the presence of the congregation, and in the Name of God. Friends utterly repudiate the authority of any man to exercise personal authority in spiritual matters. We deny the right of any organization to prescribe what another shall believe. We deny the Sacraments as essential to

Salvation. Friends deny the necessity of ordination as a requisite to preaching the Gospel. We acknowledge the necessity and validity of education, but deny the necessity of a theological education as a requisite for a witness to the Truth.

CONSTRUCTIVE CITIZENSHIP. It was an axiom among Friends that a member should make some useful contribution to human society. They would not admit to membership any one whose occupation and means of livelihood was tainted with suspicion, nor one connected with the theatre, or "places of unwholesome diversion," nor one who gained wealth at the expense of others. It was also their philosophy that one should acquire a "competency" by the time he was 55 or 60, and then retire and devote himself to public service. This was an integral part of their concept of religion and of citizenship. The present practice of living on the installment plan and beyond one's income and then retiring upon pensions provided by the government would have been abhorrent to early Quakers. They used to say "every tub should stand on its own bottom." To provide for one's family and one's own future was part of the Gospel the Quakers practiced. They cared for their own impoverished, and allowed none to be sent to "the poor house."

CONCERNING CREEDS. As to creeds. Friends believed that Truth was cumulative and progressive. God and Christ were beyond definitions, because definitions limit. Friends also perceived that writers of the Scriptures and preachers of previous generations necessarily expressed themselves in terms of the concepts of the day, which might become uncouth in a later time. Friends, therefore, exercised charity, and permitted members to possess their own view upon matters outside objective demonstration. They would say to a sincere person "Come with us and help us to find more perfect Truth." Thus, in early days especially in London Yearly Meeting and Philadelphia Yearly Meeting, some Friends interpreted Scripture literally and others figuratively and poetically. These views are further justified by a knowledge of the circumstances under which the creeds were formulated. Some are the outcome of the worst of political squabbling and are shot through with Greek metaphysics and are as far removed from the words and Spirit of Jesus Christ as could be imagined.

AS TO SINCERITY AND SIMPLICITY. Coming into the presence of the Eternal Mystery, which we in confidence call "Heavenly Father," in fellowship with others is the sublimest function of human beings. It is our own especial prerogative. The reality of the Unseen and the presentation to consciousness of the Holiness of the Eternal and of the Saviour brings the worshipper into a deep sense of his own unworthiness and creates a longing for inward purity. There can be no pride, no sense of superiority, no sham or pretense as the Image of the Invisible God appears before the soul. Worship is an occasion to face the Eternal Realities and to become conscious of one's imperfections and deficiencies. Quaker worship is divested of symbolism; outward aids detract and tend to divert attention to the emblem rather than to the eternal spiritual reality. Quakers, probably, are less dependent upon objective devices than other worshippers. Sincerity has been a characteristic of Friends ever since George Fox customarily said "verily." A true appreciation of the marvellously balanced character of our Lord is calculated to strip any sincere worshipper of pride, arrogance, conceit, ostentation and self-righteousness. In our manner of living Friends avoid unnecessary adornments of dress and the public display of jewels. Mere possessions do not constitute personal worth, and the Society has evaluated persons for what they are rather than what they own. No one who is sensitive to poverty and misery can thoughtlessly flaunt evidences of great wealth. Friends have discarded "the plain clothes," yet we cannot indulge with "the world" in those exhibitions of riches which are likely to inflate with pride and arrogance the wearer, and distress the "have-nots" who witness such spectacles.

It is contrary to Friends views to speak of clergy and laity; no one has more right to be styled "reverend" than another. The obligation to be holy rests equally upon all. Friends are a fellowship, a Society, a Household of Faith, and the Holy Spirit can reveal His will for the group to any member. The parts constitute the whole, and no member is supreme over the others. It is this Fellowship of Saints which is one of the characteristics of the body. The term Society of Friends has especial connotation. There is but one Church — the Church of the Lord Jesus Christ, and it is an affront to style any body of worshippers such and such a "church."

CHAPTER THREE

LET ALL THINGS BE DONE DECENTLY AND IN ORDER

CHRIST THE HEAD OF THE CHURCH. No person has ever been recognized as the Head of the Society of Friends. George Fox received no title, and was given no office or distinction. Christ is the Head of the Church, and all believers are members of His Body. No person has authority among Friends. In all probability they are the only religious body whose business meetings are open to all members, and where there are no secret discussions or secret financial reports.

Fox had no intention of founding a new sect, neither did any of his early associates. At first the little group of preachers and believers was known as "Publishers of Truth;" later they were styled "Children of Light;" but in course of time the name "the Religious Society of Friends" was adopted as the official title. It is believed that George Fox in 1668 suggested the outline of the organization to his closest friends. It is certain that there was some conversation and that he was not dictatorial, though he did possess the gift of organization, which is an essential to a great leader.

Among the earliest records are reports of "Second Day Morning Meetings." This was primarily a gathering of Friends who were travelling in the Ministry, to arrange schedules, to receive reports concerning gatherings, and to provide ways and means. Later it became a depository of writings in favor of Friends' views and also critical of their views. This body was consulted by groups throughout the country concerning future missionary activities. Ministers from all parts attended the "Second Day Morning Meeting" which was usually held in London.

THE MEETING FOR SUFFERINGS. Out of these informal gatherings developed the Meeting for Sufferings. Under the tempestuous times in which Quakerism arose it was common for Friends to be arrested upon charges of violating the Test Act, the Corporation Act, the Conventicle Acts, the Five Mile Act, for refusing to doff the hat, for meeting at forbidden places. Families were thus left in need, and it became the custom to report the circumstances to the committee in London. The Meeting for Sufferings would provide clothing, food, medical care and money for Friends so imprisoned, and would see that the needs of the family were attended to. They were also active in presenting appeals. In course of time this body became the legal representative of the Society. North Carolina Friends had a Meeting for Sufferings for many years, but in recent times upon the American continent the body became known as the Representative Meeting. Today the Permanent Board of the Five Years Meeting may be regarded as the descendant of the Meeting for Sufferings.

THE CLERK. At all meetings for business a clerk presides. He is in no way an authority, and a nominating committee may recommend a new person if it is considered desirable. The nominating committee is named annually "in the face of the meeting." The clerk arranges the agenda, recognizes the speakers, who usually rise and say: "clerk, please," before making remarks. It is the function of the clerk to preserve harmony. If it becomes evident that there is no prospect of unanimity, the clerk will rise and suggest that further consideration be given and the matter brought up again at the next meeting. No vote is ever taken. The clerk is supposed to respect the opinion of "weighty Friends," and is a person familiar with the faith and practice of the Society, and his judgment is respected and seldom challenged. The "minute" he prepares represents the "mind of the meeting." He is now assisted by recording, reading and announcing clerks.

PREPARATIVE MEETINGS. At first small meetings were known as "preparative meetings," or "allowed meetings." These were subordinate gatherings and had no authority to act independently. They met as a business group for a few moments after the period of worship and named representatives to the forthcoming monthly meeting held at some other locality. Few such subordinate meetings survive on this continent. Most congregations now have the standing of an autonomous monthly meeting.

MONTHLY MEETING. This body is the heart of the Society. The gathering opens with a period of worship, and the clerk reads the "opening minute," which establishes an authorized business session. All members may attend and take part in the proceedings. Nothing is kept from the congregation. There are no secret committees. This body is a legal entity and may make contracts, control the local properties, and appoint representatives to attend quarterly meeting.

QUARTERLY MEETINGS. A group of monthly meetings constitute a quarterly meeting, which convenes at various centers in rotation. At one time these were large gatherings, and it required effort to come long distances, but it was regarded as a great occasion and was an opportunity to meet Friends and perhaps to hear some distinguished preacher. One must recall colonial history and its camp meetings and great revivals to visualize what quarterly meetings used to be. The multiplicity of modern interests has taken the significance from quarterly meeting, and some members are talking of its discontinuance, but one can hardly imagine Quakerism without the beautiful fellowship which such occasions provide.

YEARLY MEETING. A group of quarterly meetings constitute a yearly meeting. London Yearly Meeting was established in 1671, although local gatherings had been held at various places other than London from 1657, and are loosely referred to as yearly meetings.

In America the yearly meetings (Orthodox) affiliated with the Five Years Meeting were established as follows: New England, 1661; Baltimore, 1672; Virginia, 1673 (this united with Baltimore in 1845); New York, 1695; North Carolina, 1698; Ohio, 1813; Indiana, 1821; Western, 1858; Iowa, 1863; Kansas, 1872; Wilmington, 1892; Canada, 1867; Oregon, 1893; Nebraska, 1908; California, 1895. (Also London, Mexico, Jamaica and East Africa Yearly Meetings).[1] Kansas and Oregon are now independent.

There are several other groups scattered throughout the country known as General Conference (Hicksite), Conservative and Independent.

The yearly meeting sessions extend over about five days, and are times of great inspiration and fellowship. The business sessions are interspersed with meetings for worship. In previous years many visiting ministers were expected, but the custom is declining.

REPRESENTATIVES. At the yearly meeting the appointed representatives meet for separate sessions and executive matters are attended to. Reports are received from the various boards and committees, such as Peace, Temperance, Social Service, Foreign Missions, Education, Evangelism, Church Extension, Statistics and Finance.

QUAKERS AND WOMEN. Women have a unique place within the Society. So far as it is known it is the only religious body which has given to females from the beginning the same standing as males. They may be ministers, elders, overseers or clerks; they may speak in both the meetings for worship and business. At one time women held their own business meetings, but that has been discontinued. The women have been active in supporting missionary enterprise.

MINISTERS. The Friends have an unusual attitude toward the ministry. George Fox said college learning "did not make a minister," and he himself had little formal learning. It cannot be denied that for a century or more Friends discounted scholarship, and the Society suffered grievously in consequence. The preaching among early Friends was not expository, but mystical. It became the custom to "record" those who spoke acceptably in meeting as "having received a gift in the ministry." This gave them no authority, but they were asked to sit upon the "ministers' gallery." Gradually a change has been effected, and there is now a general recognition that a minister should be a well informed person, and that "one should love the Lord with the mind as well as with the heart." In recent years a pastoral system has been adopted. This will be discussed later.

ELDERS. A body of elders was appointed in each Meeting "to exercise a loving and faithful care over the ministry." It was their duty to encourage suitable persons to exercise their gifts, and to advise others if necessary "that their remarks were not according to Truth, and they had better keep silent."

OVERSEERS. The Overseers were appointed to "exercise care over the membership," especially to care for the poor and the education of the children. In case of members behaving unseemly the overseers seldom were remiss in their duty in visiting such and "dealing" with them.

MEETING ON MINISTRY AND COUNSEL. It is usual for the ministers, elders and overseers to meet as a group prior to monthly, quarterly or yearly meetings. At first known as meetings on ministry and oversight they are now styled meetings on ministry and counsel. Many Friends question the continuance of these "select" meetings. In many places this body is little more than a committee for hiring and firing a pastor.* If, however, the meeting is blessed with informed and inspired leadership this body can be of great service to the congregation. It must be said, however, that eldership as

---

* Birthright and Conservative Friends vigorously object to these terms.

an aid to the ministry has entirely disappeared. So little is known of Quaker doctrine and history by the members that in many meetings the pastor exercises leadership and historic Quakerism is disregarded.

The distinction between elders and overseers has disappeared and some meetings now only appoint elders. This body approves applications for membership and forwards the same to the monthly meeting. It also appoints delegates to attend the meetings of this body which occur at quarterly meeting and in like manner the quarterly meeting names representatives to the yearly meeting on ministry and counsel.

QUARTERLY MEETINGS were established in North Carolina as follows: Eastern, 1680; Western, 1759; New Garden, 1787; Contentnea, 1788; Deep River, 1818; Southern, 1819; Yadkin Valley, 1889, Surry, 1898. Quite a few meetings were established in Georgia and South Carolina in colonial times but they have all disappeared. In like manner at one time there was a strong meeting in Virginia, now the few Friends who remain are included in Baltimore Yearly Meeting.

THE PRESENT MONTHLY MEETINGS. CONTENTNEA QUARTER: Bethany, Bethesda, Goldsboro, Hood Swamp, Nahunta, Neuse, New Hope, Oakland, Rhodes, Woodland.

DEEP RIVER QUARTER: Archdale, Deep River, Hickory Creek, High Point, Oak Hill, Springfield.

EASTERN QUARTER: Piney Woods, Up River.

NEW GARDEN QUARTER: Chapel Hill, Glenwood, Greensboro, Kernersville, New Garden, Raleigh, Spring Gardens, Winston Salem.

SOUTHERN QUARTER: Asheboro, Back Creek, Bethel, Cedar Square, High Falls, Holly Spring, Hopewell, Marlboro, Poplar Ridge, Prosperity, Randleman, Science Hill, South Plainfield.

SURRY QUARTER: Ararat, Center Valley, Friends Union, Galax, Mount Airy, Mountain View, Old Siloam, Pilot Mountain, Pine Hill, Reavistown, Union Hill, Westfield, White Plains.

WESTERN QUARTER: Cane Creek, Centre, Chatham, Concord, Edward Hill, Graham, Liberty, Plainfield, Providence, Rocky River, South Fork, Spring.

YADKIN VALLEY QUARTER: Brannon, Deep Creek, East Bend, Forbush, Harmony Grove, Hunting Creek, Mount Carmel, Pilot View, Union Cross, Winthrop.

BIRTHRIGHT MEMBERSHIP. Friends adopted the practice of recording the minor children of members as Friends and infants as
birthright members at the London Yearly Meeting in 1737. The
"minute" says that all Friends shall be deemed members of the
meeting within whose limits they dwell . . . and the wife and
children shall be deemed members of the meeting of which the
husband or father shalll be a member, and that such membership shall continue after his decease."[2] This fundamentally affected the future of the Society. Heretofore the body had grown
by "convincement," from now on it tended to become more and
more a preferential organization consisting of inter-related families.
The writer was well acquainted with an English Friend who said
he had four hundred relatives who were members of the Society.
They were supposed to be raised as Friends. It is too true that
they were in manner of living, but many lacked the conscious
presence of the Inward Christ. There existed nothing analogous
to a class of instruction leading to confirmation. The recording
of children was adopted by the various yearly meetings on the
American continent, but in recent years there has been an endeavor
to distinguish between associate and active membership. In
course of time Friends prided themselves upon being birthright
members, and those who joined by convincement seldom felt that
they were truly members of the family group. So distinctive was
the family life of Friends, in deportment, dress and especially in
speech that it was almost impossible for a convinced Friend to
avoid errors, so that it was common to hear the expression, "It's
plain to see he wasn't raised as a Friend."

Whether the recording of children was due to the loss of the
original evangelistic fervor, or whether it resulted in the loss of
that inward spiritual life which was the source of the missionary
enthusiasm some future historian must determine. One fact is
certain that after about 1737 the burning, ardent urge to propagate
the faith of Quakerism declined. So conservative and selective
did Friends become that most yearly meetings passed through
a period in which there was little likelihood of any normal person
being "convinced," and applying for membership. The majority
of the American yearly meetings abandoned birthright membership when the Uniform Discipline was adopted. This had been
prepared by a conference at Richmond, Indiana, 1887. In its
place associate membership was adopted. The Five Years Meeting assembled at Richmond, Indiana, in 1907, and requests were
received from Indiana, California and Western Yearly Meetings

that the Discipline be revised and birthright membership restored, but as a sufficient number of the yearly meetings failed to support the amendment the change was not made.

As to Marriage. The Quakers denied priestly authority in every form. They believed in the priesthood of all believers; they denied "apostolic succession" and the so-called "indelible character" received at ordination; they utterly denied the right of any priest to pronounce absolution, and repudiated the pretensions of priests to perform miracles and their claim that the bread and the wine at the elevation of the "host" were transformed into the veritable body and blood of the Christ. It followed that they denied the authority of any minister of any religious body to "pronounce a couple man and wife." The Quaker position will be best understood if we regard Quakers as carrying the Protestant Reformation to its logical consequences. The Friends are the only important religious body which was wholly democratic from its inception.

The Friends resorted to what was the "common law" custom of marriage, but with decided safeguards. The procedure established was as follows: The couple would announce their intentions in writing to their respective meetings, and the request would be considered at the next monthly meeting for business. A committee would be appointed to visit the parties and usually to obtain approval by the families. They disapproved what they styled "improvident marriages," and had to be satisfied that the proposed marriage was suitable, and that both parties were "clear of entanglements," which included debts as well as personal obligations. A time would be set for the marriage, and a regular meeting for worship would be held. There would be a period of silence, and probably one or two Friends would speak or pray. Then the couple, who had been sitting on a front seat would rise and face the meeting, and taking each other by the right hand would take each other in marriage. The man would say something to this effect: "I, A. B., in the fear of God and the presence of this assembly, do take this my friend, C. D., to be my wife, promising with Divine assistance to be unto her a loving and faithful husband until it shall please the Lord by death to separate us." The woman would then make a similar declaration. They would each sign a certificate which had been specially prepared. The clerk of the meeting and others would sign.* Sometimes the parties sat down

---

* This formula was used by the writer at his marriage to Margaret Lambie, at Newmarket, Ontario, Canada, in 1909.

and the meeting for worship was resumed; sometimes they left right away, the ministers at the head of the meeting shaking hands to indicate that "minds were clear." Among early Friends there were no flowers, no decorations, no special wedding clothes and no music. Afterward there was usually a reception and as many as cared to, signed the certificate. Gradually the original custom became changed, and "worldly evidences of pomp and ceremony" crept in, until in North Carolina the former Quaker manner of marriage ceremony is seldom used.

Because of the absence of Episcopalian priests many people upon the frontier in early times resorted to the common law form of marriage, and law and custom recognized that if man and woman had made a declaration of intention before competent witnesses and had lived together in wedlock continuously and were known as man and wife, the marriage was legal and any children were legitimate. In North Carolina a law of 1666 permitted local magistrates to act as witnesses and to record such proceedings. A Vestry Act of 1715 continued this authority to magistrates, but in 1741 an act was passed by the North Carolina legislature which legalized only such marriages as were performed by a minister of the Church of England, but if such were not available, a magistrate might officiate. This angered the Presbyterians especially and the Dissenters generally. At first Baptist ministers did not conduct marriage services. The Presbyterians ignored the law of 1741, and of course the Quakers paid no attention, except that they were careful to have the proceedings registered by a magistrate or by some public official. Because of Quaker influence chiefly, but enforced by public opinion, a modification of the law was secured in 1766. In 1770 the legislature legalized marriages conducted by a Presbyterian minister, but the King of England vetoed the measure.[3] Special legislation has been enacted recognizing the Quaker form of marriage in North Carolina. Complete liberty was not secured until the Revolution for one of the ordinances adopted at the Constitutional Convention of 1776 was to the effect that "all regular ministers of the Gospel of every denomination having the care of souls shall be empowered to celebrate matrimony according to the rites and ceremonies of their respective churches." Divorces among couples "married in meeting" are virtually unknown.

CONCERNING FUNERALS. The same simplicity applied to funerals. A meeting for worship would be held, and Friends would be dressed just as they were for a wedding a day or so before. They would sit in silence as in a First Day morning meeting. The casket would be placed before the ministers' gallery, but it would not be opened. There would be no music, no singing, no prescribed funeral service or liturgy and no flowers. A few Friends would speak briefly or offer prayer, those at "the head of the meeting" would shake hands and the undertakers would remove the casket. Usually the Friends had their own burying ground where the casket would be lowered after a short prayer and some moments of silent worship. All the graves would be marked alike with a small stone marker, in some places erect, elsewhere prone. If a family could not afford the usual stone, the meeting provided it, so that there should be uniformity. No matter how wealthy the family, no elaborate markers were permitted. In some burial grounds remains of children were placed in a separate section. No widow's weeds or crepe were in evidence among Friends. It was customary to provide for widows and orphans who needed assistance.

For those who remember the former manner of conducting funerals, there is something about present day funerals that smacks of artificiality, display and wasteful expense which detracts from the real significance of the occasion. Friends would do well to take this to heart and to do their part individually to take the commercialism and ostentation away from these occasions. Men Friends should consider that one of their obligations to their loved ones is to lessen the anxiety that inevitably comes when the head of the family is taken by death. He can render a great kindness to his family by arranging for his funeral in advance. It is a heartbreaking experience for a stricken widow to be called upon to select a casket and decide on other particulars. This should be done by the husband when he is able to attend to it without emotional disturbance. There is a growing tendency among Friends to resort to cremation, and to have a memorial service rather than a traditional funeral service.

QUAKERS As REFORMERS. Quakers were not so much concerned about getting to Heaven after they were dead as they were about the establishment of the Kingdom of Heaven upon Earth. They said they were quite satisfied to leave any after death conditions to Heavenly Father, as such matters were beyond their knowledge and understanding, but they had been taught by the Saviour to pray "Thy Kingdom come; Thy Will be done on Earth as it is done in Heaven." Friends perhaps are the only religious body which really believes this is the Divine will and that it is possible to bring it about. Friends believe in progressive creation and progressive revelation, and they implicitly believe that the Holy Spirit is adequate to transform human nature, and that all sorts and conditions of men, including barbarians and heathen, can be transformed into saints if they will "obey the Voice Within." Therefore they addressed themselves to remedy every social evil as much as their ability and opportunity permitted.

THE WORD WITHIN. They undertook redemption by moral suasion, not by political, military or social revolution. They adopted a unique technique; they challenged a wrong doer: "Is there not within thee something that tells thee thee is doing wrong?"* It was their practice to appeal to the Light Within. The only authority upon which they relied was that of the individual conscience. They counted upon the word of Scripture "there is a Light, lighting every man coming into the world."4 Truth carries its own conviction; genuineness speaks for itself. Friends possessed a remarkable fearlessness in rebuking evil because they relied not upon their own ability to convince, but upon "that of God" within.

They believed that persons could be saved from sin and live together as Children of God; they believed as George Fox expressed it that "the ocean of darkness could be overcome by the ocean of light;" that good could overcome evil; the only remedy for wrong was right; the only alternative for hate was love; the only way to transform wrong-doers was the way of forgiveness, patience, kindness and trust. They believed that ultimately graciousness would break down churlishness; they dared to believe that the only way to change enemies into friends was not by violence or defeat or threats, but by loving, sacrificial service. However, there was no passive acquiesence in wrong doing; their condemnation was out-spoken but in love. So this little band of men and women who relied upon the Voice and the Power Within set out to transform human society. That they have not fully succeeded is no evidence they were mis-guided, but only proof they were too few.

A NAME THAT THOU LIVEST AND ART DEAD. The first mission was to reform the religious practices of the time. Romanism and ecclesiasticism had lapsed into dead formalism and ceremonialism; Puritanism was cold and negative; Presbyterianism was then

---

* This is not grammatically correct, but was the Quaker language.

bound by stern Calvinism. It was the calling of the early Friends to bring back to Seekers the consciousness of an ever-present Saviour, and to quicken dead church members into active evangelists. In this they were amazingly successful, for not only in England and Ireland but on this continent a great spiritual fire was lighted, which has not yet been extinguished, though at times it has burned very low.

The Friends brought to the world a new sense of democracy and brotherhood. In the time of Fox the gentry had become fopish and extravagant in style and manner of living, with every possible ostentatious adornment; class distinctions were manifest everywhere, and in Fox's day the Cavaliers and the Roundheads came to blows. In the Civil War (1642-1646) hundreds of the gentry perished, and in 1649 Charles I was executed. The preaching of Friends produced a great Revival. It is to be regarded as a phase of the Puritan revolt, but it had distinct characteristics which may be defined as vital. The doctrine of Divine Guidance was certainly a new note, and the idea that anyone might act as his own priest and that Christ was the last and true High-Priest and that through him any soul might have direct access to Heavenly Father was an interpretation of Scripture which created violent opposition; a new and simple method of worship was substituted for the complex and costly forms then prevalent; there was a new concept of the Church and of the Sacraments. The Scriptures also had a new meaning.

HUMAN EQUALITY. Of particular importance was the belief that women as well as men might be bearers of the new Truth, and might share on equal terms with men in the various fields of religious activity — this was something radical at that time. Then there was the wider implication that all human beings were equal in the sight of God. The early Friends preached to Negroes, American-Indians, Turks, Moslems with the calm confidence that the Truth would register, and that the illiterate and the heathen would "feel the Life rising up within them."

A MERCIFUL MAN IS MERCIFUL TO HIS BEAST. Friends were distinctly humanitarians. The seventeenth century was an age of cruelty. The treatment of prisoners, the mentally afflicted, the deformed and the helpless aged was terribly cruel. Beatings were common and capital punishment was imposed for scores of offences. The new revelation of Christ which the Quakers experienced caused them to be crusaders in every field of social reform.

It was an age when the rich lorded it over the poor, an age when there was no sense of democracy or representative government. Friends refused "to bow and scrape" before persons of social distinction. They disregarded titles and man-given honors and addressed persons by their name, as did Fox when he addressed the Lord Protector as "Friend Oliver." Haggling was the common custom of the day, as it still is in Oriental countries. Friends' concept of Truth led them to the adoption of fixed prices. If a Friend were asked how much he would take for his horse, and he said twenty pounds, he would not accept one farthing less nor one penny more. Of course this was regarded as stubbornness and churlishness, but how could we do business today if we could not depend upon descriptions and quotations in trade catalogs. Because of the reputation for honor and integrity that Friends gained, they were occasionally asked to take care of surplus money held by others. In this simple way some Friends became bankers of national repute. From similar concepts of righteousness Friends did much to establish the practice of fair and fixed wages, and of the non-payment of workmen from within saloons. Friends naturally refrained not only from hunting and cruel sports but discouraged professionalism of any sport. They regarded sports as a waste of valuable time.

YE KILL. YE FIGHT — YET YE HAVE NOT. Historians will agree that the testimony of Friends against war has been more consistent and forceful than that of any other body. They persist in regarding all war as utterly incompatible with the teaching and Spirit of Christ; they regard as revolting the hanging of battle flags in places of worship and the building of tombs of military heroes within such buildings. They blame, in large part, the ecclesiastical churches for the continuance of war. Friends protest against armed conflict not only that it is a remnant of savagery, that it is fundamentally cruel and stupid, and creates more problems than it settles, that it is basically wrong; their chief objection developed from their concept of what Kant called "the moral law within." In taking an oath of allegiance and obedience, the soldier has to promise to do exactly what he is ordered to do by any one possessing a higher rank; he has no "right to reason why." From the very nature of war, it is certain that he will be commanded to do all manner of deeds fundamentally wrong. A Quaker is quite ready to "render unto Caesar the things that belong unto Caesar," but he cannot give to Caesar "the things that belong unto God."

He cannot destroy his own personality by yielding his will unreservedly unto another in an un-Christlike undertaking. It is not only that he is called upon to kill others, he is called upon to destroy himself. How can a soldier pray "Thy Will be done upon earth?" and how can he pray "lead us not into temptation?" A member of the armed services is not at liberty to follow the leading of the Spirit. Friends in North Carolina bore their testimony against war, as will be told in a later part of this story. The testimony of Friends has not merely been negative; they have not been slackers, but have sought to render sacrificial service of love in war-time, and have done relief and reconstruction work in every devastated area.

LET MY PEOPLE GO. Concerning the curse of slavery Friends have taken the lead in protesting against and in eliminating this evil. This will be developed in its proper place. Friends have likewise done their part in the development of education. George Fox when in this colony in 1672 advocated the establishment of schools and "that girls as well as boys should be taught everything civil and useful in creation." In course of time a number of "monthly meeting schools" were established. Fox also urged that Negroes be taught religion, be treated kindly and after certain years of servitude be set at liberty. These services are regarded by Friends not as social service apart from their religion; it is not that they substitute works for faith but that the obligation to forward the establishment of the Kingdom of God on earth is the expression of their religion. A Quaker did not suppose his religion consisted in attending meeting regularly; it was what manner of man he was and what he did during the week that counted.

Friends were among the first to champion the cause of temperance. At the time of the rise of Quakerism there was no running water system anywhere and there were none of the non-alcoholic beverages now existing. In the early days some Friends operated taverns and some drank beer and wine, but as the sainted Dr. J. Rendel Harris so characteristically put it "when the Quakers were willing to give up the liquor the Lord gave them the cocoa, which he thought was ever so much better." In Britain the cocoa and chocolate industry is almost wholly in the hands of three families of Friends — the Cadburys, Frys, and Rowntrees. It was not easy to abstain from fermented beverages when there is nothing else to drink save impure water, and the writer has visited in areas where drought and scarcity of fresh water created a genuine problem. Friends in Britain and in this country were leaders in temperance reform. Friends believe that the real stimulant is the Holy Spirit, of whom the Lord Jesus said "If any man drink of this water he shall never thirst, but it shall be within him a well of water, ever springing up into newness of life." Alcoholic liquors are a spurious substitute for the reality. Few Friends are habitual users of fermented or spirituous liquors.

THY KINGDOM COME. Inevitably Friends were among the advocates of woman's suffrage, and women Friends have been encouraged to participate in every worthy form of social service. Elizabeth Fry and her efforts towards prison reform have become a familiar page in history, and Elizabeth Comstock's ministrations in American hospitals and prisons are almost as well known.[5] Their labors in aiding escaped and freed Negroes are also matters of common knowledge.[6] Thus Friends do not regard religion as creeds to be believed, but rather the living as Children of God in the present.

CHAPTER FOUR

GREAT MULTITUDES FOLLOWED HIM

HOW QUAKERISM CAME TO NORTH CAROLINA. From the beginning the eight Lords Proprietor of the "Carolanas" offered what were then considered liberal terms to settlers as to the exercise of religion, except that Catholics and atheists were barred. The Charters of 1629, 1663, and 1665 took it for granted that the dominant religion would be that of the Church of England, and that provision would be made for the building of churches and the support of clergy. The proprietors also guaranteed to the settlers "the rights of Englishmen." They were therefore as much committed to toleration and freedom as they were to the establishment of Anglicanism. Speaking generally, the majority of the colonists up to 1700 were nominally Episcopalians, that is, most of them had been baptized in infancy and were of English descent. However, for nearly fifty years, according to some authorities, the church dignitaries had done nothing to care for the spiritual needs of the colonists.

> "The first voice of a Christian preacher heard in North Carolina was that of a Quaker, William Edmundson, who came to the colony in May, 1672. He was a worthy bearer of the faith, and true interpreter of Quakerism; he personified the Christian virtues of simplicity, piety, zeal and charity. Undaunted by difficulties, discomforts and dangers he courageously plunged into the wilderness and carried his Gospel message to the scattered settlers whom the church had neglected and forgotten. He found the people famished for the Gospel and the Word of God. Many were truly converted, and became members of the Society. His visits to the settlements were great occasions; the news was spread with eagerness and multitudes assembled to listen to the preacher. Many heard the message of Salvation for the first time."[1]

CONDITIONS IN THE COLONY. Needless to state conditions were primitive. It was impossible for the average colonist to maintain proper manners; there were no schools or cultural gatherings; some children were permitted to run almost wild; language became debased; life was terribly hard; what we would consider evidences of good breeding disappeared. The frontiersman had to do practically everything for himself; he had to be tough and courageous; he had to clear the land, plant his crops, supply himself with animal food, build his cabin, make and repair harness, secure a source of water, defend himself from Indians and beasts of prey,

and occasionally make long journeys to a distant market for necessary supplies.   Some of them for years received no mail and no
newspapers.   As there was no bell to call them to worship, Sunday
soon became just another work day.   God was forgotten; Bibles
were almost non-existent and few could read.   What was true of
the men was more true of the women.   What the last chapter of
the Book of Proverbs says of an Eastern woman was true of the
woman of the frontier.   It would require pages to enumerate the
tasks she was required to perform.   If she could not meet the
exigencies of the hour she perished.   A great book remains to be
written entitled "The Women of the Frontier."   It is well said that
the frontiersman had to do everything for himself except bury
his dead body.   At that time there were no organized religious
services in the colony; no church; no ministry; no baptism for
babies; no marriages by clergy; no burials in consecrated ground.
Many had grown to manhood utterly ignorant of the implications
of religion.

The coming of Edmundson was a welcome relief and break
in the monotony and drudgery of early colonial life.   His message
came to weary men with hungry hearts, and hundreds came long
distances often on foot to hear the Gospel.   We do not have many
details, but from later accounts of the great revivals the scenes
can be reconstructed.   Many who came on horseback or by wagon
brought supplies for a day or so; many would sleep out; some in
wagon boxes or in stables.   Often the meetings were held under
the trees.   It was a great time for visiting, for neighbors were
few and far between; it was time to hear the news — especially
the happenings in England and the actions of the Lords Proprietor
and the Governor and his Council.   Many seized the occasion to
trade, and the revivals were great occasions for the young people
as it gave opportunity to indulge in love making.[2]   Edmundson
says that the colonists were crude and some of them smoked while
he and Fox were preaching.[3]

WILLIAM EDMUNDSON was a most extraordinary person, but his
true measure is overshadowed by that of George Fox.   He was
born in the beautiful mountain country of Westmorelandshire.
His mother died when he was but four, his father when he was
eight, and an uncle who sheltered him was severe and unkind.
It is not surprising that he married early.   He was in Cromwell's
army in 1651.   How be became convinced of the Quaker faith is
not known, except that it does not appear to have been due to

personal contact with Fox. He was sent to Ireland by the Lord
Protector as a "settler," and was so vigorous in preaching that
neighbors considered him bewitched. He became known as "the
Hammerer" or "the Hammerer of Ireland." The first Quaker
meeting in Ireland is believed to have been held in his house.
He possessed psychic powers, had ecstatic experiences and had
a correct premonition that his store would be robbed. He met
Fox in England and the conversation between the two may rightly
be regarded as one of the most significant conferences of all time,
for the outcome was momentous. They exchanged spiritual experiences and found in each other corroboration of his own convictions.

Edmundson returned to the Emerald Isle and travelled extensively and was so vigorous in preaching and proselyting that
he was imprisoned "many times." In 1661 Charles II was restored
to the throne, and all who supported Cromwell were under the
ban. Persecution of the Quakers flared up, and Quaker meetings
in many places were often violently disturbed.

Edmundson was among the twelve (including two women)
who sailed with George Fox on the ship *Industry* on August 12th,
1671. At sea a providential fog shielded the vessel from pirates.
They landed in Barbadoes where Fox was detained for three
months because of ill-health. During this period meetings were
held and several "convinced." From there the party crossed to
Jamaica, where they labored for seven weeks with some success,
after which Fox and the others left in a great storm and reached the
shores of Maryland and proceeded to New England. Edmundson
was a recorded minister, and undoubtedly a superior and convincing person. He made history in a famous debate with Roger
Williams, the radical founder of Rhode Island. From there he
went to Virginia, and reached and "convinced" persons there.
In company with Fox he attended a "general meeting" at Patuxent,
and then Fox went north and Edmundson turned south and made
his historic entry into North Carolina in May, 1672. His coming
was almost an epic and is thus described in his *Journal:*

"I was moved of the Lord to go to Carolina, and it was perilous travelling,
for the Indians were not yet subdued, but did mischief, and murdered several.
The place they haunted much was in that wilderness betwixt Virginia and
Carolina; scarce any durst travel that way unarmed. Friends endeavored to
dissuade me from going . . . so I delayed some time. In the meantime I
appointed a meeting on the north side of the James River, where none had
been, and there came several Friends a great way in boats. There came also
the widow Holland's eldest son, with whom I walked near two miles the

night before the meeting, advising him about some disorders in the family, and so we parted; but before morning a message came to me saying the young man was dead. Then the Word of the Lord came to me saying 'All lives are in My Hand, and if thou goest not to Carolina, thy life is as this young man's; but if thou goest, I will give thee thy life for a prey!' The next day I made ready for my journey, but none durst venture with me save one ancient man, a Friend."

"It was all wilderness and no English inhabitants or padways, only some marked trees to guide people; the first day's journey we did pretty well, and lay that night in the woods, as we often used to in these Parts. The next Day being Wet Weather we were sorely soyled in Swamps and Rivers, and one of the two that were with me for a guide, was at a stand to know which way the Place lay we were to go unto; I perceived he was at a Loss, turn'd my mind to the Lord, and as He led me, I led the Way. So we travel'd in many Difficulties until Sun-set; then they told me, They could travel no further; for they both fainted, being weak-spirited Men; I bid them stay then and kindle a Fire, and I would ride a little further, for I saw a bright Horrizon appear through the Woods which Travellers take as a mark of some Plantation; so rode to it, and found it was only tall Timber Trees without Underwood: but I perceived a small path, and I followed till it was very dark, and rain'd violently; then I alighted and set my back to a Tree, till the Rain abated: but it being dark, and the Woods thick, I walked all Night between the Trees: and though very weary, I durst not lie down on the Ground, for my Cloaths were wet to the Skin. I had eaten little or nothing that Day, neither had I anything to refresh me but the Lord. In the morning I returned to seek my two Companions, and found them lying by a great Fire of Wood: I told them how I had fared: he that should have been the Guide would have per-suaded me that we were gone past the Place where we intended: but my Mind drew to the Path which I had found the Night before: So I led the way, and that Path brought us to the Place where we intended, viz. Henry Phillip's house, later known as Phelp's Point, near Hertford by Albemarle River.

"He and his wife had been convinc'd of the Truth in New England, and came there to live, who having not seen a Friend for seven years before, they wept for joy to see us: yet it being on a First Day Morning when we got there, although I was weary and faint, and my Cloaths all wet, I desired them to send to the People there-away to come to a Meeting about the Middle of the Day, And I would lie down upon a Bed, and if I slept too long they should awake me. Now about the hour appointed many People came, but they had little or no Religion, for they came and sate down in the Meeting smoking their Pipes; but in a little time the Lord's Testimony arose in the Authority of His Power, and their Hearts being reach'd with it, several of them were tender'd and received the Testimony. After Meeting they desir'd me to stay with them, and let them have more Meetings."[4]

GEORGE FOX COMES TO NORTH CAROLINA. There is a tradition that because of harsh laws passed by the Virginia House of Burgesses against Dissenters that several Quakers had fled into the adjoining district of North Carolina about 1660, but there is no record of such after Edmundson appeared. Henry Phillips evidently be-came one of his enthusiastic supporters and spread the news far and wide and "opened the way" for Edmundson to hold many meetings with the colonists, and "many were turned to the Lord."

Another person who accepted the message of Edmundson, and who apparently did much to establish Quakerism in the colony was Francis Toms, a magistrate. Meetings were held in his home, and he held important positions in the Society and exercised much influence. Edmundson left North Carolina and visited many meetings in Virginia, and in the fall of 1672 he met Fox at Shelter Point, near Newport and told him of "the opening" in what is now Perquimans County.

Thus in October, 1672, there happened what may certainly be regarded as one of the greatest events in the history of North Carolina. This man of God, named George Fox, came into this territory. He stayed only eighteen days yet he sowed such good seed that the harvest continues to be reaped until this day, and perhaps in the Providence of God the greatest harvest is yet to come. Such was the power of God expressed through him that meetings in Virginia and North Carolina were established which continue to the present. The colony was stirred in a manner incomprehensible to us at this time. Fox found a group of persons already "convinced." He met a man named Hugh Smith who lived near the Chowan River, and a meeting was held at his house, and "many persons of other professions" came to hear the evangelist. Further down the river they found a captain who was "very loving," and who loaned them a boat, as the missionary band was wet with water splashing into the canoe in which they were. They journeyed to the house of the Governor at Edenton, but the water was so shallow that "the boat would not swim." "We were all fain to put off our shoes and stockings and wade through the water some distance. The Governor with his wife received us lovingly."[5] "A doctor at the Governor's house would needs dispute, and he denied that the Light and the Spirit was in every one, declaring that it was not in the Indians." "Whereupon," says Fox, "I called an Indian and asked him whether or not when he lied or did wrong to any, there was not something in him that reproved him for it. He said that there was such a thing in him that did so reprove him and make him ashamed. So we shamed the doctor before the Governor and people." The Governor kept them all night, and treated them very courteously. The party then went by Sound, about thirty miles, to the house of Joseph Scott, who was a "representative of the country." The people here were "tender and much desired meetings." Four miles further on another meeting was held, to which the Governor's

secretary came, "the chief Secretary of the Province," who was
"already convinced."   On their way back they visited the house
of the Secretary of the colony, had an illustration of "the great
power of God who carried them safely twenty-four miles in a
rotten boat, the water being rough and the winds high," and
held a precious meeting at Hugh Smith's. Fox and his companions
were convinced there was "an entrance of Truth upon the people."[6]

It is impossible to imagine or describe the effect of Fox's
personality and preaching.   Everywhere he went he exercised a
most extraordinary power.   Unhesitatingly we ascribe it to the
working of the Holy Spirit, yet Fox had most unusual endowments, for it was said of him: "he was of God's making, and like
none other'."   So great was the number who accepted Friends'
doctrine that Governor Henderson Walker wrote to the Bishop of
London in 1703 to the effect "George Fox did so infuse the Quaker
principles into some small number of the people, which did and
hath continued to grow ever since more numerous.[7]   Six years
later William Gordon, of the Society for the Propagation of the
Gospel (an Episcopalian) wrote: "There are few or no Dissenters
in this Government but Quakers. . . . Some of the most ancient
inhabitants, after George Fox went over, did turn Quaker."[8] John
Blair, an Anglican priest thought "the Quakers were very ignorant
of what they professed;" and John Urmstone, another Anglican
missionary referred to the Quakers of Perquimans as "being very
numerous, extremely ignorant, insufferably proud, and consequently ungovernable;" while those in Pasquotank were "factious,
mutinous and domineering."

Fox appeared possessed of incredible vitality. "He was at the
very height of his efficiency as a preacher and organizer. His
physical endurance seemed unlimited. "He was almost continually
in a boat when not holding a meeting, often rowing himself." He
held meetings in barns, in tobacco houses, in Friends' houses,
and in the wigwams of the Indians, the weather being sometimes
too cold for out-door meetings. He had as usual an eye for public
officials and "high people," and the meetings of this period saw the
"convincement" of "a great many people of account in this world
— justices, magistrates, majors, captains, and divers others of considerable account in the government."

Another illustration of his stamina is given by Samuel Bowden:

"Having spent a short time in Virginia, and having many large and precious
meetings, to which a great many magistrates, officers and other high people
came . . . the people were wonderfully affected . . . the power of the Lord

was gloriously seen and felt . . . and a victory over the bad spirit in some
. . . having finished the service which lay upon him . . . Fox set sail in an
open sloop for Maryland. The voyage was unusually tempestuous; for they
were a great deal of the time completely wet and almost frozen with cold,
for it was in January. Part of the time Fox sat at the helm and steered the
sloop, but as soon as they reached the Patuxent the precious meetings began
again, and the people were convinced."[9]

To show how far ahead of his age Fox was it is to be recorded
that he advised Friends in the colony to treat their Negro slaves
kindly, to provide religious instructions for them, and after several
years of servitude set them at liberty. He advised also that schools
be established, and that "boys and girls should be taught everything civil and useful in creation," and this in a day when in
England it was commonly supposed "that girls had no souls — no
not so much as a goose."

These extracts clearly indicate the extreme hardships "the
First Publishers of Truth" experienced in bringing the Gospel
to Carolina. They were often "in perils of water," and hazarded
their very lives; they also illustrate the implicit confidence they
had in Divine Guidance, not hesitating to trust God in the darkness of a primeval forest, when experienced guides were too
scared to venture; they further illustrated the forcefulness of their
messages and the readiness of the frontiersmen to respond to the
invitation to "follow the leading of the Spirit." It is also clear
that before the Quakers came many of the colonists were wholly
without religion.

YEARS OF INCREDIBLE GROWTH. Great multitudes were gathered
by the "First Preachers" in this colony. There was a hunger for
the Word of God, and there was an extraordinary outpouring of
the Spirit. The great gatherings were times when at almost every
meeting for worship many were "convinced." Fox and Edmundson
were powerfud preachers, but often the "convincement" came to
persons who for years had lived without regard to religion during
the protracted periods of silence customary at that time. The
gatherings supplied a social need for they gave the people a
chance to meet their neighbors and create friendships, and that
leads to some remarks as to the name of the Society established
by Fox.

In course of time the name "Society of Friends" was common,
and later, the date is uncertain, the name "the Religious Society
of Friends" was adopted. Christ said to his believers "ye are My
Friends if ye do whatsoever I command you," and "henceforth I

call you not servants but Friends." Friends believe the name is appropriate, and there exists a warm fellowship among the members.

WHY CALLED QUAKERS. There are two explanations. One, that the members were subject to "shakings" or "jerks." Such expressions of emotion were indeed common, but Quakers by no means had a monopoly of such physical manifestations; but there is no connection whatever between the Quakers and the Shakers. The truer explanation is that on the occasion when George Fox was being tried before Justice Bennett at Derby, in 1650, he warned the court to "tremble at the Word of the Lord," and Fox was in derision dubbed a Quaker, but it was the powerful preaching of the early Friends that caused scoffers to experience the quaking.*

In colonial days the term "Friend" was much valued, and many became members of the Society here and in Pennsylvania for the prestige gained and particularly to enjoy the fellowship, for nothing was more needed to relieve the dreadful monotony and loneliness of the frontier. For nearly fifty years Friends were the only organized religious body in Carolina. Dr. Stephen B. Weeks writes:

> "When the eighteenth century opened the Quakers by their thorough organization, and by their earnest preaching, by their simple and devoted lives, by their faithfulness and love, had gathered into their fold many men and women who primarily belonged to other denominations. They became Friends, and remained faithful to their new-found form of religion."[10]

Bancroft also adds his testimony saying: "the sect of which opposition to spiritual authority is the badge was the first to organize a religious government in North Carolina," and the Bishop of Eastern Carolina, the Rt. Rev. Joseph Blount Cheshire, said:

> "Quakerism was the only form of religion in the colony with no rival worship among the people for the rest of the XVIIth century. It drew to itself a number of the intelligent and well-disposed inhabitants of Perquimans and Pasquotank. . . . These zealous and self-sacrificing men deserve to be held in honorable memory who at the expense of so much time, labor and bodily suffering cultivated the spiritual harvest in that distant and unattractive field. Quakerism did not begin the work of settlement and of reclaiming the wilderness, but it has the greatest honor of having brought some form of organized Christianity to the infant colony, and of having cared for those wandering sheep whom others neglected."[11]

Upon hearing of the great harvest in North Carolina a veritable stream of "Visiting Friends" came from Philadelphia and

---

* *Journal* Pg. 85.

other Yearly Meetings and not a few from England. These visitors were in a real sense missionaries. They were not satisfied to preach; they labored to "convince" persons who attended the meetings. It was an era of fervor, and it is difficult for those who remember when Friends were Quietists to form an adequate concept of this extraordinary outpouring of missionary zeal.*

---

* The story of the progress of Eastern Quarterly Meeting will be told in a later chapter.

CHAPTER FIVE

AN ENEMY HATH DONE THIS

THE PERIOD OF OPPOSITION. Quakerism spread like wildfire in the first quarter of a century in this colony. Settlers poured in, and many united with Friends because there was no other active denomination. Quakerism became the dominant religion, and office holders and proprietors of considerable plantations became Friends. A great impetus was given to the Society when John Archdale, a Friend, was appointed Governor (1696-97). He was one of the eight Lords Proprietor, having purchased the share of Sir John Berkeley, and assumed office about 1694. He had the right to name his Council, and a majority were members of the Society. For some years the Quakers exercised great influence in the lower elected Assembly, and liberal laws were passed; they were also presiding in several of the courts and fulfilling many public offices. Because of the important place that Quakers occupied in the colony, many settlers deemed it prudent to unite with the Society.[1]

By the original charters the Church of England was to be established in the colony, churches were to be built and clergy maintained at the public expense. For nearly fifty years the clergy slept upon their rights, and nothing whatever was done to establish Episcopalianism in the colony.[2] At length Henderson Walker (Governor 1699-1704) wrote to the Bishop of London, within whose diocese the colony was supposed to be:

"For fifty years the colony had been without a priest or altar, and that George Fox some years ago came into these parts, and by strange infatuations, did infuse the Quaker principles into some small number of the people, which did and hath continued to grow ever since more numerous. By reason of the yearly sending in men to encourage and exhort them to their wicked principles; and there are none to dispute nor to oppose them in carrying out their pernicious principles for many years."[3]

Rufus Jones is also authority for stating that the Church of England did nothing for the colonists till 1700 and had no minister here, and that for a quarter of a century Quakerism was the only organized form of religion in these parts.[4] Connor confirms this, and says "forty years passed before an Episcopalian minister found his way into the Carolina wilderness."[5]

The Quakers had become so influential that it became incumbent upon the Episcopalians to exert themselves in earnest if they expected to see the Church of England supported. The church party for years lacked a competent leader, but eventually they found an energetic and determined person in Henderson Walker, who had been President of the Council, and who took over authority temporarily upon the death of Thomas Harvey in 1699.

> The next year the Bishop of London "did send to the colony the Reverend Daniel Brett to establish Episcopalianism, but the record says he turned out to be 'ye monster of ye age.' His conduct was so shameful that it caused Walker, himself an ardent churchman, to send a bitter cry of protest to the Bishop of London in which he said: 'It hath been a great trouble and grief to us who have a great veneration for the church that the first minister who was sent to us should prove so ill as to give the Dissenters so much occasion to charge us with him'."[6]

Governor Walker was a person of great ability and set himself to find a way to checkmate the detested Quakers and secure a firm standing for the established church. His knowledge of English Parliamentary law brought to his mind the Five Mile Acts, the Conventicle Acts, the Test Acts and especially the Corporation Act of 1661 which was to the effect that no one could hold public office in an incorporated borough unless he first partook of the sacrament according to the Church of England. The Test Act of 1673 was more discriminatory. It was construed to mean that not only office holders but any person might be approached by authorities and asked whether he were loyal to the Crown and required to swear to it. As the Quakers regarded it as inconsistent to take an oath upon the very book that forbade the taking of oaths and in the name of Him who said: "Let your yea be yea, and your nay be nay," they were regarded as traitors. One account says that probably 15,000 suffered fines or imprisonment and 366 died in England in consequence during the second half of the seventeenth century.[7] Walker found in these Acts a means of checking Quakerism in the colony, and getting Episcopacy supported by taxation.

THE VESTRY ACTS. The Governor caused a Vestry Act to be passed in 1701 which laid off the land into parishes, provided for the building of churches, and the maintenance of the clergy by tithes. The Act proved very unpopular not only with the Quakers but with the colonists generally. The Quakers were very influential and Walker wrote that in 1703 the Legislature included more than half its number who had been chosen by the Quakers and "they have designs of making void the Vestry Acts."[8]

In 1705 there appeared upon the scene Thomas Cary, who had been involved in a rebellion in South Carolina, and about whom much might be written. He is said to have been ambitious, restless and without settled convictions. He was appointed Governor, and the Quakers at first assumed he would be a sympathizer, but they found him more to their inconvenience than his predecessors. When he found the church party in power, with the support of the Crown and the Proprietors, he kept Quakers out of public office and caused the legislature to impose fines for any person who exercised public functions without having taken the oath. As settlements were scattered and newspapers virtually non-existent, and certain public affairs had to be effected, it was common for Quakers to be asked to act in petty or important local matters. Common law is a necessity in primitive communities, yet these deeds rendered Quakers and others liable to serious punishments. In 1708 the Council stood for the Church, while the Assembly favored liberal measures for the Dissenters. Conditions remained most disturbed and the Crown and Proprietors decided to establish separate governments for each of the Carolinas in 1712. They were regarded as one political unit till that date. Connor says that the period following the attempt to impose the Test Act and the Vestry Acts was "one of the stormiest periods in its stormy career," resulting in the bloodshed of the Cary rebellion, but as this did not primarily concern Friends it is not within this record.

A new Vestry Act was passed in 1715 which divided the colony into nine parishes, named vestrymen in each and prescribed their duties, and empowered them "to raise and levy money by the poll" for the support of the Establishment. Clergy now came to the colony and in general visited the same areas in which Quakerism was first established, to wit, Chowan, Perquimans, Pasquotank and Currituck. One of them, named Rainsford vigorously criticized the Quakers. Several of the early priests produced disturbance, and Connor goes so far as to say: "Historians are agreed that the Establishment was a hindrance to the development of religious life in North Carolina. One says it was due to the character of the priests; others to the conditions incident to a frontier civilization."

WICKEDNESS RAMPANT: Stephen B. Weeks says:

"The wickedness and carelessness of the people was induced, in part, no doubt, by the badness of the missionaries . . . the chief fruit of the labor was civil dissension and bloodshed, culminating in foisting on the colony an Establishment which was to be a constant source of annoyance and which is directly responsible for a large share of the backwardness of the State."

Weeks further remarks that "during the Proprietory period a majority of the people undoubtedly adhered to the teaching and preferred the liturgy of the Church of England, and would have been glad to see that Church strong and flourishing . . . but even then many of the ablest churchmen seemed to have an instinctive feeling that an established church was an anomaly in the New World, and out of harmony with the spirit of civilization they were developing here."[9] The Dissenters were not slow in perceiving that the Act of 1715 gave to the colonists "the rights of Englishmen," and as the Act of Toleration of 1689 had given Quakers exemption in England, they had the right to be free from penalties in their nonadherence to the State Church.

The same colonial legislature which enacted the Vestry Act of 1715 also passed an "Act for Liberty of Conscience" which allowed "all Protestant Dissenters within the Government to have their Meetings for the exercise of religion without molestation." It also granted to Quakers the right to affirm, but denied them the right to act as jurors, to testify in criminal cases, or to hold public office. This had a serious effect upon the moral development of the colony, for it virtually ousted the Quakers from public office and positions of responsibility. It further had the result in debarring many others who were desirous of remaining in public favor from uniting with the Society. Popular sympathy was with the Quakers for in spite of some narrowness and self-opinionatedness they were respected for their integrity. Delegations were sent to England from time to time to complain of injustice; among others petitions were sent asking for the removal of Col. Robert Daniel, Sir Nathaniel Johnson and Thomas Cary. On one occasion the Proprietors instructed the Council to elect a new President who should execute temporarily the functions of the Governor. William Glover obtained *de facto* but not *de jure* control, and barred Quakers from taking seats and offices to which they had been duly elected. This he did under the authority of the Test Act as the Quakers would not take the oath of allegiance. Just at this time when passions were running high, some representatives of the Society for the Propagation of the Gospel arrived. They were energetic in advocating Episcopacy, and many Dissenters, not Friends, were stirred to indignant and forceful resistance. There was a defect in the appointment and authority of Glover, which need not be detailed here, but it was adequate to give the Dissenters a decided advantage, and John Porter, who had been one of those sent to England to protest laid his charges before members of the old and new legislature, and they declared Glover's appointment to office null and void.

Great excitement prevailed, but the situation was temporarily relieved by the Lords Proprietor who vetoed the measure on the ground that the Act had not made proper provision for the clergy. Matters now reached a crisis, for the Crown, the Proprietors, and Governors Daniel, Cary and Glover were determined upon the establishment of episcopacy, and the majority of the colonists were in opposition. A curious legal situation arose. There was no printing press in the colony; legislative acts were in manuscript form and copies were scarce; communications were irregular; and many public officials were uninformed concerning new laws. Thus it was that judges, magistrates and lawyers were in a state of uncertainty in regard to law enforcement.

To aid in bringing some order out of the confusion, the Assembly enacted in 1737 that all laws enacted to 1715 were null and void, unless expressly named, and at the same time declared that the colony was "a member of the Crown of England," and the original charter assumed that laws in England were in force in North Carolina. This in a subtle way implied that the State Church of England was the established church in the colony, and the only religion to receive official recognition. According to Weeks:

"When the XVIIIth century dawned, the Quakers, by their thorough organization, their earnest preaching, by their simple and devout lives, by their faithfulness and love, had gathered into their fold many men and women who primarily belonged to other denominations. They became Friends and remained faithful to their new found form of belief."[10]

Governor George Burrington also attributed the growth of the Society "to the regularity of their lives, their hospitality to strangers, and kind offices to strangers. . . . They were busy making proselytes and holding meetings daily." Weeks also says that no less than 17 missionaries of the Quakers visited the colony between 1700 and 1729, and that three of the preachers were women.

At first the membership was confined to the eastern section chiefly Perquimans and Pasquotank "provinces." The Perquimans Monthly Meeting minutes date from 1680; Bath was reached by the middle of the century. Monthly meetings were established in Cartaret in 1733; in Dobson in 1748; Northampton in 1760. In this last instance it was due to an overflow from the adjoining county, Southampton, in Virginia. A detailed report of the development of Eastern Quarter will be presented in chapter xix.

CAUSES OF THE DECLINE OF QUAKERISM. There are in nature the principles of Spiral Movement and Acceleration. Even the stars are born, mature, survive for aeons and then die; vast mountain ranges are uplifted, endure for millions of years, and ultimately become base-levelled by erosion. Some anthropologists assert that ninety-nine per cent and more of the history of the human race belongs to the Stone Age. In this generation we have witnessed the abolition of the monarchy in more than a dozen countries. It is difficult for us to realize that for thousands of years this was the form of government supposed to have Divine sanction. As the poet says "Our little systems have their day; they have their day, and cease to be." It was, therefore, in accord with the universal law that the fervor of the first generation of Quakerism should pass and be succeeded by an era quite different. In view of all the buffetings that the Society received it is a wonder that it survived. We shall briefly enumerate the circumstances which changed Quakerism from a dynamic missionary enterprise to one of the most static religious organizations the world has known.

Probably the first influence was the cessation of persecution. It has been well said that "the blood of the martyrs is the seed of the church." So long as it was hazardous to be a Friend there was no lack of adherents; so long as the governments of England and America denied Friends the fundamental principles of liberty patriots came to their defence.

The Glorious Revolution of 1688, the Acts of Toleration of 1689, the revocation of the Test and Corporation Acts, and especially the Affirmations Acts (1689, 1695, 1702, 1712-13-14, 1722) removed some of the penalties under which Friends had suffered. The disqualifications had dissuaded many who would otherwise have joined, for some who shared their convictions were not willing to ostracize themselves, be debarred from public office and be subject to penalties imposed by law. With the gradual removal of disabilities came naturally a relaxation of the passion to proselytize, and Friends "settled down" to a pattern of Puritanism, which led to Quietism.

THERE AROSE ANOTHER GENERATION. The first generation of preachers passed away, and the next generation lacked the spiritual fervor of the "First Friends." They were children of the frontier. This was especially true of the third generation which had no personal knowledge of England and English culture. To understand this story one needs a knowledge of frontier conditions, and a good imagination. Towns were few, the population was sparse;

there was little knowledge of the outside world; schools were few, and those existing were pitiful; illiteracy was common; Bibles were scarce and few Quakers of the third generations possessed books. Life was hard and rugged; labor was exhausting. Quakers upon the frontier could hardly be expected to have time or interest to do missionary work, yet whenever visiting Friends arrived there was always some one ready to conduct the ministering Friends to other centers of Quakerism.

There was a new age — psychologically and theologically. In Europe Puritanism declined and Theism, Deism and Rationalism prevailed. What was termed Latitudinarism became popular. It was a decline of Dogmatism and became an Age of Toleration in regard to theological views. This influence was felt in the South, although the population, speaking generally, was too occupied with the conquest of the frontier and too little educated to be concerned with philosophical questions.

No provision other than the regular meeting was made for the children. They were dressed in regulation Quaker garb, the girls in plain dresses, with "poke bonnets;" the boys with "stove pipe pants" and coats with stand-up collars without any buttons. There was no children's furniture in those days, and the writer well remembers the boredom of a child being required to sit still with nothing to do for an hour with his feet dangling in mid air. Maybe it was worthwhile training in self-control, although there are better forms of such discipline.

Another potent reason for the decline was the mania for disownment which prevailed largely for a century, from 1730 to 1830. The principal cause was for "marrying out." One authority says that 100,000 in America were so disowned.*[11] Birthright membership was adopted in 1737, and a Quaker historian says:

---

* "Informed Friends of today are agreed that it was a mistake for so many members to have been disowned, especially for "marrying out," but some also believe it was a mistake for a Friend to marry a non-Friend. Naturally they refer to the classic Scripture "How can two walk together unless they be agreed?" Quakerism is not merely a belief; it is a way of life; it is an unique relationship; the concept of corporate worship and fellowship in service is fundamental. One who is a true Friend has concepts of Heavenly Father, of personal holiness, of public service, of family responsibilities which are the gradual development of association with Friends. One has to be acquainted with the homes "of Friends of long standing" to be aware of the calm, sincerity and purity of a Quaker home. How can family worship after the manner of Friends be maintained if one of the spouses is indifferent? Can there be a proper marriage unless husband and wife share together and equally in their yearnings for the Highest Good? Can the children be expected to develop a balanced personality if father and mother are not of the same mind concerning spiritual realities?

"The vast importance of this step was not appreciated for some time. It changed the Society of Friends from a church of believers, at least in theory, to a corporation or association of persons some of whom always would be of those who were not spiritually minded. Youth had been no hindrance in the early days, provided the person was believed to be spiritually minded; after the adoption of this regulation membership for a large number had no connection with change of heart."[12]

In time the Society lost its evangelical fervor, and depended upon its growth by the natural increase of the members' families. To "marry out" became a serious offence, especially if the parties were married by "a hireling minister," and not in meeting. The records of the several meetings are regularly sprinkled with references to disownment. Not only for marriage, but for wearing "worldly clothing," or colored garments, colored hats or hair ribbons, for wearing jewels or adornments, for drinking, gambling, hunting, using "the language of the world," engaging in unseemly occupations, in frequenting taverns or degrading places of diversion. It is a common experience to find persons who are active members of other denominations who say they are of Quaker stock but an ancestor was disowned for some disregard of discipline.

The Quakers were themselves the most to blame for the doldrums into which the Society sank. The meeting houses were unattractive, with plain unpainted wooden benches — sometimes without backs; the men and the women sat separately; the men retained their hats except in time of vocal prayer. There were two "facing benches," the upper for ministers; the lower for the elders and overseers*; there was no pastor; no planned order of service; the worshippers gathered in silence; not infrequently there was not a word spoken; no one made any preparation for a sermon — such was contrary to Friends' doctrine. They were to wait "till the Spirit moved them." The concept was mystical, that "God (or Truth) could be revealed to the speaker without any sensory experience." The preachers (women as well as men) were to rely utterly upon

---

* In rare instances there were three "facing benches;" The ministers sat upon the highest — the men to the right of the women; the next bench was for the elders, and the lowest for overseers. Concerning the "tone" as late as 1875 Yardley Warner wrote: "Singing (intoning) is dangerous to the minister. The danger is in his dependence upon the flow of the melody rather than on the flow of the sap of the Divine life." — *Yardley Warner* p. 245. The writer remembers many instances of intoned messages, especially one that terminated hilariously. An English Quakeress was addressing a college audience in this country. She developed a sing-song delivery, and her voice swayed up and down with a decided tendency to rise higher and higher. At last the expected happened and she "hit the ceiling." The students broke up the meeting with their merriment. The custom of intoning prevailed for centuries among preachers of many denominations.

inspiration, and not permit their reason or judgment to qualify the message.

Needless to say the preaching was sometimes unprofitable, especially as it became the custom to use a sing-song chant, commonly known as "the tone." The message was unacceptable unless it were delivered "in the tune." Cases are known in which the elders refused to recommend persons to be "recorded" as ministers because it was clear they "had received a gift in the ministry, but they had not received the tone."

THE LORD WILL BE GRACIOUS UNTO THE REMNANT. The preaching was seldom expository. To prepare a sermon would have been a rebukable offence; that was "creaturely activity;" "the fatal gift of eloquence" was severely rebuked; no reference must be made to thought or reason. A case is on record in which a minister began his remarks by saying "Friends, I've been thinking. . . ." Afterwards he was "eldered," and told "he should say what the Lord gave him to say, and not think about it." One writer says the lingo that some of the preachers used was so mystical that a glossary is needed to comprehend it.

It is not in order to condemn these worthy people; they were, like the rest of us, products of the age in which they lived. Their background, their ancestors, their environment made them what they were, and probably future generations will laugh at us, just as we smile at the frontier Quakers. It was impossible for them to hold modern ideas. They were true to their convictions; they developed character and integrity and "preserved the Seed, even though they did not scatter it." The reading of the Queries and Advices constituted an essential part of the Discipline. Periodically, at the close of the meeting, which was signalized by the Friends at the head of the meeting shaking hands, the clerk would come to the front and read the Queries or the Advices. The writer will add this testimony, that although he does not recall a single message delivered in meeting for worship in his youth the Queries and Advices registered and became guiding principles throughout life. One especially seems utterly foreign to the spirit of the present age, yet undoubtedly is sound advice:

"Are Friends careful to live within their income?
Do they avoid involving themselves in business beyond their capacity to manage?
Are they prompt in the payment of their debts?
And punctual to the fulfillment of their promises?
Do they avoid defrauding the public revenue?
Do they make suitable provision for their old age?

Do they provide for the religious instruction of their children?
Do they refrain from the use of spirituous liquors?
Do they avoid places of demoralizing diversion?"[18]

It is the opinion of the writer who was reared in such a meeting (although not upon the frontier) that the original form of Quaker meeting is worthwhile if it indelibly impresses upon its members such Queries and Advices. This is written in the hope that Friends will obey our own Discipline and attend to the reading of the Queries and Advices in our meetings. If read periodically they will be remembered when sermons and solos are forgotten. A major cause of the decline of Quakerism was the competition of other Protestant bodies. The Episcopalians enjoyed patronage, and pomp and ceremony naturally appealed to many; the Baptists with their insistence upon the infallibility of the Bible, and their public baptisms also made an appeal; the Presbyterians received substantial additions by emigration from the Highlands and from North Ireland. These persons were highly intelligent, industrious and frugal, and their denomination grew rapidly.

John Wesley was born in 1703, and it was in 1738 that he received the spiritual experience which made him a flaming torch whose light and warmth is spreading even yet. He lived till 1791 and saw the revival spread throughout the American colonies, Methodism possessed a warmth, spontaniety, virility and adaptability which Quakerism never possessed. Here again, it is futile, to compare Wesley with Fox. The men were representative of different ages and different cultures. It is sufficient in this connection to say that Quakerism could not withstand the competition of these other denominations — especially Methodism.

Now I Know in Part. Again, it must be acknowledged that early Friends presented too narrow a view of the Gospel. They ignored the importance of education, and the frontier preachers knew nothing of systematic theology. There are many important phases of the Gospel, and it is a grave reflection upon the ministry of every denomination that the ministers generally have no plan for the presentation of all the fundamentals of the faith. Probably the only expositors who do so are the Scottish Presbyterian preachers, who are noted for their doctrinal sermons, and incidentally for their insistence that the members of the congregation bring "the Word of God" with them to the kirk, and follow the reading of the Scriptures.

The Quakers became unpopular because of their refusal to

take oaths, to bear arms, their opposition to slavery, and in many instances their objection to tobacco and secret societies. One has said:

> "There were some who appeared to the outward very exact and zealous against pride and worldly customs, but for all that, the inside was not right, so that I found very close exercise among them in warning them against the leaven of the Pharisees, which was equally, if not more hurtful to religion than that of the publicans; yet . . . they were too much taken up with the world, and the riches of it, making haste to increase their substance, which was a very great hindrance to their growth in the life of religion, and made them dwarfish therein; setting forth that a form, without life, whether by education or otherwise, would not avail."[14]

Of the Quakers of this period it must be said that when persecution gave way to peace; peace gave away to passivity. The western revivals, the anti-slavery movement and the westward migrations were factors so important in the decline of Friends that they each require separate treatment.

Elbert Russell thought that one of the causes of decline was that the Elders exercised a repressive influence; they subdued the ministers, and were too liberal in administering "doses of elder wine, which too often tasted of the vessel."[15] Friends tended to become wealthy, exclusive and self-righteous. Interviewing applicants was a protracted and painful ordeal; the person was not asked if "he loved the Lord," but was he "convinced of Friends' doctrines?" The Great Quaker Revival had run its course; another era in history had arrived; the informality of the "First Publishers of Truth" became formalism to the Quietists. But the Society survived because "there was something of God" in the membership which made for integrity.

The Society survived in England and in Pennsylvania in its original form because these Friends were generally wealthy and educated. The Philadelphia Friends possessed the lands adjacent to the rivers, encouraged trade with the Indians, established schools and colleges. Furthermore they never experienced the frightful impact of slavery, armed invasion and political upheaval that the Southern Quakers endured. The rigors of the frontier made the survival of primitive Quakerism impossible.

DID THE QUAKERS PREACH THE GOSPEL? It is the opinion of this writer that the principal cause of the decay of Quakerism between 1750 and 1850 was the neglect by the ministers of the historic Jesus of Nazareth. Throughout the South in this period there were few schools; illiteracy was prevalent; the Bible was neglected (any knowledge of the ministry of Joseph John Gurney is conclusive proof of this). Woodman says that until 1860 the Bible was seldom read in meeting[16] and from the writer's own personal knowledge of over thirty years it was rarely read in any non-pastoral meeting. Friends until the great revivals had no Sunday Schools. The Bible was studied in few elementary day schools.

The preaching and the meditation concerned the Holy Spirit. The sermons fell into a definite pattern concerning the Inward Light, the Seed, the Truth, Divine Guidance, the consciousness of the Inward Presence.

The writer never heard in an unprogrammed meeting any exposition of the Nature of God. The term "the Holy Trinity" was taboo; Friends said the term was not in the Holy Scriptures therefore should not be used. Yet, this writer cannot hold to Christianity intelligently without an opinion satisfactory to himself as to the significance of the term.

The three-fold revelation of the Creator is essential to faith and understanding, and the writer says emphatically that God as Creator is incomprehensible. Jesus said "God is Spirit," and that makes sense. No thinker ascribes to the Deity any physical attributes — such as form, shape, substance, size, weight, location. Apart from the revelation of the Father in the person of the Lord Jesus no one would have any awareness of the moral character of the Creator. The statements "He that hath seen Me hath seen the Father" and "I and My Father are One" refer to unity and not identity.* The love, compassion and forgiving grace of the Father are revealed in the life of the Son, and God is like Jesus of Nazareth in character — not in outward form. The sacrificial life and death of our Lord constitute for believers the unveiling of the Will and Character of the Eternal Creative Power we call Heavenly Father.

Jesus told his followers that "it is expedient for you that I go away, for if I go not away the Comforter will not come." It was necessary for the physical presence of the Savior to be removed in order that we might know Him and God spiritually, but Jesus also said: "When He the Spirit of Truth is come He shall testify of ME."

That is what the Friends for a century ignored. Jesus also said "Ye shall be witnesses of ME." Quakerism at that time witnessed to the Holy Spirit and did not witness to the historic Jesus of Nazareth. Consequently the personal touch and appeal was

---

* See John XVII, Verses 11 and 20ff

lost. They did not stress Jesus Christ as the Savior, they preached the Inward Light as the Guide to Truth.

The Friends acknowledged they were Mystics. Mysticism is valid, but there must be a norm, a pattern, a standard by which the subjective concept must be evaluated. A good definition of Reality is: "the proper agreement of the subjective with the objective." Applied to Christianity this implies that the concept of the Inward Spiritual Christ must be in conformity with the Life, Character and Work of the Historic Jesus. How can one know that the Mystic Christ within conforms to the "Word made flesh," if one be ignorant of the Gospels and the Scriptures? The writer is aware that religious experience preceded the Scriptures, and that the Scriptures are (in places) the outcome of religious experience, but no thinker would or could maintain that since "the Word was made flesh and dwelt among us" that the essentials of the Christian faith could be properly understood or presented without the Scriptures and the historic Jesus of Nazareth.

This was the main defect of Quakerism of the Quietist period. The lack of schools, colleges, and reading matter, and the prejudice against learning were the inescapable outcome of the rigors of frontier and pioneer life.

It was not until the Revivalists put the historic Jesus into their preaching and sought to expound the Scriptures that the decay of the church was checked and lives were changed, and instead of sermons about the Inward Light preachers read from the Bible in meeting, sought to expound the Scriptures and presented the Lord Jesus Christ as a Living Savior. Then the Blessing came, and the Dry Bones began to live again. The author believes these conclusions are undeniable. Rufus Jones epitomized his ministry when he approved the saying of an Asiatic who said: "Men natively, naturally love Christ and want to follow Him when they really see Him in His true Beauty and Loveliness. The *personality* of Christ has everywhere an almost irresistible attraction . . . the Christ of Galilee and Gethsemane, the *personal* Christ of the evangelists, makes an instant appeal to their hearts and minds . . . To see Him is to love Him."[17] The emphasis is here rightly put upon *Personality*.

No blame can be attached to the Seekers after Truth of more than a century ago. The hardships and limitations of the age in which they lived determined their concepts. This is true of all periods and cultures. The challenge to this generation is: Do we appropriate the Truths now available?

As to Convincement. Readers of Quaker literature will find the word "convinced" in frequent use. The early journals are proverbially "full" of the expression "many were convinced." Conservative Friends still use the term. The meanings of words change with time, and today the word "convince" commonly implies a new understanding concerning something. The word "convict" implies a sense of guilt; "convert" means to turn away or to renounce, or "a change of heart." The well-known passage: "When the Spirit of Truth is come He shall convince the world of sin, of righteousness and of judgment" (John 16:8) offers a good illustration. The Authorized Version uses the word "convince" or "reprove;" Weymouth uses "convict;" so do Moffatt and the American Revised Version;" the new Revised Standard Version uses the word "convince," which is a pity. It may be a correct translation of the MSS, but surely the word "convict" is a better presentation of the sense of the passage. Luther uses the word "strafen," (to beat or punish). The writer considers it a misfortune that the Quakers clung to the use of the word "convincement." His own experience was that he was "convinced" of Friends' doctrine years before he was "convicted" of sin in such a manner as produced "conversion." He believes that is the common experience. It is undeniable that the Society of Friends was much weakened by having in its membership those who were "convinced" but never "convicted" or "converted." It would be helpful if some learned Friend would tell us what Friends originally meant by the term, and what it implies to Conservative Friends at the present time.

CHAPTER SIX

WHITHER THE TRIBES WENT UP

THE SETTLEMENT OF THE PIEDMONT. It is not clear who first induced Friends from the North to settle in the Piedmont area of North Carolina, nor why it should have been considered such a desirable location. There is no navigable river or extensive lake within many miles; there were numerous streams that afforded excellent mill sites, but there were no mountains or graceful hills visible; it was an unbroken forest, described as "magnificent," and abounding in game. Crevecoeur wrote:

"No spot on earth can be more beautiful; it is composed of gentle hills, of easy declivities, excellent lowlands, accompanied by different brooks which traverse the settlement. I never saw a soil that rewards men so easily for their labors and disbursements."[1]

This language is extravagant. The almost universal wanderlust may have been the principal cause of the migration; many Friends would have said they were Divinely led to trek to the Southland; the long series of frontier wars and the rising ill-will toward England and hard times may have had something to do with it. They heard from some sources of the mild winters in the Carolinas and of its fertile soil to be had for almost nothing. Individuals and groups do not migrate unless they feel satisfied that such procedure will better their economic conditions.

Some Friends were at New Garden by 1750, and a meeting for worship was held the next year. There was no meeting house when William Hunt visited the community in 1752, and it is known that Friends sometimes met for worship at the home of Thomas Beals. There was an organized meeting at Cane Creek before the one at New Garden, for in 1751 Friends at Cane Creek requested the Quarterly Meeting at Perquimans and Little River to grant them the status of a monthly meeting. This was granted, and at the very first matter to come before the newly established business meeting was a request from Friends of New Garden on the seventh day of tenth month, 1751, for permission to hold a meeting for worship. This was approved and three years later on fifth month, twenty-fifth, 1754, New Garden petitioned the same for the status of a monthly meeting "by reason of the hardship they underwent in attending the monthly meeting at Cane Creek forty miles away through a trackless forest."

Among the first families at New Garden were those by the name of Beals, Beeson, Cook, Dillon, Hunt, Mendenhall, Mills, Ruddock, Thornbrugh, Vestal and Williams. There is no evidence that they presented minutes (credentials).

The news that Friends were satisfied in their new location reached their home meetings and a veritable tide of migration set in. The first groups came from Pennsylvania and Virginia between 1754 and 1770; the second from Nantucket Island from 1771 to 1775; the third began with a few members from eastern North Carolina in 1760-1761, which developed into an almost mass migration after 1800.

THEY CAME FROM PENNSYLVANIA. Among the early settlers were a host of Friends from Warrington, in Pennsylvania, bearing the names of Beeson, Cox, Dennis, Elliott, Frazier, Fisher, Harlan, Hough, Johnson, Jones, Kendall, Lindley, McGrew, Ozburn (Ogburn), Pidgin (Pigeon), Pope, Reynolds, Ruddock, Smith, Waters and Wilson. From the Bradford meeting in Pennsylvania came families named Mendenhall, Millikan, Worth and Woodward; from Chester county there came others named Dennis, Maris, Mendenhall and Reynolds; from East Nottingham there arrived James Brown, James Jonson and John Rich; from other parts of the Quaker Commonwealth came members by the name of Bradley, Pearson, Stanfield, Thatcher, Unthank, Wall and Widows.

From Virginia came substantial Friends named Ballinger, Beals, Beeson, Brooks, Elmore, Harris, Hoggatt (Hockett), Johnson, Payne (who became the father of Dolly Madison, whose home is preserved near by), Sanders and Stanley. Another group from Virginia included families by the name of Brittain, Hiatt, Langley, Potter, Taylor and Wright. Still another invasion brought members named Bailey, Brazelton, Hiatt, Kersey, Norton, Pattison and Stanley. These are by no means all the early Friends, but they represent the families which established Quakerism in the Piedmont.

From eastern North Carolina came the Lambs, to be followed later by scores from Eastern Quarterly Meeting where slavery was more prevalent, and therefore it was more difficult for free labor to survive.[2]

THEY CAME FROM NANTUCKET ISLAND. From Nantucket Island between 1771 and 1775 no less than 43 certificates were received by the New Garden Meeting. The list includes large families named Barnard, Barney, Beard, Bunker, Clasby, Coffin, Coggeshall, Davis, Dixon, Gardner, Gifford, Macy, Ray, Reece, Russell, Stanton, Starbuck, Swain, Sweet, Way, Wickersham and Worth. The War of Independence put an end to this movement for between 1783 and 1800 only thirteen such certificates were received.[3]

Volumes could be written upon this movement. Nantucket Island is twenty miles from Cape Cod, is about fourteen miles long and three and a half miles wide. At one time more than two-thirds of the inhabitants were members of the Society. The principal industry was whaling and for a while there was great prosperity, but changes in the business caused decline, which was accentuated by the increase of the population. Monthly and quarterly meetings were established. It was recorded that "the inhabitants were those who ministered only to the useful, to the necessary and indispensable comforts of life." Weeks says the causes of the mass movement to the Carolinas were the smallness of the island, and the unproductiveness of the soil.[4] Rufus Jones said he could not understand why so many abandoned security to face the hardships of the long journey to New Garden. A Friend who knows the Island gave the writer what is perhaps a better explanation. The frontier wars were heading up trouble with England, and Nantucket off the coast of Massachusetts was in an exposed position, and the Quakers felt it prudent to remove to the South.

Contemporaneously with the last mentioned invasion came devout members from Pennsylvania and Virginia named Adams, Bills, Clark, Haworth, Iddings, Pierce, Pugh, Rees and Stuart.

The records say practically nothing concerning land titles. We know from other sources that the Lords Proprietor entrusted the allotment of lands to agents who generally lived at Edenton or near the coast; we know that the counties had not been adequately surveyed; we know that land grants conflicted, and that a particular agent was often not available; that agents were careless and often granted land to a person when that parcel had already been taken up; and also that "squatting" was common, and that there was a general refusal to pay "quit rent."[*]

---

[*] *Concerning land titles.* The two Carolinas were granted by Charles II to supporters of the Crown during the Commonwealth, being the Earls of Clarendon, Duke of Albemarle, Earl of Craven, Lord John Berkeley, Sir William Berkeley, Sir George Cartaret, Earl of Shaftesbury, Sir John Colleton. In 1728 the Lords Proprietor surrendered their charters to the king, but Lord Cartaret, afterwards Earl of Granville, decided to retain his interest in his share of land which constituted the northern fourth of North Carolina extending "as far west as the South Sea!"

From all this we are sure that many Quaker settlers had almost endless trouble in finding home sites before they faced the herculean task of clearing the land, felling and facing timber, and building their log cabins. And what about supplies? Who went periodically to some far distant market to get tools, manufactured goods, medicines and other necessities, especially salt, tea and sugar? It is said that at first the nearest grist mill was eighty miles away.

There is a tendency to cast a glamor over these early settlements, but the naked truth is that everything was primitive and lacking in all that we would now regard as essentials of civilization. It was the First Day Morning and the Mid-Week Meetings that constituted the bond of fellowship, relieved the strain, replaced the solitude, and kept alive hope and courage.

These godly and industrious families intermarried and produced citizens of more than usual merit; they remained loyal to the Society and quite a number of subordinate meetings were established especially Centre in 1757, which became a monthly meeting in 1773; Deep River in 1758, which became a monthly meeting in 1778 and a quarterly meeting in 1818; Westfield and Mount Pleasant meetings composed Westfield Quarterly Meeting in 1803.

New Garden Quarterly Meeting dates from 1787 and the first

The northern boundary coincided with the southern boundary of Virginia. Earl Granville and the Crown each appointed five commissioners in 1742 to manage the vast domain, with a land office at Edenton. Certainly in some way the Quaker settlers obtained title deeds, but we have ample evidence that the land agents were corrupt, and that in 1755 the Colonial Assembly received complaints concerning the abuses, which later led to the Regulator uprising. After the Revolution the estates of the Proprietors were confiscated, and the writer has examined a large number of deeds transferring land from "the State of North Carolina" to certain individuals. Here is a sample: "In 1804 the State of North Carolina conveyed to William Rutledge two hundred acres of land on the Deep Creek for the sum of fifty shillings." This would be at the rate of four acres for one shilling (24 cents). Another deed shows that another Rutledge bought 94¾ acres in Surry County for $143.62½ cents. (We find ½ cents mentioned in the construction of Founders Hall, New Garden Boarding School.) It is to be remarked that the land was unsurveyed; there were no roads or bridges; the domain was at that time an unbroken forest. Although the Continental Congress had adopted decimal coinage in 1775 local deeds were drawn up in terms of shillings nearly thirty years later. Any sort of money had value at that period. The Piedmont settlements of the Quakers were within the Granville grant. — From many old records in the possession of Robert M. Allgood, of Winston Salem. Connor: *Hist. N.C.*, pp 32ff and 222ff; Lefler and Newsome: *North Carolina*, chap 3. Friends at New Garden apparently made some attempt to buy the land from the Indians (Cheraws or Catawbas) and in 1764 a committee was appointed, but "the matter seems to have been dropped." — Weeks, *Southern Quakers and Slavery*, p 107 footnote. Many ancient deeds are on file at the Registrar's Office in Greensboro.

yearly meeting was held there in 1791. So many Friends had settled at New Garden that they requested that the monthly meeting be separated from Cane Creek "it was a burden to Friends to
have to travel thirty miles through the wilderness to attend quarterly meeting."*

A PERMANENT QUAKER CENTER. The New Garden community
grew and prospered till in course of time it became the center of
Southern Quakerism; a school was established about 1816 and the
Boarding School in 1837. One cannot examine the minutes of
these early meetings without being impressed with the sincerity
of these Friends, but more and more they tended to become a
separate people, in dress, speech, deportment. From the Revolution to the Civil War the Friends at New Garden led Southern
Quakers in preserving the distinctive beliefs of Friends. During
this period there were many accessions from the Eastern Quarter.

A marked feature of early Quakerism was the concern of
"public Friends" to visit new and distant meetings. It is on record
that between 1752 and 1778 no fewer than ninety-three Friends
"travelling in the ministry" visited this new community. Several
of them were women. It needs a knowledge of frontier conditions
to appreciate the hardships of such long journeys. Among the
leaders of this new meeting the names of Thomas Beals, Thomas
Hunt and Richard Williams should be mentioned.[5]

They builded better than they knew, for when they felled
the first tree and prepared the first log cabin they could not have
foreseen that within two centuries there would be on that historic
spot a thriving business center, a first-class dairy and general farming community, an accredited college with nearly eight hundred
students, assets worth $4,219,000.00 and an endowment of
$1,760,871.00; while within a few miles would be a port from which
one could take an airship which would carry him to New York
or anywhere else in the wide-wide world within a few hours.

In 1787, just after the war when conditions were stabilizing
a quarterly meeting was authorized. The community now began to
exceed in importance the original Quaker settlements in the Eastern Quarter, so in 1791 the first yearly meeting was held at New
Garden; from that date until 1883 it alternated between these two
centers, except that from 1883 to 1904 it assembled at High Point,
and then returned permanently to New Garden.

Like all frontier settlements this Quaker gathering place was

---

* Cane Creek Monthly Meeting Minutes, 10th mo., seventh, 1751.

a community — a cooperative society. Logging bees, the cabin and barn raising were joint undertakings. Those who have in recent times attended threshings and barn raisings can visualize the scenes with the women folk preparing the noon meal, but the happy fellowship of such occasions was frequently beclouded with the dread that some one might be injured in the raising of the logs upon the pike-poles.

A meeting house was constructed near what is now the grave-yard adjoining the college campus, and history and not mere tradition says that during the Revolutionary War (1776-1781) wounded soldiers both American and British were brought from the field after the near-by Battle of Guilford Court House, March 15th, 1781, and cared for by the Friends in the place of worship.

Of course the Quakers were not the only people who poured into the Piedmont about this time. Friends were thinly scattered over a wide area before the close of the century, and many small meetings were started, but the young people of the second and third generations preferred the more spirited church services of other denominations. The Moravian settlements in the adjoining county of Forsyth almost coincided with the Quaker colonization. More will be told of the New Garden Quarterly Meeting in a later section of this work.

THE ANABASIS. Some future Quaker historian must write a descriptive account of these brave and hardy folk who abandoned security in the North to establish Quakerism in the Piedmont of the Carolinas. This writer has not had opportunity to do the necessary research; surely there must exist in various hands letters, diaries or papers giving particulars of these many treks. The writer has found details concerning the contemporary migrations of the Moravians from Pennsylvania to Wachovia which almost adjoins the Quaker settlement at New Garden, and there are many works concerning the opening of the Middle-west. Is there not a Xenophon who will let us know how many parasangs the Quakers traversed each day. What a thrilling saga it would be.*

Picture the home meeting as one young Friend tells of his "concern" to move to North Carolina. Probably for weeks it was

---

* The first Moravian expedition consisted of eleven unmarried men, each capable of performing a different necessary service. They left Bethlehem, Pa. on October 8 and reached Bethabara, N. C. on November 17, 1753. The journey of about 500 miles thus occupied 40 days. They encountered rain and snow, crossed mountains and rivers, and were delayed by straying horses. The wagons were so heavily laden the men had to walk.

the chief topic of conversation. Did Friends approve; how long was it before others felt "the same leading." Picture the scene at the last morning meeting before the departure; perceive the anguish of elderly mothers as their children pack up for departure; let your mind dwell upon the necessary preparations by the men — the wagons, the teams, the harness, the necessary feed. What tools did they take? Were there guns for the capture of game upon the way. Were they careful to take supplies for the future — shoes, clothing, bedding? They dared not forget such necessities as ropes, pails, axes, crowbars. Then about meat supplies. Did they take salted meats of various kinds? Happy were the women who took needles and thread.

What arrangements did they make as to the route? Did they join Friends from other meetings? How many were there in the caravan? How many wagons, and were there two horses or four horses to each? Were they conestogas or prairie schooners? How far did they travel each day? How long were they on the journey? They travelled at least four hundred miles, maybe some over five hundred. How many miles per day could a two horse team pull a heavily loaded wagon through an unbroken wilderness? How long were some of them upon the journey? Was it twenty days or forty days? How we would love to know. What happened upon the way? Were there accidents? What was the consequence if a wagon wheel became broken, or a horse lost a shoe? Did they have spare shoes? Were they molested by Indians or frightened by wild beasts? Did they lose the way — and how many times? Did they have difficulty in securing water? What did the women do in preparing meals? Probably they had camp fires at night.

Is it likely that caravan after caravan made this long trek without some person becoming ill or injured or maybe dying? Can you picture a burial service in some distant forest?

We are sure they had a period of worship each morning before continuing their southward journey; but there was no music to enliven the march and Quakers did not encourage singing as did the Moravians.

How did they find the way to New Garden? Who knows. Did they have a guide? We know that at a later period Addison Coffin acted as guide to Quakers fleeing to Free Soil north of the Ohio.

Did the courage or fortitude of some of the adventurers fail? It is not unlikely.

And what joy and gratitude on arriving! How the news was spread. Let your mind and imagination dwell upon the next morning meeting when everybody came to welcome the new arrivals.

The questions raised here are not idle speculations — they were the vital issues the founding fathers and mothers of North Carolina Yearly Meeting faced when they undertook to establish a great civilization here in Dixie Land. How long shall we wait for some gifted Quaker writer to pen this record for us.

CONCERNING THE INDIANS.   The writer has looked in vain for items concerning the relation of the Quakers to the Indians of the Piedmont at the time of the settlement. On an earlier page of this chapter there is a reference to an attempt of the Quakers to purchase land in 1764 from the Cheraws or Catawbas, but "the matter seems to have been dropped." This is all the writer found. It is likely that there may be other material, but in the absence of the Custodian of the Records (Dorothy Gilbert Thorne) nothing was discovered. What is the explanation? There is abundant evidence that at this time the French and Indian War (1756-1763) was in progress and that at the near-by Moravian settlement at Bethabara the settlers armed themselves against an Indian attack, and it is generally believed that the ringing of a bell or the playing of trombones scared the Redskins.

It is most likely that the natives of North Carolina had learned of the attitude of the Quakers towards the Amerinds, and that they experienced the friendly spirit of the settlers. Perhaps there were close relations and some trading. Why was it not entered in the minutes? The *minutes* are as meagre as can be, and nothing is entered except official business. Good will toward the natives was taken for granted among the Quakers; relations were normal and natural. It is probable that the members of the two cultures fraternized and were mutually helpful. At any rate it is clear that no antagonisms developed and that the Quaker settlements were undisturbed by the tribesmen and this perhaps is the greatest tribute to the soundness of the Quaker manner of life and religion.

CHAPTER SEVEN

THE TRIBES OF THE LORD

THE YEARLY MEETING. According to a plan established early in England, and probably at the suggestion of Fox, a "general meeting" was held annually. At first these were gatherings of ministers, "public Friends" and "weighty Friends." Gradually the custom arose for each Quarterly Meeting to appoint a number of representatives to attend what became known as the Yearly Meeting. There are records of these gatherings as early as 1657, though it is not likely that representatives attended from all parts, as means of travel were primitive at that time.[1] There were large representative gatherings in 1657, 1659, 1660, at Skipton; and 1658 at Scalehouse; at Kendal in 1661. Meetings of "ministering Friends" were held near Balby, in Yorkshire in 1658; in London, 1659; at Warmsworth, 1660; in London, 1661.[2]

A Two Weeks Meeting was held in London consisting of elders rather than ministers in 1656, in order to provide for the poor, the sick and unemployed; to settle differences between Friends (as it was contrary to Friends' concept of righteousness "to take the law;") to keep records of births, marriages and burials; to see that marriages were conducted according to the manner of Friends and to advise with women's meetings. They were also charged with the responsibility of keeping record of the "Sufferings of Friends for Truth's sake." Out of this concern developed the Meeting for Sufferings. During the days of persecution this body which received reports from the monthly and quarterly meetings met in London prior to each court term in order to petition the justices in regard to the sufferings of Friends for conscience sake.[3] In course of time this body became the Permanent Board, which acts legally *ad interim*.

What might be regarded as the first yearly meeting was held at Skipton in 1660. At this gathering there were representatives of the principal sections of England and Wales. Women apparently held some separate session at Yearly Meeting time as early as 1674. No specific number of representatives was ever apportioned. It largely depended upon the ability of individuals to attend. The system of nomination is unique; it is an exhibition of democracy

at its best, and Quakerism is the proof that democracy will work
if motives be pure. Any person is at liberty to name another as
representative. If it did not appear likely that said person could
attend, he would ask to be excused "as the way did not appear to
be open." It is practically unknown for a meeting to pack a committee or appoint representatives as lobbyists.

At the yearly meeting the names of such representatives are
called by the clerk, and committees are usually limited to such
lists, but any member is at liberty to participate in both the meetings for worship and business. This includes women as well as men.
Perhaps the Society of Friends is the only world-wide organization
that functions fully in an open forum. The Yearly Meeting is for
inspirational and consultative purposes. There is no one person
clothed with superior authority; the annual gathering cannot dic-
tate to a local congregation; it possesses no executive functions; it
appoints various boards or central committees to attend to common interests, such as Peace, Public Morals, Temperance, Education, Missions, Foreign Relief, Evangelism. These boards are composed of representatives from the various quarters. Each annual
gathering selects its officials, which include clerk, assistant clerk,
recording clerk, announcing clerk and program chairman.
Nominating committees are sometimes appointed, but usually appointments are made "in the face of the meeting." Should an unsuitable name be called the matter is rectified by letting it stand,
and covering it with more suitable persons.

THE PLACE OF MEETING. Up to 1791 the yearly meeting was held
in the Eastern Quarter, sometimes at Perquimans or Old Neck,
sometimes at Little River. Eastern Friends believe the annual assembly was held in Perquimans till the old Meeting House was
wrecked by a storm in 1788, and the sessions were then transferred
to Wells, which later became know as Piney Woods. Thus for 68
years the eastern Friends constituted the largest and most important group in North Carolina. The sessions were held at Centre
in 1787; Perquimans in 1788; at Centre, 1789. It first gathered at
New Garden in 1791, and from that date to 1813 it alternated between New Garden and Eastern Quarter; on one occasion (1880) it
was in Tennessee; from 1883 to 1904 the High Point Friends entertained the Yearly Meeting; from 1905 that date to the present
New Garden has been the headquarters.[4]

BRANCHES OF FRIENDS. All branches of Friends throughout the
world have adopted the system of monthly, quarterly and yearly

meetings. The following have affiliated with the Five Years Meeting: Baltimore, California, Canada, Indiana, Iowa, Nebraska, New England, New York, North Carolina, Western (Indiana) and Wilmington, and also the Yearly Meetings of Cuba, Jamaica and East Africa. There are also Friends connected with the "General Conference:" Canada, Genese, Illinois, Indiana, New York, New England, North Carolina, Ohio, Philadelphia and there are groups known as "Conservative" and "Independent." Official publications list over thirty Yearly Meetings, Associations and Conferences in North America, and 27 in other parts of the world, with a total membership of 174,000.[5]

The Yearly Meeting occupies a very significant place in the existence of the Society. It is first of all an occasion upon which Friends renew acquaintance. It is here that the name "Friend" has a specific connotation. The bond between members is strong and the wholly democratic nature of this branch of the church, with no bishops, no clergy, no laity, no sex discrimination gives to the common term "Friend" a beautiful and unique fellowship. No titles or "handles" are used. Each is addressed naturally, simply and affectionately by his or her name. There are no doctors or reverends or "your honor." John Brown or Susan Smith are addressed and introduced as such publicly. Distinctions of rank disappear; no one wears ecclesiastic garments or decorations or uniform. The presiding clerk has no executive authority; he is responsible for the proper conduct of the business; he is a much respected person, whose judgment is valued, and who is versed in the history of the Society. Like the Speaker in the British House of Commons he is above party and can be relied upon to exercise impartiality. He or she is as far from being a political boss as could be imagined.*

THE GREAT DAY. Many years ago Yearly Meeting Sunday had peculiar characteristics. If the weather were favorable, there would be several services upon the campus. Wagon boxes would serve as extemporized pulpits and on various parts of the campus revivalists would hold forth, and listeners would go from one speaker's stand to another. Preachers in those days were able to make the multitudes hear without such gadgets as microphones and loud speakers. It was customary for ministers to obtain from their home meetings "minutes" (or credentials) and permission to attend other yearly meetings, and part of the purpose members had for coming long

---

* See also chap. xxvii

distances by farm wagon or other animal-drawn vehicles was to receive the spiritual uplift from these sermons. Another feature was the picnic dinner. Sunday was a great day, "the Great Day of the Feast," and the feasting was physical as well as spiritual. Well-filled baskets were the order of the day, and it was a high privilege to be invited to break bread with some family of distinction.

THE FOREST PRIMEVAL. A glimpse of primitive conditions during the Reconstruction Period may be seen in an extract from Henry Stanley Newman's *Life of Stanley Pumphrey*, written in 1875:

"I had to rise soon after three o'clock to come down to North Carolina. . . . We were finally turned out with our baggage in the middle of a wood, and after a little reconnoitering found a wagon which was ready to take our belongings to New Garden while we tramped. . . . New Garden is a school house in the midst of the woods. The large meeting house lately erected stands near by, but there is no other house in sight. . . . Our lodging room is fitted up for six Friends, and has one jug and basin and soap dish. . . . The Yearly Meeting assembled next day, and wagons driving up with their curious projecting roofs,* and loaded with the families of Friends, and with bedding, provisions, and other necessities of life. Many sleep in the wagons. Some found lodging a mile or two off, and the school house is stretched to its utmost capacity, with shakedowns spread over the schoolroom floor. We had only six in our room, except that one night we made up a bed with our wrappers for a Friend on the floor. We were a lively party including Yardley Warner, Charles Hubbard, Dr. Garner and Edward Soull. . . . Many of the Friends live in log cabins, some with an entire absence of windows."[6]

NEW THINGS DO I DECLARE. This kind of yearly meeting has disappeared. The automobile has changed the whole pattern of living. No longer do hundreds of farmers in North Carolina regard yearly meeting week as the vacation for the family. The prairie schooner and the box wagon have given place to the family car (or cars). They used to load the wagon with blankets, changes of clothing, plenty of food, and fodder for the team, and were prepared to rough it and sleep in the wagon if necessary, but Founders Hall and Archdale Hall usually could accommodate all who so desired.

Now these farmers (or their descendants) have a cottage by the sea or/and a swanky "cottage" in the mountains, and the annual church gathering is just another incident in the yearly routine. Those who live near enough (and ninety miles is near for a new car), go home after the afternoon session and return next day after the chores are finished. Life affords more variety and more contacts than it did half a century ago in the good-old horse and buggy

---

* The wagons were drawn by oxen, as well as mules and rarely by horses. These animals were tethered at convenient places.

days. Business is now concluded on Saturday morning, and the next day on the campus is just another Sunday, and likely as not there remains not one visiting Friend.[7]

The annual conference is an essential part of the church organization. All the monthly and quarterly meetings are integral parts of a united Society. They are all members one of another. The parts cannot survive separated from the rest of the members; each meeting is autonomous in so far as its own affairs are concerned, but the members are conscious that they have a common fellowship in a world-wide organization with a distinct historical heritage. The yearly gathering co-ordinates the activities of the several parts; and brings about integration and a common understanding. All the subordinate parts share in the expenses of the work of the central office. Epistles are read from meetings in distant parts of the world, and replies are sent to such in return, and so the unity of the whole is preserved.

Reports are presented of the various activities and provision is made for the continuance of these, and new concerns are presented from time to time. The condition of the world is always presented by able interpreters. One cannot attend many sessions of the great convocation at New Garden in August without being challenged with some responsibility for the defects of human society.

CLERKS OF NORTH CAROLINA YEARLY MEETING. The following worthy Friends have served as Clerk of the Yearly Meeting: Gabriel Newby, William Everigin, John Symons, Joseph Robinson, Francis Nixon, Jacob Wilson, Josiah White, Thomas White, George Walton, Benjamin Albertson, Levi Munden, Exum Newby, Enoch Macy, Thomas Jordan, Barnabas Coffin, Jeremiah Hubbard, Nathan Mendenhall, Aaron Stalker, John R. Hubbard, Nereus Mendenhall, Josiah Nicholson, C. Isham Cox, Zeno H. Dixon, Lewis Lyndon Hobbs, Samuel L. Haworth, Seth B. Hinshaw, Milo Hinkle and Algie I. Newlin. These persons would grace any assembly. In latter years they have been scholars of distinction.

THE YEARLY MEETING SESSIONS. Meetings for worship were held first at the homes of members. In early days in the Eastern Quarter one day sufficed for proceedings. In 1727 two days were occupied; in 1731, three days, gradually the sessions were lengthened till by 1930 they lasted nine or ten days.

In 1735 the yearly meeting "took up subscriptions" for the building of a meeting house; in 1743 the first "assessment" was levied for that purpose; in 1784 "the maximum tax" was 4,134 pounds; in 1792 "Yearly Meeting Stock" was instituted.

SEE WHAT BUILDINGS ARE THESE. Nathan Hunt loved to tell the following story concerning some of the early meetings:

> "Two great logs were so placed as to form the long sides of a narrow triangle. Those who sat at the head of the meeting were at the point of the triangle; Friends in their sedate garb took their places on the logs and then to prevent their horses from straying during the extended silent meeting, the animals were driven into the open triangle and the end was closed by a third log."[8]

Accounts differ as to the building of the first meeting house; this is not to be wondered at, and every person who investigates events of the long ago encounters contradictions. According to records and reports in the *Friends Review* of 1860 it would appear that the first place of worship was constructed of logs south (behind) the present King Hall at New Garden. It was probably built in 1773. There is no doubt it was of the traditional pattern with "facing seats" for the "heads of the meeting." The ministers sat on the upper seats — the men on the right and wearing their hats except in time of prayer or preaching — and the women on the left. The lower seats were for the elders and overseers. In those days it was the duty of the elders "to exercise a loving and faithful care over the ministry;" the overseers had the same responsibility for the membership.*

This structure was used as a hospital for the sick and wounded troops both British and Revolutionary after the near-by Battle of Guilford Court House, March 15th, 1781, and a number who died are buried near by. This building was destroyed by fire in the winter of 1784-85. A second meeting place was erected on the same site; this was a frame structure, 35 x 70 feet, providing "two thirty foot rooms — clear of alleys; there was a youths' gallery." John and Gideon Stephens were the "head workmen." This was the "Meeting House in the forest to which the students at the Boarding School were marched two and two twice a week," and the timbers of which they scrutinized during the periods of 'awful silence' to find, if they could, traces of the blood of the wounded soldiers. Every dark spot upon the timbers attained notice and legend. It is a pity to question this story, as it was not the same building,

---

* Friends in Virginia donated quantities of tobacco for the construction of the early meeting houses. There is no record yet found that this was so in North Carolina. There is an entry dated 1698 "Meeting houses should be kept decent and in good repair." We do not know of any such meeting house at that date. Weeks, pages 50 and 76.

It may be that some of the timbers of the first building were used in the second. Thus tradition may be preserved! This place was demolished in 1876, and the material sold for $145.00, but the purchaser complained "that he found the timbers not so good as he expected," so the money was refunded. Robert H. Frazier is authority for saying that the house of Albert Peele was built from some of those boards and that when the house was being torn down he saw some of the markings upon the boards.

THE FOUNDATION OF THE HOUSE OF THE LORD WAS LAID. The third meeting house was built of brick and was near the site now occupied by King Hall. By 1881 it became evident that further provision would have to be made for the school, as it was intended to convert it into a college. There had been considerable sentiment that the school should be built at High Point, so a compromise was effected. The yearly meeting deeded "its fine new meeting house" to the trustees of the educational institution on condition that the Friends of High Point would provide for the yearly meeting. Francis T. King reported at this time that the Baltimore Association had raised $22,000.00 — $10,000 for endowment and the rest for improvement. So the meeting house was extensively re-modelled for use as a classroom, and the yearly meeting assembled at High Point from 1883 to 1904. King Hall, as it was named, was burned three years later, in 1884.[9]

The yearly meetings at High Point were reminiscent of the past, and quite unlike the assembly of the present. Friends would arrive by mule or ox team attached to a prairie schooner or a conestoga wagon and bring provision for several days. The traditional Quaker garb might still be worn by some of the older members. On First Day there would be preaching from half a dozen wagons improvised as pulpits, and vast multitudes would congregate. This house has disappeared, but recently the local congregation has built a new house of worship upon a near-by site known as Quaker Hill.

THEY BUILDED AND FINISHED IT. In 1912 as the New Garden Friends needed a place of assembly an agreement was made to erect a building that would serve the local meeting and also the yearly meeting. A structure was erected upon the Guilford campus at the junction of the property of each; so each group paid one half of the cost, and the building straddles the boundary line. The arrangement has proved satisfactory, except that the time has come when rooms of considerable size should be added on the

first floor for Bible classes and social gatherings — the existing
basement accommodations are obsolete. The premises should also
be air-conditioned, as the mid-afternoon heat in August is sometimes almost intolerable. The building was erected at a cost of
about $10,000. The location is ideal; it is within easy access of
most of the membership, and the college buildings and dining hall
provide the necessary facilities for large gatherings. Plans are now
in hand for additional rooms.

CONCERNS OF THE YEARLY MEETINGS.   The first yearly meeting to
be held at New Garden was in 1791. By then this area had become
quite a thriving Quaker settlement. The progressive migration from
the east and the increased membership in Guilford and adjoining
counties caused the transfer of the annual gathering to New
Garden.

The annual sessions of 1830 to 1837 were chiefly concerned
over the question of the boarding school. It was Nathan Hunt
who persuaded Friends to favor the New Garden location. At
each yearly meeting in the thirties committees were appointed and
reported concerning the school.

These were momentous days politically, and some members of
the Society were keenly alive to political implications. All Southerners were concerned over the Tariff Bills of 1818, 1824, 1828
and 1832. Andrew Jackson's election in 1828 and his re-election in
1832 marked a great change in the national picture. Then there
was John Caldwell Calhoun with his Nullification Ordinance and
Jackson's Force Bill. The issues of the United States Bank, and
Public Improvements and Westward Expansion were live topics.

However, there was another issue that increasingly disturbed
the saints who would have preferred to work out their destinies
without undue disturbance. That was the question of slavery.
Year after year this issue hung like a dark cloud over the annual
gathering. The atmosphere became increasingly tense. Reluctantly
some members urged the disownment of such Friends as would not
free their consciences of this evil. Then by a strange irony the
Society became the title holder of numerous Negroes who had been
manumitted by their former masters, but who could not be sent
to free territory. The Underground Railroad then occupied the
chief interest of Friends for several years. Friends tried desperately
to remain above politics. They admitted being "anti-Slavery" but
they denied being "Abolitionists," for many of the latter demanded
political action with "immediate uncompensated abolition."

To Your Tents O Israel. The question of Secession greatly distressed Friends. They regarded themselves as loyal Southerners, yet they were Unionists, and as they had completely freed themselves from slavery in a peaceful and proper way, they considered themselves under no obligation to assist in getting rid of it in an unholy way.

The meeting had to deal with those members who forsook the testimony and who bore arms. Families were divided and congregations split. Without doubt the adverse criticism aroused seriously diminished the Society. As many as could, fled to the middlewest. During the turmoil several Friends settlements were ravaged by marauders or by military, and some members of the Society lost everything.

An Enemy Hath Done This. The Reconstruction Era was a critical time. Friends gathered at yearly meeting time under a sense of impoverishment and diminution. The statesmanlike activities of the Baltimore Association inspired the remnant to rebuild the waste places.

Then came the Revival, but Revivalism was a great departure from Quietism and many were not willing to acquiesce in the acceptance of "a hireling ministry." A few seceded and affiliated themselves with the Conservatives of other yearly meetings. Many who remained tolerated the pastoral system for a decade or more, but never fully reconciled themselves to a programmed meeting, remained critical, and gave little financial support. Happily this condition has passed, and the present generation fully appreciates the services of the pastors, realizes that the financial support is inadequate, and that steps must be taken in the near future to put the Quaker ministry upon a more solid foundation, by requiring the ministers to be better prepared.

The yearly meeting became partakers in the Forward Movement of the twenties, but, in common with the other denominations, experienced disappointment in the failure "to Evangelize the World in this Generation." Friends have maintained their testimonies as to Temperance, Foreign Missions, Education, Extension, the Five Years Meeting, the various All Friends Conferences, and Public Morals.

Let Your Nay Be Nay. In regard to our testimony against the recent wars, it must be confessed that our witness was in no way as definite as during the Civil War. Then the public knew where the Quakers stood. In the World Wars North Carolina had some brave souls who refused military service, and who performed alternate public service, and some of our young men and women served with the American Friends Service Committee overseas in reconstruction work. But times have changed; society has become more complex; it is less possible now for individuals to resist the national trends; the exercise of private conscience is less evident; in doffing the Quaker garb we have largely identified ourselves with the world; we are no longer a separate and peculiar people; the outward characteristics which marked us as Quakers have disappeared; and our meetings for worship are in the main only slightly indistinguishable from the services of other Protestant bodies. Quakers and all others have now the right to affirm instead of taking an oath.

It needs no prophet to foresee that in the event of another world-wide conflict conscientious objectors among Friends will be very few. This change is, in the opinion of the writer, due to the neglect of the leaders of our meetings to publicize the case against armed conflict. This raises the larger question concerning the presentation by the pastors of Friends doctrines. With few exceptions our congregations are uninformed concerning the fundamental facts of our Quaker faith. One purpose of this book is to bring home to the minds of our ministers, elders, overseers, clerks and members generally the importance and obligation to present to our congregations Friends' views concerning worship, salvation, the sacraments, oaths, peace, reconciliation, national righteousness and personal integrity.

This yearly meeting has engaged as pastors not a few young men who had little Quaker background, and little awareness of the implications of the Quaker faith. It is futile to blame them; they did the best they could. We must reproach ourselves that few of our birthright families were willing to permit their sons and daughters to dedicate themselves to a life of public service which offered no financial security.

PHYSICAL IMPROVEMENTS. Friends were painfully tardy in realizing the necessity of modernizing their places of worship. Of course the State was impoverished by the war in the sixties, the horrors of the reconstruction era, the mass migrations to the Middle West, then by World War I, and the subsequent Great Depression. It was not till the New Deal and activities in connection with World War II that Friends in the Old North State had the means to provide adequately for the meetings. Much, however, has been accomplished in recent years.

The following congregations have either remodelled or constructed new meeting houses: In Contentnea Quarter: Hood Swamp, Nahunta and New Hope; in Deep River Quarter: High Point and Oak Hill have erected entirely new premises; and Springfield has added a chapel; in New Garden Quarter: Glenwood, Kernersville, Spring Garden Street (Greensboro) have new premises. The Asheboro Street Friends of Greensboro were compelled because of street improvements to find a new location, and most handsome premises have now been erected and the meeting is now known as the First Friends Church of Greensboro. Winston Salem which erected a handsome building in 1927 in 1958 commenced the construction of an additional educational building; Southern Quarter has verily had a face lifting for Asheboro has planned an additional educational building, Bethel, Cedar Square, Hopewell, Marlboro, Randleman, Science Hill and South Plainfield have all improved their properties. In Surry Quarter Mount Airy is modernizing; in Western Quarter: Cane Creek, Centre, Concord. Providence and South Fork have effected improvements. Yadkin Quarter is also bestirring itself, and Deep Creek, East Bend, Forbush, Hunting Creek, Pilot View and Winthrop are improving the places of worship.

For many years the provision made for ministers was a reproach to the whole Society. Friends were inexcusably slow in considering the needs of those who were called to the pastoral ministry, and several able and willing laborers were compelled to find service elsewhere as an economic necessity. However, there has been an awakening, and as Friends shared in the general prosperity they were able to make proper provision for their resident ministers. In recent years the following meetings have substantially bettered the homes for their pastors. In Contentnea Quarter: Bethesda, Goldsboro, Nahunta, New Hope, Woodland, Deep River: Archdale, Deep River, High Point, Oak Hill, Springfield; Eastern Quarter: Piney Woods and Up River; New Garden: Glenwood, Greensboro, New Garden, Spring Garden Street, Winston Salem; Southern Quarter: Asheboro, Marlboro, Popular Ridge, South Plainfield; Surry Quarter: Mount Airy and White Plains; Western Quarter: Cane Creek, Centre, Concord, Graham, Liberty, Providence and South Fork; Yadkin Quarter: Harmony Grove and Pilot View. A home at New Garden has also been provided for the Executive Secretary. Many of these residences would be a credit to any denomination. These betterments were necessary if Quakerism was to progress. Friends share with the general public in the desire to have in their homes the modern conveniences and to provide modern means of travel and communication, and it is fitting that the severely plain and uncomfortable square wooden box which served as a place of worship two hundred years ago should give place to a sanctuary in accordance with the new age.

Several of our Meetings are being equipped with electric organs, and a robed choir leads the congregation in praise. These changes are justified, as now some Friends churches have a morning meeting with 300 present, whereas there would be but a dozen if we expressed "the Old-Time-Religion" in the old-time manner.[10]

ACTIVITIES. Among the organizations which are necessary to secure the proper functioning of the church as a whole there are many boards, committees and officers. Among them must be mentioned: the Board of Trustees, the Permanent Board, the various yearly meeting, quarterly meeting and monthly meeting Clerks; committees on Recording Ministers; Missions; Service Committee; Education; Stewardship; Prohibition and Public Morals; Evangelism; Finance; Peace; Literature; Guilford College Advisory Board; Ministerial Fund; Music; Preservation of Records; Young Friends Activities and several others. The life of the church as a whole depends upon the faithfulness of individuals. There would be no "body" without "members in particular." Speaking generally there is evidence of sound vitality and steady growth in individual righteousness and corporate harmony. The pastors, ministers and other workers meet monthly for fellowship and inspiration and recently adopted a very worthy "Code of Ethics" for those engaged in the ministry.

QUAKER MEN. In cooperation with the other yearly meetings of the Five Years Meeting North Carolina has participated in what has been called "The Quaker Men." Organized in California about six years ago it has for its main purposes "the Advancement of Christ's Kingdom." A well-attended men's supper was held at the time of the yearly meeting, and 150 men pledged themselves to unite in several projects. In quite a number of our monthly meetings very successful gatherings have been held regularly. The men generally have adopted the following projects:

i   To form a local organization;
ii   To encourage inter-visitation among various Friends' Meetings;
iii   To add an additional five per cent to the local budget for

the purpose of assisting the work of expansion outside the limits of their own meeting;

iv   To contribute to the expenses of some person studying in preparation for the ministry;

v   To subscribe to the cost of building and furnishing the Friends' Central Office at Richmond, Indiana;

vi   To the establishment of a revolving fund from which local congregations might borrow for remodelling or expansion.

A very encouraging start has been made with these objectives. The Yearly Conference of Quaker Men at the gathering in 1954 appointed Chester C. Haworth as president; William A. Wolff, secretary-treasurer; Ezra Pate, the Five Years Meeting representative; chairmen for each of the quarters were named; Robert O. Crow, statistical secretary.

YOUNG FRIENDS' ACTIVITIES. In common with other yearly meetings Young Friends are shouldering responsibilities. There is a committee known as members-at-large, — a chairman for each of the eight quarters and an executive committee appointed at the time of yearly meeting. At the time of this writing Jean Parks is chairman; Caroline Pipkin, Assistant chairman; Bobbie Patterson, recording clerk; Charles Farlow, assistant; Barbara Ann Jinnette, editor of the *Young Friends' News.* There are forty-five active organizations and at the times of quarterly and yearly meeting these juveniles hold their own sessions, take an intelligent interest and make constructive contributions to the church. North Carolina has a larger percentage of teenagers than any other yearly meeting, and their manifest interest and ability is the guarantee of the future of the Society. During the sessions of 1957 they effected three organizations — the Young Friends, the Junior Yearly Meeting and the Intermediates. Each group met separately and discussed the vital issues relating to membership; and each prepared an epistle which was read in open session, and forwarded to other similar organizations in other yearly meetings. On occasion the young people made contributions to the general program, and it was the general opinion that they measured up to commendable standards of excellence in preparation, sincerity and clarity.

For several years the Young Friends have sponsored a caravan which visited Yadkin Quarter for a week-end. Over one hundred high-school students participated, representing seven quarters and eight monthly meetings. One member was delegated to attend

the Yearly Meeting in Jamaica. The writer contrasts these manifestations of vitality with a story told many years ago by the late
beloved John T. Dorland, a Canadian Friend. He overheard some
children playing at "monthly meeting," and they mimicked their
elders. When one was named as a representative to quarterly meeting he or she would rise and say: "I fear I must decline the appointment, for I do not think the way will open for me to go." Another
would say "I have a stop in my mind against acceptance;" or "I have
no expectation of being able to serve the meeting in that capacity;"
or "I attended last time and some other Friend might like to have
the responsibility this time." As in the famous parable of Jesus
"They all with one consent began to make excuse." New Garden
Quarterly Meeting has a very active Young Fellowship group
which holds its own business meeting.

MISSIONARY INTEREST. The yearly meeting shares with Quakers
throughout the world an interest in Foreign Missions. The women
as elsewhere take the lead. North Carolina does not happen to
have representatives in the field at the present, but all work is
channeled through the Board of Missions of the Five Years Meeting. Through this central agency the Quakers carry on activities
in Cuba, Mexico, Jamaica, Palestine, Kenya Colony (Africa) and
among the American Indians in Oklahoma. The Board also sup-
ports some religious workers in eastern Tennessee. The Board has
under its supervision workers from America, Britain, Germany and
Finland. North Carolina Friends contributed about $18,000 for
these activities during the last year reported. In order to increase
the interest the Board arranged to have the clerk of the Cuba
Yearly Meeting visit our yearly meeting and in reciprocation Earl
Redding, of Marlboro Meeting, attended the Cuban Young Friends
conference.

QUAKER LAKE. In recent years there has been an interesting
development among the various branches of the church to provide
means of recreation and constructive fellowship during the summer months. All over the country camps, retreats, summer conferences or lake side conventions are being held. These gatherings
give opportunity not only for vacations and bathing and sunshine,
but for Christian fellowship. Experienced speakers and leaders
are brought in, and there is opportunity for attenders, and especially young people, to meet inspiring persons.

North Carolina started feeling its way along this line several
years ago, but the desired purpose was achieved when in 1949

1 5646

a site of 105 acres of land in Guilford County with a suitable body of water was secured. There were at the time two buildings, and the purchase price was $12,500. Since its acquisition ten additional buildings have been constructed and many improvements effected, and the property is now valued at $50,000. The camp is arranged to accommodate persons in separate age groups, and for week-end conferences.[11]

OUTREACH AND EVANGELISM. In recent years the theme of the yearly meeting has been Outreach and Evangelism. There has been a conscious dynamic. We are on the march. Throughout the whole body there is a desire and intention to advance. Many meeting houses have been modernized; better arrangements made for the preparation and training of ministers and workers; provision for aged and retired ministers; both the men and women are organized and sponsor definite projects; frequent revival services are held. In order to facilitate these objectives the yearly meeting appointed a Superintendent. Lewis Macfarland served several years in that capacity. Later the appointment was that of Executive Secretary and Fred E. Carter, Murray Johnson, then Isaac Harris; and since 1952 Seth B. Hinshaw have effectively shouldered that responsibility. Victor Murchison has visited virtually all of the local meetings and conducted revivals, with satisfactory results in increase in membership and renewal of spiritual interest. In many of these services he has been accompanied by the Men's Chorus of the Winston-Salem Meeting. It is a common observation that other yearly meetings look to North Carolina as a pioneer in the endeavor to regain the vitality and growth that characterised early Quakerism.

CHAPTER EIGHT

THE LORD WILL BE GRACIOUS UNTO THE REMNANT

THERE WAS A STRIFE AMONG THEM.   In order to understand the
story of North Carolina it is well to keep in mind the structure of
the population at the time of the opening of hostilities in 1860.
The total population was less than a million (it is now about
4,250,000). Of this number one third was Negro, the figures being
331,959 slaves and 30,463 freedmen; seventy per cent of the freedmen were mulattoes; there were also 1,168 Indians.

The non-native residents numbered less than 25,000; while
nearly 300,000 Tarheels had migrated to other States. The white
population was predominantly English, with large elements of
Scottish and German stocks. The population was heterogeneous,
consisting of diverse social, racial, religious and economic groups
or classes. The census of 1860 showed 87,025 farmers, 63,481
laborers, 27,263 tradesmen, 7,436 professionals, 3,479 merchants,
1,626 clerks, 1,308 manufacturers, and 121 planters. The upper
economic group of planters, professional men and manufacturers
composed only six per cent of the total. Agriculture was the chief
occupation, and North Carolina was predominantly a State of small
farmers. There is a general misunderstanding as to the number of
slaves held. It is stated that there were only 133 families who
owned more than 100 slaves; 611 families who held between 50 and
100; while from one to three slaves were owned by 16,071 families.
North Carolina was a slave-owning state; yet only 28 per cent of
the population held slaves in 1860, and as shown elsewhere, not
one was held by a member of the Society of Friends.[1] The
Moravians at Old Salem who adjoined the Quaker communities
held few if any slaves. The poor whites numbered about eight per
cent of the total; they were in terrible poverty as free white labor
could not compete with slave labor. One contemporary writer
says "hundreds and thousands of poor men with families existed
upon half starvation . . . doomed to drag out a miserable and use-
less existence." Another observer said they "were the most degraded
people of Anglo-Saxon stock in the world."[2]

Concerning education it is interesting to note that one of the earliest references to public education is that a school conducted by Charles Griffin, a reader of the Anglican Church, soon after the opening of the XVIIIth century "was attended by a number of students, especially Quakers." Several governors urged public education, but little was done in the colonial period, except private and church related local schools. The Whig government did a little in 1839, but the few schools languished, till a memorable event occurred in 1852 when Calvin Wiley was appointed State Superintendent of Common Schools. He vastly developed the elementary system and retained his office till 1865, but the stark truth is that illiteracy prevailed. One report says that some years before the Civil War there were 3,000 common schools, with an enrollment of 118,000. The schools were operated on an average for three-and-two-thirds months, and the teachers had a salary of $26.00 per month. In many places the teacher had to depend upon his or her own exertions to collect the salary from the patrons.[3] It is asserted that North Carolina had a better system in 1860 than any other Southern State, and it was actually better in 1860 than in 1890.

The chief point to be emphasized here is that most of the Quaker settlements were rural; most of the members were farmers, and therefore the standard of education among some of the members at the time of the war was extremely low; it is no reflection upon their character, religion or intelligence to admit that there was a high degree of illiteracy. It was not the general custom to read from the Bible in meeting; there were no Bible (or Sunday) schools.[4] Bibles were supplied largely through the concern of Joseph John Gurney.* The results were at first somewhat disturbing for in some places strange literal interpretations were given to certain passages, and on the frontier, especially in the middle-west, practices arose temporarily quite at variance with historic Quakerism. In 1840 30% of the North Carolina voters were illiterate; in 1860 the percentage was 23. In a few instances Friends were able to send some of their children to Friends' schools in the North. It is the belief of informed persons that Friends were more alive to the necessity of education than other bodies. There were monthly meeting schools in quite a number of places as will be told in another chapter, and efforts were made to circulate books among

---

* See separate writing concerning Gurney later in this chapter.

Friends.* The State became known as "the Rip Van Winkle State," and historians referred to "the colossal ignorance and intellectual degradation of the people."[5]

SEPARATIONS AMONG FRIENDS. The Society of Friends is unquestionably the most democratic organized religious body. Believing as most of them do that the "Inner Light" is the final authority it is remarkable that unity to any degree prevailed. In the business meetings nothing is ever put to a vote or decided by majority opinion. Should there not be unity it is the custom for the clerk to say so and recommend a postponement of the matter till "minds are clear." In the appointment of representatives, there is liberty for any member to name a person whom he or she considers suitable, never is objection made. It is not surprising that a century and more ago some Quakers pushed the principle of individualism too far, and insisted upon their own way. Friends recognize "that the spirit of the prophets is subject to the prophets," and that if the Holy Spirit leads one member to a particular service others who share the same spirit will be in unity, and if there is no unity then Friends would advise delay till there is agreement.

The first serious division occurred in the Philadelphia Yearly Meeting in 1827-28. The story lies outside the limits of this work, and is only referred to in briefest outline so that it may be seen how it affected North Carolina.

ELIAS HICKS (1748-1830) was a powerful preacher with a rather limited education, but rationalistic in his interpretation of the Scriptures. By an over-simplification he is frequently classed as a

---

* In two articles in the *Friends Journal*, June 29 and July 6, 1957, by John H. Hobart there is a well-balanced discussion of the attitude of Friends toward the Holy Scriptures. At first "Friends knew the Bible thoroughly," then came the Quietist period when even "Bible study was regarded as a creaturely activity;" then came the Great Revival during which many evangelically minded Friends went so far as to assert "there is no other way of salvation for us than that which He hath made known to us in the Holy Scriptures . . . the unscriptural notion of the light within is another gospel." The fourth attitude is that of the modern historical-literary study. The *Friends Journal* quotes Hobart as saying "a thorough knowledge of the Bible is essential to any proper understanding of Quakerism." Hobart substantiates what this writer has stated as to Quietism, saying: "The teaching ministry practically disappeared . . . often visiting ministers would speak no word . . . John Rutty, an Irish physician wrote in 1770 that he sat through twenty-two consecutive meetings for worship in which silence was broken only once. . . . Job Scott, in 1785, attended fifteen consecutive meetings in New Jersey and Pennsylvania not daring, he said, to open his mouth at any of them."

Unitarian. He objected to the figures of speech so common in sermons. Many Friends resented his teaching as unsound.*

SAMUEL BETTLE, who was clerk from 1816 to 1830, and who had great weight among Friends, became the leader of the opposition to Hicks. A separation resulted in 1827 which spread to New York, Ohio, Baltimore and Indiana. These Friends are known as "Hicksite" or General Conference Friends. They have not adopted the pastoral system, but worship upon the basis of silence, with addresses more ethical than evangelical. A recent official report gives their number as 18,681. It may be of some interest that the last recorded action of Philadelphia before the separation was to appropriate funds to aid North Carolina Yearly Meeting in the removal of freed negroes to Indiana. This yearly meeting, Virginia and New England were not affected by the Hicksite separation.

JOSEPH JOHN GURNEY. An English Friend whose personality was indelibly impressed upon American Quakerism was Joseph John Gurney (1788-1846). He was a learned, wealthy English aristocrat who made several visits to this country from 1837 to 1840, visited extensively among the several meetings and was especially distressed by the ignorance of Scripture, theology and church his-

---

* Elias Hicks made over fifty religious missions and between 1779 and 1829 visited every yearly meeting and most of the monthly meetings north of Virginia. He did not visit North Carolina as "the small meeting did not justify the long journey." He was a dominant person, and it was generally conceded that he was the principal cause of the separation, although he blamed it upon English visiting Friends, especially Anna Braithwaite, Elizabeth Robson, Thomas Shillitoe and Stephen Grellet (French). He opposed evangelism, Bible Societies, interdenominational gatherings and especially the "hireling ministry" which he said "was one of the things which had done the greatest hurt to the children of men." (He was able to perform his visits because he received a great sum of money at the time of the death of his wife's father.) (Forbush: *Hicks,* p 74.) He opposed revivals and camp meetings, and all "creaturely activities." He emphasized "the Spirit Within" in his preaching, and almost entirely ignored the historic Jesus of Nazareth and the Holy Scriptures. North Carolina Yearly Meeting was not immediately affected by the Hicksite Separations which occurred in New Jersey, New York, Pennsylvania, Ohio, Indiana and Baltimore. Hicks rejected the plenary inspiration of the Bible, Original Sin, "the Deity of Jesus Christ" and the necessity of the Atonement. He was a Rationalist and an extreme Puritan, who said "Friends should avoid all unnecessary intercourse with people of the world . . . be separate in maxims and manners." — *Ibid* p. 53. He held that "all that was necessary of Friends was that they believe in the operation of the Holy Spirit within the soul." — *Ibid* 120. He saw no need for conversion. Hicks was a mystical Liberal and held that theology was unnecessary and all that was essential to salvation was to follow the Inward Light. To indicate the irreconcilable difference between the Liberals and the Evangelicals it may be mentioned that Elizabeth Robson wrote: "I believe there is not anything more injurious to the cause of religion than exercising the reasoning faculties in order to comprehend Divine truths." — *Ibid,* p 225.

tory prevailing among Friends. He did much to encourage Bible reading. Gurney was much criticized by London Yearly Meeting, but his learning and prestige was such that minutes were not refused him to visit the American Yearly Meetings, and no one could compete with him in scholarship over here, yet many Friends were conscious that his preaching and teaching were not in accordance with Friends views.[6] He was greatly appreciated in this yearly meeting, and many children were named for him.

JOHN WILBUR (1774-1856) challenged Gurney. He wrote letters to English Friends, and followed Gurney around on his visits here to expose what he considered his errors. Wilbur, according to Elbert Russell "was a Quaker of the Quietist school, deeply devoted to the doctrine of the Inner Light, which he construed in such a way as almost to amount to personal infallibility. He was evangelical in theology, but stubbornly fearful of innovations which he attributed to creaturely activity." He denounced Bible Schools, Bible readings and lectures — everything that savored of preparation, premeditation or organization, and considered Gurney dangerous to Quakerism. He was as much opposed to Hicks as Gurney himself, but differed emphatically upon theological matters. New England Yearly Meeting to which Wilbur belonged regarded him as contentious, and resorted to high-handed and improper methods to quiet him. The monthly meeting refused to disown him, so the quarterly meeting "laid down the monthly meeting to which he belonged and attached the members to another meeting which disowned Wilbur." This resulted in 1845 in a separation in New England Yearly Meeting, and 500 withdrew out of a body of 6,500. The trouble spread to Ohio, and the conservative element withdrew in 1854. The same year a split occurred over the same issue in Iowa, and a further separation in the Philadelphia meeting was narrowly averted. This body adopted the policy of receiving into membership Friends of both the Gurney and Wilbur groups but not to accept preachers as recorded ministers. Philadelphia's consistent attitude of remaining aloof has been of incalculable loss .to the Society as a whole.[7] The Wilburite group is usually known as "the Conservative Friends," and include separatists from New England, 1845; Ohio, 1854; Iowa, 1877; Western, 1877; Kansas, 1879; Canada, 1881.

NATHAN HUNT AVERTS A SEPARATION. There was a danger that the Wilbur-Gurney separation might spread into North Carolina, for a delegation had been sent from the New England Yearly Meeting and had persuaded Thomas Hunt, who was the clerk of the Yearly Meeting that year, to support the Wilburite cause. Allen Jay tells the story as follows: Nathan Hunt, the father of Thomas, asked the supporters of each faction to meet him at New Garden Boarding School. He waited a few minutes in silence and then asked the Wilburite committee to speak first and the others to remain silent; then the Gurneyites should present their side of the issue. This was done, and then the shrewd patriarch said: "Now Friends I want you all to go to bed," and dismissed them with no opportunity for controversy. Then he spent the whole night "waiting before the Lord" to learn the Divine Will concerning the matter. The next morning he was gracious towards all the members. When the clerk reached this particular business he said "There are two epistles on the table from New England Yearly Meeting. I propose to read the one signed by the clerk of the Wilburite Yearly Meeting," calling his name.

Nathan, who up to that time had not said a word, then said in a loud voice, "Hold, Friends, there is a lion in the camp." He took his stand by the clerk, and said slowly: "Thomas, sit down!" Then followed a scene that was unforgettable. Between eighty and ninety years of age, his voice became firmer as he proceeded and his eyes kindled with their old fire. For an hour and more he reviewed the controversy between Joseph John Gurney and John Wilbur and the attitude of the London and New England Yearly Meetings, and concluded by warning the meeting of the evils of separation. Turning to the clerk he commanded: "Read the epistle signed by Samuel Boyd Tobey from New England." The son sat helpless but the assistant clerk rose and read the epistle, and the meeting approved with the exception of the Wilburite delegates who rose silently and departed that same evening for home. Thus was this Yearly Meeting preserved from involvement from the Wilburite separation.[8]

As IN THE DAYS OF OLD. In 1904 North Carolina Yearly Meeting adopted the Uniform Discipline which had been approved by the Quinquennial Conference of 1902. This met with objection by a small group, and they withdrew and became affiliated with the Conservative Friends of Ohio Yearly Meeting. They now have a few meetings in North Carolina, the principal being at Woodland. The meeting is typical of Friends of the year 1800, but recently the young Friends have become more liberal. A *Handbook* (1952) gives the Conservatives a membership of 3,127, with 500 being in

North Carolina and the great majority in Ohio. A later report gives the membership as 1,300.[9]

Although North Carolina has not been split into hostile groups, through these withdrawals, there can be no question that the body has been much weakened. The Conservative element is needed to preserve a proper balance. The chief reason for the separation here was that the Conservative Friends objected to the pastoral system, but the tremendous increase in vitality and membership of the Orthodox group has justified the action of the meeting in adopting the Uniform Discipline and affiliating with the Five Years Meeting.

JOIN THEM INTO ONE STICK. Whilst writing this story the welcome news is at hand that on March 28th, 1955, a joint meeting was held at the old Arch Street Meeting House in Philadelphia attended by the Orthodox Friends and the so-called Hicksite Friends of Race Street, and an organic union was effected between the two bodies to be known as the Philadelphia Yearly Meeting. Thus in the place when the separations began about 130 years ago the wound has been healed. This was no sudden decision, for joint meetings and cooperation in many undertakings have been proceeding for quite a number of years. Perhaps among those who by their love, sympathy, toleration and cooperation brought about this reconciliation there might be mentioned Rufus M. Jones, Elbert Russell, Clarence Pickett and Howard West Elkinton and his wife, Katherine Wistar Elkinton, although the younger members of both branches have fraternized for a long time, and joint sessions have been held in several yearly meetings. In Canada three branches hold their sessions together at Pickering College, Newmarket, Ontario, and, influenced by the reunion in Philadelphia these bodies (Orthodox, Hicksite and Conservative) formed an organic union at the yearly meeting in 1955.

THE FRONTIER REVIVALS. While Friends were "preserving their testimonies" there came into existence a religious influence of an entirely different order. It is associated with the names of John and Charles Wesley and George Whitefield. A century after Quakerism was flourishing the Spirit of God raised up leaders to meet a changed world. The founders of Methodism were scholars, and Charles Wesley gave to the Christian Church scores of its most inspiring hymns. Friends in North Carolina were directly affected by the spread of Methodism, as active congregations developed in the neighborhood of old-time Quaker settlements, but it was upon the piedmont and mountain sections that Methodism made its greatest impression. Although the Friends were not aware of what was happening, the minds and hearts of the frontiersmen were being drawn away from the pattern of Quakerism to a more dynamic type of evangelism.

The movement may be said to have begun with Jonathan Edwards, (1703-1801). He ante-dated the Wesleys, but his remarkable power in preaching had incredible results. He was the greatest revivalist up to that time. A trained scholar and theologian, he emphasized the essential Christian doctrines of repentance, faith and righteousness. People trembled under his forceful presentations of the wrath of God and the sufferings of Christ for sinners. It was common for scores to be smitten with remorse, to fall helpless, to writhe in agony, to groan and moan and cry for mercy. Others shouted for joy, and broke into ecstatic "tongues."

George Whitefield (1714-1770) made seven visits to North America, and visited every one of the colonies. He possessed what is said to have been the most clear, musical and penetrating voice ever known in a human being. Benjamin Franklin with characteristic scientific interest paced off the distance from which he could hear clearly, and calculated that at least 20,000 could hear him perfectly at the same time. Other reports say that more than that number sometimes assembled. As in the case of Jonathan Edwards his preaching was accompanied by violent physical manifestations. It was quite common for persons to be seized with convulsions, or shout and scream. People came for miles, and camped out. Some built "brush arbors";* some brought cows for obvious reasons. The meetings would last for days, and it was nothing uncommon for the preacher to speak several times a day, and two hours at a stretch. These sermons were well thought out, and presented the essentials of the Christian faith in an orderly fashion. Then came Charles G. Finney, (1793-1815) and again vast multitudes assembled, and thousands were converted.

In what is known as "the Middle Period of American History," that is between Washington and Lincoln, the piedmont and mountain sections, commonly known as the "backwoods" were the scenes of extraordinary revival services, known as camp meetings. It was the era of the "circuit rider." This is not the place to discuss these occasions in detail; the matter is only presented because it accounts in part for the decline of Quakerism in this period. Much could be written concerning these circuit riders. Some were well-

---

* For description of a brush arbor see *Pilot View* chap. xxiv.

educated and ordained clergymen; others were laymen with little or no education, who possessed the ability to urge "sinners to flee from the wrath to come." They were a hardy group; they crossed mountains, swam rivers, camped out in the forests, slept in makeshift quarters, spoke with authority and braved serious difficulties and dangers. Often they travelled on foot, but usually upon horseback. These camp meetings often lasted for weeks; the news was spread and by the thousands came to hear and witness the happenings.

Some historians have described these gatherings as "emotional religious circuses." There was little to break the monotony of the frontier, and these annual revivals were welcomed by all as an opportunity to relieve the tensions and abandon themselves to emotion. Many expected and desired to be emotionalized; others were anxious to see who "backtracked," and known reprobates regularly backtracked.

The preaching was generally of a lurid character; the Devil was personalized, and it was common to say the preacher made Hell so real that many screamed in terror. The revivals were occasions of family reunions, of hirings, of conducting business and of love making. They are an essential page in the history of the frontier and also of the development of religious life in America. Some of these circuit riders were successful organizers, and the revivalist did not consider his work complete until he had established a congregation, appointed officials, and made arrangements to supply preachers. The Baptists also participated in this work.

The writer many years ago attended such a camp meeting. The preacher blessed handkerchiefs which he said would heal the sick. Persons went forward by the score, and some were down on all fours in the straw, with their heads spinning around like pegtops; others were "speaking in unknown tongues." A stranger said to the writer "I wish I could have an experience like that." Gradually this type of holding religious service spread throughout the colonies, and therefore removed the Quietism and Pietism of the Quakers further than ever from general interest.

THE GREAT REVIVAL AMONG FRIENDS.   The old times were passing. The purchase of the Louisiana Territory, the War of 1812-15, the acquisition of Florida, 1819-22; the Monroe Doctrine, 1823; the Nullification Issue precipitated by Calhoun in 1832, and especially the westward migration made the people of the United States conscious of a great destiny. It is impossible for us to appreciate what may be called the growing pains of the new nation. It was a nation on the march.

Not only was the country stirred politically it was shaken to its depths spiritually and emotionally. In addition to the circuit riders who have been mentioned the whole English speaking world was aroused as never before in the latter quarter of last century by the revivals conducted by Dwight L. Moody and Ira D. Sankey. Then there was John B. Gough, (1817-1886) a converted alcoholic, possessed of commanding personality and an oratorical ability rarely equalled by preachers or statesmen.

The Breath of God was certainly moving, and the spiritual lethargy which had settled upon Britain and America in the first half of the nineteenth century was being ended. Several English Friends visited the various yearly meetings and made some contribution to the awakening. In 1857 and 1858 revivals "broke out" in New York, Philadelphia and Indiana Yearly Meetings. The time had come for Quakerism to shake off the outward characteristics of its early period and to allow the spirit of a newer age to express itself. No one quite knows how it started; it was certainly not of human ordering. Evangelical messages of a new character were given by Quaker ministers; they spoke with new power; they spoke of experiencing conversion; they preached Christian doctrines in a convincing way; they pleaded with the unsaved; they asked those under conviction of sin to come forward and repent; more persons spoke in meeting; singing came spontaneously; the young people asked for special evening services, which were a great innovation; prayer meetings were held at the home of members.

To give one example. Charles F. Coffin says that at Richmond, Indiana, an evening meeting was requested, and the older Friends were asked to remain silent

"It proved to be a very remarkable meeting and lasted until nearly midnight with an almost continuous succession of prayers and public testimonies. After the close of the meeting Sybil Jones asked to meet with all who has taken part in the meeting. About 150 met with her at the house of Charles F. and Rhoda M. Coffin."[10]

Similar awakenings occurred in New York, but more especially in Western, Iowa and Kansas Yearly Meetings.

The Civil War lasting from 1860 to 1865 checked these manifestations, but the surrender of Robert E. Lee at Appomattox was the signal for a renewal of the evangelical fervor among Friends. There now appeared ministers of a totally different order from those at the opening of the century. Only a few of them will be

named here, as they were mostly Northern Friends, but before long
the fire kindled there spread to North Carolina. The leaders in the
revival were Eli and Sybil Jones, Charles F. and Rhoda Coffin, John
Henry and Robert W. Douglas, Nathan and Esther Frame, Luke
Woodward (who is said to have been the first Friends pastor),
David T. Updegraph, Lindley M. Hoag, Jeremiah A. Grinnell, William Wetherald (a Britisher),* Dougan Clark. North Carolina
contributed Nathan Hunt, Rufus P. King, Franklin S. Blair.

Naturally the older Friends were shocked at these manifestations of "creaturely activity." The *Friends Review* disapproved; so
the Evangelicals published a paper of their own known as *The
Christian Worker,* which in 1893 was renamed the *American
Friend,* with Rufus M. Jones as its first editor. The *Friends Review*
ceased publication at the same time. A revival occurred among
the student body at Earlham College, Richmond, Indiana, in 1866-
67, and a similar religious awakening occurred at Whittier College,
Salem, Iowa.** Various yearly meetings appointed standing committees to supervise these special meetings. In 1874 a veritable
wave of revivals occurred in Kansas and Iowa. At one place when
"a call was made for all who wished to forsake sin and lead a
different life to come to the front seats . . . at once a score came
forward amid great confusion, some stepping over the backs of
the benches in their haste. Some who did come forward became
the center of praying groups. . . . While some were praying others
cried aloud and, interspersed with personal pleadings, an occasional stanza of a hymn was sung.***

An account of another revival among Friends says: "Many
hearts were reached and all broken up, which was followed by sighs
and sobs and prayers, confessions and great joy for sins pardoned
and burdens rolled off. But, alas, some of our dear Friends mistook

---

* William Wetherald was one Sunday teaching a class of small boys at Pelham,
Ontario, Canada (where the writer was a minister at a later date). William noticed
that one boy in particular kept his eyes fastened upon him. He innocently presumed that the boy was greatly interested, and so asked the boy to tell the story.
The boy was blank, so William drew his chair closer and re-told the story. Again
the child was attentive — with open eyes, open mouth and open ears. Surely thought
William the boy knows the story now, but again the boy was blank when asked
to repeat the story. So in vexation the teacher said: "Tell me what you were
thinking while I was teaching the lesson." The youngster grinned and replied:
"I was wondering why it is that all your hair grows on the bottom of your head
instead of upon the top."

** Whittier College, Salem, Iowa, is now an Independent Fundamentalist Bible
School.

*** These persons had been reared upon the new frontier and knew nothing of
traditional Quakerism.

this outbreak of the power of God for excitement and wild fire and tried to close the meeting, but we kept cool and held the strings, and closed the meeting orderly."[11]

All this was so much at variance with the former ways of Friends that many elders and more conservative members were greatly shocked, and being unable to adjust themselves to the change separations occurred in several yearly meetings, which will be referred to later. So many persons were gathered in that it seemed perfectly proper that the visiting preacher who had conducted the revival should be asked to remain, and some provision was made for his maintenance. Thus it was that the revival preceded and necessitated the pastoral system. It should be clearly understood that the "so-called pastoral system" was not devised to bring about a revival among Friends.

The Westward Movement had resulted in the breaking down of the denominational walls; in fact, one of the outstanding characteristics of American democracy is that among dissenters there is little denominational antagonism. Intermarriages between adherents to other faiths are common, and attendance at other places of worship is taken for granted. It is not so in European countries, where the denominational walls are almost unscaleable.*

The revival eventually reached North Carolina. Visitors to yearly meeting told of the great awakenings elsewhere; gradually singing was participated in, and as the whole country had been moved by these wide-spread revivals there were not lacking in the South those who realized that the new wine had burst the old bottles, and gradually the meetings took on a new character. There came into the Society many who had former memberships in other religious bodies; there was therefore a loss of emphasis upon matters formerly stressed by Friends, and a new evangelical note was manifested.[12] Thus traditional Quakerism passed from much of the American continent.

A WOMAN REVIVALIST.   When but eight years of age a little Kansas girl became strangely aware of the Divine Presence and experienced a definite call to become a preacher when she became older. She became possessed of what she later described as "a holy hush"

---

* The writer recalls that he wrote to Edward Bellis, of Richmond, Indiana, congratulating him upon reaching his ninetieth birthday, and made reference to the many changes he had witnessed in his lifetime. Edward Bellis replied that "electric light, the telegraph, telephones, automobiles were wonderful, but the most remarkable development was, in his opinion, the ability of Methodists, Baptists, Catholics and Jews to be decent toward each other."

as she saw in a vision the extent of her travels in the ministry, as she put it "south, east, west and north, and even across the Atlantic." Throughout her life she treasured the memory of her father conducting family worship, and the image of his reading the Holy Scriptures made an indelible impression upon her.

Mary Moon was the daughter of John and Susannah Hollingsworth Pemberton, and was born August 27th, 1845, in Jonesboro, Indiana. She was united early in life in marriage with Jonathan Moon, near Emporia, Kansas, July 30th, 1863. Jonathan became crippled, and Mary was compelled to find remunerative occupation. Her husband weakened and died leaving her at the age of thirty-eight with three children. Her daughter, Nellie Moon Taylor, of Danbury, "the first lady of Stokes County," tells the following. "When my mother was about twenty years of age she attended a Quaker meeting in Kansas, and there was present a revivalist from New England. Something overcame her at meeting, and she returned home utterly miserable. The minister said to some of the elders after meeting 'There was a young woman at meeting with whom I must have a sitting.' Some one said it was probably Mary Moon. The preacher was taken to the home, and when some one knocked at the door, Mary refused to answer. However, the knocking continued, and when Mary appeared the minister said to her: 'Peace be unto this house. The angel of the Lord is visiting here. I must have a sitting with thee.' He told her that it had been revealed to him that the Lord was calling her, that she must cease her resistance to the Divine Will; that the Lord would provide for her."

Mary Moon told the story often in these words: "the Lord came to me in sanctification . . . I was called to answer many questions . . . Would I give my time? . . . Would I give my tongue? . . . Would I trust Him? . . . My whole being responded . . . I pleaded the merits of the Atonement, and Heaven came tumbling down, filling my heart and the whole room."

Nine years after the death of Jonathan Moon she married Franklin Meredith, a Friends Minister. She came of a long line of Quaker ministers and commenced her preaching in Indiana in 1868. This was just after the conclusion of the war, and as told in another place the great revival which was begun among Friends before hostilities and which was suspended during the days of conflict, burst forth again when peace was restored.

Mary Moon, as she was generally called, pioneered in the

days when it was a novelty for women to preach. A contemporary wrote: "Everywhere she went she was heralded with reports of wonderful revival influence. Her preaching was argumentative, illustrative and earnest; her knowledge of theology was unusual; her singing was marvellous in effect. Another wrote: "I first met her in a room of one lingering in the shadow of death. She said she would sing softly, and I shall never forget the sweetness of her song. Her prayer seemed to drive the gloom away." "Occasionally in the midst of her spoken message she would sing, and the congregation would be melted to tears." She was marvellously used of the Lord in revival services among Friends and others in Indiana, Illinois, Ohio, Iowa, Kansas, Colorado, Michigan, and North Carolina. With her husband she assisted in the organization of California Yearly Meeting. She did extensive evangelistic work in the Western States including California, Oklahoma, Old Mexico, Oregon, and her activities extended to Canada.

Her childhood vision was realized when in 1910 she and her husband visited Europe, and she found open doors of service in England, Wales, Ireland, Norway and Denmark. Her ministry was in no way limited to Friends, and much of her direct appeal was in the homes she visited.

MARY MOON IN NORTH CAROLINA. She made a permanent contribution to North Carolina, at a time when encouragement and augmentation were needed. The "western fever" had almost stripped the yearly meeting bare; then came the war; then the terrible days known as "Reconstruction," in which Federal troops remained in possession of the South. Mary Moon's gospel messages were like healing balm. She went throughout the yearly meeting, and perhaps more than any other person made possible the adoption of the pastoral system in this area. Some regarded her as the greatest evangelist of her age. One said "We have never looked upon a face beautified with higher, grander and nobler marks of Christian character." Another wrote: "She stirred North Carolina as never before," and she brought thousands into a saving knowledge of the Lord Jesus Christ. In 1878 she conducted a revival in a Methodist church in Winston, and a writer said: "Never since Winston has been a town has such a revival been witnessed here." Some contemporary reports say that sometimes there was a crowd of five thousand to hear her. Contemporary newspapers were filled for months with correspondence concerning the propriety of women preaching. One correspondent declared: "One might just as well try to stop the birds singing as to stop Mary Moon preaching." She died at the age of seventy-eight and her remains interred at West Branch, Indiana.[13]

ALLEN JAY. This gracious Friend deserves a place of honor in two chapters in this book. He had much to do with the revival of the public schools in this State; he extinguished a debt of $27,000 upon the New Garden Boarding School; he had a share in the creation of Guilford College — yet he did more. In the opinion of this writer his greatest service was in the field of evangelism. It is conceivable that there were others who could have solicited funds and given encouragement, but the Society needed a spiritual revival. Previous pages have depicted the Quietism and Mysticism into which the remnant of the Birthright Friends had fallen, and the heartwarming messages of the Gospel were needed to make "the Dry Bones Live." It would not have been of lasting benefit if the Boarding School had been metamorphosed into a great college unless the church as a whole experienced the vitalizing power of faith in a Living Savior.

Allen Jay was not an educator; he had little formal education; he was a preacher, evangelist and revivalist, so this writer includes him in this chapter. It was under the auspices of the Baltimore Association that Allen Jay came to North Carolina to take over the work after the return of Joseph Moore to Earlham College. Jay was a remarkable person; like Demosthenes he had a serious impediment in his speech; like Moses he could have pleaded a natural inability; but he endured severe operations because he determined that he would acquire some facility in public speaking. After a period of youthful uncertainty over certain "isms" of the day, he found permanent co-ordination and assurance through faith in Christ and thus became a flaming evangel. He travelled extensively in the Middle West in the ministry before he came to North Carolina. Those who remember him agree that the best explanation of his personality is to say without sanctimoniousness that "the grace of the Lord was upon him." He was essentially modest and unassuming, rather difficult to listen to, but he possessed an indescribable capacity to persuade people to conform to his suggestions. Not only could he obtain handsome subscriptions to the Quaker educational undertakings, but he was able to satisfy elderly conservative Friends and enable them to accept revivalistic methods in their meetings; he also endeared himself to hundreds of young people so that they were led to accept the Lord Jesus as their personal Savior.

He visited many families and held "general meetings" (especially arranged) throughout the yearly meeting, and was in great demand outside the Society. Largely through his ministry and inspiration the membership was increased from 2200 in 1866 to 5500 in 1876. Jay regarded the revival of Quakerism in North Carolina as the greatest work of the Society in last century. He encouraged the teachers to open the sessions with worship and also to conduct Bible classes. The revivals were free from emotionalism, but penitents by the dozen came forward, and singing became spontaneous. At first some elderly Friends were startled, if not shocked, yet when it became evident that the young folks were soundly converted and their lives changed, criticism became pointless. One typical instance may be quoted "He was invited by the Methodists to conduct meetings at High Point; he preached for thirty-one nights; there were 150 conversions; the whole town was shaken . . . and 59 wished to join Friends, although there was no Friends meeting there at that time."

In his *Autobiography* Allen Jay refers to Mary Moon, Fernando G. Cartland and wife Abby, John Y. Hoover, of Iowa, James Jones, Albert Peele, Mary Chawner Woody and Mary Cartland as leaders in these revivals. Once the new joy and enthusiasm had electrified an oldtime Quaker meeting it was impossible for the traditional manner of worship to be restored. In many instances the revivalist was asked to remain indefinitely, and thus Quaker worship became freed from Quietism.

Allen Jay returned to Earlham College and served as Superintendent from 1881 to 1887; he then became financial agent and was phenomenally successful. In recognition of his integrity and service he was appointed a trustee of the College in 1890. At his funeral in 1910 a very large number of leading citizens assembled, and President Robert L. Kelly saluted Allen Jay as "a universal man."[14]

CHAPTER NINE

SITTING AMONG THE TEACHERS

ANNE THE HUNTRESS.   Most persons with any knowledge of North
Carolina know that Guilford College, opened in 1888, grew out of
New Garden Boarding School which began operations in 1837;
but probably few have heard that there was a little brick school
house there before that, (that story will be told separately) and
that before that little school existed there was a school probably
without parallel in all the history of education.

Maybe this is tradition — but tradition must be preserved.

Forty years before this story opens, the Quakers had been
pouring into the Piedmont section of this State. They came by the
hundreds from Pennsylvania, from Maryland and New England.
There was also a stream which trekked from Perquimans, Pasquotank and Chowan "provinces." New Garden was then considered
"a thriving settlement."

One fine day in 1790 a considerable group had congregated to
hold a shooting match, and while every one's attention was upon
the competitors and the target, there stepped into the open a
stranger. It was a young woman, beautiful and attractive. She
was dressed in hunting togs with Indian leggings. She fondly
carried a highly ornamented rifle, and belt with shot pouch, a fear-
some knife and a sharp hatchet. Striding off sixty paces she turned
smartly, put her gun in position, sighted along the barrel and then
cried: "Does any one object to me taking a shot?" The situation
was so dramatic that no one considered it wise to object, so she
pulled the trigger and scored a bull's-eye to the delight of the
crowd. She then walked around nonchalantly and said to each and
sundry in the Quaker lingo "How'd thee do? How'd thee do?"

There was that indefinable something about the stranger which
attracted the children. She beckoned them to her and let them
examine her gun and belt and moccasins. She then sat down upon
a stump and told the youngsters about a wild boar she had shot.
The oldsters soon joined the enchanted listeners. Naturally she
joined the group when the "eats" were served and when an elderly
Friend asked her name she said "Call me Anne, the Huntress."

According to the custom of the frontier she was invited to spend the night. She accepted the invitation promptly and went off with Richard Dodson to his cabin a mile away. She said "Good night" to the children and "come again tomorrow if you would like to hear some more stories." The news spread, and not only the next day, but for seventeen years children sat at her feet.

She had evidently received a good education; her grammar was faultless; her pronunciation perfect. She told a story and then required the children one by one to repeat it and to use exactly the same sentence structure that she did, and insisted that they pronounce the words aright, and never to slur over a syllable or drop the final consonant.

THE LAW OF EVERY LIVING CREATURE. She told them stories of the animals and trees of the forest, and of birds and fishes, of mountains and of rivers. She made the children think. She made them realize the differences between dogs and cats. She would ask: How do their coats differ? their ears? their faces and jaws? How does each catch its prey? How many toes do they have? How do the toes differ? What can each do that the other cannot? Why?

The children did not realize they were being educated. She believed in review. Before she would tell a new story several children were required to repeat some already told. She insisted upon completeness and accuracy. They became informed of many particulars necessary for a frontiersman.

She went from settlement to settlement; she was satisfied with pot luck; she never interfered with the management of the household. The colonists were glad to share with her, for she told the grown-ups stories of the great world outside the forests, but she never said one word about herself. She paid well for her lodging, for she loved to roam the woods, and she brought back the evidence of her skill — venison, bear meat, pheasant, partridge, quail, wild turkey and rabbit. Once in a while the whole community went out to skin, butcher and share a bear or a buffalo that she had brought to the dust.

Who was she? What was her name? Whence came she? Why did she live in such a manner? Whence did she go? No one ever knew. She was Anne the Huntress, and in the winter of 1807-08 she vanished in the same mysterious manner in which she came. Although the New Garden community enquired far and near, her whereabouts was never reported. Surely a strange prelude for a Quaker college.[1]

EARLY EDUCATIONAL ACTIVITIES. The original Quakers in the colony were encouraged by English Friends to educate their children. This was not easy of accomplishment, because of the harsh frontier conditions. It is well established that for the first half century the colony had no schools whatever, and consequently illiteracy and ignorance prevailed. There is a deep seated tradition that in some of the colonies a learned person might spend a few weeks in a settlement and teach the children in return for his board. It is certain that elsewhere wealthy planters had tutors in their homes according to the English pattern and then sent their sons to England for a classical education[2] but there is no evidence that the Carolina Quakers were able to afford such a procedure. The Colonial Legislature in 1695 provided that teachers might be regarded as bound apprentices and the "master" be required to sign indentures*[3] to that effect. By 1703 we find reference to schools conducted in Eastern Quarter, one by Charles Griffin, a Friend, whose school was later taken over by the Rev. James Adams, and a person named Marshburn had a school at Sarum. In 1709 William Gordon travelled through the colony and reported "Here is no library or public book whatever . . . there is no church . . . people are ignorant."[4]

As there is no proof that Quakers possessed meeting houses prior to 1702 meetings for worship were held in residences, and the limited and primitive conditions would not permit much schooling. By 1711 there were three meeting houses and then instruction of children became feasible. Pasquotank had two meeting houses by 1806, and the children naturally were required to attend midweek meeting.

The record of the concerns of Friends for education has been so thoroughly treated by Zora Klain in his *Quaker Contributions to Education in North Carolina* that there is no need for the present writer to examine the numerous sources.

The following presents the essentials. It appears proper to consolidate the remarks into a unit rather than mention the matter in the discussion of each particular meeting — such would involve needless repetition.

The Yearly Meeting was established in 1698 and by 1714 the minutes record: "there is a deficiency found in education of the children." One can well believe this, for the official minutes are

---

* The word indenture applied to the wedged or saw-like manner in which the paper of apprenticeship was torn in two. Each party took one portion so that identification could be made by matching the serrations.

curious specimens of spelling, punctuation and capitalization. There was no printing press in the colony till 1749 and with its appearance there was no immediate betterment of culture. The yearly meeting frequently sent messages to subordinate meetings urging action concerning schools. The proceedings of Perquimans Quarterly Meeting in appointing a committee in 1787 to visit preparative meetings and encourage them in this regard is typical of many such entries.

An unusual gathering met at New Garden in 1795 consisting of representatives from North Carolina, South Carolina, and Georgia and among the matters considered was the proper instruction of children.

Stephen Grellet visited the South in 1800 and he recorded "the education of the people is very much neglected in almost every part of the Carolinas and Tennessee, there being few or no schools, so that not many children or even adults can read."[5] The minutes of the yearly meeting confirm this criticism.

The general situation can be told in the following statements: The yearly meeting urged local meetings to provide elementary education; most monthly meetings endeavored to comply and appointed committees; schools were conducted for shorter or longer periods; an average of four months; when feasible the school was held in the meeting house; conditions were primitive; there was practically no school furniture; many benches were backless; books and blackboards were non-existent; many of the teachers were from the North (especially so in Reconstruction Days;) a few of the teachers attempted to teach Latin and Greek, but these were rare; the degree of ignorance among the colonists' children was colossal; the teacher received a salary of from $15.00 to $25.00 per month; in some cases the teacher had to collect fees from the parents; monthly meetings sometimes paid the tuition of poor pupils; attendance was very irregular; generally less than half those enrolled attended; as was common some children walked miles to school; roads were sometimes impassable; the schools were "mixed,"* meaning that many of the children were not members of the Society. Colored children were not refused admission; usually a majority of those attending were not Friends; few of the teachers were members of the Society. These features caused great concern as conditions developed "contrary to Friends' principles." During the war most of the schools were discontinued; conditions

---

* In Reconstruction Days the term "mixed" implied Negroes and Whites in the same school.

were such that it was not safe for children to leave home; soldiers upon both sides occupied and defiled the school houses; some teachers went into military service others fled to the North; Confederate currency became worthless. The schools in Quaker districts were revived by the Baltimore Association, and later became absorbed by the county educational authorities. It is believed that in many places the Quaker schools were the only ones in existence. After the revival of schooling by State authority the Quakers were active in this endeavor, and the New Garden Friends aided in many ways the schools at New Salem, Muir's Chapel, Kernersville, Guilford, Greensboro, Pomona, Dover and Summerfield.

With four exceptions the Quaker schools were on the elementary level, but Eastern Quarter sponsored Belvidere Academy; Contentnea supported Woodland Academy and Western Quarter established Sylvan Academy. In each of these High School subjects were offered, and under the administration of the learned Nereus Mendenhall Greek and Latin and other advanced subjects were taught at the New Garden Boarding School.

EASTERN QUARTER conducted grade schools at Aurora, Up River, Jessups, Hickory Grove and Snow Hill.

CONTENTNEA QUARTER held schools at Neuse, Nahunta, Cross Roads Academy, New Hope, Pearson's School, Burr School House, Falling Creek and Bethany.

WESTERN QUARTER.   There were three schools under care of Cane Creek Meeting; Centre Monthly Meeting sponsored schools at Centre, Providence, Hockett, Reynolds and Concord.

NEW GARDEN QUARTER was in part responsible for the Brick School House, and later the New Garden Monthly Meeting School, and gave assistance at various times to schools at Dover, New Salem, Muir's Chapel, Kernersville, Guilford, Greensboro, Pomona and Summerfield (though most of these were not directly under the charge of the monthly meeting).

DEEP RIVER QUARTER cared for elementary schools at Deep River, Hickory Grove, North Branch, West Branch and the Springfield Monthly Meeting was responsible for common schools at Springfield, Bush Hill (which later became famous as Archdale), Oak Hill, Prospect, Pine Woods, Oak Forest, Caraway and Deep River.

Richard Mendenhall, a classical scholar, a member of Deep River Meeting, conducted a night school at his tannery at Jamestown for sixteen years, charging no tuition fees and furnishing supplies at his own expense. Youngsters and adults attended his classes. He also encouraged and supported his daughter, Judith, who had been educated at a Quaker school at Germantown, Pa., to operate a boarding school for girls at Jamestown, which institution became known as the Little Brick Schoolhouse. A brother of Richard, George C. Mendenhall, also made distinctive contributions to education. Not only did he train some of his Negroes to be carpenters, harness makers, tailors, cooks and farmers, but between 1820 and 1830 he aided his slaves in acquiring the rudiments of an education. He was also active in the establishment of a Female College at Jamestown, the attendance at which sometimes reached one hundred.[6] It would appear that these were personal concerns and not responsibilities of the meeting.

Mary M. Hobbs also gave some particulars of an elementary school for girls at Florence, N.C. Margaret Davis and Penelope Gardner, members of the Society, taught there from 1850 to 1865. After a while boys were admitted. To take care of some boarding pupils Winslow Davis built an addition to his home. It is of interest to learn that Mary Mendenhall Hobbs taught at this school.[*]

SOUTHERN QUARTER was not established till 1816, and prior to that time Friends in this scattered area were members of other meetings. Back Creek Monthly Meeting operated schools at the Back Creek Meeting House also at Belvidere, Davis and Science Hall. The attendance averaged about 20 at each school, and here again the Baltimore Association rendered very great encouragement through John Scott their agent. Holly Spring Meeting cared for schools at Holly Spring, Bethel, Middleton, Pine Ridge, Woody's and Tabernacle. Yardley Warner assisted here.[**] Hopewell Meeting was urged by the yearly meeting to educate their children, but a minute of 1911 says "the Monthly Meeting owns no schools, but there are fourteen public schools within its limits."[7]

MARLBORO MEETING showed concern about the education of their children, for the records show that there were five schools within the area by 1834, but not under the care of the Society, although there were three Quaker teachers. The number of children under five years of age steadily declined from 136 in 1835

---

[*] The writer was well acquainted with Mary Mendenhall Hobbs who gave Klain this information.

[**] For Yardley Warner see chap. xii.

to 96 in 1840 — probably an evidence of the "western fever." This Monthly Meeting operated schools at Marlboro, New Salem, Cedar Square, Flint Hill, Poplar Ridge, Glencoe and Plainfield. In one of these schools Latin was taught. The report says that these schools passed through a crucial time between 1870 and 1890.[8]

YADKIN VALLEY QUARTER. Augusta Preparative Meeting was under the care of East Bend Monthly Meeting. In 1898 or thereabouts two acres of land and a two story building was purchased for $521.00, which was said to have been worth $2,600.00. Funds came from other yearly meetings very largely. An Academy was established and attendance varied from 17 to 26, although 53 were enrolled. This is a typical example of irregularity. The school continued till 1905, when in all probability it became merged with the county system. There are slight references to a school at Deep Creek, prior to the war, and one was established under the care of the Monthly Meeting. The Baltimore Association rendered assistance and John Scott mentions a visit there. Forbush also had a small school. Few details are preserved. Hunting Creek was a small Quaker community, John Scott urged Friends to do something. In 1866 there was a six months school; one teacher; salary $15.00 per month; 35 pupils, of whom sixteen were of Quaker families. For some time there were Quaker activities at Swan Creek, but that is just one of the many meetings which lanquished. In the Westfield Quarterly Meeting (discontinued) we read that in 1831 "there were several schools; the course of the present year have taught same; and all the schools we have had any part in have been in a mixed situation — much the greater part not members of our Society — and no school under the care of our monthly meeting."[*9] Winthrop had a Monthly Meeting school from 1866 to 1882.

SURRY QUARTER. The chiefest educational activity of this comparatively young meeting was the Blue Ridge Mission. This institution was supported by aid from several yearly meetings. It was of a mission character and at times poor children were boarded. David E. Sampson was superintendent, and was assisted by Mary C. Marshburn and Mary J. White. The work continued from 1888 to 1914. The maximum enrollment was 150, the lowest 60; the attendance varied from 73 to 31; some of the students walked three miles to attend; the school term averaged about six months.[10]

---

* Minutes Westfield Quarterly Meeting, 1831. For a description of one of these schools see the story of Charles Hutchens in chapter on Yadkin Quarter.

At the time of the concern for the erection of a Boarding School it was reported that there was not one school in the Yearly Meeting operated by Friends. Previous to the Civil War there had been a committee on education consisting of two men and two women from each of the nineteen monthly meetings. This had been appointed in 1848, and in 1851 it was stated that there were 804 children between the ages of five and sixteen and 334 between 16 and 21. Of these 1,104 were receiving some education. During the war most of the schools were discontinued; the committee did not function; nothing was attempted. In 1865 a committee consisting of Joseph R. Parker, Isham Cox, Thomas J. Benbow, Thomas Pearson, Allen U. Unthank and Nathan F. Spencer were appointed to cooperate with the Baltimore Association.[11]

THE LITTLE BRICK SCHOOL HOUSE. No record of colonial times would be adequate without reference to "the little red school house." This institution is as American as the Bald Eagle. The writer more than half a century ago visited several one-room-one-teacher school houses. To see school children in over-alls, bare-footed was common. Some children were lying upon the floor, others were sitting upon the window sills. There was the big pot-bellied stove and the pile of stove wood; the stove-pipes rambled all over head; there was the pail of water and the gourd from which all and sundry drank. The teacher had one group of children gathered around her to recite their lessons. Some bright youngsters knew the stories by memory as they had heard their older brothers and sisters tell it a year or two before, so the younger kids could rattle off the stories and hold the book up-side-down, and the teacher supposed they were reading, when now and again a child did not know one letter from another. What heroines those teachers were! Often the school, so called, had no equipment, and the teacher not only had to teach six grades in one room at a promised salary of twenty dollars a month for three or four months, but she had to collect her salary — if she could. Well, all this is to lead up to the story of the Little Brick House which followed Anne the Huntress and preceded New Garden Boarding School. This time we are on sure ground and not in the realm of legend.

JEREMIAH HUBBARD must be mentioned as one of the Founders of New Garden Boarding School. He is described as a remarkable man with a commanding personality. He stood over six feet and was a most eloquent preacher. It is established that he taught at the Little Brick School House. Whether he caused it to be built is not known by this writer. The building was located back of the Old Meeting House and was a one room structure. Jeremiah was a trained and a born teacher, who possessed a passion for helping children and grown-ups to continue their education. Dorothy Gilbert Thorne says that the father of L. Lyndon Hobbs, also named Lewis, taught at this little school as also did Horace F. Cannon.*

It was at the momentous yearly meeting of 1830 when the destiny of the Boarding School was at stake. At first Jeremiah had his doubts, but the patriarch Nathan Hunt, so tradition says, told Jeremiah that if the school were established, he (Jeremiah) would probably be appointed principal. At any rate Jeremiah with great eloquence supported the earnest solicitations of Nathan, and the meeting was persuaded to commit itself to the venture. In human probability, without this strong support there would be no Guilford College today.

Jeremiah was for several years clerk of the yearly meeting. He exercised much influence throughout the whole of North Carolina. One writer says that "when he spoke in meeting, his eloquence rode on the wings of a storm," and that he sometimes spoke "in a strange prophetic note." It is on record that to arouse some slumbering sinners he cried aloud: "Sleep in mercy, and ye wake in judgment!"[12] He followed the procession to Indiana, in 1837 and so did not teach at New Garden, but he occasionally returned as a visiting minister at yearly meeting time.**

The school house was in existence by 1816, but it is not known how long before that date it was built. Jeremiah was teaching there in the twenties, but it was not in operation in 1830. Horace F. Cannon taught some time later. He did not teach in 1834, but did in 1837, and he likewise trekked to that Quaker mecca north of the Ohio River. The little school continued its existence under the care of local Friends after the Boarding School was conducted by the yearly meeting. How much longer is not known, but the historic little place was demolished in 1885.

---

* Horace F. Cannon was the father of Joseph Greenleaf Cannon (Uncle Joe) the famous Speaker of the House of Representatives from 1903 to 1911. Joseph was born within sight of Guilford College.

** Edward R. Murrow, a well-known broadcaster, is a direct descendant of Jeremiah Hubbard. Robert H. Frazier, of Greensboro, says that the article published in the Reader's Digest, Dec., 1957, is misleading. It is true that he was born on a farm not far from the present Guilford College, but "the Murrow family was one of Guilford County's outstanding families. Edward R. Murrow's grandfather, Josh Murrow, was a distinguished political leader. His wife was a member of the Coltraine family, and a sister of the father of Mrs. Charles A. Cannon."

ALLEN FRAZIER is another Quaker who played a part in laying the foundation of the educational institutions of North Carolina. Allen took advantage of the limited opportunities of acquiring an education, and in 1832 he began to do something to help others gain some intellectual awakening. He built a little log school house on the "old Brown place," a mile due west of the old Trinity College site, and opened a school in the fall of that same year. Bruce Craven, son of Braxton Craven, says the foundation stones were visible in 1927, but the building was demolished in 1890. The community was jointly occupied by Quakers and Methodists, and so Allen called his school the "Union School." Sentiment quickened in the settlement for a "community school," with several teachers, and in 1835 a committee was appointed to consider the construction of a Union Institute. Opinion was developing at this time for the Quakers and the Methodists to have their own institutions, so Allen Frazier built for himself a new school house a mile south of the first one, and this became known as Frazier's School House, and it stood from 1839 "till it crumbled to earth around 1910." Allen taught the youth for many years, regarding it as a service befitting a conscientious Quaker. This Allen Frazier school is said to have been the first school from which grew Union Institute, Trinity College and Duke University.

It appears that there was a disagreement between the Quakers and the Methodists, and each faction wanted a teacher or teachers of their own denomination, and here comes a story of true historic value. The contention prevailed from about 1832 to 1843, and the account says:

"The Quakers and the Methodists disagreed again, and in 1842 the Quakers demanded that there be a Quaker teacher elected for that year. A compromise was effected by getting a Quaker as assistant teacher. Accordingly a committee went to New Garden (afterwards Guilford College) and the Mendenhalls in charge of the school recommended Braxton Craven, then nineteen years of age. He came to Trinity and taught with Mr. York (the Rev. Brantley York) that year, and in 1843 Mr. York left, and Braxton Craven was elected principal. . . . You can figure it out for yourself how it came about that Braxton Craven raised in the good Quaker home of the Cox family, and educated in a Quaker school, later became President of a Methodist College (Trinity — which later became Duke University). He was married to Miss Irene Leach (daughter of James Leach, a distinguished educator, 1798-1881). At her funeral in 1904 she was referred to as "the Mother of Trinity College."

BRAXTON CRAVEN has become somewhat of a legend. He came to New Garden Boarding School as a poor boy wearing blue jeans, "stitched down shoes" and carrying his books, shirts, and socks in a big handkerchief. Though he brought a recommendation signed by Jonathan Cox and other Friends he was not a member of the Society, and some were chary about the admission of "worldlings." He proved to be "the greatest student of the period," and was afterwards styled "a rough and rural reproduction of Dr. Arnold, of Rugby." For two terms his grades were perfect, except that once he received 95 instead of 100. It must be recalled that at that time Dr. Nereus Mendenhall and the small faculty offered courses in Greek, Latin, composition, mensuration, geometry, geography, astronomy, mechanics, surveying, philosophy, chemistry. In Braxton Craven, the master teacher found a worthy pupil.

When the committee came seeking a teacher for the Methodist school, Nereus Mendenhall did not hesitate; he named Braxton Craven, and that boy of nineteen commenced an educational career in North Carolina that is unsurpassed. From the teacher of the little school near Trinity he advanced till be became the principal of Trinity College, became the first professor of law, and laid the foundations of Duke University, now one of the most illustrious educational institutions of the world.[13]

NEW GARDEN BOARDING SCHOOL. This institution owes its existence to the faith and energy of Nathan Hunt and Jeremiah Hubbard. The concern had been slowly developing in the minds of Friends, for from the beginning there had been the consciousness of the need for education. As far back as 1668 George Fox had advised Friends to set up schools and teach "whatsoever things was civil & useful in ye creation." He recommended the same when he came to the colony in 1672. There is on record a minute of advice from the North Carolina Yearly Meeting in quaint language: "frineds . . . be . . . careful . . . in . . . Scholisng . . . their . . . childrin." Some of the monthly meetings set up schools before New Garden was established, but these were local endeavors, and not the responsibility of the whole Society.

The yearly meeting of 1830 proved to be a memorable one, perhaps the most significant in its 133 years of existence up to that time. After the reading of the query: "Do those who have children endeavor to train them up in the principles of our religious profession; to reading the Holy Scriptures, and use the necessary restraints for their preservation?" There came a hush over the congregation, for there was a common understanding that all were remiss. There was not at that time one single school in the yearly meeting under the care of Friends. At length the patriarch Nathan Hunt arose, and with considerable emotion (as was his wont) urged Friends to do something for the education of their children. Jeremiah Hubbard followed with a like concern, and as a teacher he spoke with understanding and conviction. A committee was appointed to prepare an epistle of advice. Each quarterly and monthly meeting was advised to raise subscriptions for the purpose of a school and select young men and women to be trained as teachers, and to report at the next yearly meeting.

On this occasion a committee presented an elaborate set of very strict rules, but they could not agree upon a site for the school. The sum of $1200 was subscribed in the face of the meeting for the project. Eventually it was the venerable Nathan Hunt who persuaded Friends that the New Garden site was the proper one. New Garden was then described "as a thriving settlement;" it was the place where the yearly meeting was held and was a school center. It appears that the name had been brought from Ireland by way of Pennsylvania. A charter for the school was received in 1834, and as it was thought the legislature might hesitate to charter a school bearing a reference to Quakers, the name New Garden Boarding School was adopted. In 1835 building of Founders Hall was commenced, and much of the labor was donated by local citizens. By the next year the building was almost complete, and there was an indebtedness of $3,600.00, and cash in hand but $377.48. Money was exceedingly scarce at this time, but the Friends in England, New York and New England made generous contributions.

The institution was opened in 1837 with 25 boys and 25 girls; Dougan Clark, and his wife Asenath,* a daughter of Nathan Hunt, were named as superintendent and matron. The early teachers found conditions primitive and there were many changes in personnel until Nereus Mendenhall took over in 1839.

Dorothy Gilbert Thorne in her most excellent story of New Garden Boarding School says:

"Going to meeting twice a week was a regular part of the school program; students lined up in pairs and marched behind their teachers through the woods to the meeting house. During the long silence they often lifted their eyes to the dark stains in the ceiling and wondered whether they really were blood stains. Soldiers wounded in the Battle of Guilford Court House (March 15, 1781) had been brought to an earlier meeting house at New Garden and placed on crude beds formed of the new boards stored there. The planks had been used in building this meeting house and the students were sure that the stains they saw were made by the blood shed long before. The boys asked Nathan Hunt about it and he replied: 'Whether the red marks thee speaks of and which I have often seen are blood marks of the British soldiers I cannot tell'!"

---

* For an extraordinary story concerning Asenath see "Crossing a Washed-Away Bridge" in this same chapter.

The tradition is substantiated by stone markers which show the supposed site of the old house, and further by a grave marked to the effect that British and Revolutionary soldiers who fought at Guilford Court House are buried there.

The students also marched to quarterly meeting when it was held there and the school was in session; when it met elsewhere those students whose families could provide transportation and accommodation were allowed to attend.[14]

HE ROSE EARLY IN THE MORNING. It is of interest to state the schedule prepared by the first committee and which appears to have been adhered to in the early days. Rise at five; grammar, six to 7:30; breakfast, 7:30; lessons nine to 11:30; lunch at noon; lessons, 2:30 to five; supper at six; to bed before nine. The boys and the girls were taught separately, dined separately, and walked sedately to and from classes in pairs. Unless boys and girls could claim kinship, they had few opportunities to meet. It is not surprising that genealogical trees were constantly climbed in order to establish relationships.

The plan may have been the unexpected fruitage of George Fox's dictum: "Students must be meek, sober & ientell & qvite & loving and not give one another bad word noe time, in the skovell nor ovt of it," and that all things be kept "clean, svet, & neat & hansom." It need hardly be mentioned that Nereus Mendenhall, with his wider knowledge of human nature greatly modified and liberalized these restrictions.

The story of Founders Hall is told in connection with the various buildings in another place. Slowly the little school got under way, and the attendance grew gradually to 191 tn 1888, when through the munificence of Francis T. King and the Baltimore Association and the optimism of North Carolina Friends the little school became Guilford College.

NATHAN HUNT. Among the illustrious exponents of the Quaker faith the name of Nathan Hunt stands high. He is described as a prince among men; he is also referred to as a seer and a prophet; none would question that the term patriarch fitted him well. According to one account his paternal grandfather, Jacob Hunt, settled in New Jersey about 1700, whose son, William, was born in 1733, and was taken to North Carolina at an early age by an aunt, who was a strict Friend. At the age of fifteen William began to "speak in meeting." The elders encouraged the exercise of his gift, and at twenty he was recorded a minister. His son, Nathan, was born in

NATHAN HUNT

1758, and, like George Fox, loved to be alone as a boy. He only experienced six months schooling, but such was his natural ability and his extraordinary "growth in grace and the knowledge of the Lord Jesus" that he was able in maturity to meet with learned and distinguished persons without them ever suspecting ignorance or limitations. His father had a gift in the ministry and was much away from home visiting the various yearly meetings on this continent, and whilst on a religious visit he died in England in 1772, when Nathan was but fourteen years of age. Nathan struggled to educate himself and borrowed books one at a time from a Presbyterian minister who lived three miles away. It is hardly necessary to mention that he walked both ways, and also that he read the books stretched out on the floor by the light of a pine knot fire. Nathan's wife, Martha Ruckman, died at the age of thirty-one leaving six children. Later Nathan married Prudence Thornburgh, who became a true mother to his children.*

Nathan is believed to have engaged in business in his early days, but details are lacking. His chief interest was in the meetings for worship. He says he had "visitations of the Spirit" when he was thirteen and again when he was seventeen. He was subject to ecstatic experiences. Once after he had preached in Tennessee he was so overwhelmed with emotions that he says "tears fell like rain." In visiting distant cities for the first time he would "find the streets and houses familiar, for he had been there before;" occasionally he would speak in meeting so specifically to some one's condition that the self accused person would believe Nathan Hunt had been informed of all the circumstances.

SPIRITUAL DISCERNMENT. Another story is told in connection with the raising of funds for the establishment of the New Garden Boarding School. At the yearly meeting in 1837 the views of Nathan Hunt prevailed as to the need of the school. He made a donation of $25.00 which was a considerable sum at that time, and the first amount subscribed upon that occasion. George Howland said that if his whaling ship returned with a good cargo of oil, he would contribute $1,000. Some time later Nathan had a vision and saw the ship coming into harbor, and told his family the particulars and assured them that the promised money would be forthcoming. The ship arrived exactly as he had foreseen. Mary Mendenhall

---

* There are six known spellings of this Scotch-Irish name. There are many other names spelled indifferently. Before elementary schools became common there was no standardized spelling.

Hobbs says "he was a psychopath, but with this mystic sense he possessed an unusually healthy and sane mind, so that it never acquired the undue prominence which makes it a dangerous thing for its possessor and renders him an unsafe religious guide." Upon the occasion of the Wilburite separation he spent the whole night in prayer before the matter was to be presented to North Carolina Yearly Meeting, and by his clear understanding of the issue was able to steer this Yearly Meeting clear of becoming involved in the controversy.

He may well be called the father of Guilford College, for he was one of the first to perceive the need of an educational institution for Friends' children, and by his personal influence he did much to raise the necessary funds. After the founding of the Boarding School one of his chiefest delights was to visit the school and talk to the children.

He was probably the most travelled minister among Friends of his day. He did not lightly leave his wife and family, for he says he was sorely tried in his spirit concerning this and received assurance of the Lord that "his family would be cared for in his absence." It is characteristic of the man that he says he undertook to visit Friends in South Carolina and Georgia; that he travelled seven hundred miles in six weeks, "and he returned with the same money that he had when he started."

Another side light is thrown upon his personality when attending London Yearly Meeting he requested "a special meeting for the servants and waiters." Concerning slavery, he said: "He would rather listen to the braying of an ass than the preaching of a man who held slaves." In meeting he was without doubt "the leading Friend," and "sat at the head of the meeting." He was a striking figure, one that immediately commanded attention; his large head, silvery long hair, big white shirt collar, his large hands, and the stout stick he carried all were marks of interest, but it was his enormous broad brimmed hat, (preserved at Guilford College) which marked him out in any assemblage.

He was an impressive speaker, highly emotional and seemingly frequently on the verge of tears. He was modest and never domineering. It is said that he possessed an extraordinary capacity to remember names and faces and would identify grown up people whom he had not seen from childhood. He preached in meeting after he was ninety years of age and lived within five years of rounding out his century. He is regarded as the most unusual man that North Carolina Quakerism produced.[15]

CROSSING A WASHED-AWAY BRIDGE. Mention has been made of Asenath Hunt Clarke, a woman of marked personality, and an extraordinary incident in her career is vouched for by Sara Richardson Haworth, a Quaker historian of High Point. Asenath was away from home upon one of her characteristic ministrations, and her husband, Dougan, became concerned because of torrential rains. He went to a bridge over which she would cross Deep River, and while waiting he saw in dismay the flooring of the bridge washed away by the swollen stream. Concluding that his wife could not possibly cross he returned home. Some time later he heard sounds which indicated that a horse and vehicle had arrived. He went outside and was utterly astonished to see his wife seated in the well-known vehicle. In amazement he cried: "How did thee get here, Asenath?" She replied nonchalantly "In the usual way, Nathan." "No, thee didn't," replied Dougan, "for I went to the river and saw the bridge washed away." She replied: "I don't know what thee saw, but here I am, and I must have crossed the river." Dumbfounded they went to the site of the bridge. It was not to be seen, but upon examination they found that the woodwork had been washed away, but the metal framework remained intact. The animal had evidently placed its hooves upon a metal runner in the center, and the wheels had been supported by the metal sideframe. Asenath had noticed nothing unusual when she crossed!

ISHAM COX must be mentioned in connection with the founding of the Boarding School. He performed a very necessary service. He was a son of William and Lydia Cox and was born near Holly Spring, Randolph County, North Carolina, fifth of eleventh month, 1815. His mother passed away in his infancy. He writes "I was early instructed to heed the working of the Spirit of Truth in my own mind." This, we may remark, is the essence of the Quaker faith. Parents did not impose their will upon their children, but encouraged them to "listen to the Voice within," and "do what thee thinks is the right thing to do." He married Lavina Brower, and soon both were appointed elders. He took the greatest interest in the founding of the Quaker school and was named in 1857 one of the managers and later a trustee. The first years were lean years, and a deficit of $27,000 was accumulated. The Civil War was in progress, and days were dark. Many Friends had their homes pillaged; live stock taken and molested in many ways.

It was imperative that something be done to save the school

and the credit of the Society. The invaluable assistance of Francis T. King and the Baltimore Association will be told in another section of this story, but local Friends did their bit, and Isham Cox was appointed financial agent of the Boarding School and raised considerable sums of money in the various yearly meetings. He was active in relief during the conflict and visited several battle fields, ministering to the sick and wounded; he visited the Governor of that State, various members of the Confederate Government, the Secretary of War, and interceded for war prisoners. Isham was greatly interested in education and was at some time Superintendent of the Examining of Teachers. He collaborated with Francis T. King in the work of reconstruction. He became one of the most valued members of the Society. His death occurred at Liberty, North Carolina in 1894.[16]

JONATHAN COX ASSUMES RESPONSIBILITY. Because of the mounting indebtedness some of the trustees thought it would be wise to close the school, as they could not conscientiously defraud their creditors. In this emergency Jonathan E. Cox offered in ninth month, 1860, to assume responsibility and manage the institution as a private undertaking for the next school session, and to receive for his services what he could make above expenses. His offer was accepted as there was no prospect of selling the property as war was in progress. The magnanimous offer saved the day and for thirteen years Jonathan and his wife cared for the school. The trustees knew he had been a judicious and careful manager. His wife Elizabeth acted as matron; Nereus Mendenhall was teacher of the boys; and Mary E. Harris instructed the girls. Dorothy Thorne says that these voluntary sacrificial services "affected the lives of hundreds of young people."[17]

NEREUS MENDENHALL. According to tradition the Mendenhalls trace their ancestry back to supporters of William the Conqueror. It appears certain that there was an estate in Wiltshire, England, held by the Mendenhalls in the XVIIth century and that some of the family came to America at about the time that William Penn received his grant of land which became the Commonwealth of Pennsylvania. Three brothers — Moses, Benjamin and John and a sister, Mary, obtained a grant of land in the Quaker colony. John became the ancestor of the Carolina Mendenhalls. The record runs: John begat Aaron; Aaron begat James (who came to North Carolina in 1759 and established Jamestown just a few miles away from New Garden); James begat George; George married Judith

Gardner and begat Richard; Richard married Mary Pegg and begat Nereus, who was the fourth child and the second son of his parents.

Nereus was born in 1819, and grew up among some of the finest people in the world for among his kinfolk were the Barkers, Coffins, Colemans, Folgers, Gardners, Husseys, Macys, Mitchells, Russells, Starbucks, and Worths — all of whom had originally hailed from Nantucket. As a child Nereus was very delicate and almost supersensitive and at times seemed overwhelmed by the wickedness of mankind. He was possesed of a love of learning, and he sought every opportunity to improve his mind. He eagerly drank in all the information that could be imparted by local teachers, and it became an axiom that one could accomplish anything upon which one set one's mind. At the age of thirteen he was learning the printing business at Greensboro. At Haverford College, he completed the four year course in one half the regular time and received his degree at the age of twenty.

He taught awhile at Penn Charter School and then at his Alma Mater. He married Oriana Wilson and was soon thereafter called to New Garden as Principal in 1839 and remained two years; he returned and served the school 1843-44; 1846-47; 1849-51; 1861-67. After school hours with little assistance he gave himself to the study of Greek, Latin, Hebrew, German, science and philosophy. He was attracted also to medicine and entered the Jefferson Medical College at Philadelphia, and earned the degree of M.D.

Conscious that he needed outdoor exercise he studied engineering and did surveying for a railroad during summer vacations. As if this were not enough he served two terms in the State legislature. Between 1851 and 1861 he taught near Deep River and engaged in recreation as an engineer. He also acted for forty years as one of the State Board of Examiners of public school teachers, and was chairman of the county school board, and on the board of trustees of New Garden from 1847 to 1855. It needs also to be mentioned that the catalog of 1858 lists a full course in both Latin and Greek, besides analytical geometry, descriptive astronomy, chemistry, botany, geology and physiology. Pedagogs might well spend some moments comparing this list of subjects with the collection of odds and ends presented by many modern aspirants for a college degree.

Nereus Mendenhall added luster to the struggling little Quaker school, and established its reputation. It was due in large measure to his sacrifice that the institution was preserved. During the Civil War the conditions were discouraging. The few students who attended could bring little money, but they contributed oats, wheat, sorgham, flour, meal, meat, coins, gold, cloth, shoes and especially labor.

HE AFTERWARD REPENTED AND WENT. The story has often been told that Nereus became discouraged and decided to join his many Friends who had gone to the Middle West. He sold some of his goods, had a few packed and hauled to Jamestown for shipment. He says that during the night the "Lord told him it was his mission to stay." In the morning he told his family, with tears streaming down his face, that he could not leave the little, struggling, debt-ridden institution. They bravely accepted his decision as the Will of God. It is generally agreed that if Dr. Mendenhall had faltered in this crisis, there would be no Guilford College today and probably no North Carolina Yearly Meeting.

There were others who helped save the day. Among those should be mentioned Isham Cox, who heroically became the financial agent in 1859 at a time when the Boarding School appeared hopelessly in debt, and Jonathan E. Cox, who with his wife Elizabeth took over the school as a private venture, at the risk of bankrupting himself. He acted as superintendent and his wife as matron. Alethea Coffin (the mother of Addison Coffin) also served as matron; John and Achsah Carter also cared for the struggling school from 1864 to 1866 — the terrible war years; others were Mary E. Harris, William Lowe, Hymelius and William Hockett, Josiah and William Nicholson, Allen U. Tomlinson, Aaron Marshall Elliott and John Crenshaw, of Virginia.[18]

The enrollment between 1842-44 was 30; in 1866, 126; in 1869, 45; in 1873, 79; 1874, 58; 1875, 42; 1880, 99; 1887, 162; 1888, 191. This was the last year of operation under the name of New Garden Boarding School.

JEREMIAH PIGOTT. This Friend was one of the worthies of the early Quaker settlement. His traits exemplified the life of a number revealed by the investigations of the records of the various meetings. His memorial is among those of the Springfield Meeting Memorial Association, which has held gatherings since 1907 commemorating goodly and successful men and women whose lives were characterized by simplicity, sincerity, thoroughness and integrity. They were forwardlooking and constructive citizens. The writer is overwhelmed by the volume of material in these memorials. They are pure gold and should be preserved in print.

Jeremiah Pigott is chosen as an outstanding example. Like most of his fellows, he was born and reared upon a farm. He was the son of William and Elizabeth (Welborn) Pigott and was born in Rowan County, twentieth of eighth month, 1797. The Pigott (sometimes spelled Pickett) family migrated to North Carolina from Cecil County, Maryland and settled in the Cane Creek Community. On fourth month fifth, 1817 Jeremiah Pigott married Hannah Coffin Hedgecock (sometimes spelled Hitchcock), a devoted Quakeress daughter of Joseph Hitchcock. His education was limited but thorough, and he became a teacher. His capacities were manifold and early in life he manifested superior ability. He was in turn proprietor of a typical crossroads general store; he had an interest in a smithy and operated a stagecoach. (This book would not be a true picture of colonial times unless it referred to the stagecoach, crossroads store, the grist mill and the smithy.)

Jeremiah Pigott had a share in the founding of New Garden Boarding School (Guilford College); he was one of a committee of three named by the Yearly Meeting in 1833 to secure from the General Assembly of North Carolina a charter for the institution. This committee had to overcome the opposition to a Quaker related school so it required finesse to gain the necessary enactment. When the institution was opened in 1837 Jeremiah was one of the members of the first board of trustees. He was a "weighty" Friend and served on numerous committees named by the monthly, quarterly and yearly meetings. He was one of the committee appointed to build a new meeting house at Springfield, which was completed in 1858. This building is still in use as a museum in connection with the Springfield Meeting.

He had a large share in the construction of the plank road connecting Fayetteville and Salisbury; he was instrumental in extending the North Carolina Railroad from Goldsboro to Charlotte; he was active in the incorporation of the Town of High Point and a member of its first town council; he shared the views of the times that ownership of land was the mark of a man and a guarantee of security. In 1847 he purchased 247 acres of land near Springfield. Later he secured additional holdings of property, which was divided into lots and is now in the heart of the City of High Point. He built the Belleview Hotel (later called Hotel Arthur and later called Biltmore Hotel) of High Point. At the time of its building it was the largest brick building within one hundred miles of High Point. On the 21st of ninth month 1859, at the age of sixty-two, Jeremiah Pigott ended his earthly service.[19]

THE MONTHLY MEETING SCHOOL. In common with the usual practice of Friends almost everywhere the New Garden Meeting provided an elementary school for neighboring children who did not attend the Boarding School. It was a two-roomed affair located near the meeting house. Just when the school was started is not known, but it is on record that among the early teachers were Mary Lamb, Sybil White, Sallie White, Annie Ray Anderson, Mollie B. Roberts (who married a man named Edwards and later one named Jones) and Gertrude Smith (Mrs. Lee Smith). The school was discontinued in 1902 when the district voted a special tax for schools, and the first rural graded school supported by public funds in the State was established at New Garden. The newly built home for the Yearly Meeting Executive Secretary near Guilford College is close to the site of the monthly meeting school.[20]

JONATHAN E. COX

NEREUS MENDENHALL

JOSEPH MOORE

FRANCIS T. KING

CHAPTER TEN

YE ARE MY FRIENDS

THE BALTIMORE ASSOCIATION. As is mentioned in the Introduction the writer made an intensive study of the work of the Baltimore Association from the original Records preserved at Baltimore for partial compliance with the requirements for the Doctorate at the University of North Carolina. This work is entitled *The Contribution of the Quakers to the Reconstruction of the Southern States*. He also examined every Friends publication issued between 1860 and 1890, and every one of the various yearly meeting minutes, and also the works dealing with Slavery and Reconstruction. The barest summary of that work is here reproduced and for the sake of economy references are reduced to a minimum.

The following circumstances led to the origin of the Baltimore Association. "One Sunday morning, toward the close of the war, two men appeared in the front of the meeting house on Courtland Street, Baltimore. They informed several of the congregation that there were some Friends from North Carolina at one of the wharves in destitute circumstances. A committee was appointed and found about fifty persons of various ages and conditions, whose homes had been ruined by Johnson's and Sherman's armies. They were anxious to go to their friends in the west. They were assisted, and permission was secured from President Lincoln to send provisions and agricultural implements to Friends remaining in North Carolina. A short time later another 450 Friends fugitives from the South passed through the city, and they also received assistance. A permanent organization developed which became known as the Baltimore Association.[1] Among the refugees was "a valued Friend, with his wife and six children. He had been the owner of 1,300 acres of land. His live stock, implements, cotton, and other produce and all his money had been taken or destroyed. He and his family had lived for weeks on boiled corn."[2]

The Association was organized as follows in 1865; Francis T. King, president; Isaac Brooks, Jr., secretary; Jesse Tyson, treasurer; Miles White, Thomas Wilson, James C. Thomas, M.D., John C. Thomas, R. M. Janney, William Hopkins, Francis White, Joseph Merrifield, Julia Valentine, Rachel Brooks, Matilda Reed, Mary Ellicott, Sarah F. Smiley, Margaret H. Janney, Mary W. Thomas,

Mary T. King and Jane E. White, managers; Francis T. King, Miles White, James C. Thomas, Jesse Tyson, Caleb Winslow and John C. Thomas, executive committee.

The Association found a great field of service in ministering to the physical needs of the war victims. Dire distress prevailed; the railroads had been seriously damaged, dirt roads had been neglected; the whole South was prostrate. Plantations were deserted; destitute Negroes were roaming and pillaging; many breadwinners had been killed, and hundreds of women and children were destitute. Sherman's foraging army had passed near Goldsboro, and most Friends as well as others were stripped of all possessions. John Scott was the first to be sent to supervise relief. He rode horseback and distributed supplies, especially welcome were needles, thread and clothing. The first winter $184,173 was spent in this manner. Richard M. Janney, of Baltimore, visited in 1865, and distributed clothing, shoes, bacon, flour, coffee, sugar, salt and plows to the value of $2,500 within the limits of Contentnea Quarterly Meeting. The timely surrender of Johnson's army saved the Friends of several Quaker communities which were between the two rival armies.[3]

Sarah F. Smiley, of New England, was also early in the field. She subsequently became identified with the Friends' Freedmen's Association, and ministered in Virginia as well as North Carolina. Later she labored under the direction of New York Yearly Meeting. She raised money to place libraries in each monthly meeting in North Carolina.[4] Joseph James Neave, of London Yearly Meeting, who visited North Carolina bears testimony to the importance and efficiency of the ministrations of Janney and Smiley. He says that all but one of the quarterly meetings had been ravaged. He went through Guilford and Randolph Counties where Johnson's army had been, and made arrangements for supplies and Bibles and school books to be sent from Baltimore. Joseph Crosfield, also of England, saw conditions at first hand, and called the attention of British Friends to the need of relief. The English and Irish Friends contributed about $300,000 in money and supplies. Crosfield says that he found a Friend with six children literally in rags.

The Association at first expected to retire from the work by 1869, but failure of crops and droughts in 1865, 1866 and 1869, compelled Baltimore to continue assistance.[5] Another account says people were crying in the streets because of hunger, and that thirty-thousand able-bodied men with their families left North Carolina and Virginia because of the unbearable conditions.[6] Since relief and educational work in the South had also been carried on by the

Friends of Philadelphia, who had spent $10,931 by May, 1866, the Association refrained from appealing to that body, but the distress became so acute that Francis T. King, Allen Jay, and Joseph Moore laid the facts before Philadelphia Yearly Meeting in 1867. This meeting raised subscriptions. Friends in Indiana and Philadelphia spent about $18,000 mostly for physical relief in Eastern Tennessee and North Carolina by February, 1866, and then left the Association to supervise further activities. Relief was not limited to members of the Society, nor to the Whites. In 1869 Francis King wrote that the Federal laws relating to bankruptcy and homesteads and the States' stay laws had added to the universal miseries, and that the Quakers were the only people who had not availed themselves of these laws, which favored debtors. Many Friends who had held considerable property now found themselves dispossessed. The Association assisted many such in rehabilitating themselves. The annual report of 1872 says that every dollar loaned had been repaid.

CONTRIBUTION TO EDUCATION. Perhaps the most conspicuous phase of the work of the Association was the restoration of the elementary schools in Quaker communities. S. S. Ashley, the State Superintendent of Public Instruction, is authority for the statement that before the war North Carolina had one of the best educational systems in the whole country, but, of course, it was wrecked by the war; the schoolhouses were damaged or destroyed, the teachers scattered, and the school funds were converted into Confederate currency, and became worthless. At a conference of local and visiting Friends at the yearly meeting in 1865 it was agreed that the best means of restoring Quakerism and stable conditions was to restore the elementary school system. The Association made it clear that the responsibility rested with the yearly meeting, and the Association would assist with funds and supplies. John Scott became the superintendent temporarily.

JOSEPH MOORE was, in the opinion of concerned Friends, the person best equipped for the undertaking. He was an outstanding scientist and a member of the faculty of Earlham College. As he was in poor health he was advised that a sojourn in North Carolina would be to his advantage. It was Francis T. King who possessed the vision to check the mass migration from the South; it was he who canvassed this country and England collecting the necessary funds; but it demanded an educator possessed of administrative genius to come and live among us, to survey the wreckage, to particularize the needs, to inspire the impoverished and discouraged war victims, to formulate plans and create the zeal to re-establish the elementary schools in the Quaker districts. That was the accomplishment of Joseph Moore. His parents had been Tarheels, but were among the thousands who fled the slave states because of the "Impending Crisis."

At the conclusion of hostilities he came south on his monumental undertaking. The State was "Prostrate" and the sick man traversed the several quarterly meetings and visited many monthly meetings in order to ascertain conditions. At that time the roads were execrable, and accommodation mostly of the crudest sort. He extended his investigations into Virginia and Tennessee and informed Francis King of the conditions. Moore called public meetings, interviewed prominent citizens and laid before them the necessity of restoring the school system, and assured them of the help of Quakers throughout the land. Gradually local schools were revived until there were more than forty and 2,258 students under the care of the Baltimore Association. At one time these schools were the only such in the State — and the further South the worse the conditions.

Perhaps even more important was Moore's work in the provision for the continuance of these schools by establishing teacher training institutes. The first was conducted at Springfield in 1865; this was followed next year by one at Deep River; then for the next three years at Springfield; in 1871 the sessions were at Cane Creek, with over one hundred in attendance; the last two sessions were at Greensboro — all under the inspiration of Moore. After this session the Baltimore Association handed the responsibility to the local authorities. This undertaking is rightly regarded as the beginning of the teacher training system of North Carolina, which has grown to gigantic proportions with several great colleges being devoted almost exclusively to this accomplishment.

Braxton Craven, was a stanch supporter of Moore in all his undertakings, and Governor Jonathan Worth said: "the work is quite the most important move in the way of reconstruction that has come to my knowledge."

Joseph Moore also had a share in the concern to raise New Garden Boarding School to a college level. He was invited to become its first President, but preferred to return to Earlham, and in course of time became the head of that great institution. The famous Natural History Museum of Earlham is named for its first curator, and no name is more honored among Hoosiers and Friends than that of Joseph Moore.[7]

Allen Jay continued the work after Joseph Moore was appointed President of Earlham College. Dr. E. W. Knight, in his *Public School Education in North Carolina* says the Baltimore Association by 1869 had established 44 schools for white children; there were 65 teachers (many of whom were from the North) and an enrollment of 3,000 pupils. The schools were located in Guilford, Yadkin, Iredell, Randolph, Alamance, Orange, Wayne, Northampton and Perquimans counties. Between 1865 and 1869 the Association built or repaired 32 schoolhouses in the State. S. S. Ashley also praised the Quakers for their labors.[8] A leading citizen remarked that the Quakers were doing more to reconstruct the State than all the legislators.[9] Governor Jonathan Worth made a similar commendation.

To understand the situation it is necessary to remark that until after the election of Rutherford B. Hayes in 1876 the Southern States were under the control of Federal troops; that "the States were in a state of suspended animation," and treated as "conquered territory;" "carpetbaggers," Negroes and "scalawags" controlled the legislatures, and insisted upon "mixed schools" — that is, Whites and Negroes together. As most of the colored children were illiterate and uncouth, white mothers would not permit their daughters to attend such schools. A writer declared "when you do not in travelling a hundred miles see a school house or church outside a town, you get an idea, not only of the prevailing ignorance of the whites and blacks, but of the enormous efforts necessary to establish anything like a general system of education. . . . The well-directed efforts of the Friends have stimulated the patriotic citizens to devote attention to a work so vitally connected with the general well-being.[10]

By 1872 the Association was caring for 38 schools, with 62 teachers and 2,358 pupils; Franklin S. Blair who took over the work under the care of the yearly meeting in his report for 1879-80 gave the following statistics:

In Eastern Quarter	9 schools;	12 teachers;	418 pupils
In Contentnea Quarter	5 schools;	7 teachers;	269 pupils
In Western Quarter	9 schools;	11 teachers;	322 pupils
*In Southern Quarter	16 schools;	12 teachers;	489 pupils
In Deep River	12 schools;	12 teachers;	486 pupils
In New Garden Quarter	5 schools;	8 teachers;	249 pupils
	56 schools;	62 teachers;	2,233 pupils

* Report incomplete.

Other schools are mentioned in other reports, and other incomplete reports show that from 1865 to 1881, 32,515 children (adding totals reported in various years) received instruction.[11]

The importance of this endeavor can hardly be over-estimated, as there were very few other elementary schools in operation at this time. The financial statements show that about $72,000 was spent by the Association upon educational work in North Carolina. As a large part of this was contributed in gold, it had a purchasing value far beyond that of the depreciated paper in general use. In addition to the assistance given to elementary schools it is to be mentioned that the Association was responsible for the establishment of Normal Schools, which paved the way for the great work now being done in the training of teachers.

The Association made great contributions to the reconditioning of New Garden Boarding School. New Garden was one of the very few educational institutions which continued uninterruptedly during the war and the Reconstruction era. Times were very distressing, and the record says that students and teachers were reduced to a diet of green corn.[12]

THE MODEL FARM. In addition to their contribution to Education the Association established a Model Farm at Bush Hill, later known as Archdale, near Springfield. The Nathan Hunt farm consisting of about two hundred acres was purchased. As the Association was not incorporated, the land was held in the name of Allen Unthank Tomlinson, who more than any one else except Francis T. King was responsible for the undertaking. Additional lands were purchased, Allen Jay became superintendent, and William A. Sampson, of Maine shared the work. King purchased equipment for the farm, and introduced methods of crop rotation, fertilization, and improved methods of agriculture. Good quality live stock was shipped to the farm, and farmers were invited to attend "institutes" to discuss improved agriculture. The influence was phenomenal, and one of North Carolina's governors said "it was the only green spot in the State." This work was continued for fifteen years, and may be regarded as one of the chiefest phases in the rehabilitation of North Carolina.

REBUILDING OF MEETING HOUSES. The Association appealed to Friends everywhere for help in restoring the meeting houses, many of which had been mistreated. The report says that 58 houses were rebuilt or repaired. These operations extended beyond North Carolina, and in all $7,300 was expended for this purpose.

LIBRARIES. From early days it had been customary for each monthly meeting to possess a library. During the war reading material was virtually unobtainable in the South. Sarah Smiley drew the attention of Friends elsewhere to the great need. She visited almost every Quaker meeting in the South and enquired as to the opportunities for improving the mind. She caused appeals to be made throughout the various yearly meetings including abroad for magazines and books. Among the Association's records are complete details of this much needed enterprise. In addition to the restorations in this State the Association did valuable service in Tennessee; notable among this was the almost incredible accomplishments of Dr. Jethro D. Garner of Ohio.

FRANCIS THOMPSON KING. Further mention must be made of Francis T. King, the president of the Baltimore Association. He was born in 1819, and was one of the charter students at Haverford College. He determined at an early age to follow the old-time advice of Friends "to gain a competency by the time he was about sixty, and then retire and devote the rest of his life to public service." His public services were many and varied, and he became one of the leading citizens, although he declined to accept public office except that he had much to do with the establishment of the water supply in Baltimore. He was connected with the Baltimore and Ohio Railroad; was founder of a savings bank; executor of several large estates; a director of some insurance companies; president of the Maryland Bible Society, and president of the Thomas Wilson Sanitarium. He was an intimate friend of Johns Hopkins, by whose will be was appointed president of the board of trustees of the hospital which bears his name. He assisted in the organization of Bryn Mawr College, and became president of the board of trustees; he was also a trustee of Haverford College.

At the outbreak of the war he had an audience with the city authorities, he also interviewed the Governor of the State and it was largely due to his influence that Maryland did not secede.[13]

His chief interests were with the Society of Friends. He was successively overseer, elder and clerk, first of the monthly meeting, then the quarterly meeting and then the yearly meeting. This latter office of responsibility he filled from 1856 to 1885. He participated in many conferences to consider the condition of the Negroes and furthered the instruction of the colored people in Maryland, inaugurating elementary and normal schools for them. Many other activities of a philanthropic character might be enumerated. In matters of business he was scrupulous and would not accept orders for war goods. His religion pervaded his whole life, and he regarded his connection with the Baltimore Association as a practical exposition of the Quaker conception of Christianity.

The work of the Association was largely his work. He conceived the undertaking; it was his inspiring personality that created and developed the wide-spread interest; he collected most of the subscriptions. On him fell the task of conducting the voluminous correspondence; on him rested the responsibility throughout the whole undertaking. No less than forty times did he visit the South to ascertain the actual conditions. He made two voyages to Europe to present the situation to English and Irish Friends. He had frequent interviews with President Lincoln, with Cabinet officials and public officials. His travels entailed great hardships; he rode over the worst sort of roads, and frequently had miserable accommodations. He paid his own expenses on these missions, and sacrificed valuable time with no thought of material rewards. So much was he away from home attending to North Carolina and Indiana affairs that one of his friends asked him if he would not apply for a minute to stay at home! His letters show clearly that these visits were thorough tours of inspection; and they might almost be regarded as apostolic visitations.

He familiarized himself with conditions and knew the meetings and schools thoroughly. He had a keen perception of the character of the persons whom he met. He knew the details of the Model Farm, and himself drew the plans for the house and barn. A comprehensive set of rules was drawn up with which teachers and superintendents were expected to conform. Uniform reports were required.

King was at all times careful not to interfere with State authority nor the responsibility of local Friends. One story may be told which illustrates the situations he encountered. Tea was non-existent during and after the war, and Francis King missed his favorite drink. On one of his journeys he brought with him a pound of tea. He handed his precious package to a woman at whose house he was staying and asked her to make him a pot of tea. In a few moments she put a bowl upon the table. He looked at it; then he looked at her. There was nothing he could say. His pound of tea was all there, steaming in the pot! On the occasion of his death in December, 1891, the *Baltimore American* declared that his undertakings were more numerous than any other Baltimorian.[*][14]

One of the buildings at Guilford College was built with funds King collected. That building was burned and partially restored. In the past few years it has been completed and is now the chief instruction building, and is appropriately named King Hall.

The following summary of the financial statement is taken from the minutes of the Baltimore Association:

INCOME

London Yearly Meeting	$ 38,750
Philadelphia Yearly Meeting	30,150
Dublin Yearly Meeting	16,250
Baltimore Yearly Meeting	14,700
New York Yearly Meeting	10,200
Indiana Yearly Meeting	9,750
New England Yearly Meeting	9,000
Western Yearly Meeting	5,500
Iowa Yearly Meeting	2,400
Ohio Yearly Meeting	1,600
	$138,300

EXPENDITURES

For Physical Relief Including Cost of the Model Farm	$ 36,000
Friends' Schools	72,000
New Garden Boarding School (Now Guilford College)	23,000
Building and Repairing Meeting Houses	7,300
	$138,300

It is proper to draw attention to the fact that but for Francis T. King and his labors through the Baltimore Association it is altogether probable that there would be no Guilford College today, and Quakerism in North Carolina might have disappeared.[15]

---

[*] The writer made an exhaustive study of the work of the Baltimore Association for his Doctoral Dissertation presented to the University of North Carolina in 1926. The portion reproduced here is but a fragment. The fully documented writings may be found at the University of North Carolina at Chapel Hill, at Guilford College, at Salem College and with the Baltimore (Charles Street) Friends.

CHAPTER ELEVEN

PUT THEM IN MIND TO OBEY MAGISTRATES

NORTH CAROLINA QUAKERS AND POLITICS. The dictum of the Savior: "Render unto Caesar the things that are Caesar's and unto God the things that are God's" is among the greatest of maxims; it is bright, clear light, yet paradoxically it has been the cause of much strife and suffering. The difficulty lies in determining just which things belong to God and which to the civil authorities. From time immemorial brave souls have declared: "We ought to obey God rather than man."

THE QUAKER CONCEPT OF THE KINGDOM OF GOD. Friends believe that the Will of God should be accomplished by each generation and that the Kingdom of God will become established upon earth when a sufficient number of people determine that it shall come and do what they believe to be the Will of God irrespective of what others choose to believe and do. From the beginning the Discipline of some of the yearly meetings encouraged Friends to participate in public affairs, "engage in some honorable occupation and secure a competency by the time they were about sixty and then retire and devote themselves fully to public service." Their participation in public life was an essential phase of their concept of religion.

The Quakers in colonial times were active in politics. George Fox and William Edmundson were only in the colony of North Carolina a few weeks in 1672, yet within twenty years it was virtually a Quaker colony, not only in numbers, but with members, who, apparently were fully "convinced" of Quaker doctrine, and established meetings for worship upon the original manner.

GOVERNOR JOHN ARCHDALE was born in England in 1642. His lineage goes back to persons of distinction in the days of the Virgin Queen Elizabeth. He was in Maine in 1664 as the agent of the proprietor Gorges; he was then no Quaker, but a colonel of the militia. He returned to England and "was the leading gentleman of the village." Probably about 1681 he encountered Fox and his whole life became changed, so much so "that he became separated from his father's house . . . and the whole village bewailed his apostasy." He became possessed of that portion of North Carolina which had formerly been granted to Sir John Berkeley. Considerable lawlessness prevailed in the colony, and Governor Smith had written: "It is impossible to quiet the country unless a proprietor is sent over with full authority." Archdale came in 1694 and was able with judicious words to pacify the commissioners of South Carolina, and his management of affairs in the northern province has met with commendation by historians. The Quaker influence became paramount, for Archdale selected a Quaker Council, as he had a right to do, and as the leading colonists were members of the Society they elected a Quaker Assembly, and many of the justices and other public officials were likewise Friends.[1] As was mentioned in an earlier chapter the Episcopal Church had slept upon its rights and no serious attempt had been made in the seventeenth century to establish the State church. During a period of about thirty years Quakerism flourished, and practically every person religiously inclined or politically ambitious united with the Society. In South Carolina Archdale did not exempt Quakers from military service, but in the northern province he did. Archdale was later elected a member of the British House of Commons, but as he would not swear allegiance he was barred, although he offered to affirm.

Among the very early Quakers who held public positions in this colony were Daniel Akehurst, a judge; Emanuel Lowe, a son-in-law of Archdale; Thomas Symonds, a judge; and Francis Toms, a Provincial Councillor, was one of the earliest supporters of Fox and Edmundson.[2]

THE EARLY COLONISTS WERE STANCH QUAKERS.   As an indication of the firm roots of Quakerism in the colony it is on record that as early as 1680 nine Friends were imprisoned for refusing to attend military musters. Their names were: William Bundy, John Price, John Phelps, James Hogg, John Thusstone, Henry Prows, Richard Byer, Samuel Hill and Stephen Hancock. One of the first records of refusal to enroll in the military service occurred in 1680 and the defendants were each fined one hundred pounds of tobacco; this was in Virginia.[3]

To check the Quaker influence Governor Henderson Walker in 1701 caused the first Vestry Act to be passed. This divided the diocese into parishes, and authorized the building of churches, the appointment of clergy, and the imposition of tithes for the upkeep of the Established Church. The Quakers led the opposition, which was widespread as the colonists generally objected to taxation for the support of a religious body of which they were not members. Walker was familiar with certain Acts passed in England to restrain dissenters, such as the Test Act, the Corporation Act, the Five Mile Act, and the Conventicle Acts; and he applied the Test Act to the colony. It was to the effect that no person could hold public office unless he first confirmed his loyalty to the Sovereign with an oath. This device in time put members of the Society out of public life.

Sir Nathaniel Johnson, the Governor-General who succeeded Archdale, would not grant exemption to Friends for military service, and by 1705 those who refused were subject to fines, distraint of goods or imprisonment.[4]

QUAKERS AND THE COLONIAL WARS. The Culpeper Rebellion of 1677-78 attracted attention to the Quakers although they were in no way responsible; the same was true of the Cary Rebellion of 1711, which some early historians referred to as "the Quaker War." It was just the inevitable consequence of not being jingoistic in times of disturbance. The Cary Rebellion had two phases, the first political — in which the Quakers participated; the second military — from which they refrained; but Emanuel Lowe, a Quaker and a son-in-law of Archdale, was brought to trial by the meeting for his share in the uprising. A committee was appointed in 1711

"to inquire into the action of Lowe in stirring up a parcell of men in Arms, and going to Pamlico, And from There to Chowan In a Barkentine with Men and Force of Arms contrary to our Holy Principles."[5]

He was deposed from his position as a member of the Executive Committee of the Yearly Meeting — "the said Lowe having acted diverse things contrary to our ways and principles." The Yearly Meeting was very firm concerning this, and a minute was made to the effect that:

"Those Friends who have given away their Testimony of Hiring, Paying and Working to make any fort or defence against enemies do give from under their hands to the monthly meeting for the clearing of the truth."

This meant that they present a written apology and perhaps submit to questioning or else be disowned.

In 1738 the Assembly exempted Quakers from military service if they would provide a substitute, but this did not suit the conscience. Many Friends were imprisoned because they would not attend musters or pay fines, provide a substitute, or submit to the distraint of goods to cover the fine. In 1748 some of the members refused to pay a tax for the construction of a powder magazine in each county, but some who paid justified themselves by saying they were not responsible for the manner in which the money was spent. In 1756 an act was passed requiring every twentieth man in each county to be drafted and sent to the frontier at Winchester under Colonel Washington. This exempted only the Episcopal clergy. The Quakers came into conflict with the authorities again when the Assembly sought to mollify them by passing a law to the effect that they might make an affirmation to the Crown instead of an oath.[6]

THE REGULATOR MOVEMENT. It has been averred that Friends were insincere concerning their peace testimony, and the accusing finger was pointed at Herman Husband. Undoubtedly he and a few other Friends were involved in the Regulator Movement. Herman was born in Pennsylvania, but removed to North Carolina and became a member of the Cane Creek Meeting. The Regulator uprising had its origin in the excessive fees and taxation imposed by the Lord Proprietor, in this case Earl Granville, and his lordship's admission that fifty per cent of the taxes collected were embezzled by his agents. Husband had little formal education, yet he possessed leadership, and was at one time a speaker of high standing among Friends. He was disowned by the Cane Creek Monthly Meeting on the ground that he made improper personal remarks concerning the transactions of the meeting, and for disorderly conduct. There are entries to that effect in the monthly meeting records 12 - 8 - 1755 and 1 - 7 - 1764. Opinions concerning him differ widely. The members of the faculty at the University when the writer was there from 1920 to 1926 described him as tricky; one who fomented disturbance but always contrived to be out of the way when trouble occurred. Others, however, regarded him as "the Thomas Paine of the South," and it is said that Dr. Frank Graham once called him "North Carolina's first great liberal." E. W. Caruthers in his *Life of Dr. David Caldwell* says that

"Husband was certainly a man of superior mind, and much given to reading and reflection. He was very grave in his deportment and usually had all that reserved and cautious manner of expressing himself in conversation for which the people of the Quaker Society are remarkable; but when animated he could speak in private or in public with sufficient fluency and with a great deal of force. . . . He has been generally represented by historians as a man of a turbulent and seditious character; an arch demagog. . . . Such were the representation of his enemies or of the government party, and historians seemed to have copied them without sufficient inquiry or making the proper allowance."

Husband wrote the much discussed poem *Impartial Relation* in 1770; the Battle of Alamance, which is sometimes regarded as the first battle of the War of Revolution was fought May 16, 1771. Husband fled from North Carolina at the time and his connection with the battle is a matter of dispute. Some say he tried to prevent fighting; others that he was a coward.

It is certain that Husband created trouble in his monthly meeting, and was disowned and was not a member of the Society at the time of the Regulator disturbances. It is common talk at Snow Camp that when he was disowned he went to the step of the meeting house, sat down, took off his shoes and shook them in symbolic repudiation of the Quakers. On one occasion he was arrested, accused of inciting to riot, but was acquitted. He was twice elected to the Legislature, but was expelled on charges of libel. He later participated in the Whiskey Rebellion of 1794.[7]

A QUAKER REVOLUTIONIST. Joseph Hewes (or Hews or Hughes), a Quaker resident of North Carolina, was one of the signers of the Declaration of Independence. His ancestors were in New Jersey before William Penn received his memorable grant of land, and his great-grandfather William was one of the founders of the Quaker meeting at Chichester in Delaware County, Pennsylvania. He died in 1698, leaving a son also named William, who became the father of Aaron, who married Providence Worth in 1727 and they became the parents of Joseph, the subject of this sketch.

Joseph was born in 1730 of a prosperous and numerous family. He became a member of the Chesterfield Monthly Meeting in New Jersey. There is a tradition that he studied at Princeton College, but this is not substantiated. When he was about twenty he settled in Philadelphia, and in 1752 became a merchant. It is on record that he had some intention of engaging in business with the Virgin Islands, but there is no evidence he voyaged there. In 1763 he came to Edenton, North Carolina, by the schooner *Friendship*, brought a consignment of merchandise, established himself as a trader near the Albemarle Sound and soon became a leading citizen. He became engaged to marry but the young woman died before the union and Joseph remained a bachelor.

At the outbreak of the events which led to the War of Independence Joseph Hewes was named by the Assembly of North Carolina as a member of the Committee of Correspondence. He attended the Continental Congress in 1774, at which time there was no openly expressed intention of separating from England. He returned to Edenton and in 1775 was a member of the General Assembly of the colony. By this time he was recognized as a leading citizen, not only of this area, but as a weighty person in the Congress. He was one of a Committee of Five to raise money for the Revolution; later a member of the Committee of Three to make regulations for the army; and still later a member of the committee to secure supplies (especially lead and salt) for the revolutionary troops. In fact, he was on all the important colonial committees, as it was known he had accumulated much experience and exercised much skill in trading and shipping, for he possessed a wharf and participated in privateering during the conflict.

In 1776 he was one of the signers of the historic Declaration of Independence and was elected in 1777 and 1779 by the new State as a representative on the Continental Congress. He also had a share in the preparation of the first Constitution for this State. He seldom spoke at the sessions but he proved a trusty adviser on committees. He was possessed of great business acumen, and it was in this connection that he served the new nation. Because of his general usefulness he was sometimes referred to as "the first Secretary of the Navy of the United States."

He retained his membership in the Society of Friends, as did many others who were thoroughly in sympathy with the movement for Independence. It was a trying time for the Quakers, for to have opposed the Revolution actively would have meant extinction for the Society. Only a comparatively few members participated in arms.

I WILL ABIDE BY IT.   Joseph Hewes had great searching of heart before committing himself to Revolution. John Adams wrote concerning Hewes:

"For many days the majority depended upon Mr. Hewes, of North Carolina. . . . He had constantly voted against separation . . . then started suddenly upright and lifted both hands to Heaven as if he had been in a trance, cried out: 'It is done, and I will abide by it.' . . . I would give more for the perfect painting of the terror and horror upon the face of the old majority at that critical moment than for the best piece of Raphael."

During his last few years Hewes was much weakened by illness and it was with great difficulty he attended to public business. At one time he remarked "When I am no longer useful in Council I should be willing to take the field; I think I would rather fall than to be carried off by a lingering illness." It was common knowledge that if any of the leading Revolutionists were captured by the British dire consequences would follow. Hewes wrote:

"Some talk that members of the Congress might be seized and carried to England as rebels . . . I have no fear on that head, but should it be my lot no man on earth could be better spared. Were I to suffer in the cause of American liberty should I not be translated immediately to Heaven as Enoch was of old."

Hewes was again elected in February 1779 to the Continental Congress, and in July, much enfeebled, he undertook the arduous journey from Edenton to Philadelphia. The great heat of the summer prostrated him and he died November 10, 1779. Congress attended the funeral in a body, each person, according to the custom of the time wearing a black crepe arm band. In 1932 a monument to his memory was erected at Edenton by the United States Government, and there is a small marker in a brick wall at the north-east corner of Main and King Streets indicating that at one time Joseph Hewes resided there.[8]

It is not fitting for those who in later generations reap the advantages of living in a "Land of Liberty" to criticize a conscientious Quaker who believed it his religious duty to gain political liberty for his native land.

FRIENDS AND THE WAR OF INDEPENDENCE. With the Declaration of Independence Friends were thrown into the greatest distress. It was and still is, an axiom of their faith to obey the civil law, except when it clearly violated conscience. The yearly meeting advised members "to refrain from overt acts of disloyalty," and to have no part in the election of delegates to attend the Constitutional Convention. In 1772 the yearly meeting

"Asserted its loyalty and attachment to George III . . . and gave forth their testimony against all Plottings, conspiracies, and insurrections against the King and Government, whatsoever as works of darkness."[9]

This coincided with the occasion when the Society was disturbed over the Regulator Movement. In 1776 the Provincial Congress enacted that all suspected persons should be required to

"solemnly and sincerely swear on the Holy Evangelists of Almighty God that . . . they had not by example, opinion, advice or persuasion endeavored to prejudice any in favor of parliamentary measures or against those recommended by the General and Provincial Congresses."[10]

Before Independence had been proclaimed severe measures had been enacted in this colony against Tories. In 1777 the Assembly enacted that all who committed acts against the State were guilty of treason, the punishment of which was death, with the confiscation of the estate of the person so convicted. Those who were not directly implicated in overt acts, but who had spoken against Independence should suffer imprisonment and forfeit to the State one half of their goods, chattels, tenants and lands. One section of the Act specifically exempted the Quakers from military service, but Friends, Mennonites and Dunkards were required to give an oath of allegiance.[11]

At the yearly meeting of 1777 Friends decided that they could not take an oath of allegiance to the newly established Government of the United States, and they recorded as follows:

"As we have always declared that we believed it to be unlawful for us to be active in war, and fighting with carnal weapons, and as we conceive that the proposed affirmation approves of the present measures, which are carried on and supported by military force, we cannot engage or join with either party therein; being bound by our principles to believe that the setting up and pulling down kings and governments, is God's peculiar prerogative, for causes best known to Himself; and that it is not our work or business to have any hand or contrivance therein, nor to be busybodies in matters above our station; so that as we cannot be active either for or against any power that is permitted or set over us in the above respects; we hope you will consider our principles a much stronger security to any State than any test that can be required of us; as we are now and shall be innocent and peaceable in our several stations and conditions under this present state; and for conscience sake are submissive to the laws, in whatsoever they may justly require, or by peaceably suffering what is or may be inflicted upon us, in matters for which we cannot be active for conscience sake."[12]

The yearly meeting confirmed this the next year, and decided to labor with those who took the affirmation or oath of loyalty . . . in love and tenderness; if they remained stubborn they were not to be considered active members. Some favor was apparently granted as we find the meeting "expressing its thanks to the Assembly and do humbly request that you will be pleased to grant us the privileges we have hitherto enjoyed until proof be made that our behavior manifests us to be unworthy thereof and we hope our conduct will manifest our gratitude." In the same year they declared "they could not take the oath of allegiance . . . as it was uncertain . . . whether the matter still had to be settled by military force."

THE FREE QUAKERS. Some of the younger members who took arms became known as the "Free Quakers" and they effected some kind of organization, retaining membership in the Society and styling themselves Quakers until disbandment in 1798. Some of these affiliated with their former meetings.[13] Caruthers says: "Many of the Quakers, although they tried to be neutral had been with the Americans from the first in feeling and if the British had remained much longer among them they would have become Whigs to a man — at least in principle."[14]

Because of the general refusal of North Carolina Friends to bear arms they suffered the following fines (in round figures): 1778, 1,200 pounds; 1779, 2,152 pounds; 1780, 841; 1781, 4,134; 1782, 741; 1783, 718 pounds. In 1781 Western Quarterly Meeting reported that over 2,148 pounds had been taken by the Revolutionary army, and over 765 by the British. Friends refrained from active participation in the new government and many felt they could not conscientiously accept Continental currency nor the scrip issued by the several States and by numerous business concerns. This attitude was understandable as paper currency was subject to rapid depreciation and became of lesser value the further it was removed from its place of origin, but the actions of Friends hastened the deterioration.[15]

WHY FRIENDS COULD NOT SUPPORT THE NEW GOVERNMENT. So sincere was the Quaker objection to the recognition of a new revolutionary government based on force that in 1787 "a member was brought to trial before the meeting for becoming a justice of the peace." Friends were warned against participating in the new government. The reasons for this attitude which we might now regard as strange were: first, it was an unlawful government established upon violence and lawlessness; second, office holders would be required to take an oath of loyalty; third, they would be called upon to do official acts at variance with pure conduct; fourth, they would be called upon to administer oaths; fifth, they would have to enforce the slave laws; and lastly, they might be required to enforce capital punishment, against which Friends had persistently protested.

In 1809 the yearly meeting took a still stronger stand and it was recorded that "any Friends who accepted office in the Federal or State Governments should be disowned." This ruling applied also to "all magistrates, sheriffs, clerks of court, coroner or constable." The situation was the same in Virginia.* It may help to explain this decision if it be remembered that North Carolina was tardy in ratifying the Constitution. At a Convention at Hillsboro in 1788 the vote was against ratification, and when President George Washington took office in 1789 North Carolina was in dire economic straits and political confusion.

Frederick William Marschall, the head man or "Inspector" of

---

* Several years' *minutes* are missing from the Yearly Meeting Records at this period.

the Moravian community at Old Salem (in an adjoining county) wrote in 1783

"This country is in the condition of a patient convalescing from fever, who begins to be conscious of his weakness, and still needs medicine and care. The land itself, the people of property, commerce, public and private credit, the currency in circulation are all laid waste and ruined."

Archibald D. Murphy added his testimony: "When the war ended, the people were in poverty, society in disorder, morals and manners almost prostrate."

CONCERNING DEBTS. Weeks testifies to the high standard of honesty manifested among Friends during the frightfully disturbed period during and following the war. Because of the general devastation, confusion and poverty debts could not be paid when due. The State passed several Stay Laws and Bankruptcy Laws which prohibited legal distraint upon non-fulfilment of contract. Many repudiated obligations, but it is not known that a member of the Society did so. The Discipline required Friends to settle their debts and it was the custom to refrain from issuing certificates of removal unless "Friends were clear." It was regarded as a disgrace and a disownable offence for a member to become bankrupt. Lefler and Newsome describe the time as:

"a critical period for North Carolina . . . the 350,000 people in the State's forty-seven counties were confronted with grave problems — a weak and inefficient State government . . . economic depression and general social demoralization . . . public money unaccounted for . . . public credit almost sunk . . . utter insufficiency for payment of public officials . . . no regular system of jurisprudence. . . . Radicals constituted the great bulk of the people . . . many of them uneducated, poor and in debt . . . gold currency non-existing."[*16]

ON TAKING THE LAW. During this trying period Friends endeavored to obey the command of Christ to refrain from suing others in court in order to maintain their rights. Quakers regarded this injunction not just as a regulation to be observed, but as a fundamental concept of the Gospel. When differences occur the primary consideration should be to restore right relations. This can not be accomplished by punishment but by love and patience. It became the custom of Friends to say to a defaulter "Friend, I leave it with thy conscience; whenever thou art ready to straighten the matter thee will find me agreeable." It was one form of over-

---

* North Carolina now has a population of approximately 3,000,000 native Whites; 18,000 foreign born Whites; 1,250,000 Negroes; 4,000 Indians and perhaps 500 Asiatics. There are now 100 counties.

coming evil with good, and Quaker history is replete with instances where this conduct was highly successful. To sue a member required the consent of the elders, and this was not likely to be given as it was usual for a committee to be appointed to deal with the matter. This involved a trial conducted by Friends, a very serious affair. Curiously enough it was at one time permissible to sue a person who had been disowned. As details are not available it is not proper to regard this as a general rule. In case of suing without notification to the elders a member was required to present "a paper of condemnation" at the next monthly meeting, and also to publish a full statement of his confession at the courthouse door.* If his explanation were not satisfactory he might be disowned, and this involved ostracism.[17]

IN ALL THINGS CHARITY. Thus the Quakers came close to the repudiation of Caesar in their endeavor to obey God. We cannot condemn them, for it is impossible for us who have always known liberty and suffered no inconveniences from such disturbed conditions to realize what a constant trial of faith beset our Quaker forebears upon this continental frontier. To recapitulate their troubles we recall the hardships of breaking ground in a wilderness, building primitive habitations, digging wells, fending off wild animals, almost continuous frontier fighting, the presence of slavery, the impossibility of conciliation with a political system which required oaths and military service, and a State church which exacted tithes. Then there came decimation through mass migration to the West and neighbors who ostracized them because of their scruples, and to crown all, civil war — for such the War of Independence actually was. In North Carolina the people were sharply divided into three groups — Tories, Whigs and Neutralists (the Quakers and the Moravians who were pacifists).[18]

With the cessation of fighting came the beginning of a new era. In 1784 the Assembly granted Quakers the right to affirm their loyalty to the new government, and the yearly meeting withdrew its objection to its members participating in politics. The next year conscientious objectors were excused from attending musters. About this time a law was passed permitting a citizen to will that his slaves should be freed at his death. Another benefit was the

---

* See Letters of Condemnation in chapter xvii. It is a very ancient custom (still observed) in England for public notices to be affixed to the main portal of the parish church.

legalization of marriages according to the manner of Friends.*

The attitude of most of the citizens toward slavery was not, however, changed by the securing of political independence, so the Friends continued to petition the Assembly for amelioration of the harsh laws, known as the "Black Code." The venerable Nereus Mendenhall was called to account by the local authorities for possessing and circulating anti-slavery literature such as Stowe's *Uncle Tom's Cabin* and Helper's *The Impending Crisis*.

---

* Weeks says: "So far as I have been able to find out there were no provisions for Quakers to celebrate their marriages after their own peculiar manner before the law of 1780. A similar law was enacted in 1784. These two acts legalized all marriages which had been previously made according to Friends' Discipline. Till that time such marriages were regarded as illegal, although in keeping with Common Law. The situation was similar in Georgia, Virginia and South Carolina." — *op. cit.* pp 168-169.

CHAPTER TWELVE

LET MY PEOPLE GO

QUAKERS AND SLAVERY.   The basic concept of Quakerism was that
"there was something of God in every man," and that if one would
heed the Inward Voice, the Seed could be quickened, and one
would become a Child of God. The Quakers believed this to be
true even of uncivilized persons and therefore true of the American
Indian and of Negroes. Slavery was wrong because a bondman had
no opportunity to develop his own personality. How could a slave
pray "Thy Will be done . . . Lead me . . . deliver me from evil."
It was not merely that slavery was cruel — it destroyed the possibility of fellowship with the Eternal. Quakers were probably the
first religious body to protest against the evils of human bondage.
Edmundson spoke against it in his visit to the colony in 1672;
George Keith advocated religious instruction for Negro slaves as a
preparation for manumission; William Penn favored emancipation;
George Fox in his visit to this colony in 1672 advocated that
"Negro slaves be treated kindly and after certain years of service
be set at liberty."

The first known official protest was by the Germantown Meeting of Friends in Pennsylvania in 1688. The Philadelphia Yearly
Meeting of 1696 condemned further importation of slaves, and in
1730 the same body censured members who held slaves. In 1768
that meeting appointed a committee to deal with members who still
retained human beings in bondage. It is a coincidence that in the
same year that the Thirteen Colonies proclaimed Independence,
Philadelphia Friends decided that the holding of slaves was a justi-
fiable reason for disownment. By 1783, the year that the Treaty of
Independence was signed, it was reported that Friends in Pennsylvania, New Jersey and Delaware possessed no slaves. The other
yearly meetings took similar action, but naturally the slave States
were slower in coming to definite decisions. New England Friends
were clear by 1782; New York by 1787; Virginia by 1817.[1]

THE NORTH CAROLINA MANUMISSION SOCIETY.   Charles Osborn is
said to have been the very first American abolitionist. He visited
this State in 1814 and two years later organized the North Carolina
Manumission Society. It was supported by Friends in Guilford,

Randolph, Chatham, Forsyth and Orange Counties. One account says that in 1825 there were 40 branches (Boyd), another report (Lefler) says there were 25 chapters. At an annual convention in 1819 there were present 281 persons; six years later only 141 attended. The objectives of the organization were to bring about the amelioration of the conditions of slavery; to work toward emancipation; to encourage the emigration of Freedmen to Liberia or Haiti; to petition the authorities both Federal and State repeatedly. The press of the State as well as the authorities were hostile to the Society. Eventually the organization collapsed over the question of the emigration of Freedmen.[2]

How North Carolina Friends Freed Themselves of Slavery. It is the settled conviction of Friends that violence is not the proper remedy for any evil, but that by patience, love and firmness every wrong can be righted in time. The Quakers, therefore, resorted to moral suasion to cleanse their hands of the wickedness of slavery. Among the first steps recorded are messages from the Virginia Meeting in 1722 and 1739 recommending that Negroes be treated humanely.[3] From 1758 to the Emancipation Proclamation by President Lincoln in 1863 the question of slavery was paramount in the yearly meeting. In 1759 the sainted John Woolman visited North Carolina with slavery as his great burden. He addressed epistles to New Garden and to Cane Creek upon the subject.[4] John Griffith upon visiting here in 1765 exclaimed: "Alas, great deadness, insensibility and darkness were felt to prevail . . . concerning Negroes in perpetual slavery."[5]

In 1768 Friends appointed a committee to hold religious services among the colored people, and also ruled that members should not engage in the slave trade, although they did not at that time prohibit workers in bondage. In 1771 they addressed a petition to the Colonial Legislature in which bondage was characterized as "iniquitous . . . and a great evil and abomination."

The minutes of 1771 show that Friends were ready to take a more definite stand, for it is recorded:

"Having weightily considered the evil practices of buying and selling Negroes . . . we do give it as our judgment that no Friend in unity shall buy a Negro of any other person than a Friend in unity . . . and shall not separate husbands and wives nor parents and children. . . . Those who have received slaves by inheritance should treat them well . . . and discourage them from evil."[**6]

---

* The laws of several, if not all, of the Southern States did not recognize marriage among the Negro slaves, and the children were the property of the master of the mother.

The minute is very lengthy and is well written. The object was to keep Friends clear of trafficing in slaves, which business involved terrible cruelties.

In this same year the Friends sent a message of gratitude to the Assembly for some relief from obnoxious laws and sent another petition on behalf of the enslaved population.[7]

AN ADDRESS TO THE THRONE.   They also went further and addressed a petition to the Throne of England, which read in part:

"In order to be as eyes to the blind and mouths for the dumb, and whether it succeeds or not we shall have the secret satisfaction in our own minds of having used our best endeavor to have so great a torrent of evil effectually stopped at the place where unhappily it had the permission to begin."[8]

The yearly meeting was greatly concerned over conditions in the Eastern Quarter, for here the colored population was very numerous and at one time quite a number of Quakers held slaves. The meeting

"Advised members to cleanse their hands as soon as possible . . . and none be permitted to buy or sell Negroes to any except to members of the Society. . . . Members may be disowned if not yielding after having been labored with."[9]

A committee was appointed to visit the Quarter and see that the Discipline was carried out.

In 1777 it was reported that a considerable number had been liberated, and

"There was a great willingness, even beyond expectation to release Negroes from bondage."[10]

KIDNAPING OF FREED NEGROES.   The gratification of Friends was marred when it became known that racketeers had formed gangs which kidnaped freedmen and caused them to be re-sold into slavery.   It was reported that Friends in Pasquotank and Perquimans knew of forty such instances.   The law at that time allowed slaves to be manumitted only as a reward for long and meritorious service.   It should also be mentioned that any freeholder could challenge any colored person, and if he or she could not produce evidence that they possessed a pass or papers of manumission they could be seized, delivered to the sheriff, and sold at the court house next court day.   The Black Codes also denied a colored person the right to testify on his own behalf or to call witnesses.[*][11]

---

[*] The writer recalls that President L. L. Hobbs told him forty years ago that he remembered when any colored person could be questioned by any white person. For an extensive account of the relation of the Quakers to Slavery see Jorns, Auguste: *The Quakers as Pioneers in Social Work*, translated from the German by T. K. Brown, Macmillan, 1931.   There are numerous other works.

The approach of the War of Independence brought great anxiety to the Society. As will be told in another place the peace testimony of Friends barred them from participating, in any form of local government. The historic Battle of Guilford Court House, March 15, 1781, was fought within a few miles of New Garden. The tenseness over slavery became greatly accentuated by the armed conflict, and many Quaker families became divided. The Negroes throughout the South remained in general loyal to their masters, and no serious uprisings occurred.

At the sessions in 1780 Friends re-asserted their advice that members should only employ free Negro labor, and that same year they resorted to the ancient inalienable right of free citizens to present petitions.*[12] This practice was not limited to the yearly meeting for in 1786 one of the Quarterly meetings addressed the Assembly on behalf of "an enlargement of the rights of the enslaved Negroes."[13]

SLAVE HOLDERS TO BE DISOWNED. The Quakers by now had developed a fixed policy, which was recorded in the official records in 1780, 1781, 1784, 1786 and 1788 to the effect that "no member use enslaved persons as workers; that they were not to engage in the slave trade and that offenders should be visited by the elders and warned and if they did not conform they should be disowned."[14]

More complaints from the Eastern Quarter reached the yearly meeting in 1788, as some Friends were accused of running contraband goods.[15]

Although Friends in this period were careful to abstain from politics that did not debar them from sending a petition to the Assembly of Georgia pleading "for an enlargement of the rights of the colored people."[16]

Joshua Evans, a Friend from the North, visited the Carolinas in 1796, and was one of a delegation which presented a petition at Raleigh. His *Journal* furnishes a very interesting account, from which these particulars are culled:

"We attended the house of Common Council and had a number of private conferences with members, who received us friendly, but seemed mostly opposed to the freedom of the black people. My Great Master endued me with an innocent boldness, in which I could use much freedom of conversation with the leading men. . . . I was therefore the more free to make use of private opportunities with the members of the Legislature and others; there being now here a large number of the first rank, called gentlemen, most of them being

* The Assembly met that year at Halifax.

men of some office, civil or military. These opportunities were generally to my satisfaction, and I thought the respect they showed me was marvelous. . . . At the tavern where we put up, there were about fifty boarders, all men of note . . . and a number of them invited me to come to their rooms. . . . All this furnished me opportunities to touch on their cruel laws and the hardships to which the poor blacks were subjected. . . . When we came to settle for our board at the tavern the man would take no pay, he was so well pleased with the visit."[17]

The petition is inscribed in full in the yearly meeting minutes of 1796, and by Weeks, who observes

"The address towers in the plain and simple grandeur of its appeal to that body, and not directly for the slave, but for the rights of freemen, which had been denied to themselves."[18]

The Legislature acted adversely to the petition, and a new law was passed in November, 1796:

"To amend, strengthen and confirm the acts against emancipation that no slave shall be set free in any case, or under any pretext whatsoever, except for meritorious services, to be adjudged of and allowed by the county court and license first hand and obtained therefore."

AUTHORS OF THE COMMON MISCHIEF. Friends received the dubious compliment of "being the Authors of the Common Mischief." It is not surprising that the epithet came from the Eastern Quarter, for, as previously stated, there were at that time more Quakers and more Negroes in that area than elsewhere. A Grand Jury at Edenton made a presentment to the following effect:

"The Quakers were the authors of the common mischief in this quarter . . . for great peril and danger was caused by their proceedings . . . the idea of emancipation was openly held out to the slaves, their minds were corrupted, and alienated from service . . . runaways are protected, harbored and encouraged by them. Arsons are committed without probability of discovery."[19]

Friends began to cast around to find some other source of assistance and Judge William Gaston was approached in 1809 as to whether it were lawful for the Society to hold in trust such persons as might be liberated by its members. He made an historic decision, and resorted to the contention that if slaves were property, then laws relating to property could be applied to them, consequently:

"It was lawful for any religious Society to elect trustees to purchase property on behalf of said congregation. . . . It followed that such trustees could hold property of any kind, including personal property, money or slaves."[20]

Friends were careful to obtain from the judge a draft of the legal form which would be necessary. At first the plan that members who could not afford to emancipate their slaves should deed them to the Society did not meet with general approval.

THE YEARLY MEETING HOLDS SLAVES. Thus the most ironic situation developed. A religious Society which disowned its members for the holding of slaves became itself the holder of such persons. A central committee was appointed and agents authorized to receive in the various quarters the title of such persons as were freed by its members. These were hired out as workers for wages. Cane Creek at first had scruples, and declined to appoint agents, but eventually the plan received support. By 1824 Eastern Quarter had five hundred freedmen under its care; by 1826 there were six hundred. Steps were taken to convey them to "free territory" north of the Ohio River. This movement led to the development of the Underground Railroad, which will be told in a subsequent section.

It is impossible to state how many persons were thus "owned" by the Society and eventually conveyed to the north, especially to Indiana, Ohio, and Illinois.* The records give details of an individual who was conveyed to a meeting, which was to be his guardian, hire him out for wages, and set him at liberty when and where circumstances permitted. The minutes say that in 1824 the following were "under care": Eastern Quarter, 500; Western, 13; New Garden, 32; Contentnea, 156; Deep River, 7; Southern, 31. Another item says there were 727 in all.[21]

Friends also assisted those who so desired to migrate to Haiti or Liberia.[22] The Society appointed a committee to examine and report on the laws of other States concerning the liberation of bondmen, but the writer failed to find any such report. In this connection it may be said that several States denied the entrance of free Negroes and that the Fugitive Slave Laws were iniquitous and favored kidnaping.[23]

It now seems that the lines of battle were drawn, and the Quakers and the Legislature strengthened themselves for the contest, for in 1830 an Act was passed requiring all freedmen to put up a bond of $1,000 for good behavior. This of course, was intended to make manumission impossible.[24] Friends were quick to protest, but the Legislature continued to pass harsh laws, similar to those in many of the Southern States which became known as "the Black Code." For a time the activities of Friends and other antislavery groups were paralyzed.

---

* It is likely that the numbers given in various reports contain duplications. Learned Friends are of opinion that the figures given by Weeks and Coffin are exaggerated. The writer has examined all these reports and is of opinion that the number of colored people aided by Friends to get to non-slave States must have exceeded one thousand.

ANSWERING THE SIXTH QUERY. The minutes record that in the sessions of 1851 when Query Number Six was under consideration:

"Friends were brought into deep feeling upon the subject, and after weighty consideration it was felt to lay the subject before the yearly meeting for consideration."

But at the following year the meeting was non-committal, and decided:

"The yearly meeting regards it inexpedient to take any action concerning slave labor . . . but such of our members as feel conscientious scruples must pay attention to their feelings in this respect."

By 1854 the meeting was prepared to take more decisive action, for the minute says:

"It is our continued concern to prohibit members from holding in bondage our fellow men. Friends are to avoid becoming executors of estates involving the disposition of Negro slaves . . . if such . . . they shall be disowned."

It was the custom at the annual sessions for the clerk to read the Queries one by one and each quarterly meeting to reply with a written report. In course of time the replies became stereotyped, and the words "Friends appear to be clear" was the usual reply. The Query concerning slavery was number six, and from 1853 to 1873 the answer appears in almost identical language to the effect:

"Friends appear to be clear, except in a few cases of slaves held by heirship, which is under notice . . . and two of hiring which are under notice."

The words "under notice" imply that a committee was appointed and that they would visit and "labor with" the offender and that if such person would not comply with the Discipline the committee should so report to the meeting and recommend disownment.[25]

In 1862 the yearly epistle contains the curious combination of protests:

"Friends bear a testimony against war except in a few instances and mostly against a hireling ministry; our testimony against war and slavery are plain and explicit."[26]

In 1864 there occurs a slight variation "two of keeping slaves for board and lodging through sympathy."[27] Ten years later there is an entry "fear that in one or two instances laborers have been defrauded."[28]

During all these years there does not appear in the yearly meeting minutes any direct reference to the Underground Railroad. A perusal of Levi Coffin's *Reminiscences* gives the impression that the undertakings were purposefully secret, and probably the suppression of information was deliberate.

THE DIFFICULTIES OF MANUMISSION.   There was far more involved than the moral issue in the freeing of their colored servants by Friends. Thomas Jefferson had become convinced that slavery was an abominable nuisance and he would gladly have liberated his workers but he knew that they would become vagabonds if he did so. The adjoining States forbade the entry of freedmen. It was the general testimony that colored persons regarded freedom as the opportunity to refuse work, to wander about and to "tote" whatever they could.

Then there was the pecuniary loss. Slaves were valuable. A "stanch wench" would fetch at least $600.00 and a "prime field hand" sold for $300.00 in 1804; $800.00 in 1840; $1,000.00 in 1860. Many sincere Friends could not afford these sacrifices. Then, again, the word "slavery" had several connotations. The slave trade was one category; the term "field hand" was something else; there were hundreds of highly skilled craftsmen who were greatly esteemed and who were indispensable; then there was the "house servant."   There was a tendency for a Northerner to think of slavery in terms of Harriet Beecher Stowe's Simon Legree, but to a Southerner the distinctions were vital. In countless cases the house servants were second or third generation persons who had been reared upon the plantation, and who were in almost every instance kindly treated and who were contented and happy. They were necessary to the economy of that period. In colonial times many families were almost wholly self-supporting. Every home had its spinning wheel; nearly everything was homemade — clothing, caps, rugs, candles, soap, furniture, buildings; all the food was home grown. The blacksmith, mason, wheelwright and miller were colored folk. Large families were the order of the day. There was no free white labor. In truth the "poor white trash" were despised by the Negroes, and pitied because "they had no massa to care for them." To realize this helps one to understand why Friends deeded their slaves to the Society and encouraged their workers to remain as paid helpers. Before we laud the elders for disowning those members who did not free their slaves it is fitting that we consider the circumstances. Without question many who were disowned were overwhelmed by the difficulties of operating a farm or plantation or business without the former help. It was bad enough to be ostracized by his neighbors for being a Quaker and refusing to fight, but then to be denied Christian fellowship by his "Friends" meant for many "a cupful of confusion and pain and sorrow." Then came war and desolation and abandoned properties. Emancipation spelled chaos and the end of the so-called "Era of Southern culture."[29]

LEVI COFFIN AND THE UNDERGROUND RAILROAD.   No account of this chapter of Southern history would be complete without mention of Levi Coffin. He was born at New Garden (now Guilford College) in 1789, and was reared as a farmer. He had little schooling, but became a teacher. Early in life he developed sympathy for the Negro slaves, and established a Sunday School for them at Deep River in 1818, but their masters objected and the project was discontinued. After his marriage to Catherine White in 1824 he removed to New Port (now Fountain City), Indiana. So active did Levi Coffin become in this work that he became known as "the President of the Underground Railroad." His house contained numerous secret hiding places. His autobiography says that several hundred fugitives passed through his hands, and that he never had one recaptured and that he never told a lie. He was, however, a past master in the art of evasion, and his book contains scores of exciting moments when the disguised fugitive walked away before the eyes of his pursuer. His wife, Catherine, was an able and willing participant in collusion, and she devised signals to indicate that it was clear for Levi to let the searchers into the house and look wherever they pleased. Friends were careful never to go upon other's plantations, and urge Negroes to flee. They were accused of so doing, but it was unnecessary, as the attitude of the Quakers was as well known as their manner of dress.

The Underground Railroad continued operations for several years; many others besides Friends participated. A system of secret signals was developed; travel was usually by night; main roads were avoided; the stages of the journey were usually short; changes of routes were frequent so as to avoid detection. The refugees were passed on from one "station" to another, and the "agents" exchanged few words. In this way hundreds of fugitives were conveyed to free territory. Levi Coffin travelled extensively in this country and in England in the interests of the Anti-Slavery movement to collect funds. He was in 1867 a delegate to an international Anti-Slavery conference. He died at the age of eighty-eight in 1877.[30]

It is not surprising that the people in Indiana and Ohio objected to the continued dumping of destitute Negroes upon their frontiers, and in 1831 the last mentioned State forbade whites to bring in blacks in order to free them; Indiana followed suit; then forbade the entry of free colored persons.

Elbert Russell quotes Thomas in saying:

"By the close of the eighteenth century there was not a slave in the possession of a Friend of good standing, except where slaves were held by trustees, and State laws did not allow them to be set free."[31]

Russell further says that the emancipation of the slaves was always accompanied by provisions for their economic welfare and efforts to educate them.[32]

SUPPOSE ALL DENOMINATIONS HAD FOLLOWED THE QUAKER EXAMPLE. Thus by the time of the opening of the Civil War the Quakers everywhere had freed themselves of all association with chattel slavery. John Spencer Bassett remarks: "It was reserved for Friends to show the world that the question of slavery could be debated and settled without passion." Had all the denominations followed conscience as did the Quakers there would have been no Civil War.

In 1871 the yearly meeting addressed a memorial to the King of Spain and to the Cortes on behalf of the slaves in the Spanish dominions.[33]

QUAKERS AS CONSCIENTIOUS OBJECTORS. Quakers have adhered to the pacifist views which characterised the believers in Jesus Christ in steady succession for centuries until the time of Constantine. Before the Emperor professed Christianity and caused Christianity to become a state religion no Church Father whose work is extant condoned believers participating in warfare. It was generally known and understood by non-Christians that believers abstained from all forms of violence. The pagan Celsus, writing in the second century, declared that if all men were as the Christians the Empire would be overturned by barbarians. The Empire did not adopt the pacifist policy, yet was overwhelmed by barbarians. Many Quakers have been as steadfast in their pacifist views as the early Christians and some have in consequence suffered humiliation, condemnation, physical torture and death rather than forego their convictions that violence, destruction and murder are completely at variance with the Spirit of the Christ and are not the proper or enduring remedies for any evil. As the Quakers had solved the question of domestic slavery in a peaceful way, and as at the time of secession there was no member of the Society in good standing holding a person in bondage, the Friends did not feel obligated to assist in attempting to solve it in a way of violence which was thoroughly at variance with their religious scruples. They were Unionists, and loyal to the United States Government, yet they could not bear arms — either for or against the Confederacy. The peace testimony of the Quakers was well known for the population of North Carolina was meagre, and Friends constituted a sizeable and noticeable proportion of the population.

First the draft and then conscription was applied by the Confederate Government. It was, therefore, no surprise that ablebodied young Quakers received orders to report for service. Many — perhaps most — of those drafted stood by their peace convictions, and pleaded that members of his Society had shown the way to settle the slavery issue aright.

Fernando G. Cartland in *Southern Heroes* has given a full account of the experiences of North Carolina Friends. Many lost much of their property through marauding by foragers of both armies; some had their livestock seized; others witnessed soldiers wantonly destroy or carry away the furnishings of their homes and all their stock of food. Some draftees consented to perform noncombatant service; some refused to comply with any military orders; others drew the line at the bearing of arms. For this many were most brutally tortured; some died of the abuses. Quite a number when mustered with the Confederates seized opportunities to desert and settle in free territory. To understand this it must be kept in mind that thousands of Quakers and others had already forsaken the slave-holding States and as ruin approached there was a natural urge to escape.

Cartland gives particulars of the following Friends who were brought face to face with the issue, and who in one way or another bore their testimony against the wrongness of war. They represent practically every monthly meeting. The names include: Thomas and Amos Hinshaw, Cyrus and Nathan Barker, Solomon Frazier, Jessie Milton Blair, Jesse and William Hill, D. W. and Clark Millikan, W. F. Ball, J. R. Beckerdike, Seth W. Loflin, William Low, Jackson M. Anderson, W. and D. H. Jones, Lewis Caudle, Joseph, William B., Jesse, and Himelius Hockett, Nathaniel Woody, John Newlin, James Lindley, James and Mahlon Woody, Zeno and William Woody, Miles, William and Stephen Hobson, Mahlon Thompson, Joshua Kemp, Joseph Dixon, A. C. Swain, Rufus B. King, William Morgan, Thomas Kennedy, Tilgham Vestal, Thomas B. Elliot, Needham Pearson, Jesse Hollowell and Isaac Harvey.

The treatment of William B. Hockett was especially revolting, and the story occupies several pages in Cartland's work.

RUFUS P. KING. The story of Rufus P. King is unusual. He was born near Chapel Hill in 1843, received little education and had a hard time as a youngster. He was drafted in 1862, and at that time although he knew nothing of Friends possessed an intense horror of war, and avoided combat service and devoted himself to the care of the wounded and dying among the troops. He was captured by the Federals, taken to the mid-west, and became converted at a Methodist camp meeting in Indiana, and shortly afterwards attended a Friends meeting for the first time. He joined the Society and in time was recorded a minister. Then began an extraordinary career — in some respects unique. He possessed a most persuasive address; in a curious way he combined innocence and guile. He travelled extensively in the ministry on this continent visiting probably more Friends' gatherings than any contemporary. Then he received credentials to travel abroad and he preached throughout Canada, England, Ireland, Germany, France, Denmark, Australia, New Zealand, Syria, Palestine, Haiti, Jamaica and Barbadoes. Surely a marvellous accomplishment for a person with so limited a background. He was a rare person; a frank biographer could present a queer story; only those who knew him can appreciate his foibles.[34]

As one ponders this chapter in Quaker history and becomes aware of the steadfastness of Friends to their peace principles even in the midst of devastation and compares and contrasts that period with the behavior of Quakers in recent years one wonders whether Friends of today possess the same devotion to convictions that their ancestors did a century ago.

THE FREEDMEN AT THE CLOSE OF THE WAR. As the Union armies advanced into the South the Negroes had a tendency to abandon their masters and attach themselves to the troops. They were at first encouraged to do so, with the object of depleting the Confederacy, and they were put to work at the several camps. General B. F. Butler styled them "contrabands." That they received food and shelter was potent reason for their flight. However, they soon became a serious problem, causing confusion, and impeding the movement of the troops. By the Emancipation Proclamation issued by President Lincoln as a war measure in 1863 all slaves in territories occupied by the Confederate army were declared to be free. In addition thousands of Negroes were set free by Emancipation legislation in West Virginia, Missouri, Maryland and Tennessee. Concentration camps were improvised at many places, including North Carolina. Make-shift quarters were used — old buildings, school houses and tents. Many refugees could not find shelter, and freedom simply meant the opportunity to wander, plunder and subsist in continual fear and want. Under such circumstances it is little wonder that suffering, disease, pestilence, starvation and death were inevitable. Some accounts say that in the two years following the cessation of hostilities as many freedmen perished as combatants in the war. Unaccustomed to care for themselves, and ignorant of the first principles of hygiene the Negroes fell victims of exposure, malnutrition, vice and contagion. Naturally it was the women and the children who suffered most. The plantation system was wrecked; the economy was ruined; there was no chance for the Freedmen to secure gainful occupation.[35]

THE FRIENDS' FREEDMEN'S ASSOCIATION. Such wide-spread conditions called into being the Friends' Freedmen's Association. The women of Philadelphia Yearly Meeting were among the first to be concerned over these pitiful and dangerous conditions. Under the leadership of Dr. James Beasley, Elizabeth Farnum and Elizabeth J. Sharpless, clothing and other supplies were collected and distributed to various concentration camps. At one time the group employed seventy colored women in making garments and hospital supplies. An appeal was made for funds, and of $4,078.29 received $3,339.53 came from Philadelphia, most of which was used in making or purchasing clothing. The need became so great that the men Friends effected an organization to assist, and Samuel R. Shipley was appointed to visit various concentration camps and ascertain conditions. In all $430,875.03 was expended. In addition to clothing, Bibles, books and tracts were distributed. Schools were conducted for the unfortunates. It is a moving story. Friends were not the only organization to share in this redemptive work, but by universal consent they played a conspicuous part. In many places the "schoolhouses" had no furniture, no doors and no windows. It was not uncommon for three generations to be present in the same room. In some parts the freedmen were virtually barbarians, especially those from the South Carolina islands. Some had no real names. At roll call some would answer to such terms as "Honey," "Squash," "Mealbag," "Baby," "Punkin." Some gave their former master's "title." Many did not know the names of the days or months. Their clothing was truly nondescript. In most instances the teachers were educated young people from the North; local Friends provided lodgings wherever possible, but the war had impoverished the whole populace, so they had little means and less inclination to assist. In a few places the teachers could find no accommodations except among the Negroes. This infuriated the Whites. At Burlington a cripple teacher was badly abused by the Ku Klux Klan.

YARDLEY WARNER. Among the names which should be mentioned is that of Yardley Warner. He was a Philadelphia business man, who had previously taught Negroes as a personal undertaking. He gave up all other interests, and attached himself to the Philadelphia Association. He went to Europe and raised money for the undertaking; one account says he "possessed a zeal which amounted to a passion." He came to North Carolina, visited the sick, interviewed public men, spoke at Quaker Meetings, set up printing presses, instructed colored boys in printing; called public conventions, organized elementary and normal schools, and drew the plans for the Maryville Institute, Tennessee. He says of the colored people in the neighborhood of the Model Farm "visits to the homes of the freedman reveal a grade of heathenism incredible to persons not familiar with the vicinity. . . . The apathy of the whites to the future of the colored is alarming." He literally wore himself out in their behalf. He started a movement to enable worthy Negroes to secure land of their own. In Greensboro his name became a household word, and here he died, and such was his influence that a portion of the city is still known as Warnersville.[*36]

The records of the Philadelphia Association contain the names of 246 teachers and missionaries who labored in 153 centers in the South. Work was done in 26 counties of North Carolina, principally in Alamance, Buncombe, Craven, Davidson, Durham, Forsyth, Guilford, Orange, Randolph, Rowan, Rutherford, Wayne and Yadkin.[**]

Another service that Friends rendered was in cooperation with the Freedmen's Bureau (a Government organization) in finding shelter and work for the Freedmen. There were many "abandoned

---

[*] While writing this story the interesting news was received that Stafford Allen Warner has just published a biography of his father entitled *Yardley Warner, the Freedman's Friend*, published by the Wessex Press, Didcot, Berkshire, England.

[**] The boundaries of the counties in North Carolina have been subject to frequent change and sub-division, one motive being to enable the politicians to keep power in the older Eastern portion of the State.

lands," and until the owners appeared and claimed possession in countless cases the refugees were temporarily housed there. Barracks and tents were erected in other places. The colored people were not used to work as hired men, and many difficulties were encountered. The chiefest difficulty was the prejudice of the Southerners who regarded all Northerners as "furriners" or "Carpetbaggers."

WHITE LEADERS DISFRANCHISED. The native leaders of the South were disfranchized under the "Iron Clad Oath," and carpetbaggers, scalawags and Negroes controlled the States legislatures, and Federal troops supervised the ballot till after Rutherford Hayes became President in 1877. Little wonder that there was a general feeling that Reconstruction should be in the hands of the "lily white Democrats." The obvious answer is that relief had to be rendered immediately and that the Southerners were neither able nor willing to render organized relief to the freedmen.

Perhaps the most important and humane service has yet to be mentioned. Owing to crowded conditions and the lack of even elementary sanitary precautions disease and pestilence soon appeared at the improvised concentration camps. Milk was lacking for babies and children. A terrible epidemic appeared at Newbern in the summer of 1865. The Hicksite Friends, of Philadelphia, devoted themselves to relief among the sick and destitute. Nurses, doctors, medical supplies and clothing were sent to this and many other areas. The details cannot be listed here. It is, however, necessary to state that fevers of various kinds manifested themselves at many places, and that every yearly meeting shared in this work in caring for the sick. Disease is no respecter of persons or of races, and the alarming situation threatened the whole population. Almost everywhere the colored people were afraid of vaccination or inoculation. It must be remembered that the Confederates had suffered terrible casualties, and every community had more than it could do to care for the Whites who were wounded or destitute or bereaved.

Wherever possible local Friends rose above the common prejudice and assisted as best they could, but it was met with resentment, and it was quite common for Quakers to be publicly jeered as "nigger teacher." The presence of Friends from other yearly meetings gave needed strength to the enfeebled local meetings, yet it was not an unmixed blessing, as it brought further reproach. Cases are on record of persons being publicly whipped for teaching Negroes.[37]

CHAPTER THIRTEEN

GET THEE OUT OF THY COUNTRY

THE MIGRATION OF FRIENDS. It is an axiom in philosophy that in order to understand the whole one should see all the parts in relation to each other and in relation to the whole. Therefore, in order to appreciate the prolonged and extensive migrations of Friends it must be remembered that the vastness of the American continent and the lure of free or cheap land provided the greatest incentive to ambitious people to seek the most promising homesites. All the colonists were aware that their ancestors of only a few generations back had come from old countries in Europe. Wanderlust possessed multitudes of people; the Quakers shared the common urge, though perhaps due to their attitude toward slavery, they had a greater incentive than others to abandon the Southern areas.

To show the inducement to go West the following extract from a letter from Solomon Frazier Jr., who had left North Carolina, to his brother, Isaac, the grandfather of Cyrus P. Frazier, written in 1832 will be revealing:

"And it is my desire that some of you will come to this goodly land; there can be good land bought for twenty-five cents the acre. By taking prairie land where the grass is waving like a rye field in June, the cattle as fat as they can roll, and you can take your scythe any time and cut what hay you please, and the soil is from three to four feet in depth."

No wonder the "western fever" spread! Robert H. Frazier in reading the Memoir of his grandfather, Harrison Frazier, at the Springfield Memorial Association, in 1928 said:

"This was alluring, for the average farmer who lived in North Carolina had a strenuous, and what we would now call, a hard life. Farming implements were crude and ineffective; the mowing machine, the reaper, the sulky plow, the cutaway harrow and the improved threshing machine had not come into use. The virtues of the pea vine, clover and other leguminous crops were scarcely known, and it was thought that commercial fertilizers damaged the soil."[1]

The early colonists in New England had become aware that the rocky soil was a terminal moraine, and that the more they "cleared" the land the more boulders they unearthed, and that the soil of the Middle West was the rich black mud of the ancient Lake Algonquin, the sediments of the last glacial melting area, and also that the winters in Indiana, Ohio and Illinois were mild compared with those of New England. There was thus sufficient reason why thousands besides the Quakers abandoned their properties in the northeast and made for the middlewest.

HE BEHELD THE LAND. Elbert Russell says that the first Friend to explore the region north of the Ohio was Thomas Beals from Western Quarter. He had become interested in this area as an outcome of a visit to Indiana in 1777, in company with William Robinson and two other Friends. He removed with his family to Ohio in 1779. George Harlan went to the same general area in 1796, and the next year Jesse Baldwin and Phineas Hunt followed. After this the trek of Friends was almost constant. In 1799 John Dew returned to his home meeting at Trent River, North Carolina, after exploring the Ohio territory and predicted to his meeting, "I see the seed of God sown in abundance, extending far northwestward." As a result of his exhortation virtually the whole meeting removed, and within two years two meetings were established in the new territory.[2]

A similar story may be told concerning Zachariah Dicks, of New Garden. He travelled extensively among Friends in Virginia, the Carolinas and Georgia and urged Friends to leave. He had become frightened on hearing of colored uprisings and massacres in Santo Domingo. His admonitions persuaded the Friends of Bush River, South Carolina, to migrate *en masse*. Within three decades Georgia and South Carolina lost virtually all their Quaker adherents, and the few remaining in Virginia became united with Baltimore Yearly Meeting. North Carolina was greatly affected, and it is estimated that between 1800 and 1860 about 6,000 Friends departed from the Southern States. At the same time Friends were leaving New York, New England and Philadelphia Yearly Meetings for the Middle West so that the loss and gain of the yearly meetings was phenomenal.[3]

David Hoover, from Randolph County, was one of the first Friends to explore the Indiana territory in 1806, and that same year about twenty Friends settled in Whitewater, which in course of time became the flourishing center of Quaker activities known as Richmond. In 1809 Whitewater Monthly Meeting was established with 265 resident Friends. It has been estimated that about 1200 Friends from the Southern States migrated to the Whitewater region between 1809 and 1819.

OUR FATHERS WORSHIPPED IN THIS MOUNTAIN. Mention should be made of Charles Osborn (1775-1850) a Friend from North Carolina, who removed to Tennessee in early life and who became one of the most fearless and outspoken opponents of slavery. He travelled extensively and urged Friends not to be satisfied with moral suasion, petitions and gradual manumission, but to support the Abolitionists who demanded "immediate and unconditional emancipation." He did not receive much support from Friends who, in general, avoided political and radical procedures.[4]

Thus, like an advancing tide, the population, Quakers among them, surged westward. It is almost standard procedure for visitors from one area to challenge a Quaker audience as to where their ancestors came from. A Philadelphia Friend would challenge a Tarheel congregation; and in turn a North Carolina visitor would challenge his audience at Richmond, Indiana, and ask those who had forebears who came from the Old North State to stand, and probably more than half would rise. The same would be true of Indiana and Western; of Western and Iowa; of Iowa and Kansas and Nebraska; and if one put the same query in California or Oregon, the test would show that many families came from Iowa.

I WILL MAKE THY NAME TO BE REMEMBERED. Just as fossils reveal the existence of old forms of life so do the names of many Indiana meetings reveal their origin. Greensboro, Back Creek, Rich Square, Fairmount, Oak Hill, Jonesboro, New Garden and a dozen others tell the historian that the original Quakers in those communities were some of those who left North Carolina.

All that has preceded is well-known to students of Quakerism, but a mystery remains, and no satisfactory answer so far has been offered. The question is: "Why did so many Friends who were well established in Pennsylvania, New Jersey, Rhode Island, New England and Massachusetts abandon good prospects, suffer financial loss, endure great hardships and privation in order to settle in Piedmont, North Carolina. Perhaps the chiefest motive was that of self-preservation. Frontier wars involving the Indians, the French and the English had occurred frequently from 1689 to 1763 and friction between the colonial leaders and the British was increasing, and it became evident to far sighted persons that differences would eventually lead to war and prudence suggested migration to a settlement not so likely to be an area of conflict. This applied especially to those Friends in Nantucket Island. If this were the dominating motive they were disillusioned, for war came within a few miles of the New Garden settlement in 1781.

There is another reason. The Quakers were "a peculiar people." They were unusual in speech, in dress, in deportment. They rarely participated in public sports and largely kept aloof from public affairs unless they were definitely involved. They were quite sincere in their endeavor to live a godly life, but as all would-be saints have done, they found it difficult to live in the world and yet not be of the world. It is noticeable that wherever they settled they formed little self-contained communities. The writer is of opinion that the Quakers who came from northern areas to the Carolinas came for the purpose of establishing Quaker colonies, where undisturbed by "worldlings" they could develop a social, economic and religious fellowship without interference.

The early Quaker settlements in the northeastern part of North Carolina grew by propaganda; non-Friends were brought into membership. Missionary work prevailed, and sinners were converted and joined Friends. In the Piedmont the original fervor was lacking. From 1750 to nearly 1850 this Quarterly Meeting grew mainly by accretion or transfer of membership and by birthright. However, Dorothy Gilbert Thorne in her valuable monograph on "The First Friends of New Garden" gives extensive lists of the membership showing that there were also numbers who joined by request.

The yearly meeting archives are rich in genealogical records.* It is revealing to examine them and observe the tendency of Friends to marry within the Society. Hundreds were disowned for "marrying out." But what did it do to those who married "in"? Two things. One: it produced persons of great integrity, resourcefulness, diligence, godliness and superior ability — citizens who are the salt of the earth, but, two: at the same time it made them a "separate" people, essentially conservative and selective. They became a social caste, and dress and address became more and more important, and morality tended to be substituted for religion. It is not far from the truth to say that before the holocaust of 1860 the Society in the Piedmont area consisted of about fifty very much inter-related families, who sought to maintain a definite pattern of life.

BE YE SEPARATE. Friends did not intend to establish social islands, perhaps, but their ideas concerning oaths, war, slavery, tobacco, worship, the sacraments, priestism, marriage, hunting, amusements, playing cards, secret societies, sport, besides dress and address

---

* Many Friends of North Carolina have deposited copies of their genealogy in the Quaker archives. A perusal of these records (many of them professionally prepared) reveals the extent to which the leading families are inter-related.

actually constituted them a separate and aloof group and consequently misunderstood.

But they were not permitted to settle down and continue indefinitely as social islands. Circumstances compelled the descendants of those who fled to the South from the Northeast now to flee from the South to the Middlewest; and in a later generation still further to the Pacific Coast.

"As the eagle stirreth up her nest, fluttereth over her young, spreadeth abroad her wings, taketh them, beareth them upon her wings, so the Lord alone did lead him."

Quakers are no longer a "peculiar people," but will the Society produce in the future men and women of such integrity?

The first venturers went on horseback with pack horses and followed the buffalo trails. Later two horse wagons and two wheeled carts came into use, and in difficult places it was customary to double or treble the teams; in crossing the mountains it was necessary at times to put a man at each wheel to help propel the vehicle; and others were required to push or to chock the wheels to prevent the wagon rolling backward. The vehicles were usually covered with some kind of awning, and were tarred instead of being painted. The animals wore husk collars and the traces were rawhide. The party took with them cooking utensils, and game was caught along the way. Addison Coffin, who made several of these trips, says that it was common for runaway Negroes to join the party and thus escape to freedom. These of course would render assistance with the animals, baggage and necessary chores. The journey lasted a week or more according to the distance, but even in fine weather it was a harrowing experience.[5]

The mass migration of Friends from North Carolina to the Middlewest is so comprehensive that it deserves to be rehearsed in detail. In 1768 a few Friends crossed the mountains and settled in Tennessee; three years later the Regulator troubles caused others to escape from unpropitious circumstances; then came the Revolutionary War and the whole economic and social system was thrown out of gear. Because of their views on peace and war the Quakers were taunted as Tories and cowards, and many became convinced the South had little future. Peace was made in 1783, but New Garden Friends had become disillusioned; there was no longer any expectation that more members would come from the North, and quite a few Quaker families fled to Eastern Tennessee, and settled as squatters and set up Quaker meetings without authorization from any parent meeting. So serious did this become that Western

Quarterly Meeting in 1792 made a minute to the effect: "No Friend should move to the West without permission of the meeting of which he is a member."[6] This is a typical revelation of the extent to which the "elders ruled the membership."

In 1799 the Yearly Meeting took the matter to heart and recommended subordinate meetings "to attend more strictly to the Discipline in respect of Friends removing without the limits of an established meeting." We are also informed that many members who wanted to migrate hesitated to do so "for fear it would break up the meeting and destroy the church." Others departed without notification and were lost to the Society.

New Garden followed the example of Western and "forbade members to go to unexplored territory without the consent of the meeting." Contentnea experienced a great exodus, but most of the members obtained credentials. Because of this depletion meetings at Cartaret, Beaufort, Hyde, Craven and Jones were discontinued about 1799. By the end of the century the once strong meeting at Core Sound was depopulated. In 1835 Sutton's Creek Monthly Meeting was laid down; four years later the Narrows in Eastern Quarter ceased to be; Newbegin meeting disappeared; in 1846 Symonds Creek became greatly enfeebled, and in 1854 ceased to exist.

Trent River Meeting in Jones County decided to remove bodily; they all took certificates; presented them at first to Red Stone Quarterly Meeting in Philadelphia Yearly Meeting; they then moved to Ohio; on the way they slept and worshipped in the woods. In one year they so increased that they had two preparative meetings in the Monthly Meeting of Concord. Weeks says this is the only known instance of a whole meeting moving as a body. Other reports say they carried along the church records, and retained the same clerks, elders, overseers and membership, and continued the business of the same meeting — only in another State and yearly meeting.[7]

A curious Minute of Advice appears in 1860:

"It is to be feared that some have their minds so much on moving away from this part of the land that they are neglecting their proper duties. Whatever may be right for us in this respect may we not forget that there is an emigration for us all, and endeavor so to walk that when the period for it arrives it may indeed be to a better country — that is, a heavenly."[8]

TIMOTHY NICHOLSON'S ESTIMATE. Timothy Nicholson wrote to Stephen B. Weeks in 1855 that "between 1809 and 1819 when Whitewater Monthly Meeting was set up at Richmond, Indiana, the records show that 120 certificates were received from Cane Creek, North Carolina, and Piney Grove, South Carolina, and also at least one thousand persons including women and children were received from Guilford County and environs and 85 from Eastern Quarter." Nicholson also believed that at least 6,000 Friends settled in the Middle West between 1800 and 1860 and that three-fourths of them came from North Carolina. Allen Jay also informed Weeks that the Miami Meeting in Ohio between 1804 and 1806 received twelve hundred Southern Friends. Addison Coffin estimated that in 1850 one-third of the population of Indiana was composed of Carolinians and their descendants.[9]

To mention by name all those who left the Old North State for better land and economic security would mean a repetition of the names already given in the invasion of the South, for virtually some of the descendants of all those who settled in the Piedmont within a generation or so once more were on the move. These migrations, however, were not a dead loss, for meetings were established throughout Indiana, Ohio, Illinois, and in the next generation in Kansas and Nebraska, and still later in Oregon and California.

To show the extent of this mass movement the following statistics (which are incomplete) are copied from the very important work by Weeks.[*]

MIGRATION OF N. C. FRIENDS TO THE WEST

Dates of Migration	Name of Meeting	Number Leaving	Meeting Laid Down
1801-1807	Bush River, S. C.	111	Laid Down
1796-1837	Cane Creek, N. C.	156	
1800-1843	Contentnea, N. C.	111	
1799-1840	Core Sound, N. C.	46	Laid Down
1806-1860	Deep River, N. C.	89	
1802-1860	Dover, N. C.	71	
1824-1848	Hopewell, N. C.	37	Laid Down
1805-1812	Jack Swamp, N. C.	26	Laid Down
1802-1825	Mount Pleasant, Va.	99	Laid Down
1801-1860	New Garden, N. C.	195	
1805-1815	Piney Grove, S. C.	33	Laid Down
1802-1830	Piney Woods, N. C.	29	
1802-1860	Rich Square, N. C.	31	
1831-1839	Spring, N. C.	22	
1795-1850	Springfield, N. C.	150	
1812-1835	Sutton's Creek, N. C.	54	Laid Down
1803-1854	Symon's Creek, N. C.	49	Laid Down
1801-1822	Westfield, N. C.	50	Laid Down
	Wrightsboro, Ga.	19	Laid Down

[*] Copied from Weeks, Stephen: *Southern Quakers and Slavery*, p 269.[10]

ADDISON COFFIN.   In order to understand some phases of this movement mention must be made of Addison Coffin.   He was a nephew
of Levi Coffin, was born in Guilford County, North Carolina, in
1822, and was early active in the Underground Railway, in con-
junction with his father, Vestal Coffin and his uncle.   He made
several trips to Indiana on foot.   Fearless to a fault, he was soon
acting as guide for parties of emigrants to the Middle West.   Thus
he found his mission.   His name is inextricably associated with
the phenomenal removal of Quakers from the Southern States.   He
became an enthusiast upon the subject.   Possessing a facility of
speech, he repeatedly visited the various Quaker meetings, gave
glowing accounts of the wonderful country north of the Ohio River,
and urged his hearers to lose no time in removing from the devastated Southland.   In an age of the rapid opening of the West, and
the construction of railroads, he became a paid agent of these
transportation companies, and he devoted his fertile mind and
energies to the shipment of Quakers in particular and anybody in
general to the prairies of the West.   He was no sooner back from
one trip than he organized another migration.   Between 1866 and
1872 he arranged for ten emigrant trains each year, and he claims
the migrants numbered about 14,000, nearly half of whom were
children.*   He regarded his work as a Divine mission.

YOUR COUNTRY IS DESOLATE.   It is difficult to visualize the condition in North Carolina during and after the war.   The railroads
were wrecked; there were practically no imports; live stock was
decimated; buildings were decayed; many great plantations abandoned because of devastation; new clothing was unobtainable;
school houses were damaged and defiled; the Confederate currency
was worthless; gold had disappeared; the land was poverty-stricken;
needles and thread were unobtainable; farm implements were
carried away or smashed by the Union army; marauding bands
of freed Negroes were a menace; the South was indeed "prostrate."

Addison Coffin preached that the Quakers had fulfilled their
mission; they had protested against the curse of slavery; they had
freed themselves of its blight; there was no occasion for them to
live longer in a cursed land; let them go to Free Soil; where the
land was rich — the black mud of an ancient lake bottom; where
they and their children could be free from the "disgusting use of
tobacco."   It is little wonder that his words seemed convincing,
especially when their neighbors who had already settled in Indiana
and Ohio corroborated his words.

---

* Responsible Friends consider these figures exaggerated.

A Very Small Remnant. Addison travelled extensively in this country and abroad. His *Autobiography* is worthwhile in so far as it relates to the migrations, but in the latter part of the book he attempts to explain certain geological formations. He lacked the scientific knowledge to do this accurately. More than any other individual Addison Coffin unwittingly worked to destroy North Carolina Yearly Meeting. He is largely responsible for the disappearance of Yearly Meetings in its northern and southern neighboring States. Had Coffin not been frustrated it is probable that the migrations would have continued till Quakerism disappeared in North Carolina.

Mary Mendenhall Hobbs told the writer that she remembered a conversation between Dr. Nereus Mendenhall (her father), Francis T. King, of Baltimore, and Addison Coffin in the home of her father. King remonstrated with Coffin, and told him he was mistaken; that the South was not irreparably ruined, and that Friends had better remain rather than sacrifice their property and incur indebtedness for western lands; he believed Quakerism was not played out in the State; that Friends still had a mission here, and that the New Garden Boarding School and the yearly meeting could be made to flourish again.

At first the Friends in Baltimore assisted Quakers fleeing from North Carolina to the West, but after Francis T. King had visited the stricken territory he told the Baltimore Yearly Meeting that the policy should be changed and Friends encouraged to stay. The Meeting for Sufferings adopted this view and officially urged Friends to remain.

So great was the migration that Alethea Coffin, the mother of Addison, and at one time matron of New Garden and later a matron at Earlham College, Richmond, Indiana, asserted when nearly ninety years of age that she was able to give the names of three hundred families that had removed from the South to Indiana.[11]

King set himself deliberately to checkmate Coffin, and as a result the Baltimore Association was organized and many forms of assistance rendered to the South. So successful were these activities that according to the second annual report the latest emigrant train numbered only 518 persons, of whom 300 were under 14 years of age, and only eleven, including children, were Friends.[12] The next report said "an intelligent spirit of inquiry was manifest, and the disposition to remove to other States, at one time so general, had given place to a desire to settle down and improve the old homesteads."[13] The *Baltimore American* said "the establishment of schools had stopped all emigration from North Carolina and had increased the membership of the Society from 2,200 to 4,541, and the number of meetings from 28 to 52." Many who had left considered returning, and advertisements were issued advising such to communicate with Timothy and John Nicholson, of Richmond, Indiana, who would act as agents of the Baltimore Association in making arrangements.

IN PERILS OF ROBBERS. The hazards these adventurers braved is shown by the terrifying circumstances which befell a Friends' party from Friendship, (location uncertain). Joseph Marshall had witnessed the departure of many of his friends and had just said "the Lord be with thee" to an Irishman and his family who like others gave up in despair because of the prostration caused by the Civil War. Marshall was shocked at the burnings of the homesteads when the settlers departed. Unless one is familiar with frontier and war conditions one would never guess why a migrant put the torch to his home before departing. It was to retrieve any nails and hardware that might be found in the ashes. Such necessities were irreplacable in an unbroken forest. A few days after the departure of the Irish family a caravan of five wagons came from the east. There were as many Quaker families escaping from the general ruin. Marshall decided to join them as there was some safety in numbers. The third day out the party came to a small clearing near the Carolina-Tennessee line, and a woman gave the party permission to stay in a barn overnight. This was gratefully accepted, and the women made what preparations were possible.

The men endeavored to put in position one of the barn doors which had fallen inward. When they had lifted it they were horrified to see the bodies of a man, a woman and two children. Marshall immediately recognized them as his Irish neighbors, and it was evident that they had been murdered.

One of the men started to run to the house, but he experienced an inward warning not to cry out in alarm. As he neared the house he overheard several persons talking, and among them the voice of the woman who had told them to stay. They were plotting to murder the travellers and seize their horses and wagons. The man crept cautiously away and a hurried parley was held. It was decided to flee as quickly and as quietly as possible. It was no easy task to harness the horses, gather up the baggage, turn the wagons around in the dark without any noise. The women prayed the babies might not cry or the children create trouble. The men left a lighted lantern where it would be visible so as to give the impression they were still there, and thus made good their escape. Such was the story told by Flora Marshall Osborn to her daughter, Nonnie Bissell, of Chapel Hill, and Flora was a baby with the family of Joseph Marshall, when the incident occurred.[14]

CHAPTER FOURTEEN

SEE WHAT BUILDINGS ARE HERE

GUILFORD COLLEGE.   As far as human understanding goes there would be no Quaker College in the South and no North Carolina Yearly Meeting of Friends, but for the faith, labors and sacrifice of the heroes already mentioned in this narrative, especially Nathan Hunt, Jeremiah Hubbard, Dougan Clark and his wife, Asenath (the early superintendent and matron), Nereus and Oriana Mendenhall, Jonathan and Elizabeth Cox, and Isham Cox. These devoted persons (and very many others) perceived by faith "the substance of things hoped for" and "things not seen" were "evident."

THE BOARD OF TRUSTEES: The properties for the administration of an educational institution are committed to a Board of Trustees; and the institution's advancement is due largely to the intentions, vision, labors and good judgment of that body. So it has been with Guilford College. Devoted service, sacrifice and wisdom on the part of its Trustees have brought the College to its present high standing.

The first committee appointed in 1831 by North Carolina Yearly Meeting to prepare a plan for the school was composed of Dougan Clark, Jeremiah Hubbard, Nathan Mendenhall, Joshua Lindley, David White and Zimri Stuart. The first Board of Trustees named in the charter enacted by the North Carolina General Assembly in 1834 was composed of Joshua Stanley, John Beard, Thomas Hodgin, John Russell, Elisha Coffin, Henry Macey, Zacharias Coffin, Thomas T. Hunt, Jeremiah Pickett, Nixon Henley, Peter Dicks and Phineas Nixon, Jr. A number of trustees have served very long terms: Jeremiah S. Cox served forty-nine years; J. Elwood Cox, thirty-eight years; Joseph D. Cox, thirty-six years; John Van Lindley, thirty-three years; John Russell, thirty years; Elisha Mendenhall, thirty years; Cyrus Pickett Frazier, thirty years; Charles F. Tomlinson, twenty-nine years; Joseph Newlin, twenty-nine years; David White, twenty-nine years; Dudley D. Carroll, twenty-eight years; Joshua Lindley, twenty-seven years; Robert H. Frazier, twenty-seven years; A. Wilson Hobbs, twenty-six years;

Isham Cox, twenty-five years; and Joseph J. Cox, twenty-five years.[1]

Providing the leadership as clerks and chairmen of the Board have been John Russell, 1834-35; Phineas Nixon, Jr., 1835-45; Joseph Newlin, 1845-66; Jonathan Harris, 1866-71; Paris Benbow, 1871-75; Elihu E. Mendenhall, 1875-1902; Joseph J. Cox, 1902-03; J. Elwood Cox, 1903-32; Dudley D. Carroll, 1932-48; Richard L. Hollowell, 1948-50; Robert H. Frazier, 1950-.

Included with those named above should be these others who have also rendered service with energy and efficiency in recent years: Ralph Parker, Elbert Russell, Herbert C. Petty, Robert R. Ragan, Mary M. Petty, J. Milford Edgerton, David J. White, Nereus C. English, Jr., Edwin P. Brown, Horace S. Haworth, Duval Craven, Eunice Anderson Parker, William A. Wolff and Luby Casey.[2]

THE BUILDINGS. The war over slavery and secession reduced Quakerism in the Old North State to a remnant, and the Heavenly Father raised up a deliverer in the person of Francis Thompson King, of Baltimore. This story is told fully in another place, and Dorothy Gilbert Thorne has written so ably and satisfactorily concerning Guilford College that it is unnecessary to repeat particulars in full. Here, we shall tell of the physical plant and of the great souls who dedicated their lives to education at this institution. We now mention the buildings.

FOUNDERS HALL was, as its name indicates, the first building. It was constructed in 1835-36 at a cost of $7,686.87¼. It is curious to notice that eight of the twelve specified items express the cost in odd cents and fractions of cents. Local Friends gave time and materials, and the building was considered a very substantial structure for that period. Improvements were effected in 1883 and again in 1908. In 1955 the building was subjected to extensive modernization. The dining hall was much enlarged, a new and modern kitchen provided; also an infirmary and laboratories for the Home Economics Department. A small dining room has been added. This work was completed soon after the opening of the academic year 1955-56. The facilities in the dining hall had long been inadequate; and a new day has dawned for the Quaker institution now that proper accommodation has been made for its ever increasing student body.[3]

KING HALL. The first building of this name was the old meeting house. As it possessed a very high ceiling it was converted into two stories, and the upper floor used as a boys' dormitory. It was burned in 1885, and a second building upon the same site and named for Francis T. King went up in flames in 1908. This was a great loss and inconvenience. Steps were taken to rebuild immediately, but funds did not permit the erection of an entire building, so only the rear portion was constructed. Just a few years ago the general economic situation justified the fulfilment of the hopes of forty years. The front portion like the top bar of a "T" was added. Now Guilford has class rooms and science laboratories which would be a credit to any small college. An appreciation of Francis T. King is given in connection with the account of the Baltimore Association.[4]

MEMORIAL HALL. In the seventies the brothers Benjamin N. and James B. Duke were sent by their father, Washington Duke[*] to the Quaker institution to study particularly a course in business methods for there were few schools of commerce at that time. A sister, Mary Elizabeth (Lyon), also attended the school. In 1897 the brothers gave $10,000 for the erection of a Science Hall in memory of their sister. Above the doorway is an inscription: "This building is erected to the memory of Mary Elizabeth Lyon by her brothers Benjamin N. and James B. Duke. "This woman was full of good works and alms deeds which she did!" — Acts 9:36. Allen Jay selected the site and at a celebration of the gift Dr. T. Gilbert Pearson was one of the principal speakers. In 1905 the brothers Duke gave another $15,000; in 1924 they subscribed $25,000 each, and in the next year they presented the college with 500 shares of stock in the Duke Power Company. The lower floor was occupied by the President's office, science lecture rooms and laboratories and the rear contained the natural history museum, largely the collection of the distinguished ornithologist, Dr. T. Gilbert Pearson. The upper floor was the auditorium with small rooms at the rear of the stage with practice rooms for the music department. Mention must be made of the work in the Department of Chemistry of Robert N. Wilson, who adorned the institution by his character and achievements in 1898-1905 and 1906-1910.

When the addition to King Hall was completed in recent years, it provided opportunity to remove the Science Department to the new wing, and Memorial Hall was rearranged to provide more space for the President and other officials. In the near future another auditorium will be constructed and then the present hall

---

[*] The Dukes of the American Tobacco Company and Founders of Duke Hospital and Duke University.

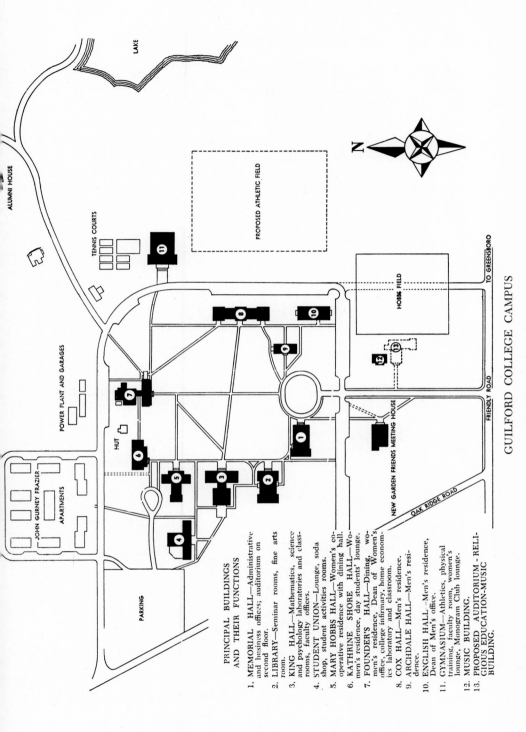

**PRINCIPAL BUILDINGS
AND THEIR FUNCTIONS**

1. MEMORIAL HALL—Administrative and business offices; auditorium on second floor.
2. LIBRARY—Seminar rooms, fine arts room.
3. KING HALL—Mathematics, science and psychology laboratories and classrooms, faculty offices.
4. STUDENT UNION—Lounge, soda shop, student activities rooms.
5. MARY HOBBS HALL—Women's co-operative residence with dining hall.
6. KATHRINE SHORE HALL—Women's residence, day students' lounge.
7. FOUNDER'S HALL—Dining, women's residence, Dean of Women's office, college infirmary, home economics laboratory and classroom.
8. COX HALL—Men's residence.
9. ARCHDALE HALL—Men's residence.
10. ENGLISH HALL—Men's residence, Dean of Men's office.
11. GYMNASIUM—Athletics, physical training, faculty room, women's lounge, Monogram Club lounge.
12. MUSIC BUILDING.
13. PROPOSED AUDITORIUM - RELIGIOUS EDUCATION-MUSIC BUILDING.

GUILFORD COLLEGE CAMPUS

will be converted into much needed class rooms and faculty offices.

The trustees have adopted a distinctly forward-looking attitude. Provision has been made for a student body of seven hundred and fifty and modern necessities will be provided. Guilford in a few years time will rank second to no such institution of its type.[5]

ARCHDALE HALL, named in honor of the Quaker governor* was constructed by the students with some competent supervision largely from materials salvaged from the ruins of the burned King Hall. It served as a dormitory for boys. It was a two story brick structure and was considered a good building at the time, but it was not equipped in modern style. For a time after Cox Hall was built and during World War I when few students were at College, it was not in use. Recently steps were taken to overhaul the building, modernize it, and render it a worthy dormitory. It may be of interest to mention that before Archdale was built, there were upon the campus a few simple cottages. When the writer went to Guilford to teach in 1918, some of these "little wooden boxes" were still standing. Poor boys lived there and fended for themselves. This condition prevailed in many institutions for learning in the South prior to the first World War and was typical of frontier conditions.[6]

JEREMIAH S. AND MARGARET COX, were among the long-time friends and supporters of Guilford. Away back when the institution became a college they were laboring as superintendent and matron, and he was a trustee for 49 years and secretary of the Board from 1895 to 1905. He was courageous and optimistic enough to believe another and better dormitory was needed for the boys even when Archdale was not fully occupied. He first offered an annuity of $15,000 and three sections were constructed; later he made other donations equalling $38,000 for the building and $10,000 for endowment.[7]

The modernization of Guilford may be said to have commenced in 1912 when the Cox Dormitory was built. This building was equipped with showers for each floor, an innovation for rural North Carolina. The handsome red brick building was in five separate but adjoining sections. Three were built in 1910, and in 1912 the donor, Jeremiah S. Cox, gave a further sum, and the two remaining portions were built. These apartments were a great improvement upon those of Archdale, and the college looked forward to expansion, but World War I swept the boys into military

---

* See Chap. iv and other references to Governor Archdale.

service, and lean years for all colleges followed. During this period some members of the faculty resided in the northern section. Then in 1918-19 the influenza struck Guilford, and a large number of girls were hospitalized in one of the new sections. Fortunately no deaths occurred, but we were all quarantined upon the campus for about ten weeks. Then the power house was burned, and Guilford was without adequate water, heat and light for several weeks. The temporary use of oil lamps throughout the institution created a painful hazard, but fortunately there were no untoward incidents. Cox Hall shared in the general overhauling of the buildings recently.[8]

THE LIBRARY. It is worthy of note that the Library came into existence with the inception of the school, for before any student was received some worthy Friend from Providence, Rhode Island, contributed a Quaker classic. Now a classic is a book that everybody buys and nobody reads. It was a copy of Robert Barclay's *Apology*. It is considered the best exposition of the Quaker faith. Within a few years eight more copies of Barclay were given to the school. Other Quaker tomes were also contributed, and slowly a library was accomplished. Alas the books were housed in King Hall, and when in 1908 that building was burned, much of the library went up in smoke, for of the ten thousand volumes only nine hundred and seventy two were saved. A second King Hall was burned, and then the trustees decided that the Library must be a separate building. With the assistance of the Carnegie Corporation a handsome building was erected in 1909. This served the purpose till the student body was greatly increased. Between 1947 and 1950 the administration concentrated efforts to raise $200,000 to create a Library which would serve for a future generation. The General Education Board contributed $50,000 and the remainder was raised by the friends of the college. The dedication of the new building occurred in 1950 and Dr. Homer Halverson, the librarian of Johns Hopkins University, was the principal speaker. Very substantial changes and additions were effected; additional stacks and study desks; offices upon the second floor; an art room upon the third floor; seminar rooms; storage and utility rooms in the basement. The most appreciated addition, however, was the Quaker room and the vault for the safe keeping of the records of the church. Here the old monthly, quarterly and yearly meeting record books are properly cared for, and quite a number of the more ancient have been micro-filmed. Guilford College is now the custodian of one of the several great collections of Quakerana in the world, and is frequented by visitors from all parts.

One of President Binford's projects was the revision and integration of the curriculum. Syllabi of some of the courses were done in his administration and others have been prepared since under President Milner. The students are required to follow through a course of related readings which necessitates the regular use of the Library. The attendance is phenomenal, and few institutions such as Guilford could match the record. In 1935 the lowest daily attendance was 239; the highest, 461; and this with a then enrollment of 300.

During the scholastic year 1953-54, 2,007 reserve books were used in the summer session; 8,711 the first semester; 9,242 the second semester; total of reserve books, 19,960 for the year. The two weeks books used by the faculty, 1,618; by the students, 9,720; total: 10,338. The Library now has over 40,000 books, besides a vast collection of music and records and many art treasures and rare Quaker books.

Among those who have rendered professional service in the Library are Mary E. Mendenhall Davis, 1882-1897; Laura D. Worth, 1897-98; Henryanna Hackney White, 1898-1901; Julia S. White, 1901-1922; Katherine C. Ricks, 1922-1927; Virginia Helms, 1927-28; Mildred Farlow, Treva W. Mathis.[9] Dorothy Gilbert Thorne is the Archivist and custodian of the Quaker records.

MARY HOBBS HALL. From time immemorial one great problem has been for poor persons to secure a higher education. Many charitable schemes have been devised, but charity cannot be the right solution for any problem. Guilford had a few little cottages upon the campus where husky boys could rough it and fend for themselves while they continued their learning. One thoughtful woman while worshipping during a yearly meeting session had an inspiration, and from that came into existence the Mary Hobbs Hall. Here in a substantial brick building arrangements have been made so that about sixty girls may cooperate in doing all the necessary housekeeping chores and thus reduce the living expenses to a minimum, while at the same time getting practical experience in housekeeping. A matron was put in charge, schedules prepared and the girls, apportioned in companies, took turns in doing all the various daily tasks, cooking, serving meals, washing dishes, sweeping, cleaning and so forth. In the early days girls brought supplies of various kinds from their homes, so that at one period the cost was only one dollar per week for board; $12.00 per term for room; about $306.00 per school year. Hundreds of girls, since Hobbs Hall was opened in 1907 have not only mastered the usual subjects of a college curriculum, but have learned to keep house and, what is perhaps more important, to share and cooperate in domestic affairs.[10]

Those who served as matrons include Rhoda Worth, Olive J. Hodgin, Myra Binford, Rachel Farlowe, Inez Wilson, Bertie Dix, Emily R. Levering, Alice Gons, Dovie Chenault, Lucy S. Trickett, Bertha S. Ginn, Anne Fordham, Hassie C. Johnson.

VIRGINIA RAGSDALE.   Unique among the college buildings is the Alumni House. It is a handsome and substantial brick building designed in accordance with Guilford architecture by the celebrated New York architect, Alfred Busselle. It is hard by the home of the President, in a lovely grove of trees at the far end of the campus. It is elegantly furnished, and there is overnight accommodation for nine persons. To account for it one must tell the story of a truly gifted and consecrated woman. Virginia Ragsdale was descended on the female line from the Coffins and was kin to many leading Quaker families. She was born at Jamestown, North Carolina in 1870, and as a child attended private schools in that little village. There she learned algebra "forwards and backwards," and was qualified to enter Salem Academy as a junior. She was graduated from that Moravian institution in 1887, being the possessor of a diploma in music and was class valedictorian. She was graduated in 1892 from Guilford College, and was the first girl to merit the scholarship for a year's study at Bryn Mawr. Here she came into her own, and not only received the A.B. degree in 1896, but won the highest honor of "the European Fellowship." She went to Germany, and at the University of Gottingen distinguished herself in her chosen field of mathematics. Bryn Mawr was glad to use her ability upon her return, and she excelled as a teacher of science. She also taught at Balitmore. In 1901 to 1903 she pursued graduate studies in New York, and in 1906 was appointed the Head of the Department of Mathematics at the Baldwin School of Bryn Mawr. In acknowledgement of her extensive studies she received the degree of Doctor of Philosophy from Bryn Mawr. In 1911 she accepted a call to teach mathematics at the North Carolina Women's College (now the Women's College of the University of North Carolina). In 1926 she was appointed Head of that Department and introduced a course on statistics.

Dr. Virginia Ragsdale became known not only as a competent teacher, but also as a warm friend, a wise counsellor and a consecrated woman. She retired in 1928 and devoted herself at Jamestown to her aged mother. After her mother had passed on Dr. Ragsdale gave considerable thought as to where she should spend the remainder of her life. Jamestown was too small and too out-of-the-way. She wanted to be near a good library, and she wanted to be near young people, so she built a lovely home upon the Guilford campus and for eleven years delighted to entertain Friends of the College. She willed the house to the College, and it is a living memorial to her artistic taste and her benevolence. It is now used for receptions and for the accommodation of visitors. The Forsyth County Alumni Association at a recent annual meeting raised funds to equip the house with a television set.[11]

THE KATHERINE HINE SHORE RESIDENCE. This new building, erected in 1954-55 is a notable addition to the college. The residence provides a third dormitory for women. It was designed by Mr. Alfred Woodruff, of Greensboro, is of Georgian colonial design of red brick, and is in keeping with the new buildings upon the campus. It will house fifty girls and is most handsomely finished and furnished. It is probably among the best appointed women's college dormitories in the State. It was ready for occupancy at the beginning of the 1955-56 school year, and is used to capacity. The extensive basement has been fitted up as a play room. The building was a gift of B. Clyde Shore, of Winston-Salem, in honor of his wife, Katherine Hine Shore. Clyde distinguished himself as a student at Guilford, and participated in the athletic activities, the Y.M.C.A., the literary societies and the Sunday School. He was graduated in 1925, and served in France with the American Friends Service Committee. He has been successful in business and has manifested his interest in the Society of Friends in many ways. He is chairman of the finance committee of the local meeting; a member of the Permanent Board and treasurer of the yearly meeting, also a member of the Board of Trustees of Guilford College. He also is active in civic affairs. His wife, Katherine, holds a degree in music from the Woman's College, Greensboro, and is active in local church work. In addition to the fund for the building Clyde authorized to be set aside from his gift of $150,000 about $30,000 as a scholarship fund "for worthy students, especially those who are being trained for service and leadership in the Society of Friends." Clyde is just one of the many Shores from Yadkin County who have made distinctive contributions to church and society.[12]

THE JOHN GURNEY FRAZIER JR. APARTMENTS.   It is not so long ago that a married man college student was a rarity, and the boys regarded him as being out of place, and if a girl student married she was willy-nilly expelled as though she had committed the unpardonable sin. The passage of the G.I. Bill of Rights by Congress opened the way for thousands of veterans to continue their education. Many of these were married, and as the Government gave some monetary assistance, wives as well as husbands desired to continue their education. Married women in college no longer were curiosities. The attendance at all colleges and universities took an unprecedented upward swing. Something had to be done, and two new things appeared in the land. Thousands of trailers upon the campus afforded make-shift homes for married couples. Then with the termination of the war the government released thousands of prefabricated huts and barracks which had been used at training grounds. Cities, medical schools, colleges and universities utilized them, and it enabled multitudes of married students to continue their education. Guilford received a number of these temporary structures, and they were set up at the back of Hobbs and Founders Halls.

Through the munificence of John Gurney Frazier, Jr. they have been replaced with twenty-two substantial apartment houses at a cost of $125,500.00. Ten of these units were ready for occupancy at the beginning of 1954-55 term and the rest were finished by the next fall. These structures are one-story of brick and concrete, with metal doors and window frames. They may be occupied by married couples, if either or both are Guilford students. They are in great demand.

John Gurney Frazier, Jr. was graduated at Guilford in 1924. During his undergraduate days he was elected each year into the so-called "All Southern-basketball team". His prowess as an all-round athlete spread far and wide while his musical tents were also acclaimed. He came of old-time Quaker stock. His grandfather, Harrison Frazier, was one of New Garden Boarding School's earliest students. His father, John Gurney Frazier, Sr. and his uncle, Cyrus Pickett Frazier, were active in the development of Guilford. John Gurney, Jr. organized the North Carolina State Automobile Association in 1929 in Charlotte, North Carolina. Its growth, with his dynamic salesmanship, was rapid.

In 1946 the National Automobile Association was organized with his promotive assistance, and he became co-chairman of its Board of Directors. He has shared his successes with his Alma

Mater and his gift has supplied a much needed improvement, enriching, with other modernization projects the prestige and efficiency of Guilford College.

RELIGIOUS EDUCATION BUILDING. Another handsome addition to the college equipment is projected. The work has been approved and construction will be undertaken as soon as funds are assured. It is the intention of the trustees to provide a modern building for largely attended public events, such as student gatherings, public addresses, plays and entertainments. It is also intended to become the center for the training of religious and social workers; several conference chambers will be provided; also an ample stage with dressing rooms. Modern lighting and amplification will be installed.[13]

THE GYMNASIUM was for years just a plain wooden structure, like a big box, with some raised seats at one end, but the student body of forty and more years ago loved it, and many an exciting basketball game was played there which led to a bonfire and a jollification afterwards. About twelve years ago the hut was replaced by a very creditable brick building, with ample bleachers, dressing rooms and suitable furnishings. Utility rooms and offices were provided on the various floors. Guilford now has nothing to be ashamed of either in its "gym" or the games the Quakers can play.

THE Y.M.C.A. HALL. This little building right opposite the meeting house was constructed largely by student labor in 1891 when the "Y" was in its heyday. Later it was used on Friday nights by the Websterian and Henry Clay Literary and Debating Societies. Here many a young man, who later became an effective public speaker, learned the forensic art. He was taught how to stand on his hind legs, with his feet on the ground, his back to the wall, with a level head, and eyes front; to keep a stiff upper lip; his chin up and his hands under control; to observe Roberts' Rules of Order and remain unabashed at his opponent's inuendoes and aspersions. In recent years the building has been used by the Music Department. In retrospect, recalling the interesting occasions when the writer attended some of the lively debates, he much regrets that the day came when interest languished and movies and automobiles superseded public speaking. In England college debates concerning contemporary parliamentary discussions are an integral part of the education of a person who expects to participate in public affairs.

THE STUDENTS' CENTER.   One most happy development in the past few years has been the growing cordiality of Greensboro to the Quaker College six miles away. The attendance of day students has been facilitated by the use of automobiles and special buses. The Evening Classes (which will be mentioned separately) have also strengthened the bonds between the communities. One of the latest projects has been to build upon the campus west of Mary Hobbs Hall a one story building of the same general design as the Shore building, to provide a place where the on-campus and off-campus students may fraternize. There are a book store, refreshment rooms, lounges, offices and small assembly rooms. The Greensboro Advisory Board has undertaken to raise $150,000, of which $50,000 was applied to the construction of the building of the Student Union, and the remainder as a permanent endowment for scholarships at Guilford for Greensboro students. This valuable addition was completed during the 1955-56 sessions.

THE GREENSBORO DIVISION.   This is a most phenomenal development. In 1948 the Chamber of Commerce sponsored an Evening School to further adult education. As the project developed courses were offered in Accounting, Business Law, Mathematics, Stenography, Economics, Literature, Philosophy, Law and Religion. The teachers were brought from State College, the University at Chapel Hill and Guilford. A few of the courses were available for college credit. The institution became known as the Evening College, but as there developed a demand for classes during the day the school is now named the Greensboro Division. The attendance was over nine hundred for the academic year 1945-46, and it is anticipated the registration will soon be one thousand. This vast enrollment necessitates additional buildings and a fund of over half a million dollars is being raised at the time of this writing. The new Student Union just opened upon the campus and the college library are available for Greensboro students. This Division gave the trustees the opportunity to limit registration at the college to 750 and for candidates for degrees; subjects not suitable for academic credit were transferred to the Division. The President in his Report for 1958 indicated that there were 758 students enrolled in the college; the annual expenditure was $627,434.00; the endowment was $1,780,871.00; the net worth of the institution, $4,219,598.00; there were 41,740 books in the college library. The Greensboro Division had 1,193 adults enrolled; a total enrollment of 1,951.[14]

A New Dormitory for Men. Early in the spring of 1957 bids were accepted for the construction of a new dormitory for men. An alumnus, a manufacturer of Guilford County, magnanimously gave the funds to build a two-story brick building which will accommodate about fifty men students and in addition a five room apartment for a dean of men. The design is somewhat similar to the Shore apartment, and the plans have been drawn by the Greensboro architects, A. C. Woodruff, Sr. and Jr. who have designed some of the recent additions to the campus. The building is the gift of Nereus C. English, Jr. and will bear the name of "English Hall" in honor of his father. It was occupied in the fall of 1957.[15]

CHAPTER FIFTEEN

A TEACHER COME FROM GOD

THE WISE MEN. It is an axiom of the Christian faith that when the Almighty has a work to be done, He calls a particular man to that service, prepares him for the task, and sustains him in the performance of that duty. No one who knows the story can doubt that Nereus Mendenhall was Divinely commissioned to nurse New Garden Boarding School through the stormy days of its infancy, and in like manner Lewis Lyndon Hobbs was the appointed Servant of the Lord in charting Guilford College in the days of its beginning.

LEWIS LYNDON HOBBS was a Southerner of the olden school. He gave the appearance of dignity, stability, scholarship, authority, with his neat beard and stately demeanor. He was born in 1849, the ninth child of Lewis and Phoebe Cooke Hobbs. His father had been a teacher before New Garden was established, and Lewis came to New Garden when he was fifteen. The venerable Nereus Mendenhall became his teacher, and no boy could have wished for a better. He early became acquainted with J. Franklin Davis, and together they planned to continue their education at Haverford College, and they were classmates from 1872 to 1876. Franklin was graduated in 1875 and Lyndon in 1876, at which date George Hartley requested Lyndon to come to New Garden as assistant teacher. Both of the North Carolina men acknowledged the great inspiration and benefit they derived not only from Haverford, but from contacts with the worthy Friends of Philadelphia Yearly Meeting. Lyndon encouraged his bosom friend Frank to continue his studies in Germany and then join him at New Garden, for "he considered that they belonged together."

THE BURDEN AND HEAT OF THE DAY. Thus Lyndon commenced a service at the little Quaker Boarding School in an out-of-the way forest which as he said "became his bride," for six years more than a half-century. While Lyndon Hobbs was doing graduate work at Haverford, the attendance at New Garden was less than fifty, and there was doubt in the minds of many Friends that New Garden was the right place for a Friends school. It is necessary to remember

LEWIS LYNDON HOBBS

MARY MENDENHALL HOBBS

that the Federal troops had only just been withdrawn from the Southern States and that the South was prostrate; that the K.K.K. was active. Many conferences were held by Baltimore and other Friends before it was decided to continue at New Garden and not try good fortune at Springfield. Furthermore the western migration had depleted the Society, and there were probably less than two thousand adult Friends in the yearly meeting. The Confederate currency was worthless, and gold currency was non-existent. The years of 1874-75 witnessed a serious economic depression.

This was the situation when Lyndon Hobbs accepted the call of George Hartley to become an assistant teacher. From 1878 to 1884 he was principal of the Boarding School, and from 1888 President of Guilford College till 1915, and President Emeritus till he joined the Immortals in 1932. Thomas Newlin was President, 1915-1917; from 1917-1918 the College was in charge of an administrative committee, of which Howard Brinton was chairman.

HONOR TO WHOM HONOR IS DUE. Lewis Lyndon Hobbs was a great teacher. Latin was more than a subject — it was a devotion, a process by means of which he instilled principles of thoroughness and a respect for the past. He was a sound administrator; he built up a worthy faculty; he saw the erection of several much needed buildings; he greatly augmented the endowment, and lived long enough to see Guilford College attain sound scholastic standing. In 1908 the University of North Carolina and Haverford College recognized the merits of his sacrifice and accomplishments, and each conferred upon him the honorary degree of Doctor of Laws.[1] For many years he "sat at the head of the Meeting" at New Garden.

MARY MENDENHALL HOBBS, a daughter of Nereus and Oriana Mendenhall, could scarcely escape being a strong character if there be anything to the principle of heredity which declares that organisms "bring forth fruit after their kind." Mary received a great heritage; by dedication she developed her personality, and her union in marriage with Lewis Lyndon Hobbs made it possible to be identified throughout life with noble purposes and worthwhile people. It was natural that she should become associated with New Garden, and early in life she was appointed an assistant teacher in 1878. Two years later she was united in marriage to her childhood friend and neighbor, Lewis Lyndon Hobbs. It was an ideal union.

Her permanent memorial is New Garden Hall, renamed in her honor and now familiarly known, as Mary Hobbs Hall. It came about in this way. She was assistant clerk of the Women's

Meeting of the Yearly Meeting, and because of her duty sat on "the facing seat." She noticed two attractive girls in the congregation, and knew that they were the daughters of a Friends minister, and without means to continue their education. At first she was glad her father was not a minister; then she became ashamed, and was impelled to do something to help the girls obtain an education. The next day with fear and trembling she rose in the women's meeting and laid her concern before the group. She met with some encouragement, and obtained permission to visit the men's meeting, for at that time the large room was divided by movable partitions, and the men and women sat on different sides. The men Friends were sympathetic, and subscriptions were started, and Friends elsewhere were appealed to.

As a result of Mary's labors the corner stone of a new dormitory for girls was laid in 1907, and since then has been of inestimable blessing to hundreds of students. In 1939 the spacious attic was remodelled and accommodation provided for sixteen more students. Much modern furniture has recently been added.

Mary Mendenhall Hobbs developed a gift in writing, and was a frequent contributor to papers and magazines and published a number of independent articles. She was identified with every phase of the work of the church, especially temperance, peace and missions. In recognition of her character and accomplishments the University of North Carolina conferred upon her in 1921 the degree of Litt.D. She passed away in 1930.

JAMES FRANKLIN DAVIS. The writer well remembers a man past middle life telling him how surprised he was that he became a teacher in a college. He described how he was a farm boy, who usually wore overalls, with no polish such as a city-slicker might possess, entering Westtown Boarding School. Some years later he felt just the same — an insignificant farm boy — when he entered Haverford College. The world seemed so big, and he seemed so small. That was typical of J. Franklin Davis. At the time of that conversation he probably did not realize that he was one of the outstanding scholars of the South. One can hardly imagine Guilford College without Professor Davis. Born of Quaker stock, he was endowed by nature with great intellectual powers, which were supported by solid integrity. Lyndon Hobbs was early attracted to him, and they became inseparable. After graduation from Haverford he studied at Johns Hopkins University, and the Universities of Leipsig and Strasbourg, and in 1876 there began a connection with the Quaker school which extended over 45 years. In 1880-81 Davis was the principal teacher, and his continuous service commenced in 1888. He was professor of Greek, of German and of Biblical Literature; for three years he was Professor Emeritus.

The writer cannot do other than quote here some extracts from the memoir he contributed to the *American Friend* at the time of the passing of Professor Davis.

"To Franklin Davis belongs the merit of being one of the first native North Carolinians to become acquainted with the historical-literary methods of interpreting the Holy Scriptures. In this respect he was fifty years ahead of his age. Being able to read several languages, he was conversant with modern scholarship. He was able to discover the fundamental principles of religion, embody them in his own life, and distinguish between the eternal verities and the imperfections in the concepts of the saints. He was a lover of truth; he sought diligently for truth; he was ever ready to accept new truth, no matter with what prejudice it clashed. He grasped, as few of his Southern contemporaries, principles of oriental imagery in Hebrew poetry and Hebrew philosophy. This knowledge enabled him to give a sound, scholarly and scientific interpretation of the Bible. His use of the historical-literary-critical method was reverently constructive and never destructive. He was so deeply religious himself that his mission in life was to help his students discover the eternal verities. . . . Hundreds, maybe thousands of his students will remember him with gratitude and affection. He made the Bible an understandable book; he showed the difference between the transcient and the eternal; he portrayed the prophets as men of like passions such as we are, and enabled us to walk with them in their search for God and truth. He harmed no one's faith; but he spurned mere credulity. His students will be grateful that a kind Providence blessed them with a seer as a teacher."[2]

MARY E. MENDENHALL DAVIS was a typical Quaker woman of her period. Sedate, saintly, positive, practical, informed, she became a teacher in New Garden in 1877; was secretary to the faculty and reported proceedings to the trustees; she taught for 20 years and also served as librarian. In 1897 she was married to Franklin Davis and proved a worthy companion. She was very successful in raising funds and went to England for that purpose, returning with 310 pounds in gold.

RAYMOND BINFORD. The Society of Friends may not be a very large body numerically, but it never lacks qualified persons to fill important positions in the educational field or, in fact, in any position of responsibility. It may well be that proportionately to its membership it has produced a larger percentage of scholars and scientists than any other denomination.

When Dr. Lyndon Hobbs resigned in 1914, Dr. Thomas Newlin filled the vacancy for two years, and then a committee of Lyndon Hobbs, Howard Brinton and Alma T. Edwards was in charge for one year. Dr. Raymond Binford was elected President in 1918. He had been graduated in Science from Earlham College, had taught Biology at Guilford and acted temporarily as coach between 1901 to 1914, with intervals out for graduate study. In 1906 he received the Master's degree from Chicago and in 1912 the Doctorate in Science from Johns Hopkins University. He then went to his Alma Mater to teach biology. At the invitation of the trustees he returned to the Quaker college in the South with which it was his calling to be identified the most of his life. His work as president involved three distinct tasks, each of them a man-sized job. First, he had to rescue the college from the great burden of indebtedness; second, to stabilize the faculty; third, to revise the curriculum. The debt had grown considerably and two vigorous financial campaigns were carried on, and with the help of a grant from the General Education Board the Endowment Fund was substantially increased and the debt cleared. As to the second objective, with the possibility of paying better salaries many experienced teachers were added to the faculty, and their living quarters vastly improved. The third accomplishment was a stroke of genius. With the assistance of the faculty the syllabi of studies was thoroughly overhauled. Dr. Binford, as a scientist, believed that a college graduate should have a true Liberal Arts education, by which he understood first, an appreciation of the universe in which he lived, involving some awareness of the fundamental facts of the natural sciences; second, an appreciation of the society in which he lived; this involved the social sciences, literature, religion, history, philosophy and art; and third, an understanding of the body in which he lives, this includes heredity, hygiene, psychology and physiology. Syllabi were prepared for some of these subjects with extensive lists of required reading; each student was required to take certain basic subjects, but was permitted to pursue his studies as fast as he was able. If, for instance, at entering, he could pass an examination, say, in third year French, he would be given credit for such accomplishment. The student must satisfy the examining board at the end of his senior year that he had actually acquired an understanding of the subjects studied. The integration of studies met with high praise from several authorities, and the plan has resulted in an almost amazing use of the library and initial investigations by the student body.

Dr. Binford, although badly handicapped by hardness of hearing, proved to be the right man for the challenge. For years the building program had to be sidetracked because of the financial conditions, the Wars I and II, and the epidemic of influenza. The powerhouse which had been built in 1903 was destroyed by fire in 1919. This meant that for quite a number of weeks the campus was without heat, light and water. After being quarantined upon the campus for ten weeks due to the influenza we were able to take the inconvenience of "primitive conditions restored" philosophically. As soon as possible the Duke Power Company restored the instrumentalities of civilization. The President did not neglect the building program, and plans were prepared for future expansion, and these visions have in large measure been realized. Due to Binford's constructive policies the college was given full accreditation by the Association of Colleges and Secondary Schools of the South in 1926.

Dr. Binford, who was a minister of the Society of Friends, retired from the presidency in 1934, and for several years devoted himself to visiting various Friends centers in this country and in Mexico. He died in 1946, and of him it may be said "He accomplished the work it was given him to do."[3]

HELEN TITSWORTH BINFORD. Raymond was more than fortunate in his marriage. Helen was a graduate of Earlham, a teacher of languages and literature, with an appreciation of music, and became an ideal helpmate for the president. She was especially active in the community with the Parent Teachers Association, was the State president in 1929-31, and a member of the National Executive Committee.

JOHN W. AND MARY CHAWNER WOODY. These worthy Friends came to New Garden from Oskaloosa, Iowa, in 1880, with their very young children. John was born at Saxapahaw in North Carolina in 1841, on the Woody homestead that had been in the family since 1759. Soon after the firing upon Fort Sumter he walked from New Garden to Cincinnati, Ohio. From there he took a train to Thornton, Indiana, and joined his father's brother, James. This incident is typical of the thousands of Friends who fled from the South at the culmination of the slavery issue. John Woody obtained a college education and received his diploma in 1868, and in that same year he and Mary Williams Chawner were married and went to Iowa to teach.

They returned to Carolina in 1880, and John commenced a distinguished career as a teacher at New Garden. He continued when the institution became Guilford College in 1888 and retired from teaching in 1894. After retiring from the College John and Mary Woody travelled in the ministry quite extensively, and he conducted many teacher training classes, being one of the first to do so in this State. In the local meeting he was an elder and a "weighty" Friend.

From 1899-1904 John Woody was one of the managers of the Slater School which has since become the North Carolina Teacher Training College for Colored People, and is one of the leading institutions of its kind. He died at his home at Guilford College August 7th, 1920.

MARY WOODY was born in Indiana, of Quaker stock, December 22, 1846. Her grandfather Chawner was an Englishman, learned in the law, who abandoned ship at Elizabeth City, and became converted and joined Friends sometime about 1810. He became the first clerk of the Sand Creek Meeting, was a recorded minister and married the daughter of a Quaker minister. His mother was named Mary Williams Chawner in memory of the widow of John Williams, a missionary martyred in Samoa.

Mary Woody was recorded a minister in 1884 by a New Garden Quarterly Meeting held at Dover. At this same occasion David E. Sampson was also acknowledged as having a gift in the ministry. Mary Woody was for the rest of her life one of the leading spirits in the yearly meeting. She was a person of strong convictions and of unusual personal influence, and was a woman preacher of remarkable power. It is said that "her sermons were well outlined, organized, and gave food for thought, and came with a freshness and earnestness that appealed to the students at Guilford College." Another student said: "the messages of Mary C. Woody and the teachings of John C. Woody were a great blessing to me; they moulded my life." She was evangelical in her preaching and was especially interested in the Evangelistic Committee, and from 1883 to 1928 (with the exception of two periods when she was out of the yearly meeting on preaching tours) she was the secretary and a member of the executive committee of this important body. She was vitally interested in Temperance and was the State President of the W.C.T.U. from 1884 to 1894 "and laid the foundation for

RAYMOND BINFORD

CLYDE A. MILNER

North Carolina to vote dry in 1908." Mary Woody measured up to the writer's concept of an ideal Quakeress. She went to live with her son Waldo and his family at High Point after the death of her husband, and there she "finished her course" on Christmas Day, 1928, being four score and two years of age.[4]

CLYDE A. MILNER. Upon the retirement of Dr. Raymond Binford the trustees did not have any difficulty in selecting a successor. A young man had been preparing himself for the obligation, and the trustees were aware of his abilities and his accomplishments. Clyde A. Milner had been nursed in Quakerism and had unique opportunities of associating with the leaders of the Society. He entered Wilmington College, Ohio, in 1917; served with the American Friends Relief abroad in 1919; was at Woodbrooke College, England, 1919-20; received the A.B. degree from Wilmington, 1921; the M.A. from Haverford in 1922; B.D. Hartford Theological Seminary, 1924; was Dean of Men and Assistant Professor of Psychology and Philosophy at Earlham College, 1924-27; graduate student at Marlburg and Geneva, 1927-28; Dean of Men, Earlham College, 1927-28; Professor of Psychology, Earlham, 1928-30; Professor of Philosophy and Dean of Guilford College, 1930-34; Ph.D. Hartford Theological Seminary, 1934; President of Guilford College since 1934. At the time of this writing Dr. Milner has been President of a four year college in North Carolina longer than the incumbent of any other similar institution. In 1926 while studying at Geneva he was married to Ernestine Cookson, who held a Master's degree from Wellesley, and who had been Dean of Women and Assistant Professor of Philosophy at Earlham. Dr. Milner was thus not only acquainted with Guilford but with several Quaker institutions, and had a fine record for scholarship and leadership. His first challenge was to raise the endowment fund and put the college on a sound financial basis. It was right after the Great Depression, and not till Franklin D. Roosevelt became the Chief Executive and liberated vast sums of money did the situation become eased. Since then, however, under Milner's leadership the endowment has been phenomenally increased. In 1947 it was $640,000; by 1950 it had reached the $1,000,000 mark amid sincere rejoicing; in 1954 it stood at $1,233,-000. This is a far cry from what it was 120 years ago. For the first time the endowment is considered satisfactory. The income from student fees has greatly increased in due part to the G. I. Bill of Rights. The enrollment was 380 in 1942; 650 in 1947; 700 in 1948; 540 in 1952; 560 in 1954. When the writer joined the faculty

in 1918 the attendance was about 200, and many of the students
then were "preps"; because the war was in progress, young men
were conspicuously absent. The presence of married men and
married couples upon a college campus is a recent phenomenon,
but from all institutions comes word that generally speaking the
G. I.s excel as students, and give dignity to the college. Since Clyde
Milner became President, a great building program has been formulated and much of it already carried out, as already detailed. Good
roads encircle the buildings; the new faculty homes are attractive
and up-to-date, a good sized lake has been installed; the old farm
buildings have been removed.

Guilford keeps abreast with extra-curricular activities; there
is a creditable choir; amateur playmakers; and in athletic contests
Guilford can hold its own in contests with schools of its own order.
Under President Milner's guidance and the hearty and practical
cooperation of the trustees there is assurance that the Quaker College is at the threshold of an illustrious career. The foundations
have been well and truly laid; the days of storm and stress are behind; the best is yet to be. Much of the money needed for this
improvement is already in hand.

J. Elwood Cox.   No organization can long survive unless it has
among its members those who possess superior business sagacity
and who are able to accumulate and care for money. It is revealing
to read in the Gospels that Jesus and His disciples were able to
devote themselves wholly to the ministry because "certain rich
women ministered unto them of their substance." (Luke 8:3).

J. Elwood Cox, of High Point, (1856-1932), the son of Jonathan E. and Elizabeth Hare Cox, and President of the Commercial
National Bank, was truly a servant of God, and for many years
filled an indispensable place in the history of the yearly meeting.
He had the capacity to accumulate means and delighted to use his
wealth for the advancement of the Kingdom of God. He was
especially interested in Guilford College and from 1903 to 1932
was Chairman of the Board of Trustees and was largely responsible
for the physical improvements and the enhancement of the Endowment Fund. He was a prime mover in the construction of the Meeting House at High Point, and a liberal subscriber to every worthy
cause.

The progress of the North Carolina Yearly Meeting for more
than a quarter of a century was in large measure due to Elwood
Cox's wise counsel and generous contributions.

Like thousands of others in similar positions he was a victim of the financial disaster which overtook the world in 1929. It was a crushing blow to one who had been a pillar in the church and community activities.[5]

THY LOYAL SONS ARE WE. Any institution which survives and renders a public service is dependent upon the devotion of its personnel. Throughout its long career this Quaker school has found among its membership those who were willing to dedicate a portion of their time and strength to rebuilding Quakerism and culture in the Southland. Dorothy G. Thorne has devoted an entire work to the recapitulation of this story, all that this writer need do here is to name some of those with whom he was personally acquainted, and whose character and service were typical of Quakerism. Mentioning them alphabetically they include:

SARAH E. BENBOW was matron of Founders Hall from 1904 to 1926; she rendered an indispensable service.

HOWARD H. BRINTON was a member of the Guilford Faculty 1915-19; then rendered conspicuous service at Earlham; travelled extensively in the Far East; Director of Pendle Hill, a Quaker graduate school in Pennsylvania, modelled upon Woodbrooke in England; author of several valuable Quaker works.

DUDLEY DEWITT CARROLL, 1907; Graduate studies at Haverford and Columbia; Dean of the School of Commerce at University of North Carolina; Valued member of the Chapel Hill Meeting; trustee of Guilford College.

JOSEPH D. COX, of High Point, 1904; successful manufacturer; valued and reliable member of the Church; trustee of Guilford since 1922.

WILLIAM BENBOW EDGERTON, 1934; graduate studies at Haverford, Columbia, University of Maryland and Pennsylvania State College. Excels as a linguist, including Latin, Greek and Russian; accompanied the Quaker delegation to the Soviet Union and acted as interpreter; teacher of Russian language at Columbia University.

DR. NORMAN A. FOX of the class of 1923 became the physician of the College community when Dr. John Williams failed in health. Dr. Fox was reared in the community, became a worthy member of the profession, was much beloved, and his early death in 1956 was much deplored.

MAUD L. GAINEY for many years secretary to the President; later treasurer of the college; a person who meticulously fulfilled exacting obligations.

PRISCILLA BENBOW HACKNEY, served as matron for eighteen years, a worthy Friend; a necessary person in the development from 1887 to 1904.

SAMUEL L. AND EVELYN MARTIN HAWORTH must be included among the worthies who manifested a fine example of Quaker living. It would be difficult to find a more beautiful exemplification of gracious manners, high intelligence, spiritual vision, public service, extensive travel and cordial hospitality.

Samuel traced his ancestry to George Haworth, who came to this continent in 1699 with William Penn. A grandson of George, Richard by name, became a member of New Garden Meeting in 1711. On the maternal side his great, great-grandmother, Abigail Overman Pike, was a minister, and one of the founders of Cane Creek Meeting. Evelyn was a daughter of Zenas and Susan Martin, who established a Friends mission in Cuba, and devoted many years to that service.

Samuel was born near Newmarket in Tennessee, a son of Mahlon and Sarah Lee Haworth. He attended Maryville College, Chattanooga University and received the Master's degree from Brown University. Early in life he dedicated himself and prepared for the ministry, and was pastor successively at Hubbard, Iowa; Indianola, Iowa; Maryville, Tennessee; Central City, Nebraska; Fall River, Massachusetts; Minneapolis, Minnesota; and High Point, North Carolina. He was then called to teach, and served several years at Wilmington, Ohio, and later at Guilford College, where he had the privilege of "opening the Scriptures" to the students.

He also found many other fields of service, among which may be mentioned: Counsellor and Visitor to Conscientious Objectors during the first World War; member of the Executive Committee of the Federal Council of Churches of Christ in America for eight years; Ambassador of Good Will from the Churches of America to the Churches of Europe, 1923-1924; American representative to the Universal Christian Council at Chamby, Switzerland, 1936; preparing for the Conferences of Faith and Order at Edinburgh and Oxford; special speaker at many of the Friends schools in England; also with many conferences and service clubs in Great Britain, 1923-1924; American Friends Service Committee; a member of the Executive Council of the Churches of North Carolina. All this extensive acquaintance with Quakerism on two continents prepared him for the responsible task of Clerk of the North Carolina Yearly Meeting, which position he filled acceptably from 1929 to 1941. This is no mean chapter of accomplishments and the record testifies eloquently of the esteem in which he is held by Friends everywhere.

In later years he was elected by the Head of the Church to the Ministry of Suffering. For more than seven years he was physically helpless due to a stroke and a fall, yet in spite of grievous handicaps and suffering he exhibited the finest example of Christian fortitude, patience and cheerfulness and discoursed freely concerning the affairs of the Kingdom of God here and throughout the world.

Samuel and Evelyn exhibited to all who know them a supreme triumph of faith over adversity. It is of such persons the elect of the Society of Friends consists. At the age of 89 he passed away on April 5, 1957.

DR. ALLEN WILSON HOBBS, 1907; B.A. Haverford; Ph.D. Johns Hopkins University; Professor of Mathematics and Dean U.N.C.; trustee Guilford College.

DR. LEWIS LYNDON HOBBS, JR., 1907; B.A., U.N.C.; M.D. University of Pennsylvania; eminent surgeon. Died 1958.

RICHARD J. M. HOBBS, 1909; A.B. Haverford; LL.B. Columbia; Professor of Law in School of Commerce, U.N.C.

RICHARD L. HOLLOWELL, (1863-1950) was a valued member of the Board of Trustees of Guilford since 1926 and Chairman since 1947. A graduate of Earlham College; returned to North Carolina and taught for awhile at the historic Quaker center at Archdale; later he became the mayor of Asheboro. He had business connections in New York, New Jersey and South Carolina. In 1924 he settled in Greensboro and became a staunch supporter of all the interests of the yearly meeting, including service as the clerk of the monthly meeting and clerk of the meeting on Ministry and Counsel. His judgment concerning the finances of the college and of the yearly meeting was sound and reliable. He was familiarly known as "Uncle Dick," and was a splendid example of a Quaker in judgment, character, ability and reputation.

NANCY ERA LASLEY, 1913. As registrar and treasurer she has served her alma mater since 1923. Without continuous service on the part of some such persons no organization can survive.

JOHN VAN LINDLEY was a member of a distinguished family and of the committee which prepared the document for the incorporation of New Garden Boarding School to become Guilford College; founder of a nursery business which has grown to great proportions; has done much to develop the whole community. Greatly assisted in the building of King Hall and was from 1885 to 1918 a trustee.

CLEMENT ORESTES MEREDITH, 1900; graduate work at Haverford; Ph.D. Johns Hopkins University; twelve years (discontinuous) a teacher of the classics at Guilford; died 1958.

ALGIE I. NEWLIN, 1921; graduate studies at Haverford; Ph.D. Geneva, Switzerland; Head of Department of History, Guilford College; Clerk of North Carolina Yearly Meeting.

LOUISA H. OSBORNE, Professor of Latin and Dean of Women at Founders Hall; a veritable "Mother in Israel."

JOSEPH H. PEALE, B.S.; B.D. Hartford Theological Seminary; teacher at Guilford; excellent in speech; beloved as a minister; "a man full of faith and good works."

THOMAS GILBERT PEARSON, 1897; eminent ornithologist and naturalist; LL.D., University of North Carolina; established natural history museum at Guilford; President Emeritus National Association of Audubon Societies.

ELLWOOD C. PERISHO, Governor at Guilford 1887-1893; later a distinguished geologist; D.Sc. from State College, South Dakota; returned to Guilford as financial agent in 1921; an orator.

KATHERINE CRENSHAW RICKS, B.S. 1914; B.A. 1935; librarian at Guilford from 1922 for many years. It was largely through her perseverence and ingenuity that the Library was enlarged and remodeled and the Quaker Room and vault added.

DOROTHY GILBERT THORNE, A.B.; A.M.; at Guilford since 1926 as Director of Physical Education for women; later as Professor of English and Supervisor of the Quaker Records; author of *Guilford: a Quaker College;* recognized authority on Quakerism in North Carolina.

THE FACULTY OF GUILFORD COLLEGE (1957)

Front row, left to right: Stuart T. Maynard, Benjamin G. Baker, Herbert T. Appenzeller, Robert E. Shoaf, Ernestine C. Milner, Frederic R. Crownfield, Eva G. Campbell, Harvey A. Ljung, Clyde A. Milner, Algie I. Newlin, E. Garness Purdom, Philip W. Furnas, J. Curt Victorius, Thomas J. Moore, Charles N. Ott.

In back, left to right: Hiram H. Hilty, Charles C. Hendricks, Mary B. Feagins, Edward F. Burrows, Mildred Farrow, Ligia D. Hunt, Donald D. Deagon, David B. Stafford, Ann F. Deagon, Gay H. Spivey, Carroll S. Feagins, N. Era Lasley, Treva W. Mathis, Alma Martin, Edward E. Terrell, Helen Fortenberry, Norris W. Preyer (above), Maxine K. Ljung (below), Charles W. Sembower (above), Marjorie Williams (below), E. Daryl Kent (above), Edna L. Weis (below), Helen C. Davis, Carl C. Baumbach, Grady E. Love.

D. ELTON TRUEBLOOD was Professor of Philosophy at Guilford College 1927-30; Ph.D. Leland Stanford; Professor of Philosophy Earlham; a writer of distinction and a foremost exponent of Quakerism.

JULIA S. WHITE may be regarded as one of the makers of Guilford for the institution was dependent in its early days upon the fidelity of the faithful few who sacrificed their own personal gain for the sake of the school. "Miss Julia," joined the faculty in 1887, and taught till 1892 when she resumed her studies at Bryn Mawr College. After teaching at other places she returned to Guilford in 1901 and served as governess, custodian of the Quaker records and as Librarian for 21 years.

DR. JOHN AND ANNIE EDGERTON WILLIAMS cannot be omitted in any story of the New Garden community. He was for many years "the beloved physician" and his wife, a former missionary in India, was a "weighty Friend." Each was "full of good works," and both have "been gathered unto their fathers."

WILLIAM A. WOLFF. A Friend who is making a distinct contribution to society and to science is Dr. William A. Wolff, of Winston-Salem. Born in North Carolina he was graduated from Guilford College in 1923; received the Master's degree from Haverford the next year; and the Ph.D. from the University of Pennsylvania in 1932. For some years he has been Associate Professor of Clinical Chemistry at the Bowman Gray School of Medicine in connection with the Baptist Hospital in Winston-Salem. Here he has attained an outstanding record for his research in tobacco and alcoholism. He has perfected a device to determine degrees of sobriety and drunkenness by testing the breath and the blood of a patient. The local police department often calls upon him for expert opinions, and he has explained his devices to the State legislature. Dr. Wolff is also an authority in the use of radioactive and other "tracers" in the human body, so that more accurate diagnoses may be made. He is now a trustee of Guilford College.

LAURA D. WORTH. B.S., R.N. Director of Physical Education for women at Guilford, 1895-98; Nurse at Guilford. She did much to liberate girls from the restrictions of the Victorian era; she did much to classify the Quaker Library. During the influenza epidemic she rendered indispensable services.[6]

CHAPTER SIXTEEN

LOOK HOW THY BRETHREN FARE

THE STRAITS OF THE EARLY SETTLERS. Conditions remained primitive for several generations. It is quite impossible for one who has always known comfort and conveniences to imagine the circumstances of a family which has to clear the land, construct some sort of a shelter, break the soil, garner the crops and hunt their own food. Travelling Friends testify to the poverty-stricken conditions. Daniel Stanton and Isaac Zane visited the Southern Quaker settlements about 1761. The following incident occurred in Virginia, but similar conditions prevailed for many years in North Carolina:

"That night we lodged at Peter Holand's, lying down in one room like a flock of sheep in a fold, being sixteen in number with the Friends' family."[1]

A somewhat similar experience occurred in this colony:

"We stopped at a house to enquire for entertainment, where was a woman and several children. She gave us liberty for house room, and there being no bed for us we laid on the floor, and it being cold and snow falling, we were sometimes obliged to get to the fireplace to warm us."[2]

It was under such circumstances that John Griffith visited the scattered settlements, and it is no wonder that

"he regarded the conditions gloomy and discouraging . . . two small poor meetings . . . where the life of religion seemed to be almost if not wholly lost. . . . We had a meeting at Centre; it was extremely cold, and as some observed, the like had not been known in the memory of man; and being quite an open meeting house, and very little of anything to be felt among them of religious warmth, it was really a distressing time inwardly and outwardly."

Concerning the visit to Cane Creek he wrote:

"This was large, but most of the members seemed void of a solid sense of solemnity; a spirit of self-righteousness was plainly felt . . . I am persuaded many of those under our name have removed from Pennsylvania and other places to these parts in their own will, having taken counsel of their own depraved hearts, and when they have got thither, they set up for something in the church; but it seemed to me most of them were very unfit for the spiritual building, not having been hewn in the mount. We went to their meeting on First Day, but there was much darkness and death over them."[3]

Hugh Judge* who visited Southern Friends in 1784 tells similar stories. Of one place in Virginia he wrote:

> "We arrived there safely, but though it was a poor place . . . we had a tolerably good bed, and corn blades for the horses; but there was no milk, bread, cheese or butter for us. I asked whether we could have some water boiled which they did in a large kettle, for they were entire strangers to tea and tea tackling, having nothing of the kind. However, getting some hot water, I made some tea in a quart mug; and having tea and sugar as well as bread and meat with us, we fared pretty well on our own. . . . Set out before sunrise, and called at several places before we could get any breakfast or anything for our horses to eat. At length we obtained some corn blades for them, and a broken kettle to boil water for ourselves at breakfast. So sorrowfully poor is the situation of many of the inhabitants of Virginia that travellers are hardly beset to get a little refreshment . . . yet they abound with Negroes."[4]

A QUAKER HOME UPON THE FRONTIER. While attending Earlham College the writer was privileged to have some share in the ministry at the South Eighth Friends Meeting in Richmond, Indiana. There he became acquainted with Timothy and Elmina Wilson. She was a remarkable person, although aged, she possessed unusual mental vigor, breadth of interest and a commanding personality. It was always an inspiration to visit her. She probably told about her life in North Carolina, but the writer does not remember the details as he at that time had no expectation of being associated with the South.

It was a thrill and an abiding satisfaction forty years later to read the story of her girlhood not far from New Garden. Her great-grandfather came from England to North Carolina in 1730, and settled in an unbroken forest right near where the Battle of Guilford Court House was fought. At first he lived in a tent, and then in a rude hut until a log house could be built. Indians were still in the vicinity. Her grandfather as a boy of fourteen hid during the Revolutionary War. Elmina wrote a very interesting paper in which she narrates many incidents told her by her parents. She describes fully the placing of a new "back log" in the great open fireplace. At yearly meeting time a large brick oven in the yard was used for cooking and about thirty Friends were fed out-of-doors. "If a family was moving to the West grandmother would get mother to bake quantities of food for the journey.

"At harvest time primitive methods were employed, there being no machinery. To thresh the wheat the grain was spread upon

---

* Hugh Judge travelled extensively in the ministry, and is mentioned frequently in Bliss Forbush's *Elias Hicks*.

the floor of the barn and trodden out by horses, and the chaff was winnowed by a fan turned by hand.   Each family did its own weaving and so there was an array of warping bars, reels, winding blades, the big wheel, the little flax wheel, the quill wheel and shuttles; also the loom and the gears, beams and treadles; weaving was interesting but monotonous.

"Cotton picking was done by the children; the seeds were picked out by hand; all the processes of spinning were done at home.   Sheep shearing also involved the tedious labor of picking out the burrs.   Flax was pulled by hand, spread out on the grass for the woody part to decay, and then prepared for spinning.   It was quite an art to twist the flax on the distaff.   There seemed to be a halo of peace as grandmother sat day after day at the spinning wheel.   Different threads were used for various garments, and various dyes were in use.

"We had to pay 25 cents in silver for letters received.   All kinds of berries and fruits were home grown, but as canning was unknown the fruits were preserved by being dried.   As the spring was some distance from the house the fetching of water was quite a chore.   Shoes were made by a local craftsman.   As was customary the young men indulged in horse racing and running horses for a wager was a disownable offence.   As slavery was common it was not unusual to see slaves put upon the block and sold."

Elmina tells of a neighbor whose property was sold: "His Negroes and other livestock, farm implements and other goods." The daughter of the house said to Elmina, "I just can't bear to see the poor things sold."

"In those days it was considered disreputable for Quakers to attend the meetings of other denominations, but the Cannons,* who were neighbors, and my parents attended a Methodist camp meeting a few miles away.   We lived four miles from meeting, and the roads in places were very bad so most of the time we rode horseback."

Elmina's record confirms the legend of the blood-stained boards in the meeting house, and of the British and Revolutionary soldiers buried nearby.   She speaks of the candle making; of the family washing down at the spring; how the water was heated in a big kettle; of the big pounding barrel; the tubs set upon large flat

---

* The family of Joseph G. Cannon (for many years Speaker of the House of Representatives) lived close by.

stones, so that they could be easily tipped over to be emptied; of the spring-house where the milk was cooled; and of the many metal vessels, usually pewter.   She describes the plucking of the down from geese.   The fall brought the ingathering of the harvest, and winter the drying of apples and the making of cider.   The children shared the universal dislike of turning the grindstone when Father or some one else wanted an ax or scythe blade sharpened.   Here as in many other places tomatoes were believed to be poisonous, and were called "permartices."   It was a great event to go with Father to market in Greensboro.   He would take bacon or lard to sell; we regarded it as a luxury to sit in the straw in the wagon and "the bewildering splendor of the town, with its fine stores, and its big cotton factories was something to tell about again and again."

Elmina shared with all children a horror of snakes, "run-away-niggers," mad dogs and ghosts, especially headless men from the battle ground, but she says that "three-quarters of a century have made her skeptical, and she now believes this world of ours is under law."   It fell to Elmina's lot to wait upon her grandmother who was crippled by a carriage accident.   As she was unable to walk without crutches she spent much of her time knitting and spinning.   Her paper contains an interesting account of the great meteoric shower of 1833 and the terror of the Negroes as they feared it presaged the end of time and the Judgment Day[5]. . . . Unfortunately Elmina does not mention her maiden name, nor the date when she journeyed to Indiana, but it is established that she was a descendant in the male line from her great-grandfather Hugh Forster (or Foster).

TRAVELLING FRIENDS.   From the very beginning intervisitation was an integral phase of Quakerism.   As there was no hierarchy it was regarded as a function of the Holy Spirit to "burden some person with a concern for some Friends elsewhere."   He would lay this concern before his local meeting and if approved a certificate would be issued, signed by the clerk, liberating him for such service. Mention was made in chapter four that opponents complained bitterly of the activities of the Quaker missionaries in eastern North Carolina.   This cornerstone of Quakerism was brought into being by preachers and organizers possessed of a holy enthusiasm.

In like manner as told in chapter six the Quaker settlements in the Piedmont were encouraged by the ministrations of ninety-three visiting Friends between 1752 and 1778.

Special mention must be made of the visits of the sainted Stephen Grellet,* who came first in 1800 in company with John Hall, an English Friend. He came again in 1808 and 1824. On one of these missions he narrowly escaped drowning when in the Contentnea Quarter. There were twelve visiting ministers in 1853, and sixteen the next year.

After the Civil War, Friends elsewhere were very solicitous and the yearly meeting minutes show that there were twenty-two visitors in 1866; twenty-five in 1867; twenty-seven in 1868; twenty-four in 1869. Very few ministers now are widely known as "travelling Friends."

BRITISH VISITORS. There was a great sympathy in England for Southern Friends, and London Yearly Meeting authorized many members to visit North Carolina. Among the earliest was Catherine Peyton Phillips, a remarkable person. Others included Cordelia Bayes, Joseph John Gurney; Walter Robson was here in 1877 and again in 1922 when he was eighty-one years of age; Robert and Sarah Lindley, Eliza Barclay, John Allen, Joseph J. Neave, James C. Fuller, James Hack Tuke, "who was accompanied by a young Friend of twenty-four years of age, known as Joseph Crosfield"; Isaac Robson, William Forster (who died at Friendsville, Ten-

---

* Etienne de Grellet, born in 1773, in France of a wealthy noble family; reared by Roman Catholics; became a Rationalist; forced to flee to America by the excesses of the long Revolution; parents impoverished and imprisoned. In Long Island at first, taught French; became acquainted with Philadelphia Friends; converted at 22; joined Friends at 24; complete dedication to Christ; responded to call to the ministry; changed name to Stephen Grellet; visited Southern States; oppressed by the evils of slavery; two years ministry in England; visited prisons; "the Chief of Police of London gathered all known criminals to hear Grellet"; visited many parts of Europe in 1813-14; travelled 26,000 miles by land (no railroads); six months in Russia; visited "the Southern and Slave States" 1798, 1808 and 1822-24; returned to America; made fourth tour of Europe. In most of these tours he was accompanied by William Allen, a British scientist. These visits were religious missions; he had no eye for scenery or art treasures. He secured letters of introduction and had personal interviews (meetings for worship) with dignitaries in England, with the Kings of Prussia, Bavaria, Wurtenburg, Spain and the Czar and Czarina of Russia. He also had a personal interview with the Pope at the Vatican. Everywhere he went he requested of the authorities permission to inspect the prisons, the galley slaves, hospitals, schools, dungeons and slums. He was moved with compassion to seek out the destitute and criminals and preach salvation to them and seek amelioration of their sufferings. He was not primarily concerned with preaching in Friends' meetings; he was burdened with the souls of those in authority and pleaded with them to govern humanely and establish justice. He visited almost every country in Europe, besides extensive visits to the West Indies, to Canada and the various American yearly meetings. His missions constitute one of the most extraordinary annals in evangelism. He died at 82.

nessee), Josiah Forster, William Edward Forster (Member of Parliament who introduced the historic Education Bill of 1870 — the foundation of the public elementary school system), Joseph Sturge, Sanford Allen, John Pease, Harriette Green (whose remains were interred in the New Garden burial ground), George Stacey, Isaac Sharpe, Joseph Bevan Braithwaite, William Holmes, Mary Elizabeth Beck, J.J. Dymond, Henry Stanley Newman, William and Elizabeth C. Hobson, Sarah B. Satterthwaite, Hannah Thistlethwaite, Jonathan and Hannah Chapman, Gurney Backhouse, Hannah Backhouse, Stanley Pumphrey and those most extraordinary persons — Thomas Shillitoe and John Woolman.

William Greene and George Grubb presented minutes from Dublin Yearly Meeting. The beloved John T. Dorland, a Canadian minister and evangelist, attended New Garden and also London Yearly Meeting. Robert Saylor and Silas R. Sing were also from Canada; William Wetherald, a Britisher domiciled in Canada also had religious service in North Carolina.

Walter Marriage and his wife, Rachel, with daughters, Lillian and Ann and George Dixon and wife obeyed the Divine leading to come from England and labor for several years among the Freedmen. Yardley Warner, mentioned elsewhere, also assisted in this particular service.

The writer has a special interest in these visitations as he was personally acquainted with quite a number of these distinguished Friends in his youth.*

Robert H. Frazier calls attention to the interesting circumstances that many Southern Friends visited Northern meetings. In her work *The Early Settlers of Nantucket,* the author Lydia S. Hinchman, lists the following Southern ministers who received credentials to travel in the ministry between 1784 and 1801 in Nantucket Island. They include, Henry Stanton, William Hunt, Zachariah Dicks, Thomas Thornbrough, John Carter, William Coffin, Ann Jessup, Lydia Hoskins, Stephen Gardner, Nathan Hunt, Matthew Coffin, Jeremiah Hubbard, Elijah Coffin. These arduous undertakings (before the existence of railroads) afford ample evidence that "the very small remnant" was possessed of abundant vitality.

---

* For a more extensive list of Visiting Friends see Russell's *Story of Quakerism,* chap. xviii; also Drake, Thomas E., *Patterns of Influence in Anglo-American Quakerism* for the significance of these visits. There were many other English visitors but this writer includes only those who are known to have visited North Carolina.

THE AGE OF QUIETISM. Charles Woodman says "the period of Quietism lasted from 1700 to 1835 and even later. . . . Friends were occupied in building fences around themselves . . . they forgot to give of themselves . . . theological concepts took primacy over sacrificial living, and the seeds that produced the great separation grew like thistles in the fair garden of their thinking and living, and choked their beautiful unity."[6] Thorne remarks: "Even when the war was very close Friends had nothing to say about it. They merely disowned a member who joined those who styled themselves Regulators of Public Affairs."[7] It can hardly be questioned that this Age of Quietism (which was almost world-wide at that time) resulted in an almost complete withdrawal of Friends from public affairs.

CONCERNING QUAKERESSES. The writer has had the privilege of being acquainted with many Quaker women in England, Canada and various parts of the United States; he has also known estimable women who were not members of the Society of Friends. There is something distinct and different about women reared as Friends. It is hard to define but not difficult to detect. It is easier to use negative terms, yet it is the possession of positive qualities which is the dominant characteristic. Perhaps the words which the writer heard concerning Woodbrookers* would be appropriate "They are sanctified, but they don't brag about it."

There we have it — the positive and the negative.

As to sanctification. With Quaker women that word does not denote sanctimoniousness; it does not suggest the coldness, aloofness, austerity and unnaturalness of seventeenth century Puritanism; it implies a natural serenity, dignity and high standard of ethics and conduct; it is the mark of a decent woman, a person who manifests self control and a Christ-like spirit.

It was recorded of a certain Quaker lady "She never wears her best dress." The Quakeress does not consider it necessary to wear the "coalscuttle bonnet" of her grandmother's day, yet she is never a walking exhibit of the latest fashion. Her clothing never attracts attention because of its expensiveness or elaborateness. No Quaker woman would display expensive jewels; she would be mindful of the feelings of others with limited incomes.

It is unlikely that a young woman reared in a Quaker home would deem it proper to resort to conspicuous make-up. Beauty

---

* For an account of Woodbrooke see chap. xxvii, footnote to topic "Friends and Higher Education."

of character is more expressive than the artificialities of a beautician's salon. Someone said a certain female "exuded a confused aroma of alcohol, perfume and nicotine." Such could never be said of a Quaker girl who was conscious that her body "was a temple of the Holy Spirit." It is the dignified bearing, the serenity and assurance, the acceptance of her lot, that graces the Quakeress. There is an absence of fussiness, of pretence, of ostentation, of self-assertiveness that so frequently mars the personalities of those who lack "the Peace of God which passeth all understanding."

The Quakeress of today is a firm believer in education; she is ready to sacrifice in order to secure for herself and her children a worth-while preparation for life; it is probable that she is more tolerant of new concepts of the universe than her spouse. Her religion is eminently practical and grounded in common sense. Not having been reared to repeat ancient creeds she is able to relate her religious beliefs not to hoary tradition but to the implications of modern knowledge.

A Quaker mother knows how to rule her family without compelling obedience. From early years the children are encouraged to "listen to the Voice Within," and often when a child asks "Mother, should I do this?" she is likely to reply: "What does thee think thee should do?" She encourages them to rely upon their own judgment and obey conscience. This characteristic is more noticeable among families where both parents "have been reared as Friends." It is a natural development of the fundamental belief of Friends in the Inward Light.

As to amusements Quakers now manifest toleration and discretion. Few would say it is absolutely wrong to attend theatres and other places of entertainment but Friends agree that it is inconsistent with our profession to "attend places of diversion which are demoralizing." Our attitude toward dancing has also been modified. The writer has heard ministers at yearly meeting rail against college girls dancing, but a long association with college and university students forbids the writer from such a sweeping accusation. No Quaker mother would fail to give her daughters proper advice. The writer does not advocate dancing, but he has known many college girls who danced when young, but who in later life became ideal citizens and church members.

One outstanding characteristic of women of the Society of Friends is that they are not dependent upon professional entertainment or amusement. The properly developed Christian woman can find within herself "the Life that bubbles up eternally." (John iii, 14). Quakerism tends to cultivate rich and full personalities that when alone one can draw upon the resources of an informed mind, a contented spirit, and the communion of the Eternal. The daily practice of quiet meditation brings this enhancement of personality. One who cannot bear to be alone or to be quiet and must attend a card party or listen to the blaring of a radio or watch the inanities of television or seek diversion to wile away the time is profoundly to be pitied.

Women of the Society of Friends possess a religion that "tends to make them equal for all circumstances and occasions." It is the consciousness of the Indwelling Spirit of the Christ which frees them from petty irritations, vexations and emotional disturbances and induces serenity and poise.

There is no notion of celibacy among Friends. Matrimony is natural and honorable; marital love is essential to maturity. Quakers believe that the normal woman finds more joy and satisfaction in the care and nurture of her own children than in any professional career, and they unhesitatingly believe that marital relations may be holy. They have liberated their minds from the degrading notions which for two thousand years obsessed our ancestors that "we were born in sin and shapen in iniquity, and in sin did my mother conceive me." Christ Jesus found a human body a perfectly adequate vehicle in which and through which to manifest a holy life and so can those who believe "the body is a temple of the Holy Spirit." We repudiate the old notion of the Dualists that "the body is vile."

Quaker women have an attitude toward church membership which differs from that of other worshippers, who are members of organizations controlled wholly by men. As mentioned earlier women may be ministers, elders, overseers, clerks, members of committees and have liberty to speak in meetings for worship and business. In the early days men and women sat separately, the original reason being that the meetings were liable to be broken up by soldiers or disturbers and the men sat in a body near the door so as to give the women protection and an opportunity to seek shelter in another portion of the premises. It was not due to any sense of inferiority as in the ancient Hebrew synagogues the women sat at the rear and their presence was merely tolerated. It was not so among Friends.

It was understood that women and girls could receive Divine guidance and were able and permitted, even encouraged, to deliver a vital message in meeting which freed them from any sense of inferiority, and enabled them to exhibit a serene consciousness that they were Children of God. In the marriage service the woman was not required to promise to obey the man; they each made an identical promise to be loving and faithful to each other till death separated them.

Quakers led the world in the emancipation of females. This has much to do with the development among Friends of women of outstanding personality and accomplishment. Such could not occur in a land such as India where females are held in virtual subjugation. It is not claimed that Quaker women have any monopoly of the full fruition of womanhood, but it cannot be questioned that the views and organization of the Society of Friends affords females a greater opportunity to develop and express their individuality.

JUST LIKE INEZ. An illustration of "the abundant life" was seen in the experience of Inez Beebe Perisho. Elwood Perisho married rather late in life a woman younger than himself. He was connected with Guilford College in early life and again in his later years, and resided upon the campus. In course of time "he became well stricken in years" and it became evident that the end was near. He died in a Greensboro hospital, and the memorial service was held at New Garden, after which the body was conveyed to South Dakota for interment. Within a day or so Inez had disposed of some of the properties locally and the rest forwarded to her home in the Dakotas. When the neighbors marvelled that she was departing so soon and had all her affairs attended to, she answered: "I thought all that through years ago when Elwood asked me to marry him." She did not collapse or go into hysterics, or enervate herself with excessive grief. She experienced "the Grace Abounding." The neighbors said, "Well, that was just like Inez."

The women referred to in this book are a few examples of the dynamic personalities which Quakerism has produced in North Carolina. They participated enthusiastically in civic affairs because they believed they could contribute to the establishment of the Kingdom of God upon earth.[8]

THE QUAKER AND HIS HAT. The typical Quaker was known by his hat. Probably many children because of clever advertizing have learned to associate Quakers with some exaggerated headgear. Who can there be who has not gasped at the famous picture of Nathan Hunt, and involuntarily exclaimed "Where did you get that hat?" There is a picture at Guilford College of George Fox with a monstrous something on his head. It seems more suitable for a pirate than a reformer. Visitors to the archives should ask the librarians to show them this curiosity. We do not know where George Fox obtained his hats, but we can tell something about the making of Quaker hats in North Carolina.

Four years before the memorable Declaration of Independence a stream of migrants from Nantucket Island were impelled by the spirit of the age to pull up stakes and adventure upon the long, tedious and hazardous journey to Deep River Quarter. Among these hardy settlers were Richard Beard and his wife, Eunice Mach Beard. They reared five children, one of whom was named David. Richard brought with him some knowledge of the manufacture of hats, and David excelled in the craft while yet in his teens, so much so that the father turned over all the equipment to his son, and later in 1795 when Richard died, David became sole proprietor of the business.

According to Addison Coffin many kinds of fur-bearing animals abounded in the Piedmont. He lists buffalo, bear, grey wolf, fox, squirrel, wild cat, otter, beaver, muskrat, mink and racoon. There were also deer and enormous flocks of destructive wild turkeys. David became known far and wide as a merchant in hides, skins, and furs, and he knew how to dress each kind and its best use. The manufacture of hats stood at the head of the list. Tanning naturally went with the preparation of hides, and David and his employees prepared all kinds of leather goods, including harnesses, saddles, boots, shoes, leather jackets, buffalo robes, rugs and furniture coverings. The chiefest use of cowhide, so the boy said, was to hide the insides of the cow, but after the slaughter the settlers knew that David could put the hide to many practical purposes.

The War of 1812-15 came on, and David went north to purchase a variety of supplies, anticipating a bull market, but a panic ensued, and David had to sell his business at a loss.* However, to return to hats, the next time you are at Guilford by all means visit the Library and in the Quaker Room you will find pictures of Quaker patriarchs "sitting in their hats" as the British parliamentary expression has it. You will also see the enormous hat worn by Nathan Hunt. Probably David Beard made it.[9]

QUAKERS AND MUSICAL INSTRUMENTS. The Great Revival among Friends inevitably brought differences of opinion concerning singing and instrumental music in meeting. Many sincere members

---

* Dr. Charles A. Beard, a distinguished American historian, was a grandson of David Beard.

objected, and in some places conservative members ceased to attend meeting.   Before relating incidents in North Carolina the writer will mention some incidents which came under his observation elsewhere.   In one meeting a man named Exam White badly damaged a small harmonium with an axe.   The youths had the instrument repaired, sent the bill to Exam, who "condemned his conduct" and paid the cost.   In another place the young folks planned an entertainment and arranged for some music.   Hesitatingly they asked the approval of a "weighty Friend."   He said he would not object to a violin, but he did hope they would not have a fiddle! At another meeting it was believed the time had come to have an organ, but it was understood that this step could not be taken without the approval of "the head of the meeting."   With fear and trembling he was approached, and to the amazement of his petitioners he replied: "If thee must praise the Lord by machinery, thee'd better get a good one," and subscribed liberally.   The writer was acquainted with a meeting years ago in which the following incident occurred.   Some of the younger Friends pleaded for an instrument, but one of the elders vigorously objected.   A youngster arose and remarked that he was astonished at the attitude of the worthy Friend who had just spoken, for it was common knowledge that he had musical instruments for sale in his store.   The dignified Friend arose, put on his hat, walked slowly out of meeting, unhitched his horse, got into his buggy, drove straight to his store, and forcefully threw all the musical instruments into the roadway.   They were jewsharps!

The following incident occurred at New Garden about fifty years ago.   The younger members were responsible for the introduction of a small reed instrument into the Sunday School services; it was noticed that the singing was improved, but the instrument disappeared and no explanation was forthcoming.   Some time later the organ was found in a dark place under a stairway in King Hall. Not for half a century was the explanation given.   It appears that Dr. Lyndon Hobbs was overheard by his son Richard to say "he didn't like the squeaky thing," so Richard obtained the help of Henry Davis and another boy and they surreptitiously put the offence out of sight.[10]

Dertha Farlowe told the writer that her grandfather, David Farlowe, when a minister at Marlboro meeting was most severely censured by the elders for encouraging the use of an instrument in meeting.

In recent years singing and music have come to occupy an

integral part of worship among Friends. There is need for a word of caution. The Great Apostle said he preferred to "sing with the understanding." Friends originally objected to congregational singing on several grounds among which was singing was not true; "for it was just as bad to sing lies as to tell lies." Many popular "hymns" express theological sentiments contrary to Friends' views, and many are gross materializations of spiritual verities. Friends value worshipful hymns, but rag-time, jazz and hill-billy stuff have no place in a Friends' meeting.

Most Friends' meetings now have music, choirs and instruments; many choirs are robed and there is now general approval of this practice. Singing is natural, and a person who has experienced the redeeming Grace of the Lord has a religion that spontaneously expresses itself in praise and song. The time has gone by when puritanism can frown upon all music, but much more care should be exercised in the selection of musical numbers.

CHAPTER SEVENTEEN

WHAT THOU SEEST WRITE IN A BOOK

THE QUAKER ARCHIVES. When the Guilford College Library was remodelled and enlarged in 1950 it was decided to provide adequate accommodation for the large collection of Quaker literature and official records. Adjoining the magazine room there was constructed a "Quaker Room" for the valuable and ancient record books. For the safe-keeping of the hundreds of yearly, quarterly and monthly meeting *Minutes* a vault was installed. The Quaker Room has three large windows, protected by heavy wiring, and is furnished with beautifully made book cases and filing cabinets and a handsome double desk from the estate of Dr. Lewis Lyndon Hobbs. The yearly meeting is very rich in its treasures; among its possessions are early editions of George Fox's *Journal,* and many scarce and valuable editions of the Holy Scriptures. Several hundred volumes of important and valuable Quaker books have been acquired by purchase and by gift, and the archives are now recognized as one of the great sources of Quakerana.

Among the treasures are ten rolls of microfilm of the proceedings of London Yearly Meeting dating from 1696 to 1754; also four rolls of records of London Yearly Meeting for Sufferings, 1675 to 1687; also Epistles to and from London and Philadelphia Yearly Meetings; also microfilm copies of Perquimans Monthly Meeting, 1734-1735; Wells and Perquimans, 1774 to 1794; Piney Woods and Perquimans, 1680 to 1762; Eastern Quarter, 1704-1793; 1794 to 1834; 1835-1836; Minutes of the Yearly Meeting held at Eastern Quarter, 1704-1793; 1793 to 1830; 1835 to 1836; Cane Creek, 1756 and 1814; New Garden, 1775-1782; Deep River, 1778 to 1807. Some of this microfilming was done at the University of North Carolina and some by Dr. E. Garness Purdom, of the College faculty. The enormous old hat of Nathan Hunt always attracts attention.

The vault deserves especial mention, for in it are housed hundreds of record books, dating back to 1680. Some of the earliest records are lost, but few yearly meetings can claim as complete a collection. The steel shelving was especially designed. Each partition is about forty inches long and about ten high. The books are laid flat, and seldom are more than six in a pile. Many have been rebound, and some repaired professionally. The quarterly and monthly meeting record books are alphabetically arranged. Among the treasures in the vault are three of the original books of the yearly meeting clerk in manuscript covering the period from 1704 to 1845. There are also the records of the Meeting for Sufferings, many Boards, the Boarding School and Guilford College, and countless valuable documents dealing with all the various phases of the activities of the Society of Friends. Needless to state the vault has a burglar and fireproof door.

MASTERPIECE OF RESTORATION. It would be difficult to state which is the most valuable treasure in the Quaker Room, for there are so many antiques and rarities, but there is one which commands admiration. It is the old Minute Book of Perquimans Monthly Meeting in the Eastern Quarter, dating from 1680. Extraordinary to relate sections were discovered in four different places. Part had lain in the Guilford College Library for many years; part was found in an old barn on a farm owned by Dr. Elbert White in eastern North Carolina; a few pages were retrieved by Dr. Henry Cadbury in an antique shop in New York; a few additional pages were found in Duke University library. Many of the pages were loose, tattered and discolored.

Dr. Charles E. Rush, librarian of Yale and later of the University of North Carolina employed a person skilled in the preservation of records to come to Guilford especially to train Laura D. Worth, the chairman of the committee on Records of North Carolina Yearly Meeting, to repair old volumes. First, each sheet was carefully sponged on each side to cleanse it; then it was pressed between blotting papers; then each sheet was edged on both sides with Japanese paper; mounted upon silk chiffon, and trimmed. So expertly was the restoration accomplished that it is virtually impossible to feel or see where the original paper terminates and the addition begins. Each page was separately strengthened at the spine, and the whole bound to harmonize with other volumes which have been remounted. The records date from fourth of fifth month, 1680 to seventh of fifth month, 1736, and constitute the oldest record in the possession of the Yearly Meeting. Every visiting Friend should peruse this masterpiece of restoration.

WILLIAM WADE HINSHAW rendered a most valuable and unique service to Quakerism. He was a birthright member of Chester Preparative Meeting, at Old Honey Creek, Iowa, and was born in

1867. After attending Friends Academy at New Providence he studied at Valparaiso University, Indiana. By profession he was an engineer, but his avocation was music and he toured with Ira D. Sankey and Dwight L. Moody in their memorable evangelistic missions. He became President and Director of the Chicago Conservatory of Music and was a leading baritone. In 1917 he became President and General Manager of the Society of American Singers, and gave the first Mozart festival in this country; he rendered over one hundred operatic roles in four languages. He developed a great interest in Quaker genealogy, and began his studies in this yearly meeting. He gradually widened his researches till he planned to cover all the Quaker records in the country. He employed a staff of experts, who under the guidance of Thomas W. Marshall, of Washington, D.C. studied the original minute books. It was a gigantic task, for many of the old volumes were tattered and stained and almost indecipherable. The principal entries were typed in uniform style. He was especially interested in genealogy, and he gave it as his opinion based upon these studies that at least fifty per cent of American families had Quaker ancestors.[1]

North Carolina possesses six volumes of Quaker genealogies in professional style, and each volume contains about a thousand pages. Marshall was assisted by his son Whitfield. The work is in alphabetical order and is furnished with a comprehensive index. It has been warmly commended by the Five Years Meeting, by Harlow Lindley, of Earlham, and later of the State Museum of Ohio, by Walter C. Woodward, of Earlham, and later the editor of the *American Friend,* and many others.[2]

This service alone would have constituted a monumental task, but an equally valuable contribution followed. Thirty-three of the oldest minute books were perused and the chief entries typed in uniform style on pages about 12½ x 8¼ inches. There are twenty-one volumes bound in uniform style, and properly labelled. These records include the history of many meetings which were laid down because of the westward movement. In the preparation of this most valuable collection much assistance was rendered by the librarians, including Laura D. Worth, Julia White, Katherine C. Ricks and Dorothy G. Thorne.

THE FIRST MINUTE BOOK OF NEW GARDEN MONTHLY MEETING was restored as part of the second centennial celebration in 1954. The volume covers the period 1754 to 1775. It was well written; at the beginning of each monthly record there is bold, beautiful two line large Spencerian script; the writing was upon each side of the paper. Time has damaged the book, and the pages were separate, torn and discolored. It was expertly restored; each page has been separately cleaned, pressed, mended and squared, strengthened at the spine and handsomely bound. There are about 255 pages.[3]

THE MINUTES OF THE YEARLY MEETING (as distinguished from the minutes of the quarterly and monthly meeting minutes). The earliest records preserved are in an old volume covering 1704 to 1793. Considering its age it is in a well preserved condition, though the leather cover is tattered and the pages stained by time. It is written in the style of the period with the letter "s" having elongated ceriphs and the "d" ending in a flourish that sweeps over to the beginning of the word. It is well written but full of curlicues and flourishes and only a paleographer could decipher all of it. A curious entry occurs on pages three and four at a meeting held in 1704.

> "It is the judgment of this meeting considering the "ondocency" (indecency) of Friends in not keeping their place as much as possible and not run in and out in time of worship and likewise in meetings of business, this meeting finds it an illconvenience in having too many Friends in our yearly meeting of business it is our judgment that our yearly meeting consist of twelve men chosen whose names are written." The "inspectors" named were Francis Toms, William Newby, Thomas Pearce, John Barrow, Timothy Clare, Samuel Nichols, Emanuel Low, James Davis, John Hawkins, Henry Kooton, Edward May, Augustine Scarborough." — Signed: William Evorigin, clerk.[4]

The explanation for this unusual procedure is that there was no meeting house at that time and gatherings were held at the homes of Francis Toms, Henry White and others, and comings and goings might well create an "ill-convenience."

There are two other MSS books — one dating from 1794 to 1838; the other from 1835 to 1846. As some of the first mentioned book was almost indecipherable part of it was copied into the later book. This accounts for the overlapping of the dates. The later volume is well written and appears to be all in the same writing, but the clerk modestly refrained from attaching a signature and a considerable search failed to reveal the name of the writer.

After 1845 the minutes were printed, and the archives possess sixteen bound volumes including proceedings from 1845 to 1948. The subsequent minutes have not yet been put in stiff covers.

The earliest printed volumes of the yearly meeting *minutes* were just little booklets about four by two-and-a-half inches with 18 pages; poorly printed on common paper; the next few numbers were irregular in shape and size, and some are falling to pieces. Most of the issues until 1852 were badly printed; the paper is discolored and deteriorated. The MSS volumes are housed in the vault; the printed volumes are in one of the cases in the "Quaker Room."

It is of interest to examine the various volumes, as it calls to mind scores of worthy Friends whom one knew in days gone by. It is a moving experience to recall Friends whom one knew forty, fifty, sixty and even seventy years ago, and to visualize them hale and hearty engaged in the service of Christ and the Church. These old books are a storehouse of information concerning Quaker ancestors and their relation to the Society. There is evidence that at least one well-remembered Friend examined the records and marked his name wherever it occurred, and inserted his initials* wherever he thought they had been wrongfully omitted. Except in the case of *Memorials* there is no mention of particulars other than in relation to the business of the Society. The *Memorial* of Nathan Hunt in 1854 occupies several pages and two years later there appears a very poignant *Memorial* concerning Dougan Clark.

CONTENTS. The minutes follow an established pattern (which perhaps is unavoidable). The usual procedure of the period up to the adoption of the pastoral system was about as follows: the opening minute; the recording of the names of the appointed representatives — both present and absent; the reading and answering of the queries by each Quarter; discussions concerning the same; the reading of reports concerning attendance; the use of intoxicants; the use of slave labor; reports upon education; the reading of the epistles. Very little can be learned of the persons or movements of the period.

The recorded minutes are skeletal. The names of visiting ministers are recorded, but their messages are not; addresses were given by prominent Friends, but they have not been preserved; lively discussions occurred concerning slavery and the use of intoxicants; the hireling ministry was roundly denounced; marrying-out came under frequent condemnation; so did secret societies and lotteries. The minutes make cryptic allusions to these matters, but we search in vain to learn what was said and imagination must be used to reconstruct the situations. Other matters which claimed the attention of Friends during the last century were the distribution to members of the Holy Scriptures; the protection and hiring

---

* F.S.B.

of Freedmen; the use of wigs; the preservation of plainness; the use of the "tone;" and capital punishment.

NEGRO SLAVERY. Without question the matter which concerned Friends the most between 1820 and 1860 was the fact that slavery was an established institution. It affected the life of every Friend and every meeting, for it barred white labor, and made it impossible to compete successfully with neighbors who utilized unpaid service. The recorded minutes alone do not tell the story; in fact they are extremely disappointing, for in answer to the Sixth Query which asked whether "Friends were clear of purchasing or holding mankind as slaves so as to prevent them from receiving the benefit of their labor" the regular reply was: "Friends appear to be clear" with certain exceptions which are briefly alluded to. There are so many aspects of the relation of the Quakers to Slavery that chapter twelve of this work is devoted to that story.[5]

THE USE OF INTOXICANTS. One of the chiefest interests was the number of Friends who used intoxicants other than as a medicine. Annually it was reported how many adults there were and how many used liquor. In 1849 there were 2031 members over 18, and 224 used liquor; in 1852 there were 1725 and 89 respectively. In 1879 Friends are laconically rebuked "for distilling and attending places of diversion;" in 1883 the "use of liquor was complained of in six of the Quarterly Meetings."[6]

THE HIRELING MINISTRY. The topic which appears to rank third in importance about a hundred years ago was the query: "Do you uphold and cherish a waiting spiritual worship and a free Gospel ministry?" This led to reports that "the hireling ministry was creeping in." One finds in the minutes of 1858, 1860, 1867, 1868, 1869 and 1870 the curious juxtaposition in one sentence: "Friends bear a testimony against war and the hireling ministry." It reminds one of the dual charge against the Lord Jesus "He is a Samaritan and hath a devil." The record of 1860 is modified by the word "mostly." In 1873 the record says: "Friends endeavor to maintain our testimony to a free Gospel, with an exception noted by one of the Quarters."

The peculiar views and testimonies of Friends were much dwelt upon by our ministers and overseers during the war and we were exhorted to be faithful in all these peculiarities. The following from a Minute of Advice in 1864 will illustrate the general attitude:

"We verily believe that the great distress in which our country is now plunged is in a large degree traceable to the hireling ministers of the present day. We fear that some of them, feeling that their places and living may depend upon the doctrines which were preached, have failed to enforce the truths of the Gospel in its fullness; while others from the same cause have advocated doctrines directly at variance with the teaching of Christ. Let us then be careful, while treating all men with kindness and love, that we do not lower this important principle — that a pure Gospel ministry must be free."[7]

In 1876 a marked change is noted by the reference to "young men who are studying for the ministry . . . which is an encouraging feature." In the same year "ministers are urged to avoid tones, gestures and all unbecoming manners which tend to mar their work. . . . Dear Friends, bear in mind these things are unnatural and injure your service."[8] These are evidences of the great revivals which had occurred among Friends.

PEACE TESTIMONY. Considering that the Friends experienced the disturbances of the Colonial Wars, the War of Independence, the War of 1812-15 and the War Between the States it is surprising that there are so very few references to Friends' testimony concerning war in the yearly meeting *minutes*. There are two explanations — one, already mentioned, that discussions and addresses are never reported (no Friend would have been allowed to present a carefully prepared and documented speech), and secondly, it was virtually forbidden for Quakers to participate in politics. As they would not bear arms they adopted the policy of non-participation and non-interference in government. However, every year at the answering of the Query "Do you maintain the Christian principle of peace and consistently refrain from performing military service?" Friends "preserved their testimony." In 1861 we read "we cannot conscientiously pay any fines which may be imposed upon us, individually, for non-performance of military duty, but rather quietly submit to have the value of the same distrained by proper officers."[9] In 1865 Friends participated in a proposal by the Ohio Yearly Meeting for a conference of Friends concerning our peace testimony, and a delegation was named. That same year a Friend was "eldered" for calling a guard to protect his property. The member later "acknowledged his action to be inconsistent with Friends' principles." The Peace Association of Friends was organized in 1867 as an outcome of the conflict just concluded.[*10]

PLAINNESS. In 1864 and 1872 "deep concern was expressed because of the deviation by some of our members from plainness of

---

* See Topic "Conscientious Objectors" in chap. xi.

dress and speech. We have retained the style of dress which prevailed at the time of our beginning. It is comfortable and convenient. . . . In this day of the display of banners it is incumbent upon us to show which side we are on." In 1872 the clerk recorded "there are some exceptions noted to plainness and moderation."[11]

PLACES OF DIVERSION. The reading of the Query: "Are you careful to avoid all places and amusements inconsistent with a Christian character?" brought rebukes in 1871, 1876, 1878, 1879 and 1883. A typical entry says "a few cases of attending places of diversion appear, which are under notice." There was another Query relating to tale bearing and detraction. No wonder that "it was not wholly avoided" in three meetings, for there must have been some tale-bearing concerning those who "attended places of diversion."[12] It is clear that the elders and overseers exercised their functions.

CHILDREN. Evidently Friends in last century were not at liberty to hand over the permanent care of their children or to adopt children not birthright members without the knowledge and approval of the monthly meetings involved. Cases were reported to the yearly meeting in 1867 and 1871. In 1891 the Yearly Meeting addressed an epistle to the children among Friends. Although some juveniles wore Quaker attire and said "thee and thou" some were not saints, for in 1853 it was said in meeting that "some of the children at the Boarding School wore unsuitable clothing and their language was unbecoming."[13]

THE HOLY SCRIPTURES. For many years the reading of the Scriptures was not stressed by Friends,* and it was the mission of an English Friend, Joseph John Gurney from 1837 to 1840 who became greatly concerned at the scarcity of Bibles and the lack of Biblical knowledge among Friends that led to an organized effort in 1871 to provide each family with a copy of the Holy Scriptures. Hitherto the Bible had seldom been used in meeting. In 1874 it was reported that "every family among Friends was possessed of a copy, but that the reading thereof in a collective capacity is much neglected." The many revivals which occurred led to a new interest in the Bible.[14]

---

* Russell: "The Bible was, of course, never read in meeting;" *Quakerism*, p 281; Woodman: "Before 1860 the reading of Scripture had never taken place in Quaker meetings." *Quakers Find a Way*, p 89.

ADDITIONS. The great migrations to the West had greatly depleted Quakerism in this State as already told and in 1863 there were only 1030 members over 18 years of age. The revivals turned the tide and in 1873 it was reported that there had been one hundred additions; there were 604 families; 451 parts of families; 4121 males; 2096 females; three years later there was an addition of 173 received by request.[15]

QUAKERS AND THE INDIANS. This writer has looked in vain for particulars concerning the relation of the Quakers to the Indians in the Piedmont at the time of the settlement. On an earlier page there is a reference to an attempt to purchase land from the Cheraws or Catabaws, but "the matter appears to have been dropped;" . . . "Land titles were very conflicting;" this is all the writer found. It is likely that there is other material undiscovered. What is the explanation?* There is evidence that the French and Indian War (1756-1763) was in progress at that very time, and at the Moravian's first settlement, Bethabara, less than thirty miles away the Brethren armed and fortified themselves against an attack, and it is generally believed that the ringing of a bell or the blowing of trombones as a call to worship scared away the redskins.

Why were the Quakers not interfered with and why are there no references to danger? It is most likely that the natives learned that the newcomers were from Pennsylvania and were friendly to the Amerinds. They probably lived together in good relations and were mutually helpful. Why was this not entered in the *minutes*? Probably because the goodwill was taken for granted; relations were normal and natural. At any rate it seems that no antagonisms developed, and that the Quaker settlements in this Yearly Meeting were undisturbed by the tribesmen. This perhaps is the greatest tribute to the soundness of the Quaker manner of life and religion.

Several missions were cared for over a considerable period and at the Yearly Meeting in 1880 reports were given concerning the Quapaws, Wyandottes, Sac, Fox, Osages, Kaws, and Cheyennes. Schools and missions were conducted. In 1897 this undertaking was transferred to the Wilmington (Ohio) Yearly Meeting.[16]

FRIENDS AND EDUCATION. In 1831 it was reported "there is not a school in limits of the yearly meeting which is under the care of a committee of either monthly or preparative meetings. . . . The

---

* See Thorne, D. G.: *Quaker Migration to the Western Waters.*[16]

Friends' children are under the instruction of non-Friends and all the schools are in a mixed state." The next few years one of the chiefest concerns of the yearly meeting was the establishment of a Boarding School, which story is told elsewhere. In 1850 "nearly all Friends' children were receiving some education." At each year after the Baltimore Association became active there is a full report included in the minutes. In 1880 the committee on education reported "there is perhaps too great a tendency to secure teachers whose low price is their main qualification."[17] The minutes refer somewhat fully to the establishment of Guilford College.

EXPANSION OF THE MINUTES. With the adoption of the Uniform Discipline in 1904 and the coming of the pastoral system the minutes included much new material especially Directories of the officers of the various meetings; the times and places of meeting; list of recorded ministers; clerks; Bible School superintendents; names and addresses of active Friends. New activities are mentioned; full financial reports and reports from the Yearly Meeting Superintendent (later the Executive Secretary) are introduced. The printed minutes are now an indispensable reference book.

JOHN AND REBECCA COLLINS from Burlington, New Jersey, visited North Carolina in 1869. He was an artist and drew and painted sketches of the meeting houses and the costumes of Friends at that time. He also wrote in most beautiful Spencerian writing, accounts of his experiences. The work was done in three volumes and is entitled *Among the Friends in North Carolina*. The volumes came into the possession of Carrie B. Aaron, of Collingwood, N. J., a 94 year old daughter of John and Rebecca Collins, and was made available to New Garden Friends by Mrs. A. L. Stephens, a sister of Mrs. C. O. Meredith, of Guilford College, who was a close friend of Mrs. Aaron. The book contains references to other meetings, but the most of the work deals with this yearly meeting. It contains a full account of the yearly meeting of 1869; a description of the meeting house, of the school house, of leading Friends, and of the conditions of the South at that time. Both the exterior and the interior of the meeting house are shown in color; the old wood stove is depicted; also a variety of benches and the "facing seats" all unpainted. There are also sketches of the gravestones; and a water color of the Boarding School.

The work is a splendid specimen of art and script, and of great historical value. It shows clearly that the "plainness of the dress was not in the color, but in the cut," for pinks and blues were much in evidence. Collins confirms the belief that many visitors slept in their wagons, and he corroborates the belief that the old school building was "behind the meeting house." He also gives a fuller account of the sessions than does the official record which occupies only 19 pages whereas Collins devotes 43 pages in color and in most careful writing. All his descriptions tally with known sources. Collins says "he left the meeting thoroughly chilled by the dampness and cold air." He "tramped through the wet leaves and the ooze to take a parting view of the time-worn place of assembly."

His three notebooks constitute an art treasure, and no visitor to the Yearly Meeting should fail to examine these beautiful sketches which are housed in the Library. Some of his sketches have been enlarged in color and adorn the walls of the magazine room.[18]

DISOWNMENTS. It is in the *Minutes* of the Monthly Meetings that we find the extraordinary record of the almost wholesale disownments and the more incredible evidence of the practice of self-condemnation by the hundreds who violated the Discipline. Perhaps the chiefest loss occurred through "marrying out;" and the next for being married by a minister of another denomination, that is by "a hireling priest." Members were disowned for attending a Baptist church; for "using intoxicating liquors to excess at monthly meeting;" for "betaking himself to the vain fashions of the world;" "for joining with the vain customs of the world, such as horseracing and frequenting places of diversion;" "for purchasing and receiving manumitted Negroes;" "for fighting and spreading a report to the injury of his neighbor;" "for marching in procession with music and weapons of war;" "for fighting and laying a wager;" "for allowing himself to be transported with passion as to utter some very unbecoming speeches, and threatening expressions to the dishonor of our profession;" "for enlisting in military service;" "for answering his name to a military muster;" "for joining the Masonic society;" "for neglecting to attend our religious meetings;" "whereas she who had a birthright among Friends has so far deviated from the known rules as to join in marriage with a man not of our religious society, we do therefore disown her from being a member of our Society until she makes satisfaction;" "for dancing;" "for taking strong drink to excess;" "offering to fight and hiring a slave;" "for moving out of the State without endeavoring to settle with his creditors."

LETTERS OF CONDEMNATION. References to "Letters of Condemnation are quite numerous in the *Minutes* of the Yearly Meeting but the writer has not succeeded in finding any originals in the Archives. It was not the practice for clerks to preserve with the *minutes* communications of any kind except under unusual circumstances. (It would be of great help to future historians if clerks and pastors were to preserve every program and message and public notice relating to particular meetings.) Fortunately a collection of confessions was made in the Cedar Creek Monthly Meeting in Hanover County, Virginia, and as there is little doubt that these follow the same pattern they may be accepted as typical of this yearly meeting. Here are a few samples:

"I, having been a member of your meeting, but going contrary to the good order and rules of Friends to be married by a hireling priest, which practice I do fully condemn, and am heartily sorry I have been the cause of trouble and sorrow to Friends and greatly desire to be re-united to my friends, which I submit to the freedom of the meeting." — 1/2/1778, signed, Richard Kirby.

"Having gone out in marriage contrary to the good order amongst Friends, and having a sight and sense of my error, I do sincerely condemn the same and myself in so doing, and hope in future to conduct myself more circumspectly and agreeable to good order, and request that you may accept this condemnation which I submit." — 1/12/1789, signed, William Terrell.

"I having married contrary to Discipline, for which I was justly disowned by you, and being lately measureably sensible of the disadvantage of such a separation, do therefore condemn my misconduct in this respect and desire to be reinstated to Friends again, and hope my future conduct will evidence the sincerity of this my acknowledgment." — 9/17/1791, signed, Millie Johnson.

Micajah Johnson "condemned his conduct by having been married by a hire-teacher." — 8/9/1805.

William Johnson "condemned his conduct in having been married in the ways of the world." — 9/1/1812.

Mildred Tyree "condemned having deviated so far as to marry contrary to the rules of Friends." — 3/14/1816.

"I have at some time past acted in a disorderly manner in fighting and thereby brought a scandal upon Truth and a wound to my own mind, the practice I do utterly condemn myself in so doing, and if Friends will pass by my conduct in that respect am in hopes through Divine assistance never to do the like again." — 2/17/1787, signed, Edward Terrell.

"Being suddenly overtaken with passion too unguardedly beat a man, which I am really sorry for, and do heartily condemn myself in so doing, and all such rash undue liberties, and believe if I had a little reflected I should have been preserved from such unbecoming conduct, and for your satisfaction can assure that it is my resolution to endeavor to conduct myself consistent with our profession for the future." — 6/20/1788, signed, William Terrell.

"Having so far deviated from the peaceable principles professed by us to suffer the spirit of anger and resentment so to prevail as to secure firearms for my safety, all which conduct I do condemn, hoping at the same time that my future conduct will evince the sincerity of this my acknowledgement." — 6/20/1789, signed, Enoch Robarts.

"We acknowledge that we have deviated from the principles of Friends in kissing the Book, etc., which we were inadvertently drawn into not knowing the difference between an Oath and an Affirmation, which we are heartily sorry for and if Friends can pass by this offence we hope in future to be more cautious how we commit such errors." — signed, Timothy and David Johnson.

"I have done amiss in hiring a slave, for which I am sorry and condemn the practice, and have set her at liberty until her year is up, and if Friends will look over my misconduct, I hope to be more careful for the future."— 11/9/1805. signed, Moorman Johnson.[19]

We can hardly imagine the strictness with which the Discipline was enforced in those days. Elbert Russell is justified in considering that the decline of the Society was in large partly due to the authority of the Elders. It is to be noticed that the words "condemnation" and "deviated from the rules and good order of the Society" occur in practically all of these confessions. Evidently the Elders insisted upon the use of these phrases.

The great Revival brought not only new spiritual vigor to the Society, but that greatest of the Christian graces — Charity.

CHAPTER EIGHTEEN

A CITIZEN OF NO MEAN CITY

QUAKERS RETURN TO PUBLIC LIFE. The influence of Quakers in public affairs has been substantial wherever they have been. In proportion to their numbers it has been said to have been phenomenal. Our "American Democracy," as it is today, stems in a large measure from the political philosophy of Quakers.*

The contribution of Quakers in politics in the State of North Carolina has been true to form. It has been shown in previous pages that in the early colonial period the Quakers figured largely in the political life of North Carolina as they also did in Pennsylvania, New Jersey and Delaware. In fact, at one time the government of this southern colony was wholly in the hands of Friends, John Archdale being Governor.

Quakers, however strongly they have advocated government and undertaken to support it, have staunchly held that governments of state must not exercise control of that of God in man. They have been ready to render "that of Caesar" to the state but "that of God" they do not surrender. For example, the command of the state's military authority to kill, they have refused to obey. Likewise the state's order to take an oath they have declined to obey. Hence, a Vestry Act enacted by the General Assembly of the Carolinas in 1701, which provided that all members of the Assembly must take an oath that they were communicants of the Church of England and, in addition, an oath of allegiance to the Queen thus denying the right of affirmation caused large numbers of Quakers elected to the Assembly to be deprived of their offices. The application of the Vestry Act eventually put the Quakers out of public life much to the detriment of civic righteousness. Friends retreated for a time to what has been given the name "otherworldliness." So strong was the feeling against any deviation on

---

* If one today would seek the spot most deserving to be called "the cradle of democracy" in America, one should go, not to Jamestown or to Plymouth Rock, but to Philadelphia, William Penn's capital city in Pennsylvania planned to be "a green country town." It was Penn's 1682 "holy experiment" in state making that first set the social pattern which we praise today as "American." — From review by Douglas Adair, *New York Herald Tribune*, Sunday, January 27, 1957.

the part of Friends in taking the oath or surrendering rights of God's world that for a period the North Carolina Yearly Meeting approved a provision in the Quaker Discipline forbidding members from holding public offices.

With the establishment of the Republic of the United States these objections to office holding became untenable. Some continued reluctant to enter the mire of politics but, in general, since then Friends have realized that public officials have an unparalleled opportunity to promote national righteousness. Friends recognize that they owe something more to the community than regard for the law, the payment of taxes and jury duty. This sense of obligation gives zest and purpose and hence Friends regard office holding as a religious service.

North Carolina Quakers opposed to slavery and strong supporters of the Union prior to secession were naturally attracted to the Republican party.* They contributed to it a stability and progressiveness not to be found in it in some other southern States, and they earnestly endeavored to make North Carolina a two-party State. This party has twice honored Quakers with the gubernatorial nomination, one being J. Elwood Cox, of whom more is written elsewhere in this book. Cyrus Clifford Frazier, a member of the Greensboro Monthly Meeting from its founding, a Guilford graduate of the Class of 1907, a very successful lawyer and public speaker, was nominated for Chief Justice and has served on Greensboro's School Board and Library Board.** A list (admittedly incomplete) of Southern Friends who have participated in government follows:

As Governors. John Archdale. It has already been told in previous pages that John Archdale restored tranquility to the two Carolina colonies; exercised prudence; won the confidence of all classes; did much to establish Quakerism in the colony; caused salutory laws to be enacted; and aided in setting the pattern of toleration which characterized his period.***

Governor Jonathan Worth. This distinguished citizen was a descendant of Quaker forebears who came from Nantucket Island

---

* Herbert Nicholson said: "Before the Civil War all the Friends in Pasquotank and Perquimans Counties and the area around Piney Woods were Whigs and at the rise of the Republican party they naturally supported Abraham Lincoln."
** Lefler, Hugh T.: *History of North Carolina*, Lewis Historical Printing Co., Inc., 1956, Vol. III, p. 281.
*** See chap. iv.

in the mass migration to the North Carolina Piedmont, and was born in Guilford County in November, 1802. His father was Dr. David Worth and his mother Eunice Gardner Worth, and he was the oldest of twelve children. Jonathan possessed great intellectual ability and became a classical scholar. He aspired to the practice of law, but a natural diffidence and a Quaker conscience debarred him from competing with others not so scrupulous. He desired to be a fluent speaker and with that in mind turned to politics. He had a broader view of public responsibility than most of his Quaker kin and did not share the Quietist views and exclusiveness of Friends.

He became elected to be Clerk and Master in Equity for Randolph County, and in 1858 was elected to the State Senate. He was challenged to a duel as a consequence of exposing corruption in connection with a North Carolina railroad. He abominated Jacksonian Democracy and believed it to be dangerous. He was an admirer of Henry Clay and a Whig. In the elections of 1860 the Democratic Party was split and Worth actively supported Bell and Everett of the Constitutional Union Party. He opposed Nullification and Secession, yet after hostilities commenced he did not hold the pacifist position. He was re-elected to the Legislature during the Civil War, and Governor Zebulon Vance appointed him to have custody of the State archives; later Provisional Governor W. W. Holden named him State Treasurer and when Holden was removed from the Executive Worth became Governor.

He rendered an invaluable service to North Carolina during the dreadful Reconstruction Era when plunder and pillage were the order of the day. He was greatly concerned over public elementary education. So judiciously did he conduct affairs that he won the friendship and admiration of General Sickles who was in charge of the Military District including that State even though he staunchly defended civil rights from the encroachment of the military.

Dr. J. G. de R. Hamilton, who edited *The Correspondence of Governor Jonathan Worth* says "he shared the Quaker characteristics of his family — including, thrift, devotion to principle and fear of God. He was of too firm a mould, too much given to forming his own opinion and then living up to his conviction; like all strong men he had his enemies. He was a fine representative of his stock."

He severed his connection with Friends when he married a

Presbyterian,* though it is evident that he shared their convictions but believed in a more forceful presentation of the Quaker faith. In a time when Friends had largely withdrawn from public functions he threw himself into the forefront of the battle to restore the Constitution and Rights of the State. He exemplified the fundamental principles of Quakerism in his personality and was acclaimed by his family connections. He probably would have been restrained if he had attempted his public affairs while retaining his membership in the Society.

False charges were brought against him and he was removed from office by the military, who controlled the South till 1877. He died in 1869 — one of North Carolina's esteemed citizens.[1]

GOVERNOR JOSEPH MOORE DIXON is another illustrious product of the Quaker settlement at Snow Camp, and a descendant of the migrants from the colony of William Penn. He was a son of Hugh Woody and Adeline Murchison Dixon, and was born July 31, 1867. He attended Sylvan Academy under the care of Friends, Earlham College and Guilford College, from which institution he was graduated in 1889. He then removed to Missoula, Montana, became a lawyer and practiced in that State. He became Public Attorney for the county of Missoula; then a member of the State Legislature; then Congressman for Montana 1902-1907; and U.S. Senator from 1907.

His activities were numerous; he owned and published the *Daily Missoulian* and also operated one of the most up-to-date dairy farms. Such a man could not be hidden and he served one term as Governor of Montana, but a severe agricultural depression caused a political upset and he was not re-elected.

Herbert Hoover appointed him first Assistant Secretary of the Interior. He died at the age of 67 and at his obsequies he was lauded by a former U.S. District Attorney as "one of the ablest and most courageous men Montana ever knew, who fought for his convictions and stood ready to risk all in their defence."[2]

QUAKERS IN THE GENERAL ASSEMBLY. Almost continuously from 1785 to 1874 there was a Quaker in the House of Representatives from Guilford County. Several other counties were also represented by Quakers. Here is the Guilford list: Barzellai Gardner, 1784-1794; Richard Mendenhall, 1805; William Armfield, 1810;

---

* According to Jonathan Daniels, his great-grandson, in an address at a Guilford College Commencement.

Obed Macy, 1813; William Unthank, 1824-1825; George D. Mendenhall, 1828-1842; Nathan Hunt, 1848; Cyrus P. Mendenhall, 1860; David Hodgin, 1868; Nereus Mendenhall, 1874; Otis E. Mendenhall was a member of the State Senate, 1891-1895; Byron Allen Haworth is a representative from Guilford, 1955-1957.

Herbert Nicholson, who passed away in 1957, was a representative from Hertford County in 1898. He informed the writer: "My first flair with politics was a desire to occupy the County Clerk's office, which coming to the notice of the Elders of the Meeting, was nipped in the bud because it would entail the administration of oaths. Instead I ran for the Legislature and was elected in 1898. The only Bill I presented to the Legislature was for an elevator at the State Capital. It was installed fifty years later upon the motion of someone else." To the same session of the General Assembly Hertford County sent Yound Snipes who said: "It was a time of unprecedented bitterness and confusion. The Republicans united with the Populists and gained control of the executive, the legislative and the judiciary of the State Government. The Democrats (the Lily Whites) regained control in 1899."

Roger C. Kiser, a Guilford graduate of the Class of 1919, has served for many years and is now serving as representative from Scotland County. J. William Copeland, a graduate of Guilford College of the Class of 1934, now represents Hertford County. Grace Taylor Rodenbaugh, a graduate of Guilford of the Class of 1917, and a granddaughter of the sainted Mary Moon,* and a daughter of Nellie Moon Taylor of Danbury, has served in the North Carolina Legislature for a number of years and is still serving.

The records of the Archdale Literary Society, Randolph County, say: "The Society enjoyed the distinction of furnishing seven members to the subsequent legislatures, namely, Harrison Frazier (died after election before taking office), Enos T. Blair, S. F. Tomlinson, Nereus C. English (Sr.), A. S. Holton, Jacob Brown, David Henderson." From this Literary Society came also two county commissioners and a register of deeds. Later Nereus C. English, Jr. was also elected to the Legislature from Randolph County.

As MAYORS. Considering the prominent place that Quakers have occupied in Greensboro, it is not surprising that on four occasions a Friend has been that city's chief magistrate. Cyrus P. Menden-

---

* For Mary Moon see chap. viii.

hall was elected Mayor in 1844; Jabez R. Mendenhall in 1892; Paul C. Lindley in 1931; Robert H. Frazier in 1951.

Nereus C. English, Jr. has served as Mayor of Thomasville; Richard L. Hollowell as Mayor of Asheboro and William P. Ragan was Mayor of High Point.[3]

As POSTMASTERS: Herbert Nicholson, who was well acquainted with the Friends of the Eastern Quarter, recalled that in that part of the State Quakers for many years served as Postmaster, especially at Belvidere and Newby's Bridge. Among the appointments were Mathias Jordan, 1827; Lewis Killenberger, 1830; Thomas Newby, 1836; Henry White, 1842; Josephus White, 1853; Jeptha White, 1854; Josiah Nicholson (father of Herbert) 1866 to 1893. (Josiah Nicholson also served as County Treasurer for twenty years.) Adelaide White, 1897 to 1913; E. N. Hollowell, 1914; Delia R. Winslow, 1915 to 1951. She was also the first woman to serve on a Federal Grand Jury.

According to Nicholson, Elihu A. White was an outstanding political leader of his day but failed in his candidacy for Congress. He did serve as Commissioner of Internal Revenue at New Bern and Raleigh. Nicholson also remembered Jonathan Albertson, of a distinguished Quaker family in Perquimans, a judge and a famous orator.[4]

OTHER OFFICE HOLDERS: James Hoge Ricks, a graduate of Guilford College of the Class of 1905, became a distinguished jurist. In 1916 he was appointed the first Judge of the newly created Juvenile and Domestic Relations Court of Virginia. After forty years he retired. In appreciation of his accomplishments he was presented with a scroll bearing: "In recognition of his long and faithful career as an outstanding jurist whose unbounded wisdom, kindness and humility have given countless unfortunate and troubled children hope, faith and courage." He was presiding clerk of Baltimore Yearly Meeting, a trustee of Guilford College, and served his community in many ways worthy of the Quaker tradition. Death came to him unexpectedly in March of 1958.

Byron Allen Haworth has served, and is now serving, as Judge of the Municipal Court of the City of High Point. Horace S. Haworth, at one time also served as Judge of the Municipal Court of that city. William Worth was elected State Treasurer; Ed Ragan of High Point served as Clerk of Superior Court of Guilford County; Rufus W. Frazier served for many years as Register of

Deeds of Randolph County. David Stafford of Greensboro served as Sheriff of Guilford County for many years. Nereus C. English, Sr., J. L. Tomlinson, Cyrus P. Frazier, and Jabez Mendenhall served as Superintendents of the Greensboro Public Schools. Juliette Ballinger Dwiggins was the first woman to serve on the City Council of Greensboro; John Haworth is now a member of the High Point City Council; B. Clyde Shore (the donor of the Shore Apartment at Guilford College) is an active member of the Winston Salem Planning and Zoning Board and David J. White has rendered valuable service in a similar capacity on the Greensboro Planning and Zoning Board.

From the Springfield Meeting David H. Blair was nationally famous as a lawyer, particularly in the tax field. He was appointed by the President Commissioner of Revenue of the United States.

Nereus Mendenhall and John Van Lindley have served as Chairmen and Shubal E. Coltrane as Acting Chairman of the Guilford County Board of Education. Charles F. Tomlinson was for many years Chairman of the Board of Education of the City of High Point and William A. Tomlinson is now Chairman. Sarah Mendenhall Brown served for a number of years on the Board of Education of the City of Greensboro.[*5]

There have been for many years members of the Society of Friends in the British Parliament (perhaps the most notable was John Bright) and they have also been conspicuous in local government. It is an acknowledged fact that their influence has been great; they have done something distinctive to raise the level of public morals. The same can be said of Quakers in this country. They have never been numerous, but we assert without pretending to be superior that the popular verdict and the measured word of historians will confirm the opinion that the participation of Friends in governmental activities has had a refining influence.

We therefore encourage the younger members of our Society to regard office holding as a part of their Quaker inheritance and as an obligation to stand for truth, justice, toleration and integrity in the body politic.

---

[*] This chapter was compiled in great part by Robert H. Frazier.

CHAPTER NINETEEN

THE BODY HATH MANY MEMBERS

EASTERN QUARTER has the distinction of being the birthplace of
Carolina Quakerism. The story of the coming of Friends to the
South is told fully in other pages. Here we mention once more
that the eastern shore witnessed in the coming of Edmundson and
Fox one of the greatest spiritual awakenings any area had ever
known. Edmundson was a very sick person when he forded the
Dismal Swamp as his *Journal* clearly shows. For half a century
Friends had virtually a monopoly in this area and Quaker meetings sprang up in many parts of the colony. It is quite understandable that after other denominations established themselves
several Quaker meetings would be discontinued. Such happened at
The Narrows, Newbegin Creek, Bath, Buck Springs (or Beech
Spring), Sutton Creek, Little River and Flinty Creek.* This did
not represent a total loss, for during the years scores of Quaker
families carried their certificates of membership to the Piedmont
area. For those who are interested in more details there is to be
found in the archives a very carefully prepared paper by Alpheus
Briggs.[1]

The Quakers were responsible to a large degree for shaping
the political and ethical character of the colony, because for over
a quarter of a century they were the only active organized religious
body, and held many public offices. A sufficient number of persons
were awakened spiritually and several meetings for worship were
established. The earliest was Perquimans Monthly Meeting, later
known as Wells. Many other centers developed and such was the
importance of Eastern Quarterly Meeting that for eighty-eight
years the Yearly Meeting was held either at Perquimans (Old
Neck) or Little River (all in Perquimans County). The present

---

* The Quarterly Meetings are arranged alphabetically in the Yearly Meeting
Minutes and other records, but a distinguished Friend suggests the arrangement
followed here as more fitting for an historical record. The records of the Eastern
Quarter are somewhat confusing because of the difference of the names used, as was
mentioned in discussing the microfilm records — some of the records are labelled:
"Perquimans, Wells and Perquimans," one "Piney Woods and Perquimans," and
others "Eastern Quarter." The same monthly meeting convened at three different
places.

meetings are Piney Woods (Belvidere), 1794 and Up River (Whiteston), 1867.

DISTINGUISHED VISITORS. In spite of the great distance of Eastern Quarter from New Garden — 250 miles — three very remarkable travelling Friends visited Eastern Quarter, namely John Woolman (1720-1772), Thomas Shillitoe (1754-1836), and Stephen Grellet (1775-1855). These Friends had much in common, save that Grellet was of noble French lineage, while Woolman and Shillitoe were of English extraction. They were each puritanical and abstemious; they practiced holiness; they were given to much walking, even incredible distances; they were great humanitarians, being concerned especially with the evils of slavery; they were diligent in visiting from house to house; they were each possessed of incomprehensible courage; they did not hesitate if they believed it to be the Lord's will to plead with emperors, kings, rulers and dignitaries; yet they also visited prisons and saloons; they were considerable penmen; and were indeed Apostles. They stirred Eastern Quarter. John Woolman says that between six and seven hundred attended meetings at which he preached. It may truly be said that these extraordinary Quakers were saints and mystics. Every Friend should become acquainted with them.

PINEY WOODS MONTHLY MEETING. According to old records there were Friends meeting here, at Belvidere, by 1754 and probably earlier. The group became a monthly meeting in 1794. The four acres of land upon which the meeting house now stands consists of one acre given by Joseph Newby and three acres purchased from Thomas Newby in 1832 for $20.00. The yearly meeting was held in 1788 at Wells located between Winfall and Belvidere. Wells meeting was discontinued and Piney Woods established in 1794. Before that date meetings had been held at five places in Perquimans — Little River, Suttons Creek, Old Neck, Vosges Creek (now Brights Creek) and Wells. This last named group set off Suttons Creek Monthly Meeting then transferred itself to Piney Woods Monthly Meeting at Belvidere in 1794. However, in an old book entitled: *Memoirs of the Life of Catherine Phillips,* an English Friend, printed in 1798 there is this statement: "On the sixth of second month, 1754, we reached Perquimans River, where the main body of Friends in the province is settled. Our first meeting among them was at Piney Woods meeting house, which was pretty large considering shortness of time allowed, to give notice of it. We visited two other meetings in this quarter." Catherine Phillips and her companion rode horseback. She encountered difficulties upon some ice over the Perquimans River and was injured by a fall.

In 1788 the meeting house at Old Neck was wrecked by a storm and the annual gathering was therefore held subsequently at Wells, which eventually became Piney Woods Monthly Meeting. The Yearly Meeting assembled in the East till 1791, when for the first time it was held at New Garden. From that date (with few exceptions) it met alternately at New Garden and in the Eastern Quarter.

In other records dated between 1736 and 1770 there is a reference to Piney Woods: "At a monthly meeting held at Perquimans second of sixth month, 1762 . . . this meeting taking into consideration the request of the Friends that desired to have the week day meetings that had been settled at Caleb Elliott's removed to the Piney Woods meeting house, and Friends agree thereto." This shows that Friends have worshipped at Piney Woods for two hundred years, but how much longer is uncertain. The records of these early gatherings are sprinkled with well-known Quaker names, including Albertson, Bagley, Blanchard, Cannon, Elliott, Knight, Maudlin, Mendenhall, Moore, Newby, Nicholson, Nixon, Parker, Sanders, Smith, Toms, White, Williams, Wilson and Winslow. There is also a record of a house of worship at Simons Creek, near Nixontown, in Pasquotank between 1702 and 1706. This was the second place of worship in the colony. The old meeting house was replaced some years ago. According to custom the early house had partitions separating the men from the women at the business sessions, and the Quaker garb of course was in vogue. There was no pre-arrangement and the worshippers sat in silence and meditation for a portion or even the whole of the hour. If a woman Friend had a "concern" to communicate to the men's business meeting, she first presented the matter to the women and asked permission to visit the other meeting. If the request were granted a woman Friend was named to be her companion and the door-keeper would take a message to the door-keeper of the men's meeting; he would take it to the clerk, who would read it to the meeting; it would then be solemnly and silently considered for a while and then discussed before permission would be given. The woman Friend would then be admitted, advance to the clerk's table and deliver herself of her concern.

The Discipline required simple living and plainness in all affairs. It is on record that Dinah Carver, a minister, was "eldered" for riding in a gig and carrying an umbrella.

At Piney Woods we have a survival of the good seed scattered by Edmundson and Fox in 1672. The latter was only in the colony eighteen days, and yet the harvest continues till this day. Like all Quaker settlements in the east the numbers were depleted as family after family trekked to the Piedmont — especially to the New Garden and Deep River settlements. Because of the lack of ministering Friends the members believed themselves justified in inviting a person who had a gift in the ministry to reside among them. Adelbert Wood in 1915 was the first minister in this area to receive remuneration. Later ministers included Absolam Knight, John C. Trivette, Herman Parker, Bertha Smith White, Howard Yow, J. Waldo Woody, Benjamin H. Millikan, Claude Bullock and Virgil Pike. The work is well maintained; there are 225 members; Bible School, 178; Grace C. Ward is clerk. A special service was held October 3, 1954, to commemorate the 160th anniversary of the organization of a monthly meeting. Clyde A. Milner, the President of Guilford College, was the guest speaker.

BELVIDERE ACADEMY. This famous Quaker school was established by Little River Quarterly Meeting in 1833, but until the school building was completed sessions were held in the Piney Woods Meeting House. Difficulties were experienced in finding qualified teachers locally as there were few institutions of higher learning in eastern Carolina so help was secured from New York and New England. The school gained reputation, and students came from adjoining counties, and for many years the school performed a valuable service. Schools were scarce and the disturbed conditions throughout the South prevented the development of a State supported elementary school system. Friends' children thus were able to secure advantages not generally shared, and it is likely that there was a higher standard of culture than elsewhere.

In 1899 the property was conveyed to Piney Woods Monthly Meeting. The most outstanding teacher was Mary J. White, affectionately known as Miss Minnie, and her service of twenty-one years is an integral part of the history of Quakerism in this community. Timothy Nicholson also served as a teacher, but his life's story is so important that it is given separate treatment here. The old building was replaced in 1903; and in 1914 the Academy was sold to the county, which then took over the responsibility of elementary education. The old building was destroyed by fire in 1935.[2]

Friends also conducted an elementary school at Aurora for

several years. The land was donated by Elias Elliott, a maternal grandfather of Mable Ward Wolff; and Jaspar Thompson was among the teachers. As was common in many places this denominational school was discontinued when the State public school system was established.

UP RIVER MONTHLY MEETING. The group of Friends at Whiteston was originally included in the Piney Woods Meeting (where members had worshipped prior to 1754), and remained such till 1901. The old meeting house was probably constructed in 1875 and the first known monthly meeting held there was on twelfth of fifth month, 1914 and Up River was granted monthly meeting status in 1946. As in all the other eastern settlements, family after family moved away to the Piedmont. Because of the lack of Friends with a gift in the ministry the members united in asking Elizabeth White to become pastor. For 52 years up to 1933 this consecrated person was the minister and pastor.* In recent years considerable improvements have been made to the property — additional class rooms, a heating plant and a suitable residence for the minister. James Rayenkamp served 1953-1955 and since then Orval Dillon has been in residence. The meeting is in a healthy condition and all departments are growing. The membership is 294; the Bible School, 218.   Linwood Winslow, Eunice Winslow and Merrill Winslow have served as clerks.

ELIZABETH ELLA LANE WHITE is a typical example of a colonial Quakeress. Probably no other religious organization could have afforded at that time such a field of service to a woman. She came of English stock, being a daughter of Columbus and Mary Winslow Lane, and was born on November 24, 1866; she was a life-long resident of Whiteston in Perquimans County. Her father passed on when she was but seven. At nineteen she was married to Robert J. White, a Friend, and it is part and parcel of the history of Eastern Quarter that the Whites and the Winslows should intermarry. Such families have been and still are the backbone of Quakerism and public service in that community.

    She commenced to speak in meeting before she was out of her teens, (and it is far more than probable that the most esteemed among ministering Friends responded to the Inward Call in their youth). For fifty-two years she was resident minister and pastor of the Up River Meeting, and her whole life was a benediction to

---

* See next section for further particulars concerning Elizabeth White.

the community. She said, "My husband was very faithful in making the way for me to attend different meetings and funerals, but he left us in 1938." Elizabeth White was a faithful minister; her testimony to Christ as a personal Saviour was clear and convincing; she supported all movements for good citizenship; her visits to members were "concerned visits" not mere social calls. She continued her courageous and steadfast service until she was within a few weeks of ninety years of age, and passed away November 9, 1956. She was survived by a son and daughter, fifteen grandchildren, thirty great-grandchildren and three great-great-grandchildren.[3]

LINWOOD C. WINSLOW one of the pillars of Up River Meeting was stricken while attending yearly meeting in 1957 and was conveyed to a hospital at Edenton, but expired after surgery. He had served the meeting in numerous capacities, such as elder, trustee, teacher of the Men's Bible Class and clerk of the quarterly meeting. His passing in the prime of life is a great loss to the yearly meeting.

TIMOTHY NICHOLSON. The Nicholsons were among the leading colonists from the first. There is a record of Christopher Nicholson acquiring land under the Great Deed of the Lords Proprietor in 1673, and early Quaker meetings were held in his house. The family became recognized as proponents of education, temperance and religion. Joseph Nicholson was born in 1797, and married a widow with three children. Three sons were born of this union, John, Timothy and William. The father determined to provide a worthy education for the children, and as there was no institution of higher learning near the Dismal Swamp the girls were sent to a Friends' school in Delaware, and the boys after attending Belvidere Academy went to a Quaker school in Providence, Rhode Island.

Timothy was possessed of the mysterious gift of leadership, and his masterful ability was early recognized. He became the most influential Friend of his generation and as he had his origin in Eastern Quarter it is fitting that he should be mentioned in connection with the birthplace of Quakerism in North Carolina.

The Nicholson family is described a happy family; the home life was based upon the products of the farm, and all the children were required to cooperate in the tasks common to a frontier community. Family worship and regular attendance at the First Day and Fifth Day meetings at Piney Woods were never neglected. The sons of Josiah Nicholson received sound religious instruction, healthy exercise upon the plantation, a broad education and high ideals which fitted them for Christian leadership. Timothy became the natural leader, not only of his family but in Quakerism in what may be termed the critical period. Upon returning from Providence he learned that the school at Belvidere had been closed because of the lack of a teacher, and Timothy, contrary to his intentions was called upon to be the teacher. The school house was dingy and poorly equipped. Timothy solicited subscriptions to improve the premises, and horrified the community by painting it white.* As a consequence the building became known as "the white school". Under Timothy's supervision the academy gained reputation, and the attendance increased. In 1852 another room was added and extra equipment provided, and his brothers John and Josiah assisted in the teaching.

Timothy and his wife Sarah (the daughter of John and Mary White, superintendent and matron) were appointed representatives to the North Carolina Yearly Meeting held at New Garden by the Piney Woods Quarterly Meeting. This involved a journey with horse and buggy of 250 miles from Belvidere. There were practically no roads worthy of the name and no towns where they might rest overnight. The accommodations they found were primitive.

So famous did Timothy become as an educator that Haverford College offered him a position as Head of the Preparatory Department. Some years later upon the death of President Harlan, he was elected Superintendent of Haverford College, having all the duties and responsibilities of a business manager. In recognition of his services there is a stone archway at the entrance of a greenhouse known as "Timothy's Arch".

During the 50's, the ever-increasing turbulence because of the slavery issue, a tremendous exodus of Friends and others from the South took place. The first lap of the journey was Indiana, and the chief center was Richmond. Among others the Whites, Winslows and Nicholsons joined the band of fugitives, for such they were, as the realization of an "Impending Crisis" became clearer year by year.

Timothy and his family left Haverford and joined his former neighbors at the Quaker settlement at Richmond, Indiana. Here he united with his brother John in the management of a book store,

---

* Within the memory of the writer any person in some rural areas of North Carolina who painted his house was regarded as "uppity" by his neighbors.

and he soon became known as "the master Quaker." He made his influence felt in every phase of civic life, not only in the city, not only in the State of Indiana, but throughout the whole Quaker world. For fifty-five years he was a member of the Board of Trustees of Earlham College, and occupied every position of honor in his own meeting and in the yearly meeting. He had much to do with the various Quaker conferences which resulted in the preparation of the Declaration of Faith, and the coming into existence of the Five Years Meeting. Through his statesmanship he helped tide the Society from the old Quietist pattern to the pastoral system. He was Chairman of the American Friends Service Committee and of Indiana Division of Russian Relief.

He was familiarly and affectionately called "the Grand Old Man of Quakerism." He was a forceful lobbyist, and he was often at the State Legislature using his influence especially for temperance and humanitarian legislation. He was a reformer, educator, pacifist and constructive citizen. No public interest was beyond his attention. In Friends' business meetings he was always "a weighty member" and his judgment was seldom unheeded.

He reached the venerable age of ninety-five, and without question was the first citizen of Richmond, Indiana. His brother John removed to Baltimore; William studied medicine, and for several years practiced at Belvidere, later removing to Kansas; Josiah Nicholson remained in his native town. All remained faithful to the principles of Friends, and each held positions of responsibility.[4]

A MEMORIAL. On June 11, 1929, a commemorative pageant was held at Hertford to mark the spot where William Edmundson first preached the Gospel in the colony of North Carolina. A goodly company of Friends assembled from many parts of the yearly meeting. Henry White, of High Point impersonated Governor John Archdale, he and other Friends wore the historic Quaker garb, and to give greater reality to the occasion several masqueraded as Indians and the writer enjoyed the fun of scaring Palefaces with a simulated war whoop and brandishing a make-believe tomahawk. The marker was a granite block 3.5 feet in height; with an inscription upon a metal plate and was erected on Church Street near the Perquimans River bridge. The marker was designed by Alpheus M. Briggs and the inscription by Mary M. Petty. The inscription reads:

EDMUNDSON-FOX MEMORIAL

"Near this spot William Edmundson, an English Friend, held in May, 1672, the first religious service on record in North Carolina. Six months later George Fox, the founder of the Society of Friends, also visited this section and held meetings among the colonists. Here were the beginnings of the religious life of a great State."

Erected June 11, 1929, by North Carolina Yearly Meeting of Friends.

RICH SQUARE. (Orthodox) Friends settled in this community at about the same time that the New Garden settlement was commenced — about 1750, and there is evidence that meetings for worship were held at Edgecomb and Hertford Counties soon afterwards. In 1760 a monthly meeting was set up by the authority of Eastern Quarterly Meeting, and in 1774 a meeting house was built at Jack Swamp in Northampton County. By 1782 a migration set in and many Friends transferred their membership from Tar River to Contentnea Quarter. A list of these Friends is extant in the old Record books which William Marshall caused to be re-typed and re-bound. By 1800 the migration to the Piedmont was in full swing and some travelled as far as Ohio. In 1812 those who remained at Jack Swamp were united with the Rich Square meeting, which retained the characteristics of the Quietist congregations, the membership being largely birthright.

In 1903 the North Carolina Yearly Meeting united with the Five Years Meeting, favored the Richmond Declaration of Faith and the pastoral system. This caused great perturbation among the Conservative element at Rich Square and resulted in a separation, a large number withdrawing from the Yearly Meeting and affiliating with the Conservative Yearly Meeting in Ohio.*

The Orthodox continued their organization but the numbers progressively declined. Gurney Wright, from Ohio, was pastor for many years. W. Jasper Thompson and Bertha V. Smith (White) also did pastoral work, but a few years ago at a Quarterly Meeting it was decided to discontinue the Rich Square meeting and recently the property was returned to the Ward family which had provided the land.

The record books which Marshall restored include five volumes of the Men's Monthly Meeting from 1760 to 1925; four volumes of the Women's Meeting from 1750 to 1928; two volumes of births and deaths; one volume of the Men's Meeting and one volume of the Women's Meeting at Jack Swamp. The births and deaths oc-

---

* For an account of the Conservative Meeting at Rich Square see chap. xxvii.

cupy 37 large typed pages; the marriages 20 pages; the genealogies 60 pages in professional arrangement. This set of books constitute a veritable gold mine. Numerous records of disownments occur; for example, in 1847 Elizabeth Johnson was dismissed from membership for "using the plural language and absenting herself from meeting;" some "for holding fellow men in bondage;" several "condemned their marriages out of meeting." Some of these offenders were re-instated, some were not.[5]

CHAPTER TWENTY

YET BEING MANY ARE ONE BODY

CONTENTNEA QUARTERLY MEETING mostly in Wayne county, was established in 1789. At first it grew rapidly, and a large number of congregations were set up, but due to the various factors which have been discussed hundreds of families moved away, and meetings at Bear Creek, Core Sound, Falling Creek, Trent, Club Foot Creek, Hood Swamp, Mattamuskee, Lower Trent, Tar River, Turner Swamp and Upper Trent were discontinued. The dates of the existing meetings supplied by the clerks do not always agree with a list prepared by Alpheus Briggs preserved at the yearly meeting archives at Guilford College library, but discrepancies may be expected in ancient records. The following meetings are active: Bethany, Bethesda, Goldsboro, Hood Swamp, Nahunta, Neuse, New Hope, Oakland, Rhodes and Woodland.[1]

Among the great services rendered by William Wade Hinshaw and William Marshall was the decipherment and typing of an old minute book entitled the "Minutes of Great Contentnea, Neuse and Woodland Meetings." The minutes date from 1748, but Contentnea Quarterly Meeting was not established till 1789. The first settlement appears to have been at Falling Creek. "The Friends in Johnson County upon the New (Neuse) River, request Friends of Eastern Quarterly Meeting to grant them the privilege of a monthly meeting till yearly meeting because of their present necessities, to be either approved or disapproved by the Ensueing yearly meeting," taken from the minutes third month, twenty-eighth, 1748. The request was approved, but few records of Falling Creek survive. In 1772 the meeting was discontinued, and some members were transferred to Contentnea. From 1772 to 1851 the monthly meeting alternated between Contentnea and Nahunta. The Women's Record books terminate at eighth month, nineteenth, 1774, and it presumed the women then ceased to hold separate business meetings. This record book contains entries which are typical and which may be found by the hundreds in the books of that period: "In 1851 John Kennedy condemned his marriage out of unity," which means he read in meeting an apology, and thus saved himself from possible disownment, and in the next year the same person was disowned "for favoring slavery." In 1847 Smithson Moore was disowned "for joining the malician" (militia). Between 1842 and 1874 eleven members of one family were disowned for various offences.[2]

Contentnea Quarterly Meeting suffered perhaps more by the mass movement to the west than any other section for the counties of Beaufort, Craven, Cartaret, Hyde and Jones were depopulated of Quakers. As related fully elsewhere the membership of Trent migrated in a body. Weeks says the flight was "sweeping and emphatic". Friends discussed the matter several times in meeting; some were loath to depart for fear it would break up the meeting. "They were concerned many times to weigh the matter in the balance of the sanctuary." Each member received a certificate of removal and then the meeting was authorized to deliver the records to the Quarterly Meeting, which was done on first month, eighteenth, 1800.

This quarter was destined to go through the fire again, for in the Civil War it was between the armies of Sherman of the Unionist Army and Johnstone of the Confederates. The Northerners occupied Goldsboro for twenty days, and thoroughly ravaged the community.

Fernando Cartland gives a vivid account of the brutal treatment that Thomas Kennedy and Lazarus Pearson suffered because of their adherence to Quaker peace principles.[3]

Among the valued ministers in Contentnea Quarter in the early part of this century were J. Addison Branson, Micajah T. Cox, William U. Grantham, George Jernigan, I. Lindley Jones, John S. Moore, D. Virgil Pike, William Pelt, Thomas Smith. Somewhat later came Palmer Holt, Robert O. Crow, Margaret Farlow, Tennyson Lewis, Absolam Knight, William Garrison, Estelle Garrison, Howard Yow, Clifton C. Pearson, Hugh W. Moore.

BETHANY MEETING was started at an inauspicious time — in 1868 — just after the area had been ravaged by the Civil War. As stated elsewhere the whole South was called "prostrate"; the Federal troops were in possession, and the K.K.K. was intimidating all office holders; anarchy ran riot in many places. The meeting never had a chance to grow and prosper; the few members have shown steadfastness and loyalty, but Quakerism proved to be unpopular in this area. The membership is 35, and there are but eight households. Ezra Jinnete is clerk; Quarterly Meeting assembles there in fourth month. The ministers have included Palmer Holt, Virgil Pike, Robert Crow (nine years), John M. Pitkin, Edward and Lola Scott, John C. Trivette, Harold Jernigan.

BETHESDA MONTHLY MEETING dates from November, 1886 as a preparative meeting; the monthly meeting was established in 1908. A meeting house was built in 1886, and remodelled in 1938. The home of the minister is valued at $5,000.00. Those who have been active in the ministry include John Moore, John S. Moore, Whitford Edgerton, Absolam Knight, Tennyson Lewis, D. Virgil Pike, Lela Sills Garner, Hershel Hill, Gene Lewis, Elbert Newlin, and at present J. Waldo Smith. The present clerk is Hubert H. Warren. Others who have rendered valuable assistance include Ann Warren, Silas W. Cox, Julius E. Lee, Virgie Warren, Blaney Smith, Bettie Smith, Iola Warren, Ettie Warren Lucas, Iva Dixon, Maggie Dawson, Lillian Warren, Dora W. Knight, Daisy Warren, Mittie Sills, Emmett Edgerton, Sr., Leonard Hodges, Hubert H. Warren. A hut was constructed in 1949 and is very useful for social gatherings. The membership is 147; the Bible School numbers 107. The church is rendering an influence for good in the community.

CORE SOUND MONTHLY MEETING. We are indebted to William Marshall for the decipherment, typing and binding of the minutes of this meeting. Core Sound was probably the first Quaker settlement in this region and the nucleus of the Contentnea Quarterly Meeting. About 1733 several Friends families settled on "Neuport River," in Cartaret County, and were "well concerned and thought it their duty to meet together on the First Day of the week and the First Day of eighth month at the house of William Borden." Permission was granted and the meeting established. The records deciphered by Marshall exhibit the familiar pattern of "eldering" and disownment. Mittie Chadwick (formerly Harris) was required on 5-14-1783 "to condemn her marriage out of unity." She was disowned, but re-instated 9-1-1787; only to be disowned once more in 8-29-1807 for joining a Methodist society. Between 1781 and 1813 there are eight entries of disownment on page 14; on the next page there are nine such entries; on 1-28-1826 Enoch Davis was disowned for marrying out, but sixteen months later he was re-admitted by request. On 9-28-1811 James Hall was severed from the Society for owning slaves. The "western fever" smote this meeting, and certificates were issued for 13 families before 1801; 12 about 1810; and 21 between 1831 and 1840. The meeting disappeared in 1841.[4]

GOLDSBORO Friends in 1906 purchased premises from another denomination. The present property dates from 1926. Waldo Woody was largely responsible for the setting up of the monthly meeting, which has steadily grown and now has a membership of 325, with an attendance at Bible School of 219. Four young men have received a gift in the ministry and have been recorded by the Goldsboro congregation. They are Clifton C. Pearson, Robert O. Crow, Theodore E. Perkins and Gene Lewis. Others who have labored in the ministry include Joseph H. Peele, William G. Hubbard, Thomas Hodgin, Alvin C. Barrett, William W. Garrison, I. Lindley Jones, Tennyson Lewis, Calvin Gregory, Bascom G. Rollins, John Permar, Elbert D. Newlin, Phillip Griffin, Frank J. Long and Virgil Pike. The following have served as clerks: Nathan D. Andrews (who will long be remembered for his great interest in Foreign Missions), Loren Pearson, Leslie Barrett, Eschol Edgerton, Estella Garrison, Cedric Edgerton, Thomas Crow, Osmond Pate, Wendell Edgerton, Eli F. Pate, Annie Bell Edgerton, Luby Casey (who in recent years has dedicated himself to raising funds for caring for aged ministers) and Rosa Glisson at present.

A FAMILY RE-UNION. On the second Sunday in September the McClenny clan holds its annual re-union at the Goldsboro meeting house. It requires just a few words to record the event, but the occasion deserves comment because of its significance. This is just one example of a wide-spread, deep-seated and ancient tradition. The practice prevails among most Protestant groups. It probably had its origin in antiquity when relatives and friends experienced an urge to visit their home folks once again, and when nostalgia overpoweringly drove wanderers back to the place of their childhood! It is fitting, and characteristic of a Christian civilization, that these homecomings should be associated with a place of worship made sacred by a thousand memories.

These gatherings are advertized, though that is hardly necessary, for they are established institutions, and in many places among the great events of the year. As one of the McClennies said to the writer: "I can meet and visit with more of my kinfolk and neighbors on this one day than I could possibly visit separately in a whole year."

The church in question makes the occasion a rally day, and a record attendance is secured; a preacher of note is invited; special singing is arranged, and of course the occasion merits a picnic lunch, which if weather permits, is partaken of under the trees.

The person is to be pitied who has not shared such an experience. These gatherings mean much to rural folk, and do much to keep religion at the heart of their social life.

HOOD SWAMP was set up by Nahunta Monthly Meeting as a Preparative Meeting. The membership was too few to guarantee continued growth. No minutes are on record from 3-5-1904 to 7-4-1908, when it was decided to re-establish the meeting. The records are missing between 1-1914 and 11-1-1919, when there was again an attempt at reorganization. In 11-6-1920 a Quarterly Meeting was held at Hood Swamp. In 1927 Benjamin H. Millikan was pastor. Dorothy G. Thorne rendered a valuable service in copying the original minutes in 1953, including a list of members and also the birthright members. At one time the pastor received a salary of $12.50 per month. Recent pastors include D. Virgil Pike, Lela Sills Garner, Howard B. Yow, Lola Simpson Scott, Elbert Newlin, Harrison Hinshaw. The membership is about 50. Velda Faye Howell is clerk.

NAHUNTA is a continuation of an earlier meeting known as Contentnea. It originated in a private house. The present clerk gives the date as 1788; Alpheus Briggs puts it as 1772, and monthly meeting as of 1856. At an early date the Friends met near Fremont not far from Contentnea Creek on the Quaker Road. Later they assembled on what is known as the Alex Aycock property. In 1896 the Pike family gave a plot of ground and a house of worship was built near Pike's Cross Roads. Still later Nathan Edgerton donated two acres of land for the site of the present meeting place, and Tom Edgerton and many others gave time and labor in the construction of the building. A portion of the Bible School department was built during the pastorate of Elbert Newlin and later additions were made during the service of Lela Sills Garner. In the spring of 1955 the property was redecorated and much improved. This Quaker settlement in the nineteenth century experienced all the vicissitudes which befell a land afflicted with slavery, war and mass evacuation, but since the adoption of the pastoral system there has been a steady growth and interest.

Those who have assisted in the ministry include Henry McKinley, Clifton C. Pearson, D. Virgil Pike, Benjamin H. Millikan, Elbert D. Newlin, Howard Yow, J. Waldo Woody, Lola Simpson Scott, Luther McPherson, Homer Barker, Lewis Dillman, Blake Wright, Paul Osborne, Lela Sills Garner and Buford Frye. The clerks have included in recent years Cora Aycock, Ora Bell Sasser,

Mary Elizabeth Davis. The membership totals 200, and the Bible School has an enrollment of about that same number.

NEUSE MONTHLY MEETING. This meeting in the Contentnea Quarter is one of the older congregations. The place of worship was built in 1782, but gatherings had been held in the home of Richard Cox for fifteen years or more before that date. The meeting house was rebuilt in 1841. The following have served as resident ministers: Abbie Hollowell, W. U. Grantham, Micajah Cox, William Pelt, Virgil Pike, Addison Branson, Absolam Knight, Robert Crow, John C. Trivette, Theodore Perkins, Harold Jernigan, Edward C. and Lola S. Scott. The following have served as clerks: Ella Perkins, Albert Perkins. The membership is 37, and 85 attend the Bible School.

NEW HOPE MEETING was established in 1876; the membership is now 103; attendance at Bible School, 154. Among those who have preached the Gospel are: Esther Garrison, Sally Foushee, Benjamin H. Millikan, John S. Moore, Howard Yow, Lola Simpson (Scott), Elbert Newlin, Thomas Smith, J. Waldo Woody, Harrison Hinshaw, Lela S. Garner at the time of this writing. Margaret Daniels is clerk. Among distinguished Friends who have worshipped and labored here may be mentioned: Annie Daniels, John B. Best, Lottie Hinnant, Eunice Hinnant, Nannie Grant, Lillie Whitley, John Daniels, Vivian Webber, Carrie Wilson, Mary Alma Anderson, Jesse Whitley, R. M. Wilson. This congregation in common with many rural areas holds Bible School regularly, but the preaching service is irregular as the itinerant ministers serve two or three and sometimes four congregations at scattered places. Until the arrival in recent years of the automobile many of these preachers spent hours upon the road travelling from one appointment to another. An understanding of the hardships and discouragements merits only appreciation. As there is no Bible teaching in the public schools, and as there is little background of Quaker practice, the rigorous life in rural areas affords little feasibility for persons reared under such circumstances to maintain a meeting for worship according to the conservative pattern. It can be said that the ministrations of these rural pastors and the community church services do bring regular attenders unto fellowship with one another and with the Heavenly Father through Christ and worthy citizens are developed.[5]

OAKLAND MONTHLY MEETING is another Quaker center within Contentnea Quarter. The congregation assembled as an outcome of a wide-spread revival movement. Extracts from the minutes of the Neuse Quarterly Meeting held January 28, 1882 read "Friends on the north side of the Neuse river request an 'indulgence meeting' to be held on the First Day of the week, with which this meeting unites and grants the request of said meeting to be held in Grantham's schoolhouse." It is of interest to note that this school house was one of the oldest in the county. It was built by David I. Grantham, who hired and paid the teachers; the students paid a small fee.

There are also on record excerpts from a monthly meeting held at Bethany, February 4, 1882 to the effect: "The Quarterly Meeting grants the privilege of setting up an 'indulgence meeting' at David I. Grantham's schoolhouse on the north side of Neuse River to be held on the First Day of the week. Isaac H. Cox, L. J. Moore, Abbie Hollowell and Mary E. Cox are appointed a committee to attend the opening of said meeting and report to our next monthly meeting. This committee was also empowered with a Christian oversight of said meeting for one year."

"On September 1, 1883, the question of circulating this meeting in order to hold the meeting in twelfth, third, sixth and ninth month at Oakland was laid before the meeting. After much deliberation it was united with." The first meeting held at Oakland was on December 1, 1883, but it was not until December 4, 1915, that Oakland meeting was set apart from Neuse. The building committee of Oakland meeting consisted of: William U. Grantham, David I. Grantham and Hilry Hastings. Much initiative and resourcefulness was exercised by these Friends, and it is recorded that they encountered much criticism, but we are not told why. The record says they labored hard to create interest. The actual construction began March 1, 1883. Lumber was donated by David Grantham, bricks by H. Weil and Brothers, of Goldsboro; John Wright, Richard and John Uzzell were the actual builders, with assistance from many local Friends. The building was completed in July, 1883, at a cost of about $1,100. The members were gratified at their accomplishment for the building was superior to the usual country church. The dedicatory sermon was preached by Nathan Perry. A small rural church encounters many difficulties, and for many years the financial burden was hard to carry, especially when it is recalled that the whole Southland had been impoverished by the Civil War and degraded by the subsequent so-called Reconstruction Period which lasted until the Federal troops were withdrawn in 1877-78.

Among those who bore the financial burden were: David I. Grantham, Isaac Cox, Jessie Hollowell and Calvin Perkins. The charter members included David I. Grantham, Polly Grantham, Curtis Hastings and wife, Maynard Grantham, William U. Grantham, Louisa Fail, John Batten, Beabie Batten, Polly Tyner, Richard Collins and wife, America Collins, Axie Howell, Josephine Fail.

Since the building of the meeting house repairs and additions have been made from time to time in the construction of rooms for the Bible School and remodelling. The lighting system and the heating have been modernized and in 1918 a piano was substituted for a small organ. To effect these improvements $1,140.50 was subscribed by local Friends and $300.00 from the Charleston fund of the Philadelphia Yearly Meeting; gifts of material and labor were valued at $365.00. Appropriate dedicatory services were held on the third Sunday in April, 1937. A burying ground has been provided at the back of the premises, and the body of Polly Cox, the wife of David I. Grantham, was the first to be interred there.

Among those who are affectionately remembered for their ministry are: L. John Moore, William U. Grantham, Barney Perkins, Louisa S. Bridges, Milner A. Cox, William Pelt, Leslie Barrett, J. Addison Branson, Henry McKinley, Benjamin H. Millikan, Elbert Newlin, Howard Yow, J. Waldo Woody, Lela Sills Garner, Luther McPherson, Blake Wright, Buford Frye and Paul Osborne. Among the clerks have been Eunice Neal, Simpson King, Julia Mae Worby, Leona Oats. The membership is about 175; the Sunday School, 200.[6]

RHODES MONTHLY MEETING is within the limits of Contentnea Quarterly Meeting. This is a new and small meeting, yet rendering a needed service to the community. The congregation was authorized in 1890, and the meeting house was secured seven years later. In common with other rural meetings it has experienced difficulties, as the membership was for years less than fifty, with an attendance of about seventy in the Bible School. Among those who have served as ministers are: John S. Moore, Robert O. Crow (eleven years), John C. Trivette, John Pipkin, Billy Britt, Margaret Brown, Edward and Lola Simpson Scott and Paul Andrew. The clerks have been Mary Pipkin, Edna Price, John Pipkin, Thomas Grantham, Emma Anderson and Wilbert Hatch. On the third Sunday of each ninth month this meeting holds its annual homecoming and charter members and others attend in large numbers. Robert O. Crow brought the message in 1957. In that same year a series of special services was conducted by James Marion, and there were a number of professions of faith and nine persons were admitted to membership.

WOODLAND* is located in Wayne County not far from Goldsboro. It is believed that some Friends were settled here about 1860 and they were members of Neuse Meeting till Woodland was set up in 1883. There was a meeting house by 1876. For a while the sessions alternated between Woodland and New Hope, but the latter was set off as an autonomous body in 1876. Later Woodland Friends purchased a former school house in 1919-20 from the Wayne County Commissioners. Among those who have been active in the ministry are: Lancaster John Moore, John S. Moore, Micajah T. Cox, D. Virgil Pike, Absolam Knight, Benjamin H. Millikan, Calvin Gregory, Bascom Rollins, Margaret Farlow, John C. Trivett, Theodore Perkins, Harold Jernigan, Edward C. and Lola Simpson Scott and Paul and Pauline Andrew. Mrs. Willie Edwards is clerk.

Recent reports indicate that the Quaker Men, the Young Adults and the Women's Missionary Society are active; improvements have been made to the minister's residence and a building fund for Bible School additions is being accumulated. There is a membership of 86, and a Bible School of about the same number. This group of Friends conducted the famous Woodland Academy** which served an invaluable purpose in the post-war and Reconstruction era. Many persons who distinguished themselves in public service received their early education here. I. Clarkson Blair and wife Stella were the first teachers. Cyrus P. Frazier followed and rendered self-sacrificial service for three-and-a-half years, Julia F. Mendenhall also participated in this service. Conditions were very primitive throughout the South. Woodland Academy was one of the schools maintained by Friends during this troublous period. As mentioned elsewhere in many districts the schools operated by the Quakers were the only ones.

---

* Woodland — Not to be identified with the Conservative Meeting of the same name. See chap xxvii.
** See chap ix under Educational Activities.

CHAPTER TWENTY-ONE

ALL MEMBERS HAVE NOT THE SAME OFFICE

WESTERN QUARTERLY MEETING which straddled Chatham, Alamance, Orange and Guilford Counties was established in 1759. This quarter, in common with the whole yearly meeting, suffered because of Friends testimony against slavery, secession and war, and was almost decimated by the same emigration engineered in large part by Addison Coffin. Meetings, many of them quite small, were laid down — including Brush Creek, Dixon, Eno, Ivy Creek, Kirby's Longs, Mill Creek, Prosperity Ridge, Sandy Creek, Tratten Creek, Tysons and also Fredericksburg and Piney Grove in South Carolina.[1] The Quarterly Meeting now comprises active congregations at Cane Creek, Centre, Chatham, Concord, Edward Hill, Graham, Liberty, Plainfield, Providence, Rocky River, South Fork and Spring.

The ministers who were active in this meeting in the first quarter of this century were: Margaret B. Hackney, Rufus Pegg, Thomas J. Dixon, Rufus P. King, Georgia G. Reece, Herbert W. Reynolds, Jeremiah S. Cox, Alfred I. Zachary, Alfred H. Harris, Oscar Cox, Edward Harris, Clarence Macon, Henry Wrenn and John Permar.

CANE CREEK MEETING. It is believed that Friends began to settle in this area by 1720, and a record book preserved in the archives says that Friends came from Pennsylvania, Maryland and Virginia by way of Cape Fear River and founded a meeting for worship in 1727. The land on which they located is described as beautiful and is within the present counties of Chatham and Orange. By 1730 there were several meetings for worship. The preserved records begin October 7, 1751. Additional Friends in the next few years arrived from Pennsylvania, Maryland, New Jersey, New England, Ireland and England. Names of two hundred persons of 48 families are known. A feature of this settlement is that large families were the rule. The record quoted says: ten families had nine children each; thirteen had ten; ten had eleven; seven had twelve; six had thirteen; two had fourteen; one had fifteen children, and that 90% of them grew to be adults. The report further says that faith in nature's medicines was almost a religious belief, for every family garnered roots, herbs, barks and nuts for medicinal purposes and the colonists were remarkably long-lived.[2]

By the authority of Eastern Quarterly Meeting the Cane Creek Monthly Meeting was established October 7, 1751, and sometime later Simon Dixon, a son of Thomas Dixon, of England, a mill-wright, settled at Cane Creek and brought quite a few relatives. Soon afterwards several members swarmed and set up Carver's Creek Meeting. It is not known whether Cane Creek ever passed through the "Preparative" stage. In 1754 William Marshall gave 26 acres of land to the Society and a meeting house was erected four years later, but as the law did not at that time permit religious bodies to hold title to real estate no deed could be delivered till 1801. It is of interest to note that New Garden Monthly Meeting was set up by Cane Creek. It was at this Quaker center that Herman Husband was disowned for his unbecoming conduct.[3] Action was taken by Friends here protesting against "mason made grave stones", and several tall stones were cut down. The troops of Lord Cornwallis camped here after the Battle of Guilford Court House (March 15, 1781) and helped themselves to hundreds of head of livestock and other provisions. The place received the name "Snow Camp" as a heavy snowstorm occurred at the time the British were encamped there. An old conventional meeting place was erected in 1879, which served till 1942, when a very substantial and commodious structure was built. Those who have rendered conspicuous service include: Eula Dixon, Oscar Cox, Edward Harris, Cora Lee Norman, Benjamin J. Millikan, Lewis McFarland, D. Virgil Pike, Elbert Newlin, J. Waldo Woody, Bascom G. Rollins and Willie R. Frye. The clerks are: Elbert Moon and Francis Coble. The membership is 352, and the Bible School has an enrollment of 220.

Laura D. Worth rendered a great service by thoroughly repairing the first minute book of 205 pages of this meeting — vol. 1, 1751-1796. The pages were torn, loose, discolored and almost illegible in places. She treated every page separately, binding the edges and attaching each page separately to the spine of the binding. It was a long, tedious, and painstaking task, and is just one example of her meticulous care and devotion.

For fifty years more than one-half of the records concern reception of members, marriages and disownments. It was the custom to give charivaris (pronounced "shivereez") a raucous midnight serenade to a newly married couple. Why that should have frequent mention in an old Quaker record book we do not know.

Among the worthy Friends who have lived, labored and worshipped at Snow Camp are families by the name of: Allen, Braxton, Cook, Dixon, Hadley, Holiday, Kimball, Lindley, Marshall, Moon, Newlin, Nicholson, Puryear, Pigott, Pike, Pugh, Scott, Stafford, Williamson, Wilson, White and Woody.

EULA DIXON.   The Society of Friends has produced many women who were possessed of far more than average abilities and who made distinctive contributions to the age in which they lived. Among such must be numbered Eula Dixon, of Snow Camp. She was born in 1872, the youngest of three daughters of Thomas and Ellen Albright Dixon, in a substantially built house of Georgian pattern. Lord Cornwallis is said to have visited the Dixon home, and the writer many years ago in visiting the home was shown the chair in which the General sat.

Eula Dixon received some elementary education at a frame school building at Sylvan and then attended New Garden Boarding School, but due to ill health could not continue till graduation. Later she enrolled at the Agricultural and Engineering College — now State College — at Raleigh. Her father died in 1899, and Eula became responsible for the management of a farm, a grist mill and a woolen mill. The business had been known as the Dixon Manufacturing Company, and under Eula's management was named the Snow Camp Flour Mill.

Eula Dixon had the reputation of being not only a successful business woman, but she passed on to the farmers of the community the knowledge and inspiration she had gained at the Agricultural College. It was a common saying that she knew more about farming than most of the men in Alamance County; she was ready to accept new ideas and to experiment. She cared little for convention, tradition or current notions and was essentially practical. Her obituary said she was the first person to be sent for in sickness, sorrow or death. She was a leader in the community in every worthwhile undertaking and a staunch supporter of the Quaker Church. She died at the age of 49 greatly beloved.[4]

CENTRE.   The history of this meeting goes back two decades before the signing of the Declaration of Independence. In 1750 William Hockett a pioneer Quaker from Pennsylvania arrived here. He met some Indians and somehow was able to let them know that he was from the land of William Penn. The natives welcomed him, for they knew of the Quaker attitude toward the Redskins. They treated him with every kindness, and with their approval and assistance he purchased from Lord Granville, one of the eight Lords Proprietor of the two "Carolanas", a section of land one mile square. Here Hockett built a rude log cabin. Nine years later he received a title to the land.

Other Quakers from Pennsylvania joined him, including John Bales, Richard Beeson, and Peter Dicks. At first there were no white neighbors within 18 miles, and the settlement became known as Centre because it was midway between the Quakers at Cane Creek and New Garden. They united in membership with New Garden which became a Monthly Meeting in 1754. As often as possible they walked or rode the long distance to attend meeting. In 1757 the New Garden Monthly Meeting granted them the right to worship from house to house. To provide a local place of worship there was purchased in 1763 a lot four rods square for twenty shillings. The little colony erected a log building, and two years later applied for the right to have their own monthly meeting. This was refused, and again deferred in 1768, but eventually granted by the Quarterly Meetings of Orange and Rowan in 1772 or 1773. By 1780 it was necessary to provide more accommodation for worship. The yearly meeting was held at Centre in 1787, at Perquimans the next year, and again at Centre in 1789. The records of the meeting for the first century were lost when the home of Obed Osborne was destroyed by fire.

Although the earliest minute book of this meeting was lost, an examination of the marriage, birth and death records reveals this as a meeting having among its members a number of the earliest settlers in this section bearing well-known North Carolina Quaker names. Among these one may find the following pioneer settlers of North Carolina families: Jonathan Anthony, Benjamin Beeson, Enos Blair, John Branson, William Coltrane, James Davis, James Dick, Nathan Farlow, James Frazier, John Henley, William Hill, Jos. Hoggatt (Hockett), Jonathan Hodson (Hodgin), William Milliken, Matthew Osbun (Osborne), Jeremiah Reynolds, David Stanton, Joshua Stanley and Daniel Worth.*

Modest markers to commemorate several of these founding fathers have been erected in the burying ground at Centre. Genealogies of the descendants of some of these have been compiled. For example, the Coltrane family genealogy contains the names of

---

* Contributed by Robert H. Frazier.

more than 1,250 descendants of William Coltrane. In this family in the present generation are the well known North Carolinians: David Coltrane, Assistant Director of the Budget; Eugene Coltrane, President Emeritus of Brevard College; Mrs. Charles A. Cannon (Ruth A. Coltrane); Shubal E. Coltrane and Edward R. Murrow.**

The Friends at Centre early became concerned over the issue of slavery. The first manumission society in the South was organized there in 1834, and Friends were active in bearing their testimony against this indignity. The first Bible School was started in 1865, with Himelius Hockett as superintendent and Thomas Mason, Perrin Reynolds, Samuel A. Purdy and a daughter of Lewis Reynolds as teachers. An elementary day school was begun in 1866 (the year after the war), with Samuel Purdy as teacher for the first two years. Here is another example where the Baltimore Association came to the rescue. By the help of funds provided by Northern Friends a school building was erected near the meeting house, and school was conducted here until the State took over the public school system. Among the early teachers were: Joseph Moore, Alpheus Mendenhall, Titia English, David Farlow, Samuel Purdy and Martha Stanton. The importance and value of this service cannot be over emphasized, for it must be recalled that the war had left the South prostrate; the school buildings were damaged or destroyed; the teachers scattered and the necessary school equipment altogether unobtainable. Radicals and Negroes controlled the legislatures, and Federal troops remained in the South till 1877. Worst of all the Radicals instituted mixed schooling, and in consequences the whites boycotted such schools. After the State took over the schools Ella Chamness (Cox) was the first teacher.

The Great Revival, referred to in another place, came to Centre. Nathaniel Gossett, a visiting Methodist minister, was the first to sing in meeting; then came Mary Moon, who stirred Friends here as she did everywhere she went. Through her ministry the objection to singing was overcome, and the character of the service became changed, and presently instrumental music obtained a place. By 1910 a new organ was installed; then came a piano, and now an electric organ.

As elsewhere expansion became necessary; more land was purchased in 1867 — three acres for $55.68. By 1879 the old meeting house, in use for over a century, became obsolescent, and a

** *Ibid.*

third place of worship was built upon higher ground. This was in use from 1885 to 1920. In 1923 a Memorial Association was formed, to take proper care of the adjoining cemetery, and additional land was acquired. These Friends have participated in the usual activities of a Quaker community, with a very active Women's Missionary Society, a Young Friends organization and summer camps. A suitable minister's home was provided in 1939 and a hut for social activities. This hut was removed to Quaker Lake in 1952. The meeting house was extensively remodelled in 1920 and 1922, and in 1948 the fourth house was constructed. As is natural in areas where a fine community spirit exists "practically every resident member, man, woman and child, at one time or another did actual work on the building," and clean up days provided occasion for a picnic lunch and good fellowship. The fourth place of worship cost about $32,000.

Among the resident ministers were: Peter Dicks, a very distinguished person; Ada Lee Stanley, David Brannon, Rodema Wright (seven years); Herbert Reynolds, Charles Osborn, Edgar Murrow, Margaret B. Hackney (15 years); Thomas Hendrix and Samuel Pickett (assistants to Margaret Hackney); Elbert Newlin, (5 years); Ben Millikan, J. Waldo Woody (seven years); Margaret Farlow (Davis), Orville Dillon (seven years); Willard Mendenhall since 1952; Elbert Newlin at present.[5] Those who have served as clerk include Beatrice Rickett and Eunice Beeson. The membership is now 352, with an average attendance of 181, and about 263 attend the Bible School. In 1954 a commitee prepared a very complete historical booklet from which these extracts have been culled.

These frontier meetings were greatly helped by visiting Friends. Among them were: Robert Willis, William Farrell, Daniel Stanton, Ann Newlin, Alice Hill, Susannah Hatton from Ireland and Jane Crosfield and Samuel Neale from England. It is a simple matter to record the names, but to imagine the difficulties of traversing an unbroken wilderness, crossing streams and mountains before the beginning of the nineteenth century is beyond conception.

The original minutes of this meeting are now easily accessible, for Thomas W. Marshall in 1932 copied over one hundred pages including a very large number of genealogies. These records are valuable sources of information and are often examined by visitors to the Quaker archives. The 200th anniversary was celebrated on August 17, 1957, with a pageant "The Silver Thread." Well over one hundred participated in the presentation.

CHATHAM is one of the oldest meetings; it was set off from Spring Monthly Meeting in 1824. A meeting house was erected in 1888, and it obtained its own monthly meeting eleven years later. From time to time additions and improvements have been made to the premises. Those who have advanced the Kingdom of God through the preached Word include: Alfred Zachary, Margaret Hackney, D. Virgil Pike, Ed. Harris, Walter Allen, Cora Lee Norman, John Permar, Victor Murchison, Allie R. Kemp, Harold Ritze, Orval Dillon, Hiram H. Hilty. Those who have presided as clerks include: James Newlin, Charles Newlin, J. Norman Osborne, W. W. Newlin, W. S. Guthrie, Kermit Newlin, Albert Braxton, Bertha Jean Newlin. The membership is 84, and the attendance at Bible School 69.

CONCORD MEETING was established in 1800; there is now a membership of 104 and a Bible School of 77. Those who have participated in the ministry include: John C. Trivette, Robert Green, Claude Bullock, James Marion, and Thomas Butt. The clerk is Alice M. Cook. The Young Friends are taking an active share in the work and in recent months they have conducted the evening service, have presented a play "The Meaning of Thanksgiving," and had charge of the Mothers' Day exercises. A junior choir is being developed. At the annual Homecoming Day in May there was a record attendance; Seth B. Hinshaw, the Yearly Meeting Executive Secretary was the principal speaker. The occasion took the form of a picnic dinner and of Memorial Service for Gurney S. Barker who had been a staunch member of the meeting for many years.

EDWARD HILL MEETING has a membership of 96; a Bible School of about the same number. Allie R. Kemp rendered valuable leadership, as also did Harrison Hinshaw, Isaac Harris and Leonard Vuncannon; Hazel Patterson is clerk. For a small meeting the activities and interest are well maintained.

GRAHAM MONTHLY MEETING dates from 1907. Three years later the meeting house was acquired. This is another meeting which owes much of its initial momentum to the blind David E. Sampson, who afterwards rendered a monumental service in establishing the meeting at Winston-Salem. Others who succeeded him in the ministry were: Margaret Hackney, Fleming Martin, John Permar, Virgil Pike, J. Waldo Woody, Robert Crow (five years), Homer Barker, Myron Goldsmith, Dallas M. Rush, James Marion.

The following Friends have served as clerk: Allen J. Marshburn, Sallie Sampson, J. Addison Branson, J. Webster Pegg, John Linens, Mollie Guthrie, J. C. Chrisco, John D. Adams, A. C. Kimrey, Myrtle Knight, Daniel Allen, J. M. McBane, Ethel Allen, Blake Wright, John Allen, Jr., Daniel Allen, William Guthrie. The meeting has provided a suitable home worth about $7,000 for the minister. The membership is given as 262; the Bible School attendance as 222. Additional classrooms were added in 1956. Steady progress is maintained.

LIBERTY MONTHLY MEETING. This new meeting came into existence ninth month, twenty-fourth, 1943. A church building was purchased from another denomination. The attendance has steadily grown till now there are 114 members, and a Bible School of nearly one hundred. The following Friends have shared the ministry: Thomas F. Andrew, Calvin Gregory, John Permar, Edward B. Harris, Luther McPherson, Howard Yow, Clifton C. Pearson and Robert Medford. The clerk is Dayton G. Newlin. The community is rapidly progressing and expanding, and there is a good opening for Friends. A substantial home has been provided for the resident minister. The congregation participates in the usual church activities.

PLAINFILELD MONTHLY MEETING is a young meeting, being established May 20, 1914 with 56 members; the meeting house was improved and brick veneered in 1945. The membership is now 132; with a Bible School of nearly one hundred. The following have preached the Gospel: T. F. Andrews, Ed. Harris, Alpheus White, D. Virgil Pike, Thomas Hendrix, Oscar Cox, York Teague, Charles and Cora Lee Johnson, Robert Green, Orah S. and Cleta Evans. The clerks have included: H. Z. Terry, Blanche Terry, Elzena Andrew, Turner Hargrove, Webb Bare, Edith B. Terry, Beulah Hinshaw. The first Quarterly Meeting was held at Plainfield in 1915.

PROVIDENCE MEETING appears to have been set up about 1769 (another account says 1792) and the Monthly Meeting was authorized in January, 1912. The first meeting house dates from 1769; the second from about 1800; the third from 1884; and the present from 1929. The following Friends have participated in the ministry: Ada Lee (Stanley), 1915-16; Oscar Cox, 1916-17; Margaret Hackney, 1918-19; Henry Wrenn, 1919-23; Nereus Hodgin, 1923-24; Robert Melvin, 1924-27; Thomas Hendrix, 1927-

31; Thomas Andrew, 1931-37; Benjamin H. Millikan, 1937-41; Victor Murchison, 1941-45; J. Norman Osborne, 1945-46; all these were part time pastors. The following were resident locally and rendered full time service: Victor Murchison, 1941-45; Cecil Nicholson, 1946; Edward B. Harris, 1947; Donald Gates, 1947-49; Robert O. Crow, 1949-55 (the first to live in the minister's home); Blake Wright, 1955.

Those who exercised gifts in the ministry apart from pastoral service included: Simeon Barker, Alpheus White, Jeremiah Cox, George Wood, Oscar L. Cox and Heimar Lowe.

The following have served as clerk: Elma J. Barker, Vanner E. Neece, Myrtle Cox. The membership is 172; the attendance at Sunday School is 78. Useful additions have been made recently to the minister's home.

ROCKY RIVER MEETING, near Siler City, is unique in that it was an organized congregation for 155 years before it became a self-governing monthly meeting. Before 1753 Cane Creek was the gathering place for Friends who were settled over a very large area. A monthly meeting was established there in 1755 and it became the mother of several meetings including New Garden in 1751. The early settlers came mostly from Quaker centers in the north. Families by the names of: Campbell, Carter, Hobson, Hinshaw, Hollady, Jones, Johnson, Stuart, Piggott (Pickett), Vestal came from Pennsylvania, although some of them tarried a generation or so in Maryland or Virginia. Oddly enough few came from Eastern Quarter but the Pikes were an exception.

Dorothy Gilbert Thorne in her very informing booklet: *Two Hundred Years at Rocky River Friends Meeting* from which most of the following particulars are culled, says that at the time that Rocky River became a monthly meeting in 1908 there were sixty charter members and most of them were descendants of the original Quaker settlers at Cane Creek. At the time of her writing in 1953 there were living fourteen members of the original number when the monthly meeting was organized, bearing the names of: Andrew, Johnson, Pike, Stout, Stuart, Thompson, Teague and Wrenn. At one time there were 22 Thompsons among the members. This confirms what is amplified elsewhere that the Society before the adoption of the pastoral system had become a distinct social group of a comparatively few inter-related families.

Other families arriving at a later date included the Albrights, Coopers, Lanes, Langleys, Loys, Ways, Wickers and Whiteheads.

In 1753 Rocky River requested permission to hold meeting on Fourth Day. It is believed that such meetings were general for a century or more in many places, but scanty references are found in the minute books because few Friends attended and no business was transacted, but no record of Quakerism would be complete without reference to the fact that "concerned Friends" considered it part of their religion to leave their work and spend an hour in quiet meditation during the week.

The next year Friends asked the Quarterly Meeting for the right to gather at Rocky River instead of journeying to Cane Creek; three years later they requested a meeting every other First Day; but in 1763 they again asked for a meeting each First Day morning. In 1766 the record reads: "Friends inhabiting on Rocky River request to have the Indulgence of their meeting removed from them under the present situation of the house heretofore met at." Dorothy Thorne believes this refers to the abandonment of the first meeting house which was probably a log structure of the conventional type with raised "facing seats" for the ministers and elders and with moveable partitions between the men and the women.

For unexplained reasons the meetings seemed to have been discontinued, for in 1770 the minute book says the meetings were resumed. The clerks were not loquacious in those days, for the records of eight consecutive monthly meetings occupy but a single page. In 1792 the Friends once more requested a continuance of their meeting. It is not unlikely that the wide-spread disturbances upon the frontier, the Regulator movement, which was close by, and the Revolutionary War made it an "illconvenience" for Friends to meet regularly. Cane Creek appointed a committee and Rocky River meeting was re-established in 1792.

In 1785 a Philadelphia Friend, Hugh Judge, visited Western Quarter, and he noted that "he lodged with David Vestal, near Rocky River, a choice elder. I wish there were more of his stamp." David is also referred to in the *Journal* of Thomas Scattergood, who said "the house could not hold all the people."

Mention of these visiting Friends renders it fitting to remark that in the opinion of many Friends and historians the Society was maintained in the period before the Civil War by these periodic visits. William Hunt, of New Garden, kept a list of the "public Friends who hath visited in Truth Service from the first settlement of the meeting in the year 1752 up to 1778." In spite of the disturbances just referred to there was the almost incredible number of 93, including several women. To appreciate this service one needs to consider the difficulties and hazards of travel in that period. These visits were serious occasions and as mentioned elsewhere in this work the news was spread, and largely because of the novelty of seeing a stranger a great concourse often assembled.

Among these visiting Friends was Catherine Payton Phillips, of England, and it will not be out of place to mention that English Friends were very solicitous concerning American Quakerism, and it would be of great interest to have a complete list of the numerous certificates issued by London Yearly Meeting to Friends with concerns to visit the colonies. Catherine wrote that "in 1754 she held a very satisfactory meeting at Rocky River . . . but that at New Garden the meeting was dead, formal professing spirit, under which the living were sorely oppressed, as well as of a flashy wordy ministry." From Western she travelled to Carver's Creek, 160 miles away, with Jeremiah Piggott and John Wright as guides and with a woman companion. "Two nights at least they slept in the wilderness, surrounded for aught we knew by bears, wolves and panthers." As they pitched the tent the men told the women that not far away a person had been killed by a panther! Two of the horses strayed and the men went to find them, leaving the women for several hours alone. Catherine wrote: "All fear was removed, and we spent the time of our friends' absence cheerfully." In the morning they saw what they believed to be the spoor of a wild beast, which "gave us room to suspect that they had been near our tents in the night, but we were preserved both from their fury, and from being affrighted by their hideous howls."

THEY UNDERSTOOD NOT. Another English Friend who encouraged the frontiersmen was William Reckett, who came in 1758. He visited the Pee Dee area and found Friends "who had nigh one hundred miles to go to monthly meeting, and very seldom missed attending." Concerning Cane Creek Reckett records "Friends had not been settled there above ten years but had found occasion to build five meeting houses, and then wanted one or two more." The Rocky River house was probably one of the five. Another visiting Friend, John Griffith, born in Pennsylvania, but removing as a young man to England, came to Rocky River in 1765. He wrote of the Friends there "he had a small meeting . . . with little of the wrestling seed therein . . . we sat the whole meeting silent . . . yet a Friend had something to offer very suitable to their states." Concerning the meeting at Deep River he said: "Friends were void of a spiritual concern;" and at Centre "there was very little of a religious warmth," while of the Cane Creek congregation he wrote: "the members were void of a solid sense and solemnity . . . and the leaven of the Pharisees seemed to prevail." We venture the opinion that said Friend had better have stayed at home, for he had no concept of the isolation, the lack of reading materials, the fewness of associations, and the deep spiritual hunger of the famished souls of the frontier in pre-Revolutionary days. It is only a few years ago that Friends in North Carolina were urged to gather at a central place to meet a distinguished English Friend. A goodly number travelled considerable distances — some over fifty miles. The visitor was introduced, but he had no "word of the Lord for us." We returned disappointed, for we could not believe that the Lord sent him and yet gave him nothing wherewith to encourage us.

Rocky River seemed to have had a succession of "worthy and weighty Friends" who were overseers. Jeremiah Piggott appears to have been the first; in 1778 Thomas Vestal was named; Joseph Kemp in 1781; Stephen Hobson, 1783; Isaac Hobson and John Carter in 1795. David Vestal was also an overseer. The original trustees included: William Hobson, Joseph Branson and Nathan Vestal. In 1779 two pillars of the church — John Piggott and Jeremiah Piggott — passed away.

As might be expected this meeting followed the traditional practice of disowning members for "marrying out", for owning Negro slaves, for "accepting an office with the military", for attending military exhibitions and places of diversion.

Migrations also depleted the membership. Quite a few families moved to Bush River, Wrightsboro and other places in South Carolina with the intention of establishing Quakerism there. Small meetings were maintained for years, but slavery conditions were such that Quakerism had no chance of survival in such hostile soil. The "western fever" also struck this community, and in 1806-07 eight families moved to Ohio; in 1808-09 four more families went north of the great river to Ohio and "free soil", and between 1815-25 twelve families went to Indiana. These migrants included members named Cox, Dixon, Hadley, Rubottom and Siler. Yet Rocky River meeting grew in spite of these withdrawals.

It would appear that the explanation for the tardiness of this group of Friends becoming a monthly meeting was that there was a close bond between the members at Cane Creek and other centers of worship. From 1820 the quarterly meeting assembled once a year at Rocky River, and from 1821 the monthly meeting alternated between Cane Creek and Rocky River. Thus the closely related family groups were able to meet frequently. So close were these ties that some members did not approve the setting up of a separate monthly meeting for Rocky River in 1908. The quarterly meeting appointed the following committee to attend the establishment of said meeting: Elma Hodgin, W. A. White, Nathan Stuart, Alfred Harris, Alfred Guthrie, Rodema Wright and Wilson White. The minute was read by Nathan Stuart. W. J. Thompson was named as clerk; Bertha Thompson assistant clerk; Alma Thompson recorder.

Thomas F. Andrew became the first pastor and with interruptions was an effective preacher for 36 years. In common with most of the membership he was a farmer. Rufus King, who is portrayed elsewhere, was a member of this meeting and participated in the ministry when he was at home — which was seldom. Others who exercised gifts in the ministry were: Henry Wrenn, Oscar Cox, Virgil Pike, Charles and Cora Lee Johnson, Robert Green, J. Norman Osborne and his son Donald Osborne. Four young men of this meeting received gifts in the ministry and rendered conspicuous service — Manley Hollady, Virgil Pike, Victor Murchison and Harrison Hinshaw. Burton Andrew is the present clerk.*

The present meeting house is the fourth. The first two were of the traditional log variety; the third was a long frame structure; the fourth was built in 1926. The membership in 1908 was sixty; it has steadily increased till now there are 237; with fifty associates (juniors) and a Bible School of 170. All departments of the work are well maintained.[6]

SOUTH FORK MEETING dates from 1818. A remarkable feature of this group of Friends is that three generations (direct descendants in one family) have produced able ministers, namely Alfred H. Harris, Edward B. Harris (son) and Isaac Harris (grandson). Some years ago when all three were living the unusual circumstance was suitably acknowledged by the community. Isaac is at present pastor of the Archdale Meeting, and has served as Executive Secretary to the Yearly Meeting. Efforts are made by the congregation to keep the premises up-to-date, and quite recently a modern home has been provided for the pastor. The membership totals 273; the

---

* See the excellent booklet by Dorothy G. Thorne *Two Hundred Years at Rocky River Friends Meeting.*

Bible School, 149; the clerk is Blanche Andrew. Among the ministers have been: J. Norman Osborne, D. Virgil Pike, Donald Gates, Benjamin H. Millikan and Waldo Smith. All departments of the work are well maintained.

SPRING MEETING is fifteen miles from Graham and a few miles east of Cane Creek. A meeting was established in 1773 and a monthly meeting was allowed in 1793. Before that time it had been under the care of Cane Creek. In common with other Quaker centers this group suffered great losses in the extensive migration to the west. To show the extent of this depletion it may be mentioned that between 1831 and 1839 families by the name of: Andrew, Carl, Hadley, Harvey, Lindley, Morrison, Newlin, Piggott, Thompson, Turner and Woody all severed their connection with the Spring Meeting. These departures continued up to and after the Civil War.[7] It is a wonder the meeting survived. The membership is now 56, and 34 attend Bible School. Mary Ruth Perry is clerk. Those who have ministered to the spiritual needs of the community include: Allie R. Kemp, D. Virgil Pike, Victor Murchison, Theodore Perkins, Charles Lamar, J. Floyd Moore, Orval Dillon, Hiram H. Hilty and J. Norman Osborne. Thomas Marshall selected one of the old *Minute* books of this meeting as one of the thirty-three such records he caused to be re-typed. The book consists of fifty large pages; many genealogies are professionally arranged and are of great value.

CHAPTER TWENTY-TWO

WORKERS TOGETHER WITH GOD

SOUTHERN QUARTERLY MEETING.   This portion of the church mostly in Randolph County embraces the following monthly meetings: Asheboro, Back Creek, Bethel, Cedar Square, High Falls, Holly Spring, Hopewell, Marlboro, Poplar Ridge, Prosperity, Rand Leman, Science Hill, South Plainfield. Meetings at Needhams Grove, Little River, Pine Ridge, Salem, Wharrie were laid down.   The Quarterly Meeting was set up in 1820, and for three quarters of a century the women maintained their separate meetings for business. In 1931 the quarterly meeting requested each monthly meeting to prepare a historical sketch of its development; these were read at various gatherings and collected and published under the care of Seth B. Hinshaw and Allie R. Kemp.[1] This is a valuable source of information and the plan is recommended to other quarters.

Those active in the ministry in the first quarter of this century included: Thomas Andrew, Elwood Cox, Milner A. Cox, William Cox, Randall E. Emmons, Michael A. Farlow, Michael C. Farlow, W. Alston Humble, Clarence Macon, Joseph H. Price, John S. Tillman, Sarah E. W. Winslow.

The following Friends have served as clerk of the quarterly meeting or in other capacities: Stephen Henley, William Dennis, Phineas Nixon, Aaron Stalker, Joseph Newlin, Nathan Craven, William Clark, Nathan P. Hill, Nathan Spencer, Isaac Lee, Thomas Hinshaw, James A. Allen, Jeremiah S. Cox, Samuel A. Henley, Levi P. Macon, David Farlow, Sr., Anderson Barker, Benoni J. Stout, Luellen Farlow, Samuel R. Pickett, Hope Hubbard.

ASHEBORO MEETING came into existence rather late in the history of Southern Quarterly Meeting.   The settlement had a rapid development, being beautifully situated in the State.   Friends from many near-by communities moved in, and Ada Lee (Stanley) who was pastor of the Archdale meeting was asked to hold a series of evangelistic services. She preached in the Baptist Church; great interest was aroused, and she was invited to reside in Asheboro and assist the local Friends in the establishment of a meeting. Permission to establish a monthly meeting was granted by the Southern Quarterly Meeting in 1915, and the meeting was established by the reading of the minute. A lot was donated and preparations for building undertaken. This meeting has had a steady growth and exercises considerable influence in the community. Elwood Cox was the first clerk. The membership is now listed as 368, and the average Sunday School attendance is 251.

The following ministers have resided in this meeting: Ada Lee (Stanley), Elwood Cox, Milner A. Cox, Eli Reece, Joseph Peele, Fred Ryan, A. C. Barrett, Thomas Andrew, Clarence Macon, George Moore, Calvin Gregory, John M. Permar, Herman Parker, D. Virgil Pike, Seth B. Hinshaw, David A. Stanfield, and Bascom G. Rollins. L. Brack Cagle is the clerk.

BACK CREEK dates from 1785, and Thomas Winslow conveyed to the meeting two years later a plot of land and a house thereon. In 1789 a log house was constructed which served the meeting for 135 years. A monthly meeting was authorized in 1792. The names of the early members are preserved, among them being Andrew Hoover, an ancestor of former President Herbert Hoover. Between 1797 and 1811 twenty-two certificates of removal were issued by Eastern Quarter, and most of the migrants settled in Back Creek. These movements developed into an almost constant stream. A First Day School was begun in 1835. By the time the war came Friends had already left in large numbers for the west. The slave question and the great difficulty of free labor competing with unpaid toil depleted the meeting. It is said that for some time the mid-week meeting was kept in existence by only two faithful Friends, William Lowe and Rachel Henley. To avoid criticism they attended alone on alternate weeks, each meditating the full hour. Similar stories are told of other meetings. One account says the man Friend would send a message to the woman Friend, asking if she had a concern to attend meeting next Fourth Day. If she said she hoped to be able to attend then he would be absent. The next week she would follow a similar procedure. In 1866 a school house was built, and with the help of the Baltimore Association local Friends sought to revive elementary education in Back Creek. Mary Moon visited this meeting and did much to revive it. The Women's Meeting record book, Vol. 1, is preserved in the archives along with extensive records of Friends marriages, even giving a full list of the witnesses.[2]

Among the ministers who have served the meeting are:

Pharaby Hammond, Elwood Cox, Sarah E. Winslow, John S. Tillman, Herbert Reynolds, Samuel Pickett, D. Virgil Pike, Allie R. Kemp, Milner A. Cox, Warren A. Pierce, Edward C. and Lola Simpson Scott and York A. Teague. The meeting now has about 80 members, with a Bible School of 36. Samuel A. Lowe, Jr. is clerk.

BETHEL MEETING is located five miles southeast of Asheboro in Randolph County. It was set off from Holly Spring Meeting in 1821, with the approval of Southern Quarterly Meeting. A member, Abner Barker, deeded an acre of land for the site, and the first place of worship was a log structure; built about 1839 and burned in 1855; another log house was built, covered with boards. All the benches were of slabs with wooden peg legs, except the two in front, which were of sawn lumber. A Bible School dates from 1857. A frame meeting house was built in 1888. The pastoral system was adopted in 1901, and Thomas F. Andrew served the community for twenty years. Another enlargement was made in 1904. The work prospered, and Quakerism became a vital factor in the community. Again there was need for enlargement and modernization and a commodious place of worship, this time of brick veneer, was constructed in 1943.

Upon the petition of 58 Friends Southern Quarter consented to the setting up of a monthly meeting at Bethel in 1921, and a committee was appointed according to practice to be present when the authorizing minute was read. William C. Winslow was named as clerk for the day. A nominating committee named D. C. Smith as clerk; Pearl Craven, assistant clerk; Carl E. Cox, Mary L. Pugh, and Alta Smith, overseers; Orlando Brown, treasurer; Mattie Craven, recorder; Theodore F. Pugh, Rufus C. Craven and James B. Henson, trustees; David J. Kemp, correspondent. Other committees were named. The minute book, which has been typed and bound, contains little information; sometimes several monthly records are on a single page; only from nine to fourteen attended; the minutes, like so many others, consist largely of references to the Queries and the representatives to quarterly meeting. In 1931 Edward B. Harris conducted a revival and later continued as pastor, but the attendance at monthly meeting continued very small. In 1940 Murray Johnson assisted the pastor in a revival.

Ministers who have labored here include: Levi Cox, Nereus Barker, John Tillman, Milner A. Cox, Albert Peele, Joseph Price, Edward B. Harris, Victor Murchison, York Teague, Harold Ritze,

Milner Cox and J. Norman Osborne. The first clerk was Daniel Smith, and later presiding officers include: Alta Smith, Pearl Craven Kemp, Virgie Smith Pugh, Carl Cox, Allie R. Kemp and Stena Cagle the present clerk. The membership totals 132, and the average attendance at Bible School is 112. Plans are in hand for the building of a home for the minister.

CEDAR SQUARE has been a Quaker community since the memory of man runneth not to the contrary. The school and meeting have been so closely connected that their histories are inseparable. Both had their origin in a little log house about one mile from the present meeting house. In 1873 Marlboro Monthly Meeting and Southern Quarterly Meeting approved the setting up of a monthly meeting "at or near the Stalker school house." For a while it was known as Muddy Creek. An interesting feature is that "on Fourth day morning the men and women would come in, and the children would lay aside their books and join in the meeting for worship."

Later Friends bought a parcel of land for $20.00 for a site; a place of worship was completed in 1876, and a square of cedars planted around the building. The quarterly meeting consented to the abandonment of the name Muddy Creek and the substitution of Cedar Square. The custom of the teachers and children of the school attending the mid-week meeting was continued. Nathan Spencer usually preached after a period of silence. "At that time there was no singing except when Jesse Frazier would sing alone."

Since the pastoral system was adopted the following have exercised their gift in this meeting: Robert H. Melvin, Thomas Hendrix, Thomas Stamey, Norman Osborne, Elbert D. Newlin, Ben H. Millikan, Howard B. Yow, Reuben J. Payne, Charles Lamar, Harold Ritze, York Teague, Chester Peele, Orah Evans and Floyd Moore. Friends have made a distinctive contribution to the community, for doctors, preachers and many public school teachers have received inspiration in the meeting. The membership is 70, with 123 in the Bible School. John C. Hinshaw is clerk.

HIGH FALLS MEETING was for several years under the care of the Friends in Prosperity. By 1907 a meeting was held due largely to the work and influence of Waldo Woody and his wife. Leonard Vuncannon became pastor in 1953 and High Falls was granted the status of a monthly meeting, with about twenty members at that time. In recent years much progress has been made in the improvement of the meeting house and its furnishings, including complete renovation, with new furnace, new lighting, furniture, organ, hymn

books and outside walkways. There is now a membership of fifty
and a Bible School of 128. The men of the church are loyal
workers and have donated much labor to the improvements. In
like manner the women under the leadership of Rachel Brady have
contributed substantially to the pulpit furnishings, windows and
heating system. Among the ministers have been: Leonard Vuncannon, Alfred Harris, Talmadge Knight, Don M. Gates and York
Teague. The few Friends here have a good record in meeting
the yearly meeting assessments. J. C. Russell is clerk; Raymond
Vaughn is the efficient superintendent of the Bible School.

HOLLY SPRING MONTHLY MEETING probably had its beginning when
some unknown Friends from Philadelphia settled there. The remains of some two hundred pioneers were buried in a near-by
cemetery, and there is a reference in the Cane Creek *minutes* of
1765 to "the Meeting of Indulgence* on Mill Creek in Cox's
settlement." This is identified as near the present Quaker community. In 1787 Richard Caswell, the first Governor of North
Carolina, deeded fifty acres of land to Benjamin Cox "for the use
of the Society of people called the Quakers." The first building
was naturally a log structure. This building was burned and a new
frame building erected about 1830; this was replaced in 1890. An
old record book at the yearly meeting library without title or
writer's name dated 1889 says: "Holly Spring Meeting was established in 1769; was suspended in 1821; and restored in 1845." A
preparative meeting dates from 1790, and a monthly meeting from
1818. From the earliest days Friends operated a school, which was
located near the first log meeting house. In all they cared for six
schools. It is of general interest that one of the early teachers
at this little country schoolhouse was Braxton Craven, who later
became the first President of Trinity College, which has become a
great institution under the name of Duke University. The westward movement, discussed elsewhere, decimated this old-time
Quaker community. The meeting also suffered by the withdrawal
of a few conservative members when the pastoral plan was adopted.
The old style meeting house is retained.

Among the early ministers were: William Cox, Franklin Hin-
shaw; Thomas Andrew was the first paid pastor. Others include:
Ed. Harris, J. F. Jones, W. M. Cox, B. B. Bulla, Don M. Gates,
Allie R. Kemp. There are about 100 members; with attendance

---

* Meaning a Preparative Meeting.

at Sunday School of 125. In 1957 Clyde and Allie Hinshaw donated an electric organ which is of great usefulness.

HOPEWELL has a curious yet very natural history. The record says that the dead had been buried in a certain plot for about a century before Calhoun Vuncannon had the solemn duty of arranging the funeral of his mother. He was distressed that "he had to bury her in the woods." He commenced the next day to canvass the community for erection of a place of worship. He met with approval and support, and in 1885 a meeting house was planned. One Friend gave the land; others donated materials or services. When the building was completed, W. R. Ashworth and Calhoun Vuncannon said "they hoped it would do well!" Thus the meeting gained the name "Hopewell".

Permission was granted in 1916 by Southern Quarterly Meeting for Hopewell to become a monthly meeting, the congregation being really an offshoot of Back Creek. There were 36 charter members, and Roscoe Branson was the first clerk. Elwood Cox was minister for thirty years. Others who labored were: John S. Tillman, Joseph Price, Thomas F. Andrew, Calvin Gregory, John Permar, Edward Harris, Allie R. Kemp, Charles Lamar, Harrison Hinshaw, Norman Carter, Charles and Cora Lee Johnson, Billy Britt, Fred Morgan and Dallas Rush. The clerks have been Roscoe Branson, Nellie Hussey, Trilby Hammond, Homer Dawson, Chloe Nance, Rosa Dawson, Jessie Dawson and Docia Parks. The membership is 69; the Bible School numbers 106.

MARLBORO MONTHLY MEETING is one of the oldest in North Carolina. It must have existed some time before the first meeting house was built in 1797. In 1816 Marlboro and Salem Preparative Meetings requested permission to "hold a monthly meeting circular between them." Previous to this they had been included in Centre Monthly Meeting. Western Quarterly Meeting approved, and Marlboro Meeting has had care over its own affairs since 1816. A minute dated fifth month, 1819, reads that a committee be appointed to visit delinquent members and "labor therein as they may be abilitated for the removal of these deficiencies."

In 1826 the meeting united with the effort of the Society and raised funds for the removal of Negroes to free territory. During the Civil War a committee was named to attend the interests of Friends who had been confined in military encampments.

More than a passing interest attaches to the *Minutes* of 1829 and 1831. A committee was appointed "to labor in love and tenderness with those who had artificial grave stones erected in the burying ground and have them removed." A few years ago Edgar Farlow, although blind, raised a large sum of money and a very tall granite marker was erected, inscribed with the names of hundreds of Farlows who had worshipped at Marlboro. The occasion was a great homecoming for several hundred former residents. Francis C. Anscombe gave the principal address.

The meeting house has been recently modernized, and fine driveways constructed. The records say that in 1817 Peter Dicks and Dougan Clark were "recommended to be in the station of ministers." No other was recorded until 1850 when David Farlow was recorded. Others later include: Nathan F. Spencer, David S. Farlow, Seth C. Barker, Michael A. Farlow, Michael C. Farlow and Margaret Farlow. In recent years York Teague and John Pipkin have been pastors. Binford Farlow is clerk. There is a membership of 217 and a Bible School of 106. Among those who maintain the principles of Friends here were families bearing the names of: Barker, Beeson, Cannon, Cox, Davis, Farlow, Frazier, Gardner, Hinshaw, Hoover, Loflin, Lowe, Millikan, Rush and Spencer. Many of these intermarried.

POPLAR RIDGE was originally within the limits of Marlboro Monthly Meeting, and in 1857 Joshua Hill deeded to the trustees a tract of land upon which to build a place of worship. Northern Friends assisted financially. There were thirty charter members. The war and migration to the west played havoc with this company of Friends and numbers were greatly reduced. In ninth month, 1906, the rights of a monthly meeting were granted by Southern Quarterly Meeting, and according to custom a committee met with the local Friends and the authorizing minute was publicly read. Nathan Ferguson was appointed clerk. Many Farlows were among the group. In 1911 a beginning was made towards the erection of a meeting house, but funds came in very slowly. An example of the Discipline is discovered in the record of the meeting of 5-20-1922 "Pedro Linthicum having failed to render an excuse for not attending Quarterly Meeting, after having been appointed as a representative, Herbert C. Lanier was appointed to notify him that the meeting expects one to be reported at the next meeting." Also on 3-31-1925 "Herbert C. Lanier gave a reasonable excuse for non-attendance at Quarterly Meeting, but those who did attend said they received nothing in charge from it for the meeting." Interest lagged and the monthly meeting records are as follows: Monthly

Meeting was not held the ninth, tenth, eleventh and twelfth month of 1928; in the next year no business meeting was held in the first, second, third, sixth, seventh, ninth, tenth, eleventh and twelfth months. The following laconic entry occurs in seventh month, 1930: "There was no meeting held at Poplar Ridge for the reason nobody was there."[3] Meetings were very irregular in 1930 and 1931. In recent years there has been revived interest, largely due to the labors of Margaret Farlow, Cora Lee and Charles Johnson. Prominent among the ministering Friends were Rufus King, Albert Peele, Mary Moon, Michael C. Farlow, Samuel Cross, Samuel Pickett, Thomas Stamey, Cora Lee, Gardner Johnson, Charles G. Johnson, Cleta Briles, Warren (Allen) Pierce, J. Waldo Smith, Nell V. Brady, Dallas Rush and Barney Pierce. Allen Nelson is the present clerk. The membership is 158, and the attendance at Sunday School is 169. The present meeting house, built in 1938 is the third to serve the community.

PROSPERITY. Another locality where there was close relationship between a church and school and all denominations meeting in fellowship is Prosperity. As the record has it "it was built in 1875 for ministers and laymen of good standing in all denominations." This was natural and necessary in early days when communities were small and possibilities restricted. In 1880 a preparative meeting was set up by Cane Creek Meeting, and later transferred to the Holly Spring Monthly Meeting. Services were held occasionally, but revival services were held at regular intervals. During this period Thomas Inman and Isham Cox were the principal preachers. About 1900 William E. and Ellen H. Woody came to live in the community and were of much value to the meeting. Levi Cox became the first pastor, and meetings were regularly held. Ministers who have been resident include: Thomas Andrew, Alpheus White, Dougan Cox, Herbert Reynolds, Joseph A. Price, Samuel R. Pickett, Edward Harris, Cora Lee, Norman Gardner, York Teague, Alfred Harris, Talmadge Knight, Leonard Vuncannon. The present clerk is Shelby Jean Short. A new and commodious meeting house has recently been provided, affording convenience and gratification.

RANDLEMAN is the baby of Southern Quarter, and dates only from 1945. The ministers include: Charles and Cora Lee Johnson, Dallas Rush, John Permar, J. Waldo Smith, and Billy Britt. In 1954 the congregation built an Annex as a Sunday School Department, bought pews, brick veneered the building and completed the payments. The membership is 57, with 84 in the Bible School. Randleman is a very small town, and Friends are greatly respected and are bearing testimony to the Truth. The clerks are: John Beane, Vance Bowman, Nellie A. Noel. A home for the minister was provided in 1956.

SCIENCE HILL MEETING appears to be a product of the evangelistic services of Mary Moon, a Friends minister from Indiana, who came into the community in 1892. The historical sketch issued by the Quarterly Meeting says: "there was a great spiritual awakening, such as this section of the country had not known. Christian people of all faiths re-consecrated and re-dedicated themselves to the great task of promoting the Master's Kingdom, and great numbers were brought into the fold of Christ. There was a felt need for a Friends Church in which they might worship, and thus this band of Friends set themselves to the task of constructing the Meeting House in which we worship today."

The local Friends requested permission to establish a meeting in 1894. There were 85 charter members, the majority being young persons. The first clerk was William C. Winslow, who served for many years; then the assistant clerk, Hope Hubbard, assumed the responsibility, which she has carried on with marked ability.

Among the ministers should be listed: Sarah E. Winslow, John S. Tillman, Alvin Barrett, Herbert W. Reynolds, Oscar Cox, Clarence Macon, Calvin Gregory, Samuel Pickett, Edward B. Harris, J. Waldo Woody, Victor Murchison, Charles Lamar, Luther McPherson, Earl Redding, Elizabeth Fields Moon, Floyd Moore, Larry Emerson and Joseph Moorefield. There are now 128 members; with an attendance at the Bible School of 99. The *Minute Book* of 1894 to 1927, which is very hard to decipher, contains the names of the 85 charter members.

SOUTH PLAINFIELD. In 1886 a log school house was named Plainfield by a Friend who had moved from a place of that name in Indiana. A day school was conducted in the winter, and a Bible School in the summer. About 1887 the log house was replaced by a frame building. This, as was common in early days, was shared by the Methodists. The present place of worship was constructed in 1893, and for some years all denominations who desired held services in the building, and it is comparatively recent that Friends had the sole use of the premises.

Those who showed special interest in the meeting include: Michael A. Farlow, Michael C. Farlow, Herbert Lanier, James and

Mary Ragan, Thomas Robbins, Baud B. Bulla, Rom and Hazel Pearce, Irene Farlow, Troy and Blanche Millikan, Samuel S. Nelson, Elwood Millikan, Charles and Cora Lee Johnson, Leonard Vuncannon, Howard Ward.[4]

In 1938 the premises were renovated, and two years later a monthly meeting was established with a membership of 38. There are now 122, and 94 attend Bible School. The meeting is known as South Plainfield to distinguish it from Plainfield in Western Quarter.

WHARRIE was a strong meeting for many years after its establishment in 1793, but it was laid down in 1870. There is an ancient burying ground, but it is badly neglected. Some markers bear initials only, some dates 1828 and 1829 are legible.

CHAPTER TWENTY-THREE

A HABITATION OF GOD THROUGH THE SPIRIT

NEW GARDEN QUARTERLY MEETING was set up in 1787. As mentioned elsewhere this settlement of Friends took firm root, and sent out many branches which have borne much fruit throughout the years. The story of each meeting is told separately. The men and women these communities produced are worthy of great honor. They have been an inspiration to the whole nation. Some of the settlements did not survive the buffetings the Society suffered. At one time there were gatherings at Piney Grove, Blues Creek, Bull Run, Mount Pleasant, Gum Swamp, Little Creek, Muddy Creek, Newberry, Sandy Branch, Sandy Spring, Summerfield, Dutchman's Creek, Dover. Many members transferred to nearby larger meetings. There are now active and growing congregations in the following centers: Chapel Hill, Glenwood, Greensboro, Kernersville, New Garden, Raleigh, Spring Garden Street (Greensboro), and Winston-Salem. The Quarterly Meeting embraces Friends in Guilford, Forsyth, Orange and Wake Counties.

This quarterly meeting has been unusually favored with able persons possessing gifts in the ministry. In addition to the early colonists named in chapter six there were the powerful preachers mentioned in connection with the establishment of the Boarding School, especially Jeremiah Hubbard, Nathan Hunt, Jonathan Cox, Nereus Mendenhall, Dougan Clark and others. Unfortunately their sermons have not been preserved, and the yearly meeting minutes make no mention of their forceful messages. A generation or so ago there were such "weighty members" as President Lewis Lyndon Hobbs, Mary Chawner Woody, Manly Holliday, Arthur E. L. Pain, Ellen W. Pain, Annie Edgerton Williams, Ada Lee Stanley, W. Alpheus White, Roxie Dixon White, Joseph H. Peele, James C. Holmes, Thomas Hendricks, John Riley, Nettie Riley, Christopher Cunningham, Charles C. Cross, Julia S. White, Mary M. Mendenhall, J. Edgar Williams, J. Waldo Woody, Samuel G. Barnes. In more recent years there were persons connected with Guilford College who made significant contributions to the spiritual life of the community, among them were President Raymond

Binford, President Clyde A. Milner, Elbert Russell, Philip W. Furnas, Daryl Kent, Frederic R. Crownfield, J. Floyd Moore.

CHAPEL HILL is the site of the University of North Carolina. Here in 1937 with 28 charter members a meeting according to the traditional manner of Friends was established. The group meets in the Graham Memorial Building and attenders sit in a circle with no prearranged program. A monthly meeting was authorized in 1944. For many years this group was highly favored with the presence and messages of Elbert Russell, but others were also open to the leading of the Spirit. The meeting is in the spirit of John G. Whittier who wrote:

> "And so I find it well to come
> For deeper rest to this still room.
> For here the habit of the soul
> Feels less the outer world's control.
> The strength of mutual purpose pleads
> More earnestly our common needs.
> And from the stillness multiplied
> By these still forms on either side,
> The world that time and sense have known
> Falls off and leaves us God alone."

Quaker students are among the several thousands now attending this institution which is rapidly becoming recognized as one of the great centers of learning in the world, and they find this quiet meeting a source of inspiration. Friends gather and quietly take their seats. Greetings are deferred to the close of the period of worship, which is indicated by the oldest Friend shaking hands with the ones nearest, and then all shake hands with those nearest. This little gathering is a healthy reminder that the old-time manner of worship still meets the needs of cultured persons. The meeting is affiliated with the Yearly Meeting and with the Five Years Meeting. Richard Hobbs was clerk for many years and was succeeded by Dudley D. Carroll, with Mary Shott as recording clerk.[1]

GLENWOOD MEETING is located in a suburb of Greensboro in a residential district. The meeting was organized in October, 1930, and at first occupied premises bought from another denomination. The present place of worship was acquired in 1949 and is simple yet beautiful and suitable. By October 19, 1952, a service of rejoicing was held that the structure was fully paid for. In addition, the congregation has provided a home for the minister at a cost of $10,000. Those who have preached the Gospel include

Robert Melvin, Talmadge Bristow, Winfred Cox, Norman S. Carter. The clerk is Roy Walker; Harold Mesimore is recording clerk; Norman Carter, assistant clerk.[2]   Robert Melvin, the pastor and founder of this meeting passed away at the age of eighty in October 1957. He had been the leader of the meeting for thirteen years, and also preached at Oak Hill, Cedar Square, Marlboro, Concord and Providence. His wife passed away thirteen days after his decease. Their services cannot be forgotten.

GREENSBORO MONTHLY MEETING is one of the substantial units of Quakerism in our midst. It was established in 1891, and the meeting house was built two years later. Owing to recent street improvements and residential changes the members decided that another location would be preferable. A lot in another part of the city was secured. The meeting vacated its site at Asheboro and Lee Streets and built a beautiful modern meeting house on the Friendly Road in 1957.

Those who have served in the ministry include: James R. Jones, Joseph Potts, Joseph Peele, J. Edgar Williams, Stephen Myrick, Earl J. Harold, Fred E. Smith, George Levering, Francis C. Anscombe, Kirby Bowen, Milo Hinkle, B. Russell Branson, Ralph Boring, Howard Cope, O. Herschel Folger, Robert M. Jones became the minister in 1957. Among the clerks are counted: James Addison Hodgin, Richard L. Hollowell, F. Herbert Nicholson, Simeon Addison Hodgin, David White, David J. White, Carson H. Grantham, Philip W. Furnas. In 1941 the Golden Jubilee was celebrated. This meeting participates in all the usual activities of an aggressive Friends meeting. The membership is 546; the Bible School has an enrollment of 190, with an average attendance of 125.

This meeting has been favored to include in its membership many persons of old-time Quaker stock, possessed of means, culture and devotion to the Society. Those who might truly be called "weighty Friends" include Mary E. Cartland, Priscilla Benbow Hackney, Nathan D. Andrews, Richard and Hettie Overman Hollowell, Cyrus P. and Lucetta Churchill Frazier, Walter E. Blair, Jabez R. Mendenhall, William D. Mendenhall, J. Van and Sandie Cook Lindley, David White, Eli Franklin Craven, Rhoda M. Worth, Ada Lee Stanley, Dr. Arthur and Cordelia Elliott Ledbetter, Alice Ledbetter Walters, Dr. D. W. C. Benbow, James Addison Hodgin, J. Walter and Martha Mendenhall McLennan, Victoria Petty, Cyrus and Mary Reynolds, Julius and Anne Cummings Pegram. Nathan L. Spencer, William Worth, Jeremiah S.

Cox, Rhetta English Hardin. Nearly "all of these have fallen asleep, but some abide unto this present."[3]

The imprint of the Quakers upon the Greensboro community is well recognized. Their activities contributed in no small degree to this city's good reputation for educational advancement, freedom from prejudice and solicitude for the welfare of the less fortunate. It will not be out of place to refer to a passage in the publication commemorating the Fiftieth Anniversary of the Greensboro Monthly Meeting. A survey made in 1927 reports: "Walter Blair as President of the Y.M.C.A., Paul Lindley as President of the Chamber of Commerce (later to become Mayor), three Y.M.C.A. Directors, ten members of civic clubs, thirty college graduates, fourteen teachers in city schools and colleges, one member of the Good Roads Commission, one member of the Police Department, six members of the Real Estate Board, two lawyers, one doctor, the head nurse of the City Health Department, two members of the Zoning Commission, one member of the Park Commission, and also a fine representation among merchants, bankers, manufacturers and governmental positions."[*]

NATHAN D. ANDREWS. A native of the State assisted in the establishment of the Friends Meeting at Goldsboro. Later he settled in Greensboro and became clerk of the Monthly and also of the Quarterly Meeting; was also Chairman of the Yearly Meeting Committee on Evangelism and Church Extension. As a salesman he was often away from home but so great was his love of the church that he planned his trips in order that he could visit various meetings. He was a useful and faithful member and was a representative on the Five Years Board of Missions, which service he rendered from 1917 to 1941.

CYRUS PIGGOTT FRAZIER. Attenders at any gathering of Friends near New Garden a generation ago would inevitably have noticed a pair of distinguished individuals in close conversation. Like Ike and Mike they looked alike. Each stood six feet two inches; each was as erect as a flagstaff; each wore a neatly trimmed white beard; each was devoted to the Society of Friends.[**] They were the brothers Frazier, Cyrus Piggott and his younger brother John Gurney. They bore an illustrious Scottish name. Some of their

---

[*] Much of this section was contributed by Robert H. Frazier.

[**] Prior to the writer's knowledge of New Garden there was a third brother, Rufus W. Frazier.

ancestors were among the Pilgrim Fathers and for a century and a half occupied plantations upon the Island of Nantucket.

James Frazier, son of James and grandson of Alexander, was among the great stream of migrants who came in 1751 to New Garden from Warrenton, Pennsylvania. He acquired a six hundred acre plantation, and became one of the early pioneers who helped to carve a vital Quaker settlement out of a virgin forest. The family ancestral tree from this James Frazier, who married Martha Millikan, may be expressed in hallowed terms: James begat Solomon; Solomon begat Isaac; Isaac begat Harrison; and Harrison begat Cyrus and his brothers, Jeremiah, Ruffin, Rufus Winston and John Gurney. Some of the male progenitors married into worthy Quaker families, so that in the Fraziers of today there may be found the seed of the Coxes, Millikans, Coltrains, Worthingtons, Thornborghs, Tullys, Piggotts (Picketts), Coffins and Mendenhalls. What a heritage!

Harrison Frazier was born in 1818, and married Gracette Piggott. He died shortly after his election to the General Assembly of North Carolina in 1872, leaving a widow and four young sons, Cyrus being the third and John Gurney the fourth. The boys had a rough time of it, working upon the farm, during the days of the war and the more dreadful Reconstruction that followed. The family biographer says however: "they received the benefits of a gentle home and Christian fellowship — but also the privations of war."

Cyrus was born, eighth month, twenty-fifth, 1853. He made good use of the very limited opportunities of study, and may be considered as one of the fruits of the labors of the Baltimore Association. He prepared for entrance to Trinity College (now Duke University) and received the Bachelor's degree in 1877. Upon the advice of Allen Jay he entered Haverford College, Pennsylvania. He earned the degree of Bachelor of Science, and returned to Trinity to teach French and German. At that time the President of Trinity was Braxton Craven — a product of New Garden Boarding School who had cheered the heart of Dr. Nereus Mendenhall with his aptitude and versatility — a rare instance where a great teacher has a student to match his mind.

In 1880 Cyrus was awarded the degree of Master of Arts, and in 1885 was appointed Superintendent of the first graded school of North Carolina, at Greensboro. Cyrus regarded teaching as his life's work, and was happiest in the classroom, but ill-health compelled him to abandon that form of public service. He was a

member of the Board of Trustees of Guilford College for more
than a quarter of a century, and was twice nominated as State
Superintendent of Public Instruction.   In 1888 he was nominated
for Congress.

Cyrus turned to business, and in 1888 helped to organize the
Greensboro Furniture Manufacturing Company.   Later he ven-
tured into the real estate business.   He saw the necessity of providing housing in the southwest of Greensboro.   He then became
interested in the Bank of South Greensboro, the Southern Life and
Trust Company (now the Pilot Life Insurance Company,) and the
Dixie Fire Insurance Company (now the American Fire Insurance
Co.).   He was quite successful so that he was able to retire and
devote his activities to church, civic and educational interests.
Cyrus ran true to form for it was an axiom among early Friends
that "they should engage in some occupation which contributed
to human needs; that they should provide properly for their de-
pendents and their honorable and independent old age; and then
should retire after securing a competency and devote the remainder
of their lives to public service."

He was a charter member of the Greensboro Monthly Meeting
of Friends and was active in the building of two meeting houses;
he was interested in the construction of Cox Hall and other buildings upon the Guilford campus.

Cyrus Frazier married in 1882 Lucetta Churchill, a daughter
of Samuel and Mary Taylor Churchill.   She was a woman of rare
charm, and a worthy helpmate.   To the union were born Cyrus
Clifford Frazier, Robert Haines Frazier, and Gertrude (Frazier)
Sellars.   The wife and mother died 5th month, 2nd, 1918, and in
10th month, 6th, 1919, Cyrus married Elizabeth Hodges, a half
sister of his former wife.

JOHN GURNEY FRAZIER, SR., a younger brother of Cyrus, also became a pillar in the church.   He was a pioneer teacher, teaching
seven grades in a one-room schoolhouse.   Like the rest of his
family, he was devoted to the Society, and filled many offices at
Old Trinity till he moved in 1899 to New Garden.   Here be became
Superintendent of the Bible School for seventeen years not missing
a Sunday.   He also taught a class, was generally recognized as a
worthy Friend, and was a staunch supporter of Guilford College
and every meritorious enterprise.[4]

LAURA PETTY HODGIN (1869-1956) daughter of William C. and
Victoria Petty, a Quakeress who manifested the beauty of the

Christian graces in a remarkable manner, served in many capacities in the church, and exhibited during protracted suffering extraordinary fortitude and patience.

CYRUS P. MENDENHALL. James Mendenhall when he departed from Pennsylvania to join the Friends who had responded to the lure of "the loveliest land in the world," and trekked to North Carolina could have had no conception of what he was conferring upon Southern Quakerism. One great historian said "the Almighty sifted whole nations in order that he might plant the choicest grain in North America." Some of that choicest grain was undoubtedly by Divine Providence directed southward.

Some of the descendants of this James have been the builders of the Kingdom of God in this community. James begat George; George begat Richard; Richard begat Cyrus, and Nereus and Mary. And Cyrus became one of the founders of Greensboro and one of its most distinguished mayors; Nereus became the historic "Dr. Nereus." On the mother's side the line was descended from the Pilgrims — the Pilgrim Mothers this time. We hear a great deal about the hardships the Pilgrim Fathers had to endure — the Indians, the hard winters and the starving times — but the Pilgrim Mothers endured all that — and the Pilgrim Fathers as well!

Tradition has it that Jamestown, a small town not far from Guilford College, was named for James Mendenhall. Cyrus who was born in 1817 studied law and in 1856 "hung out his shingle" in Greensboro, which was then "a one horse town." He became the leading citizen, and was possessed of a determination to lift the little place out of the mud and give it standing in the state. He was one of the far-sighted and progressive men who built a new court house and other public buildings; he had much to do with bringing a railroad to the town; he sponsored a gas plant; he helped inaugurate a Farmers' Bank; he became a director of a Mutual Insurance Company and had some experience as a cotton broker. in 1874 he was elected mayor. Let the date register. The Federal troops were still in possession of the South; the Confederate States had been made into five military districts. The South was still virtually prostrate.

It was a time when such a man as Cyrus Mendenhall was needed in public affairs. He was an authoritative person, with a neat beard and an impressive commanding personality. The times made him grave, yet never grumpy. He possessed the acumen of a man of ten talents and the integrity of a "man of God."

WILLIAM D. MENDENHALL was another well-known member of the Mendenhall family and was closely identified with the Greensboro Meeting. His devotion to the Bible School will be long remembered; his annual class excursions were a great event for the children. As President of the Guilford Lumber Company he occupied a substantial place in the business affairs of the city. He was married to Martha Blair and of this union were born Edwin J. Mendenhall, Robert Earl Mendenhall, Etta Mendenhall Burke, William Blair Mendenhall, Martha T. Mendenhall McLennan and Ruth Worth Mendenhall Swain.

MARY M. PETTY, a daughter of William Clinton and Victoria Haworth Petty, was born in the old Quaker settlement formerly known as Bush Hill, but later as Archdale in honor of the Quaker governor, John Archdale. She grew up during the dark days after the war, which by the way goes under all manner of names. Usually called the Civil War, political scientists say that term is incorrect. Other names are the War of Emancipation; Lincoln's War; the War Between the States; War over the Nature of the Union; the War of Secession; the War over Slavery; War between the North and the South; War between Unionists and Confederates; the War over Sectionalism. Whatever the name the result was clear.

Mary Petty entered New Garden Boarding School and was graduated in 1881. She then entered Wellesley College, Massachusetts, and was graduated with the class of 1885. For three years she taught at Statesville Female College (now Mitchell College) and in 1888 became a member of the Faculty at New Garden Boarding School, teaching mathematics, history, Latin and English literature. In 1893 she accepted an invitation to become a member of the Faculty of the State Normal and Industrial School for Women at Greensboro (now the Women's College of the University of North Carolina). At first she taught physics and chemistry, and when the institution became a college she became the Head of the Department of Chemistry. During her long session of instruction she kept abreast of the developments in scientific fields.

Mary Petty did graduate work at several institutions, including Bryn Mawr, Harvard, Columbia, Cornell, Chicago and the University of California. Few Tarheels of her time were better qualified by preparation and by character to guide the rising generation. She retired in 1931. Her teaching by no means monopolized her attention. There was no one in the yearly meeting more capable or devoted. She served efficiently on many committees in monthly, quarterly and yearly meeting; she was at one time Superintendent of the Asheboro Street Sunday School, and for years was teacher of a class of women. Her interest in Guilford College was sincere, and she was most active as a member of the Girls' Aid Committee, and as a member of the Board of Trustees, holding the distinction of being the first woman appointed to that body. She qualified as an ideal Quaker lady. Mary M. Petty was one of our most beloved and esteemed members and was a typical product of Archdale.[5] She passed away on the first day of 1958 at the venerable age of ninety-four.

ELI FRANKLIN CRAVEN has been one of Greensboro Meeting's outstanding spiritual leaders and a most loyal financial supporter. In affairs of his city and State he has had a prominent part. He served on the Greensboro City Council and for some years was State President of the Gideon organization. He established the E. F. Craven Road Machinery Company, which has been one of the most successful concerns of its kind in the southeast. He married Minnie Phipps Craven. Their children are Louise Craven Godwin, Duval Craven, Edwin Ashburn Craven and Sarah Elizabeth Craven Watt. Eli is one of the most useful and dependable members of the yearly meeting.

DEWITT CLINTON BENBOW must be included in the roster of Greensboro's distinguished citizens. This Friend was the great-great-grandson of Charles Benbow, who as a lad of fifteen was brought from Wales in 1718 to Philadelphia and bound apprentice to a Quaker named Carver in order to pay for his passage. Before long the master joined the great Quaker trek to the South and brought Dewitt with him. The arrangement evidently was satisfactory as the Welsh lad married a daughter of Carver, and settled among the Quakers. He lived from 1832 to 1902 and so was witness of the horrors of the War Between the States. He located in Greensboro, which after the conflict was over was described as "a struggling village of less than two thousand people, white and black; a way-side station on the North Carolina Railroad and the Piedmont Railroad; visited by few outsiders, who tarried only long enough to transact their business; known only for its educational advantages — Edgeworth and Greensboro Female College — and as being the residence town of a few State notables."

Dewitt Benbow established a dental practice, and being possessed of great faith and business acumen set himself to "put Greensboro on the map," according to his biographer. He built the Benbow Hotel of such proportions that it was by many regarded as a white elephant, but the number of business representatives and other visitors progressively increased. He had a hand in developing a storehouse; a row of dwelling houses; roads and graded schools. He had much to do in the development of Guilford Court House Battle Ground as a public park; he advocated improvement in livestock; the use of farm machinery. He figured largely in the advancement of education, and was active in the development of the Normal and Industrial School, the Agricultural and Mechanical College for Colored Students; and he operated a dairy and vegetable farm in connection with the hotel, but he tolerated no bar. For many years the main room in the hotel was used as a town hall, a concert hall and theater.

Dr. Benbow was a conscientious member of the Society of Friends and a supporter of all its concerns. For years he was a valuable member of the Board of Trustees of Guilford College. He was also a member of the Board of Alderman of Greensboro. His biographer, James T. Morehead, says "it is not exaggeration to say the City of Greensboro is more indebted to Dr. Dewitt Clinton Benbow than to any other of its citizens for his activities . . . and no one surpassed him in his efforts in behalf of the educational advantages she now possesses."*

John Van Lindley and Richard Lloyd Hollowell were pillars in the Greensboro Meeting and are referred to in connection with the narrative of Guilford College.

THE WORTH FAMILY. Some account of this distinguished family has been given in a previous chapter in connection with the career of Governor Jonathan Worth.** It remains to be said that William Worth came to this country from England in the time of Charles II. A grandson, Daniel Worth, was born in Massachusetts in 1739, migrated to the Piedmont and died here in 1830. Joseph Worth married Judith Starbuck in Nantucket, and was among the migrants to North Carolina. His descendants have been among the most ingenious and industrious of our citizens. Governor Jonathan Worth, was a grandson of Daniel Worth, of Nantucket Island stock. Dr. David Worth was another leading citizen and Dr. John M. Worth became State Treasurer. Laura D. Worth was

---

* Contributed by Robert H. Frazier.
** See Chap. xvii.

the efficient college nurse during the period this writer was a member of the faculty. Daniel Worth was a member of the Board of Trustees of Guilford College and ranked as a man of affairs. It would require a volume to relate adequately the accomplishments of other members of the family — including Cora, Eunice, Flora Carter, Florina, Rhoda and Ruth Worth (Mendenhall).

KERNERSVILLE. This meeting in this little historic center became established through the faith and energy of Shepherd and Myrtle Nelson. A tent meeting and revival was held in 1906, and the Nelsons were quickened to consider a gathering of Friends. The small group met for worship the next year, and representative Friends came from Asheboro Street and New Garden to set up the meeting in 1907; the next year a property was acquired as a house of worship, and a Bible School was started. William Benbow was the first clerk and served efficiently as long as he lived. The monthly meeting was set up in 1909. The persons who assisted in the ministry include Shepherd and Myrtle Nelson, Albert Peele, Hugh Moore, Hugh White, Mildred Angel Cox, Annie Edgerton Williams, Lela Sills Garner, Beatrice Camiene, Howard Yow, Carl Yow, Harold Ritze, Thomas Hendricks, Francis Carrier, Gene Clark, John Permar, C. Kenneth Wood. The Clerks include John Benbow, R. S. Nelson, Jack Angel, Ollie Angel, Charles Clark, Dosky Nelson, Edwin Idol, Richard Flynt, Charles E. Idol. In 1953 the congregation moved into a new and substantial brick building and now accommodations exist for the entertainment of quarterly meeting. There are now 131 members, with a Bible School of 178. The small meeting finds the financial obligations onerous.[6]

NEW GARDEN MONTHLY MEETING. As mentioned in a previous section, this group of Friends "found it a hardship to travel through a trackless forest forty miles to attend meeting at Cane Creek" and requested permission to hold their own monthly meeting, as there were forty families in the community. The official record says:

"The first business before the Cane Creek Monthly Meeting of seventh day, tenth month, 1751, was a request from Friends at New Garden to hold a meeting for worship;" and "at the Perquimans and Little River Quarterly Meeting, fifth month, 25th, 1754, the request of the Friends at New Garden to organize a monthly meeting was granted because of the hardships they underwent in attending monthly meeting at Cane Creek."*

---

* Thorne: *First Friends at New Garden.*

There were able ministers and there was much visitation of concerned Friends from a distance, and the phenomenal migration of Friends from northern parts caused the meeting to grow rapidly and there was much rejoicing as additional families arrived. According to custom the labor was necessarily co-operative and "bees" of all sorts were the order of the day. Optimism prevailed until about 1825 when the anti-slavery issue became acute. Few Quakers had slaves and in the adjoining county of Forsyth, the Moravians (Unitas Fratrum) also owned but few, but more and more it became evident that the question was becoming a vital national issue, and Friends began to perceive that a free labor economy could not without much difficulty compete with unpaid slave labor.

Friends became a body apart. Their views concerning amusements, hunting, oaths, war, dress, speech, marriage and worship tended more and more to make them a "separate people." This was accentuated by the disastrous practice of disowning members for breaches of discipline, particularly for "marrying out." This was not only stupid — it was cruel, for it deprived a person of Christian fellowship, despoiled him (or her) of the benefit of co-operative worship, and of "the Bread of Life" which the soul needed. In the small meetings it was often true that there was no person who suited the one anxious to marry.

As told elsewhere the New Garden Friends built a meeting house, supported a "Little Brick Schoolhouse," later established a Boarding School; and carried on the general activities of a frontier colony. Each home was a veritable factory, each family perforce owned the equipment for carding, spinning and weaving; the buzz of the spinning wheel was constantly heard; each family endeavored to produce its own clothing as far as possible; the men had their shoes and harness made by their neighbors, and in exchange other homemade goods were accepted. Smiths, coopers, carpenters, weavers, thatchers, butchers, millers were essential even to frontier civilization. Each community possessed these craftsmen, but they all realized that the youngsters needed a better apprenticeship than could be obtained in the small settlements upon the frontier, so it became necessary for boys and young men to be sent to the North to learn their crafts. Mary Mendenhall Hobbs' grandfather and a great uncle were sent to Chester, Pennsylvania, to learn the trades of potter and tanner.

The local meeting experienced its diminutions as well as its accretions. The westward movement seriously weakened the little group. Addison Coffin persuaded many families that there were better prospects north of the Ohio River, and many Friends regarded the cultivation of tobacco as loathsome if not actually sinful. The anti-slavery agitation seriously disturbed the Quaker community. Mails were pilfered; it was hazardous to possess a copy of Helper's *Impending Crisis* or Stowe's *Uncle Tom's Cabin*. There was malicious public criticism of Friends who permitted colored persons to attend Quaker meeting or who endeavored to educate Negroes. Then the manumission movement grew among Friends, and the quarterly and yearly meetings were times of heart searching as one by one members were given the grace and courage to emancipate their slaves. Thus Friends became involved in the Underground Railroad activities. The clouds darkened which brought the storm.

During the days of the Civil War the Quakers shared the general chaos and impoverishment. Some of the young men were required to respond to the call for military service. The regular meetings continued, but there was little joy in the gatherings, only the assurance that some day the human race would experience more of the Spirit of God in human affairs. New Garden Boarding School was never closed, but the few who remained were on a "subsistence level" basis.

Then came Francis T. King and the Baltimore Association as a veritable Messiah, and new hope was brought to the meeting and to the school. Later came the news and the influence of the Quaker revivals which had occurred in other yearly meetings, and gradually new life came to New Garden. The times had been so disrupting that it was inconceivable that if Quaker meetings survived they could be of the same order as before. They must manifest more vigor or else perish. Gradually the spirit and methods of revivalism came to New Garden, the presence of the student body perhaps made it acceptable. The story of Mary Moon is told in another place, but there were others who became fired with the evangelistic spirit. The movements which led to the formation of the Five Years Meeting (1902) and the adoption of the Uniform Discipline (1904) culminated in the acceptance, if not the general adoption of the Pastoral System in 1917.

The following have served as pastors: Edgar Williams, Joseph H. Peele, Herbert Huffman, Sr., B. Russell Branson, and Charles F. Thomas up to 1958.

Among Quakers of eminence who have been members must be numbered Thomas Thornborgh, William Coffin, William Unthank,

Nathan Hunt, Jeremiah Hubbard (for some time of Deep River), Nereus Mendenhall, Mary Mendenhall Hobbs, L. Lyndon Hobbs, J. Franklin Davis, Mary E. Davis, Alpheus White, Roxie Dixon White, John Gurney Frazier, Sr., Annie Edgerton Williams, Myra Binford, George W. White, Raymond and Helen Titsworth Binford, Howard Brinton, Edgar T. Hole and hosts of others who could be numbered among the intellectual and spiritual giants. The membership is over 500, and the Bible School attendance is about 175. Algie I. Newlin is clerk.

CONDITIONS AT NEW GARDEN AT THE CLOSE OF THE WAR. Allen Jay says: "Horses were all gone; few cattle, all poor condition; merest pretence at farming; tools worn out; harness mostly rope; vehicles in the last stage of the "one horse shay"; buildings dilapidated; roofs leaking; windows pasted over with paper or cloth because broken; fences gone, mostly burned because of scarcity of fire wood; houses and properties destroyed by fire; no sugar or tea or coffee, drank warm water with sorgham sweetening; little boys with help of their mothers did some farming and gardening; no stores at which to buy anything; no tallow for candles; lighting a big problem; roads in bad condition; bridges in disrepair; thread and needles scarce; mending a problem; furniture worn out and irreplaceable; kitchenware very scarce; new toothbrushes $4.00 apiece."[7]

THE NEW GARDEN GRAVEYARD. It has been usual for Friends nearly everywhere to possess their own burying ground. As mentioned elsewhere the interments were conducted with simplicity and uniform markers were placed, in many cases a small stone either laid or erected at the head. Many instances may be found in the minutes of this yearly meeting where families were required to cut down or else remove a large stone marker. At New Garden behind the meeting house and college is a burying ground of historic interest. An old record says that "Richard Williams took up 53 acres soon after 1750 and gave a plot of land for a meeting house and burial ground." The earliest graves are unmarked. The meeting was officially organized in 1754, but settlers had been there for at least four years before that date, and it is not unlikely that some deaths and interments had occurred. A yearly meeting was held at New Garden in 1791; details concerning the first meeting house and the first school house are uncertain. But it is established that wounded soldiers from the historic Battle of Guilford Court House, March 15, 1781, not far away, were brought to a meeting house in that vicinity, were cared for by Friends, and that thirteen (some say fifteen) British soldiers died and were buried six in one grave and seven in another in the graveyard, which at first was but two acres in extent. It is also established that there was a little brick school house (probably back of the present meeting house); some Friends say the foundations are still visible. Near to the grave of the soldiers is a gigantic tree which is known as "the Revolutionary Oak Tree." The burying ground has not been reserved exclusively for Friends, nor has the uniformity of markers been insisted upon. Harriett Green, a visiting English Friend, who died here while on a religious visit, was interred there. In 1928 the burying ground was brought by legal incorporation under the care of a board of trustees consisting of J. D. Cox, S. A. Hodgin and A. J. Hollowell. Additional land was acquired and now the property includes twenty-one acres. Many prominent members of the Society have their last resting place there.[8]

COLLEGE STUDENTS AND THE WEEK-END. The New Garden Monthly Meeting is unique among the Friends in North Carolina as the place of worship is on the Guilford College campus and the students are encouraged to attend meeting and participate in the regular church activities. Before the coming into general use of the automobile a considerable proportion of the students met regularly with the local congregation, but as every college and university administrator realizes, times have changed, and the week-end has become increasingly important. Students now expect to be away for the week-end and they select their curriculum, their schedules, their "dates" and their roommates accordingly. It is almost incredible the extent to which hitch-hiking is practiced. This profoundly affects the relation of students to a local church and college officials view the future developments with misgivings. Thus, although in recent years the number of college students has greatly increased the number of cars has multiplied and the cooperation of students with college chapel services is disappointing.

RALEIGH. A splendid example of Christian fellowship is being developed at the State Capital. In April 1926 the few Friends, largely under the inspiration of Elbert Russell met for worship and to consider the setting up of a meeting house at some future date. A meeting was organized, and at first the group met in a room at the local Y.M.C.A. By invitation they united in worship with the United Church (Congregational Christian). They retained their membership in the Society of Friends. Frequently Elbert Russell presented a message to the united congregation, always to the satisfaction and edification of the worshippers. Friends as a body did not assume any obligation for the church expenses, although individuals contributed as they wished. The monthly business meetings have been held at the homes of members, and the yearly meeting activities are participated in. Recently there has been a desire to hold a meeting for worship on the basis of silence, and so Friends are now meeting at eight o'clock on Sunday night in a room of the United Church. Once a month the period of worship is shortened so as to give opportunity for conducting the business. It is intended to formulate a plan so that several times a year a planned discussion shall be held, and refreshments served. Committees have been named to work out the details. There are 34 members at the present time. Mary Hoadley is the clerk.[9]

SPRING GARDEN STREET MEETING (Greensboro). This meeting was started at Pomona, a suburb of Greensboro, and the center of a tile manufacturing plant. It was through the faith and energy of Alford W. Hollady, Manley L. Hollady and Charles Roberts that a Quaker Meeting was organized here on September 22, 1909. Previous to this date these courageous persons had conducted a Bible School and a meeting for worship in the second story of an old store building.

After awhile the congregation moved to a corner of South Aycock and Spring Garden Street, and again later in 1926 across the street to a larger lot. During the ministry of Murray C. Johnson rooms were added for the use of the Bible School, and the auditorium was redecorated, and in the ministry of Charles C. Cross three more large Sunday School rooms were added and other improvements effected. The meeting has had a steady growth. Beginning with only ten active members by 1954 it had a membership of 357, and one of the largest Sunday Schools in the quarter. For over twenty years D. E. Allred gave his services as superintendent; the first ten years he served without missing a Sunday or being late. Eli Barker as chairman of the Promotion Committee for a number of years had a great part in the development of the Bible School. Eli Reece, who had been a missionary in Africa, was the first pastor, and served between six and seven years; he was followed by Charles G. Johnson, Samuel Barnes, Sarah Harvey, John Riley and wife Nettie Riley, Murray C. Johnson, Reuben Payne, Charles C. Cross, Orville D. Dillon, John M. Permar, Frederick E. Taylor, Kenneth Temple, Robert P. Miller, Frederick

Carter and Leslie Winslow. The first clerk was Adam B. Hinshaw; others include Ada Lee Stanley, Savilla Johnson, Eula Pugh, Ollie McBane, Edith Hendrix, Maurice Hollowell, Owen Osborne and Berta Osborne.

This meeting has always been characterized by close adherence to the "Old Fashioned Gospel" and the preaching of "the established doctrines" of the Christian faith, including Regeneration, Sanctification and Holiness. At one of the home comings a list was presented of thirty-eight members of the meeting who had become workers in the Home or Foreign field, with several active young members who plan to give themselves later to full time evangelistic service. In 1941 the congregation purchased a lot adjoining the place of worship. The building of a minister's home was accomplished at a cost of $5,022.98, and in January, 1944, the congregation approved the construction of a modern meeting house. A lot adjoining was purchased for $8,500 cash. Soon afterward, with a fund in hand of $23,327.24 the congregation gathered for a ground-breaking ceremony, and handsome contributions were made at that time. On November 15, 1953 the members gathered in happiness and gratitude for the last annual homecoming in the meeting house, in observance of 44 years as a monthly meeting. It was a time of great rejoicing, and over $1,000 was added to the building fund.

On July 14, 1954, the Friends held the last service in the old building, and on the following First Day took possession of the new, adjoining premises. Seth Hinshaw, the Executive Secretary of the Yearly Meeting, brought an appropriate message. The corner stone was laid with suitable ceremonies on November 21, 1954, which was observed as Home-Coming Day. B. Clyde Shore, treasurer of the yearly meeting, assisted at the stone laying ceremony. The new home for the growing and devoted congregation cost about $45,000.[10]

WINSTON-SALEM MEETING. To tell the story of this meeting, which is one of the youngest and which bids fair to become one of the strongest, if not the largest, in the yearly meeting, it is necessary to tell the story of David E. Sampson.

David was born in England, yet was called of the Spirit to come to North Carolina about 1800. He settled in East Bend and proved an inspiration to the Friends there and assisted in the establishment or restoration of Quaker gatherings in Yadkin and Surry Quarters. In 1885 he undertook evangelistic work in the mountains of Stokes and Surry Counties and extended his labors into Virginia. This work, known as the Mission, was taken over by the yearly meeting but was discontinued in 1918, and the properties were afterwards sold.

In 1886 David conducted evangelistic services at White Plains, and partly through his faithfulness White Plains Monthly Meeting and Surry Quarterly Meeeting were set up, the latter in 1898.

An official report says that there was much evangelical fervor in this period, and that in 1887 in Deep River Quarter there were 32 series of meetings; 304 conversions and 187 joined Friends. Much of this, however, was due to the messages and personal work of Mary Moon.

For fifteen years David travelled through North Carolina, bringing Gospel messages and great encouragement wherever he went. He usually travelled with horse and buggy, and was warmly welcomed wherever he went. Largely through his influence a monthly meeting was authorized at Graham in 1907, where he ministered till 1911. In his labors in Yadkin he was frequently accompanied by Myrtle Foltz (Nelson) and Annie Edgerton (Williams) who were acceptable vocalists. Then he had a concern to visit California, and on this occasion he was accompanied by his second wife, Sarah Marshburn, of New Garden. While ministering to the Friends in the West he was called of the Holy Spirit to return and seek to establish a meeting at Winston-Salem. He obeyed the Voice and contacted a number of Friends families whom he had known in Yadkin, and they formed the nucleus of a meeting. On Sunday, December 11, 1911, at the home of the late Catherine Pfaff the Quakers met for their first meeting at this city. Later a house was rented on Cherry Street, and the first gathering for worship there on January 2, 1912. Then for awhile Friends gathered at the Y.W.C.A. building. J. Dobson Long was the first superintendent of the Bible School.

Soon after this a building on Patterson Avenue formerly used by another denomination was acquired for the sum of $1,500. The yearly meeting appointed Nereus English and Alpheus M. Briggs as trustees.

The Friends thus took root with 34 charter members at the time the monthly meeting was organized in 1913.

DAVID SAMPSON was a blind man, yet his devoted wife acted as eyes for him, and he did not appear to be seriously handicapped. In this year David and "Sallie" Sampson were granted a minute to visit London and Dublin Yearly Meetings. This service was fulfilled satisfactorily, and they returned in 1915. To the sorrow of all the yearly meeting David passed away unexpectedly in 1916.* The loss of the leader and minister was a hard blow, but the few maintained courage. Visiting Friends came occasionally, although in those days automobiles were few. Among those who assisted were several members of the faculty of Guilford College only twenty-five miles away, but it was "a day's journey" at that time.

Among the early pastors were Elizabeth and Philip Moon, Ada Lee Stanley, William Rayhenhamp and Hugh W. Moore. By 1926 the Friends realized that a more suitable location would be of lasting benefit. Accordingly a site was purchased at the corner of Sixth and Broad Streets, and a handsome place of worship was constructed. Hugh Moore bravely undertook to collect subscriptions. For a while fortune smiled, but then the Great Depression hit us all. Friends who had been liberal subscribers were almost without means; many had no employment; several lost heavily through bank failures, and the meeting was not able to support a pastor. In the emergency Francis C. Anscombe did what his other duties permitted to hold the meeting together. The debt appeared staggering, and there were times when the congregation was threatened with the loss of the property. Under great anxiety and sometimes with little support the meeting struggled on. Those who assisted in these critical days were Bascom G. Rollins, Calvin Gregory, Isaac Harris, Howard B. Yow and Victor Murchison.

When the Depression passed and a war plant was established in the city, the economic situation was altered, and gradually Winston-Salem became one of the boom towns in the South. Hope was restored, and Friends were able to meet the current expenses, and new members began to join the congregation.

A YANKEE SOLDIER AND A CONFEDERATE MAID. Help came from an unexpected quarter, and hereon hangs an interesting story. During the Civil War, a portion of the Union army passed nearby, and a soldier named David Endsley being thirsty and seeing a Southern girl at a well drawing water went to her, and like the Man from Galilee said to the woman at the well: "Give me to drink." They chatted, and something about the girl intrigued

---

* David Sampson's widow, Sarah Marshburn Sampson familiarly known as Sallie reached the age of ninety-four and passed away June 7, 1957. The obsequies were conducted at New Garden.

him, so that when the hostilities were over, he returned to North Carolina and married the Confederate maid. He became interested in the Friends there and made a will leaving to his only son a life interest in a valuable farm, and at his death the property was to go to the local meeting. A few years after the death of the father the son was killed by a bull. With the acquisition of this property and with considerable faith and monetary sacrifice on the part of B. Clyde Shore and Ed. Mackey the balance was paid, and the congregation returned thanks and heaved a great sigh of relief to see the notes against the church publicly burned.

In addition to the church site the meeting owns two cottages adjoining, a large vacant lot, and a filling station which brings in a substantial income and which by 1956 cleared the indebtedness against this extra land. A minister's home has been provided.

Under the leadership of Victor Murchison the congregation has made remarkable progress. The pastor is a native son, and meets the needs. He is musical, and has great success in developing a men's chorus as well as a mixed choir.

AN ADDITIONAL BUILDING. All departments of the work flourished, and it became evident some years ago that additional premises were necessary. A fund for expansion was generously started by Dr. J. B. Whittington and the members cooperated with enthusiasm. Hopes became realization when after morning meeting on October 26, 1958, the congregation adjourned to the rear of the premises for a ground-breaking ceremony. The following persons manipulated the long-handled shovel in a semi-professional manner as representatives of the various departments of work: Francis C. Anscombe, Clerk of Monthly Meeting; John C. Trivette, Clerk Meeting on Ministry and Counsel; Dr. Whittington, for the subscribers; Charles Norwood, Building Committee; B. Clyde Shore, Finance; Martin Mackie, House and Grounds; Graham Patterson, Bible School; Mabel White, Women; Nellie McClenny, Sunday Night activities; Thad Martin, Quaker Men; Cynthia Cann, Young Friends; Clyde Williams, Architect; Victor Murchison, Pastor. The construction of several additional classrooms, various offices, and alterations to the auditorium is expected to be accomplished before the fall of 1959. The membership is now nearly 500; and new members are being received continually; the Bible School numbers 375; the meetings for Ministry and Counsel and the Monthly Meetings are exceptionally well attended. Ethel Payne was for five years the assistant pastor; Charlotte Pringle, Sarah Cooke and

Jean Cude have been efficient recording clerks.   Trudy Lane is
secretary.   The Youth Fellowship is very active.

CHARLES AND CALLIE CUDE.   Among those who are especially
remembered are Charles Sumner Cude (1874-1926) and his wife
Caroline Talbot Cude (1874-1954).   Charles was a devoted servant of God, a practical business man, who was enthusiastically
interested in every phase of the work of the Society of Friends.
He was a charter member, and was active in securing the
premises on Patterson Avenue, and later in building the new
meeting house.   He served the meeting in almost every capacity,
and invariably entertained visiting Friends.   His home was always
available for any good purpose.   In this dedication he was supported by his devoted wife, familiarly known as Callie.   In like
manner she was class leader, elder, clerk and a wise counsellor.
She attended meetings in her eightieth year, the day before she
was stricken in her last illness.

A CENTENARIAN.   Friends are famous for examples of longevity.
This Meeting joined in the unique circumstance of one of our
members celebrating the centennial anniversary of her birth.
Amanda Holcombe Trivette was born March 1, 1857.   Her husband died in 1945.   One hundred of her descendants and their
spouses gathered to honor the aged Friend.   There were present
five children (one being a Friends minister), twenty-one grand-
children; forty-three great-grand-children, and eight great-great-
grand-children.   She attended Friends' meeting the Sunday following her anniversary.   Apart from some hardness of hearing the
venerable Friend is in good health.   At this writing she has passed
her 102nd milestone.

REVIVAL OF THE QUARTERLY MEETING.   "For as long as mind runneth not to the contrary" quarterly meeting had been held on
Saturday. In early days it was considered one's duty to attend,
even though it involved travelling considerable distances.   It is
on record that if a Friend were appointed a representative and
did not attend he (or she) was required to give a satisfactory
apology to the next monthly meeting or else he was subject
to severe "eldering" (censure).   In recent years attendance had
dwindled until there were "just the same faithful few," and it
was actually suggested that the quarterly meeting be abandoned.
However, by a very simple change the situation has been recti-

fied, and since the beginning of 1957 almost two hundred members have attended the sessions of the New Garden Quarterly Meeting. And how was the miracle effected? Simply by meeting on Sunday afternoon! This movement did not originate in North Carolina, but blessings on the Friend who first suggested the change. It is likely to result in a far-reaching revival.

CHAPTER TWENTY-FOUR

BRETHREN DWELL TOGETHER IN UNITY

DEEP RIVER QUARTERLY MEETING. Quakers are not given to extravagant language; even superlatives are used in moderation. The writer confesses his inability to deal adequately with Deep River Quaker history. Could any genius describe the Grand Canyon of Arizona or Westminster Abbey in ten sentences? Could a virtuoso describe his reaction to a rendition of Handel's *Messiah* in one hundred words. Deep River Quarterly Meeting deserves not only a volume, but two dozen worthwhile biographies could be penned concerning individual members. This is not written in adulation, but as an apology. All that this writer can do is to be selective.

Much that has been written of the pioneers who established New Garden is pertinent to this quarter also, for the mass migration of Quakers from Nantucket Island, Eastern Pennsylvania, New Jersey and Maryland resulted in wave after wave of Quakers spreading themselves over territories included in the present counties of Alamance, Guilford and Randolph.[1] These settlers were largely of English stock, but there were capable persons of Welsh, Scotch-Irish and Pennsylvania-Dutch extraction.

Naturally the first meetings for worship were held in the homes almost certainly of the log cabin variety. It is believed that most of the migrants brought certificates of membership with them, but it must have taken time for organization to be effected. We would like to know more of these early gatherings and how the news was spread. It is understood that Cane Creek was the first to be organized in 1751 by the authority of Eastern Quarterly Meeting; New Garden Monthly Meeting, had been active since 1754. It is on record that in 1753 "Friends of Deep River request permission to hold a meeting every other fifth day at the house of Thomas Mills;" and there is another ancient minute to the effect that Mordecai Mendenhall and Walter Thornborgh requested permission to hold a meeting at Deep River every second first day in each month. This was approved by Cane Creek. In 1754 New Garden Monthly Meeting gave permission for a meeting at Deep

River on first day "at the house of Benjamin Beeson except when it is held at Mendenhalls." Meetings for worship were held more or less regularly at Deep River from 1760 and a monthly meeting was allowed in 1778; Springfield Friends worshipped together by 1773, and seven years later they became a preparative meeting; a monthly meeting was authorized in 1790 by New Garden Quarterly Meeting.

Gradually the information that Friends were satisfied with their new locations, reached their relatives to the north and the migrations continued and settlements of Friends were quite numerous in this area, but the adverse conditions which prevented the Quakers from living as a fellowship according to their convictions caused many families to forsake the South and slavery conditions and flee to the middle west. Meetings were discontinued at Barker, Cedar Grove, Kennett, Long Hill, Oak Forest and Pine Wood in North Carolina and Bethel and Maryville in Tennessee which were under the care of Deep River Quarterly Meeting. This was not all loss as many united with Friends in their new locations. The Quarterly Meeting now embraces the following monthly meetings: Deep River, 1754; Springfield, 1773; High Point, 1884; Oak Hill, 1908; Archdale, 1924; Hickory Creek, all in Guilford and Randolph Counties.* Many of the distinguished Friends who worshipped here are mentioned in connection with the Springfield Memorial Association — later in this chapter. Among the ministers some decades ago were Nereus M. Barker, Walter White, Lewis W. Macfarland, Samuel Haworth, Eugene Coltrane, Leslie Barrett, Ida L. Curtis, Clara I. Cox, Tom Alderman Sykes and Cora Lee Norman.

ARCHDALE. In addition to the Friends who came through the forests from the north were some who came by water to Charleston, South Carolina. Among them was Thomas English who married Margaret Flynn, a cousin of Lord Cornwallis. He and others founded a Quaker meeting at Bush Hill, South Carolina, and another at Charleston. Their daughter Anna married Samuel Tomlinson and moved to Pine Woods, in what was then Rowan but now Davidson county in North Carolina. Their descendants are numerous in the families of the Blairs, Englishes and Tomlinsons.

---

* The writer realizes that there are objections to putting the various monthly meetings in alphabetical order, but it was impossible to put them all in chronological order and a general pattern had to be established.

WILLIAM TOMLINSON accompanied his brother Samuel to the location of Archdale, which was formerly called Bush Hill. William purchased ten acres for five pounds from John Hoggart. There was a later grant to him of three hundred acres at ten pounds per hundred acres. Samuel Johnston, the Governor signed the grant. Tomlinson purchased other sites, so that it is said he owned nearly all the land within the present limits of Archdale. William and his wife Martha Coppock came to this section while the Indians were still inhabiting the forests. As a girl she had been kidnapped by Indians, lived among them for a while, but was eventually rescued and restored to her family. It is inferred from this and other incidents that the Quakers here were able to live on friendly terms with the natives as were their brethren in Pennsylvania. Between 1800 and 1820 many Quaker families came to settle in the neighborhood of Bush Hill. Mention should be made of Thomas, John, and William English, Eli and Henry Haworth, George, the oldest son of Eli, Nathan Hunt and John Carter.

Archdale became a typical Quaker community. The members of the Society in a unique manner exemplified the characteristics of Friends, in simplicity, sincerity, industry, thrift, generosity, and integrity. It is no exaggeration to state that from this little community have gone forth some of the most capable, honorable and distinguished citizens of the State.

ELI HAWORTH. Among the early settlers Eli Haworth should be mentioned. He was a wagoner, and made frequent trips to distant places with his covered wagons drawn by four or six horses. As there were no modern means of communication settlers on the frontier were dependent upon those who were daring and skillful enough to go to distant places, especially ports, to get supplies. Eli brought many worthy families to Bush Hill. It is on record that at times he had a regular caravan of vehicles, and also that he made the trip to Indiana seven times, a return journey occupying six months. Although the journeys involved great dangers he never carried arms. His sons joined in this enterprise when old enough. Eli was a pronounced Whig and enjoyed participating in the "log cabin" campaign of 1840.

JOSIAH TOMLINSON. Another worthy of note was Josiah Tomlinson, who was an expert worker in leather, especially saddles; this encouraged Allen Unthank Tomlinson to establish a tannery which grew into a large business; but it was destroyed by fire in 1845. So efficient were these Friends, and so varied their activities that

Bush Hill became known as "the Hive of Industry." At that time there was no High Point and no Thomasville, so Bush Hill drew custom from a large area. The Quakers possessed creative capacity and gained reputation for good materials and thorough construction.

THE PETTY FAMILY was a source of strength — commercially, socially, and religiously. Of course the Quakers in this settlement shared the views of their brethren elsewhere concerning slavery, and freed themselves from this blight. As they had been Whigs, they remained Unionists, and as they were pacifists their position became difficult after the State seceded and hostilities began. A conscript law was passed, which involved the enrollment of all males between 18 and 45 for military service. Many of the men here were freed from armed service because the Confederate Government needed boots for the army and W. C. Petty, a natural born mechanic, devised machines for manufacturing a variety of building supplies and for making shoe pegs, and the Quakers "felt free to make shoes for the soldiers."* Allen U. Tomlinson's factory also shared in the manufacturing of shoe pegs and lasts, and thus a number of other workers were exempt from combatant service. It required much tact, especially on the part of Allen U. Tomlinson, to preserve the community from the interferences of the Vigilantes.

HERBERT C. PETTY. The passing of this Friend marks a break in the ranks of historic Quakerism. For several generations the Pettys had been pioneers in industry, towers of integrity in the Archdale community, and leaders in all civil and religious enterprises. He was a fine representative of the past generation. He was graduated from Guilford in 1898 and was awarded the Master's degree from Haverford the year following. For thirty years he was connected with a manufacturing concern in New York, but moved back to his home in 1957. For twenty-four years and until his death he was a trustee of Guilford College, and his unexpected passing just after yearly meeting in 1957 was a distinct shock to the whole community.

GIDDUP DOBBIN. In April, 1865, Johnson's army, or that part known as Hardie's command, surrendered at Bush Hill. Disbanded soldiers committed serious depredations, especially in the stealing of horses. The story is told that Isham Cox, returning from meeting was met by a squad of soldiers who told him their captain had

---

* For more concerning the Petty family see chap. xxi.

ordered them to take his horse. He replied that he was obeying the orders of *his* Captain; that he was a minister of the Gospel, and his Captain was Jesus Christ. He jerked the reins, shouted "Giddup, Dobbin," and he vanished out of their sight.

Some of the members of the Society were conscripted. Enos A. Blair was not released till he had paid a fine of $500, and his son, Franklin S. Blair, was arrested when only 17. Solomon Frazier and Milton Blair, members of the nearby Springfield Meeting were tortured in a most inhumane fashion for refusing to bear arms. On another occasion sixteen young Friends had been drafted, and Allen U. Tomlinson went to the authorities on their behalf. By adroitly inviting Col. Pearson, who was described as "the coldest blooded man ever known," to several Quaker homes where he was well fed, and his horse carefully attended to, the Quaker took a paper from his pocket and said as the visitor was leaving: "Colonel, here is a paper I wish thee would sign for me." The officer did so, and so the release of the young conscientious objectors was secured.

ARCHDALE DURING RECONSTRUCTION. Quakers were abreast in education, and nearly every settlement made provision for an elementary school. Allen U. Tomlinson was teacher at such a school at Bush Hill. He was successful in the management of children with reputations for misbehavior. A so-called high school was opened in 1853, at Springfield, nearby, with David Marshall as principal. The war disrupted the continuance of schooling throughout the whole South, but when the war was over Francis T. King and the Baltimore Association undertook the restoration of the elementary schools in the Quaker districts. John Scott under these auspices opened about sixty schools, and later Joseph Moore was named as superintendent. One such school was established at Archdale and became conspicuous. Today there is a handsome modern school building known as the Allen Jay School in memory of the sainted evangelist who ministered in this community as a representative of the Baltimore Association. The Model Farm, also a product of the Association was located in this Friends' community.*

As soon as practicable after the conclusion of the war visiting ministers came from other yearly meetings with the Gospel of Good Will as well as material encouragement. Among those who visited Archdale and the neighboring meetings were Elwood

---

* See section concerning the Baltimore Association in chap. ix.

Osborne, Thomas and Allen Jay, Samuel Lloyd, Carolina Talbot, Joseph Neave from England, Amos Kenworthy, Eli and Sybil Jones, and John Henry Douglas; the latter was a fine specimen of manhood with a powerful and convincing Gospel message. Ada Lee Stanley for some time was a resident minister.

For many years Springfield and Archdale functioned as one monthly meeting, and Clara I. Cox from 1918 served both meetings as pastor. In 1924 Archdale was set up as a separate meeting. Reuben J. Payne followed (1926-35); Benjamin H. Millikan (1935-37); Clifton C. Pearson (1937-52); Isaac Harris since 1952. In January 1956, the Lions Club of Archdale-Trinity honored Isaac Harris as the outstanding citizen of the community including Archdale, Trinity, Allen Jay and Springfield. He was presented with a plaque in recognition of his leadership in promoting health, morals, education, religion and economics.

A HOLY EXPERIMENT. The Archdale Quaker community is a conspicuous example of what can be accomplished when a group of citizens are united in Christian love, possessed of skills and characterized by integrity cooperating to establish the Kingdom of God upon earth. They were active in promoting not only education, but temperance, the study of the Scriptures, literature, and good local government. Many of the worthies who helped to develop the community have been memorialized in the annual gatherings of the Springfield Memorial Association, and a list will be found in the section referring to that Society.[2]

The Bush Hill-Archdale Quakers were active in supporting an Academy, which was not just a community school but which drew students from many parts of the State. To some degree it was a preparatory school for nearby Trinity College (which eventually became Duke University). Cyrus P. Frazier and Nereus C. English were among those who headed this academy. Its good work is mentioned in the Collins *Journal,* which is one of the treasures of the yearly meeting archives.

DEEP RIVER MONTHLY MEETING. A large number of the Quaker migrants settled in a community which was destined to become of historic importance, for it is no exaggeration to say that the Friends in this community preserved civilization during the dark days of the Reconstruction era, and that from this center have gone forth many families who have attained eminence elsewhere. As previously mentioned Friends were here about 1750, and New Garden Monthly Meeting granted permission for a meeting to be held regularly at "the home of Benjamin Beeson, except when it is held at Mordecai Mendenhall's." The preparative status was granted in 1760, and the monthly meeting was organized in 1778. A log meeting place was erected in 1758. It is believed this was of the conventional pattern with a movable partition separating the men's and women's business sessions. One account says the place "looked very much like a barn . . . and was warmed by stoves, whose pipes extending through the overhead ceiling, discharged their contents into the space beneath the rafters. The final escape of this smoke was through the cracks between the shingles. Why the house did not burn down is an unsolved riddle." No deed was given for the forty acres of land till 1809. The original structure was replaced in 1875 by the brick building now in use. Stanley Pumphrey, a distinguished English Friend, who travelled extensively in North Carolina gave the message at the dedicatory services.

In the two hundred years of its existence this meeting became the center of the life of the community. It was an industrial settlement, and folks came long distances to secure the products of the saw mills, grist mills, potteries, tanneries and hardware stores. It became a busy trading post where furniture, clothing, wagons, looms, spinning wheels, boots, saddles and other leather goods were produced. These industrial centers were few, and skilled craftsmen were scarce. There were gunsmiths in the community, but Quakers would not manufacture guns.*

ONE OF THE EARLIEST SCHOOLHOUSES. Friends from an early date provided for elementary education, and they constructed the first schoolhouse in southwest Guilford County. It was a log building, and the site has been marked by a substantial granite monument. Levi Coffin taught there between 1813 and 1822. A second school building was provided in 1830, and this served a valuable purpose until 1858, when a brick house was provided. "This seems to have been the last of the free schools until long after the Civil War," which disrupted the whole educational system of the Southern States till after 1877 when the Federal troops were withdrawn by President Rutherford B. Hayes.

---

* Thomas Marshall has performed a monumental service for the preservation of the Quaker records, for the archives now possess retyped and rebound copies of the Deep River Men's Minute Books from 1790 to 1885; also the Women's Minute Book 1790 to 1886; and in addition are birth and death records and twelve typed pages of genealogies professionally and alphabetically arranged. The collection is said to be among the most complete in the whole country, and every Friend, especially those of Quaker ancestry, should examine these records.

Names of the early Friends are not available, partly because the Society at that time was "enjoined to maintain its testimony against affixing superfluous monuments, of any description, to graves."

It is known, however, that many whose remains are interred here in the old graveyard were prominent in the community and State. Among them may be mentioned Dr. James R. Gordon, Jonathan Harris, Stephen G. Horney, Richard, George C. and Dr. Nereus Mendenhall, J. S. Ragsdale, William Wiley and Cyrus J. Wheeler. Other notable Quaker families who worshipped here included those named Armfield, Beeson, Coffin, Cooke, Chipman, Folger, Gordon, Gardner, Haines, Howell, Iddings, Macy, Mills, Mendenhall, Starbuck, Stuart, and Thornton. Among the early ministers were Joseph Potts and George Wood.

MINISTERS OF THE WORD. According to custom the early meetings for worship were of the conservative quietist order, but Deep River followed the general movement for the adoption of the pastoral system. Among the "weighty Friends" of this meeting should be mentioned Amos Stuart. He was a trustee of Guilford College and the father of one of its valued teachers. With his entire family he moved to the West. His then small son, Elbridge Stuart became the successful founder, and for many years the President of the Carnation Milk Company. Among the many benefactions of Elbridge Stuart is his generous contribution to the Endowment Fund of Guilford College.

Among those who have assisted in the ministry may be mentioned Elizabeth Field Moon, Leslie H. Barrett, Ida Curtis, Thomas Hendricks, Clifton C. Pearson, Samuel L. Haworth, Joseph H. Peele, Elbert D. Newlin, Paul Osborne, Isaac Harris, Francis Carrier and Millard Jones. An appropriate educational building has been planned for the near future at a cost of $25,000, and a suitable home for the minister has also been provided, and named in memory of Joseph H. Peele. Deep River claims to be the first monthly meeting to have an orchestra, that being introduced in 1945. A special commemoration of the bi-centennial was held on September 12, 1954. There was a great homecoming, and addresses were given by Elbert D. Newlin and Leslie H. Barrett. The present membership is 285, with a Sunday School of 113. Allen Seifert is clerk. This center of Quakerism has unquestionably been a great Christianizing influence throughout two centuries, and will continue to be the salt of the earth in this community. For many years it was the only place of worship within considerable radius.[3]

HICKORY CREEK MEETING attributes its recent spiritual awakening to prayer. The Friends here have an experience almost unique. As many as twenty assemble on Saturday night for prayer, neighboring ministers have brought inspiring messages, and a Revival occurred in November, 1957. A fund has been started to effect needed improvements to the property. The membership is quite small, but there is a vigorous Bible School. In February, 1958, an Old Time Quaker meeting was planned, and Algie I. Newlin, the Clerk of the Yearly Meeting, was a visiting minister, dealing chiefly with Quaker history. Among the pastors have been Selena Parsons, Paul Andrews, Baxton Anthony and Thomas Hendrix. The clerk is Glen Wall.

HIGH POINT has one of the strongest meetings in the yearly meeting; its membership includes doctors, lawyers, educators, bankers and successful businessmen. It is one of those centers which benefitted by the great migration of Quakers and others from New England, Pennsylvania, Maryland and Virginia about the middle of the XVIIIth century. Many settled in that part of the Piedmont section of the State which is now known as Guilford, Randolph, Surry, Chatham and Alamance Counties. These migrants were largely responsible for the setting up of Cane Creek (1751), New Garden (1754), Centre (1772), Deep River (1778), Springfield (1790), High Point (1892) and Oak Hill (1908) Monthly Meetings. All these settlements had meetings for worship many years before they were organized as separate monthly meetings.

A LIGHT SET UPON A HILL. A preparative meeting was established at High Point in 1885. These meetings have been almost everywhere discontinued, for such were what was known as "allowed" meetings and did not have autonomy and could not make contracts. They needed representatives to the monthly meeting to which they were responsible, usually at the close of the morning meeting before the monthly meeting. High Point was set apart as a monthly meeting in 1892.

The North Carolina Yearly Meeting was held at High Point from 1883 to 1905 and then returned to New Garden. The High Point congregation then used the old meeting house for its activities. The congregation grew rapidly, and in 1903, a handsome and commodious stone structure was erected in the heart of the city. It was later extended in the rear, and an annex was provided for classrooms and social activities. The city has made remarkable growth and has become a national center of the furniture manufacturing industry. The site of the meeting house was in a congested area, and in common with many other church attenders, Friends found difficulty in parking. It became evident that a more commodious site should be secured, and the hopes of the members were brought within sight of realization on February 20, 1955, when on a bright Sunday afternoon a very large number of Friends and neighbors gathered together for a ground-breaking service on a twelve acre tract of land on Quaker Lane, not far from the site of the old meeting place. Those taking part in the service included Ed. Mendenhall, clerk; Seth B. Hinshaw, Executive Secretary of the Yearly Meeting; Cecil E. Haworth, minister; and A. Scott Parker, Horace S. Haworth, John W. Clinard, Joseph D. Cox, Anna Mendenhall, Groome Fulton, Jr., Lelia T. Clinard, Silas B. Casey as representatives of the several activities. With furnishings the new premises are expected to be worth nearly $500,000. The dedication service occurred on November 27, 1955, and the building and equipment ranks among the best of its kind in the Five Years Meeting. Here is one of the finest organs in a Quaker Meeting House, the generous gift of the family of Marvin Boren and Elvira (Lowe) Smith.

Already the attendance has considerably increased. A suitable home for the minister has been provided. The High Point Friends have long been conspicuous as leaders in all constructive activities, the Men's Bible Class, the Quaker Men's Organization, the Women's Missionary Society, and the Young Friends Meeting are but a few of the activities.

Among the recorded ministers who have witnessed for the Truth in this community were Fernando and Abbie Cartland, Ellison R. Purdy, Thomas Anderson, Frank Clark, J. Robert Parker, Mary E. Cartland, Clara I. Cox, Walter White. The pastors included Joseph Potts, 1892-94; Mead Kelsey, 1897-1900; Eli Reece, 1900-07; Enos Harvey, 1907-12; Lewis W. MacFarland, 1912-15; Dr. Sylvester Newlin, 1915-18; Samuel L. Haworth, 1918-23; Andrew Mitchell, 1919-20; Tom Alderman Sykes, 1923-37; Cecil E. Haworth, 1937 to the present. The clerks have included Otis Mendenhall, David H. Parsons, Sr., Alice Paige White, Ed. E. Mendenhall. Others who have rendered conspicuous service in leadership include J. Elwood Cox, Robert Ragan and Dr. Frederick Taylor. The membership totals 847, with an enrollment in the Sunday School of 505 and an average attendance of 291 for 1954.[4]

ALPHEUS M. BRIGGS is another worthy who devoted his chief interests to the promotion of the Kingdom of God and measured up to the high level of the Quakers of Deep River Quarter. He was a

son of B. F. and Phoebe Ledbetter Briggs, and was born at Jamestown, October 8, 1857. He married Mary Richardson and joined
Friends at Deep River in 1890. It was soon apparent he possessed
what Friends called "solid character," and he was appointed an
elder and soon afterwards in 1892 was nominated a trustee of the
local church affairs. In 1902 he moved to High Point and engaged
in the business of manufacturing buggies and carriages. One of
his sons is Gurney Briggs, whose musical talents have greatly enriched the church services for miles around.

It may well be said that from the time Alpheus removed to
High Point he was identified with everything that concerned the
Quakers in North Carolina until he departed this life. For thirty
years he was a teacher in the Bible School, instructing, as he called
them "the old folks;" he was clerk of Deep River Quarterly Meeting
for twenty years; he served on the yearly meeting Evangelistic
Committee, and was from 1915 to 1935 chairman of that important
body. He was a member of the Orphanage Committee, and its
treasurer; he was a trustee of the Tripp fund and also a trustee
of the yearly meeting from 1907 to 1929.

On the occasion of the Edmundson-Fox celebration at Hertford on June 11, 1929, he was a member of the committee of
arrangements and drew the sketch for the marker, and Mary M.
Petty decided upon the lettering. He also was a valued member
of the Permanent Board (which is the standing committee which
acts officially for the whole Society).

It is an acknowledged fact that for at least half a century
Alpheus was recognized as a man of prudence, sound judgment,
caution, grace and charity and was invariably named upon important committees of the monthly, quarterly and yearly meetings.
He was not just a member; he was known as a conscientious
worker. The Society does not seem the same without such men
as he.[5]

DR. FREDERICK R. TAYLOR is an example of a scientist who found
in the Quaker concept of worship a way to Reality. He was a
man who had a profound concept of spiritual values and who
could see beyond the materialistic and the symbols to the Truths
dimly expressed by the outward forms. In his practice of medicine
he found delight in "thinking the thoughts of God after Him," and
of ministering to humanity as a religious service. Though well
versed in philosophy and psychology he had little use for theology,
as he knew the Ultimate Realities were indefinable. Dr. Taylor

commanded attention in any group, though he was never self-assertive, it was just because he possessed so full and rich a personality, was so well informed and so universal in his interests that he also was worth listening to.

He was born in New Jersey in 1887; received a degree in science at Haverford in 1909; the M.D. from the University of Pennsylvania in 1913, and settled in High Point for general practice in 1915. During World War I he served at a U.S. base hospital in France and then did graduate work at Harvard. On returning to High Point he limited his practice to internal medicine and neuropsychiatry. He soon became a recognized authority in his chosen field, and contributed more articles to the Oxford Loose Leaf Medical Dictionary than any other person. He became a member of the faculty of the Bowman Gray School of Medicine at Winston-Salem, and was a member of many of the learned societies in the world of medicine, and among his many honors was a complimentary banquet and a silver plaque from the Guilford Medical Society.

He and his family were staunch supporters of the local meeting of which he was an elder; attended meetings when his practice permitted, occasionally spoke in meeting and always took a keen interest in the affairs of the yearly meeting. During his later years he experienced with the Great Apostle that "while the outward man perisheth the inward man is renewed day by day." "In weakness and weariness" he labored to alleviate the sufferings of others. At the age of 68, on November 1, 1955, he passed away and at a memorial service the local pastor, Cecil Haworth, read a number of poems and other writings of "the beloved physician." He was a fine representative of the Society of Friends.[6]

ALICE PAIGE WHITE. If the members of the yearly meeting were asked to name the person who most fully measures up to the ideal Quaker woman in all probability Alice Paige White would be overwhelmingly nominated. It would be difficult to imagine a more perfect exemplification of a woman Friend. This gracious lady possesses culture of the finest quality — the product of a godly home, of extensive education, foreign travel, wide acquaintance of Quaker academies, great universities, college faculties and the leading Quaker families of the nation. In addition she has participated in the leadership of local affairs and at the age of 87 is as active as the proverbial cricket.

Alice Paige was born at Cape Cod, Massachusetts, in 1871, of a distinguished Quaker family; she attended the public schools at Lynn, Mass., and received the Bachelor's degree from Boston University in 1893, majoring in Latin, and later was awarded the Phi Beta Kappa key. She made great contributions to the Quaker academies teaching at Germantown, Westtown and Oakwood, besides some private schools. She enriched her personality by following graduate studies at Columbia University for which she received the Master's degree in 1907; she also attended Harvard, the University of North Carolina and Pendle Hill.

In 1910 she married Henry White, a buggy manufacturer of High Point, who is remembered by his contemporaries as a man of integrity and leadership. Upon removing to High Point Alice Paige White identified herself with the local meeting, and it would require many pages to enumerate her activities and interests, which included that of recording clerk for many years; teacher of the Women's Bible Class. In addition she was a leader in many public bodies and was the recipient of many distinguished service awards.

Upon the establishment of High Point College in 1924 it was almost inevitable that she should become a member of the faculty, for her erudition, graciousness and prestige were matters of public knowledge. Here till she was half-way through the years of an octogenarian she was a competent instructor in Greek, Latin, Biblical Literature, English, Mythology and Library Science. She is among the most beloved members of the whole community, and in culture and scholarship occupies an eminent position.[7]

HOMECOMING. Hitherto the High Point Friends had not celebrated special occasions, but after they were in their new commodious and up-to-date building it was fitting to encourage former members and attenders to return home. The proceedings occurred on the nineteenth and twentieth of October, 1957. On the first day a program of sacred music was given by the organist, Evelyn Pearson Blair. This was followed by a reception for Dr. Alexander C. Purdy and his wife. Alexander Purdy was the guest minister at the Sunday morning meeting for worship. His father, Ellison R. Purdy, had been active in the organization of the High Point Meeting in the late eighties. The speaker was a graduate of Penn College, of Hartford Theological Seminary, and for many years Dean of that institution. He is an author of distinction and a recognized leader among Friends. The Homecoming was largely attended and was a great occasion.

OAK HILL is situated in the western portion of High Point and is a rapidly growing section. The Friends' work commenced in 1861 when in war time Jacob Addison Hedgecock established a one room log schoolhouse not far from the present Thomasville. The Springfield meeting the next year assisted in starting a Sunday School in the same little building. Parthenia Henley was in charge and was assisted by Jane Anderson, Mary Suits, Morris Marsh, Jane Albertson and Joshua Anderson. Owing to bad roads and bad weather the school could not be carried on during the winter months. Springfield Monthly Meeting appointed a committee to encourage the work. During these early years Friends were active in the temperance cause, and Springfield and High Point Friends assisted in advocating temperance at Oak Hill. It may not be out of place to let our younger readers know that in the latter quarter of the last century temperance was a live issue and many Protestant churches held regular temperance meetings and a vigorous protest against the liquor traffic was maintained. "Bands of Hope" were common and Oak Hill had its "Temperance Band." Those who remember and who actively participated are appalled at the indifference of the churches to the increasing use of alcoholic liquors by professing Christians.

The local Friends consisted of a nucleus of five families including 27 persons. Their first concern was for a better schoolhouse, which was secured in 1879 and a Preparative Meeting under the care of Springfield Monthly Meeting and Deep River Quarterly Meeting was set up. By 1905 the Friends at Oak Hill built a meeting house and three years later the Quarterly Meeting appointed a committee to supervise the establishment of a monthly meeting which was accomplished on the "eighth of tenth month," at which time the names of the 27 charter members were read, and also the minutes of the quarterly meeting authorizing the proceedings. Alta Anderson (Burton) was appointed clerk and she served the monthly meeting in that capacity for a quarter of a century. In 1923 the women effected an organization and during the years sponsored many projects for the community. The Friends took the lead in advocating better school facilities, and largely through their activities new schoolhouses were erected in High Point and at Oak Hill in 1925. The church renders a necessary service to the community; the membership has grown till it is now 295 with 246 in the Bible School. The following have served as pastors: Thomas Anderson, James White, Bertha V. Smith, Clarence Macon, Robert Melvin, Cora Lee Norman.

J. Waldo Woody, Norman Osborne, Reuben Payne, D. Virgil Pike, Elbert Newlin, Theodore Perkins, and Hershel Hill. The clerks have included F. U. Burton, Ruth Anderson, Mabel Russell, Daniel Anderson, Eva Woody, Tilmont Slack, Wade Russell.

The work outgrew the premises and preparations for a new meeting house were developed and on Sunday, April 3, 1955, a large number of Friends gathered for ground breaking ceremonies. The clerk, J. Wade Russell, presided; Seth B. Hinshaw, the Executive Secretary of the Yearly Meeting read suitable portions of Scripture and offered the invocation; Jeanette Hill read Whittier's poem "We Would Be Building;" others who participated included R. Ernest Lamb, Garland Cranford, Coolidge Murrow, Alma Burton, Blanche Farley, Ethel Newton, Ruby Cross, Bill Burton and Hershel M. Hill. The new building was completed and occupied in 1956.[8]

To celebrate the Golden Anniversary a pageant prepared by Sara Richardson Haworth was presented on October eleventh, 1958. The leading Friends of previous generations were impersonated in three scenes, representing the original Bible School, the Temperance Band and the Monthly Meeting. The pageant was appropriately named "From Small Beginnings."

SPRINGFIELD — AN HISTORIAN'S PARADISE. Here is a perfect picture of the frontier; here is an unbroken record of progress from the primeval wilderness tenanted by Indians, buffaloes and deer to as beautiful a representative of modern culture as can be found anywhere in the old North State. Here may be found by the score direct descendants of the early courageous colonists who crossed the Atlantic in sailing ships and suffered the hardships of voyages lasting from four to six weeks, and who then braved the unknown dangers of a forest to reach a settlement far from the coast. Others left the relative security of the Quaker Commonwealth of Pennsylvania to come to a location which had been described to them as "the fairest spot on earth." These early settlers were not only Men of God, they were skilled, industrious, resourceful, progressive. They founded a colony which generation after generation thrust forth its sons and daughters to be the makers of a mighty nation, mighty not in the cause of war, but in the arts of peace and constructive citizenship. From Springfield they settled in High Point and Thomasville and New Garden, and from these centers they spread away west to Indiana, Ohio, Illinois, to Iowa, to Kansas and Nebraska, and in the next generations to Oregon and California.

THE NAMES OF THE DISCIPLES. Read over the roster of the Quakers who established the Society in Deep River Quarterly Meeting, and you find the names which recur again and again in the history of the State and the nation. There are such familiar and honored names as Barker, Barrett, Beeson, Blair, Carter, Coltrane, Coffin, Cox, Curtis, Dennis, English, Frazier, Haworth, Hockett (or Hoggett), Hunt, Johnson, Kersey, Mendenhall, Millikan, Petty, Pickett (or Piggott), Pidgeon, Ragan, Reynolds, Stanley, Tomlinson, Unthank, White and Wilson.

These are not mere names extracted from some old minute books; they are living saints of the third and fourth generation of the first settlers. Throughout the years they have inter-married until the Friends who live within thirty miles of Springfield and Archdale are one big family united in the bonds of Christian fellowship. And they are not merely pious, they are substantial citizens, bankers, lawyers, doctors, teachers, professional men and women, business men, some serving with a distinction in the State legislature, the judiciary, and in every worthy department of a complex society. Few communities have so illustrious a record for producing men and women far above the average in leadership, in intelligence, in public esteem. Here can be found history in all its phases — pioneering, the frontier conditions, cooperation, creative genius, agriculture, house-building, inventiveness in the arts and crafts, establishment of craft shops which later became large and nationally known manufacturing establishments, frontier schools which in course of time became models for the State — and it was all religion. Everything that was done was performed as a religious service. The common simple faith of Quakers inspired them. Consciously they were building the Kingdom of God on earth.

THE BUILDING OF THE TEMPLE. Here is the history of the meeting houses. There have been four. The first was built in 1773 and was of the log cabin variety. This was about a score of years after Friends began to settle there, so we may be sure that till that time they met for worship in the homes of members. As roads were non-existent worshippers probably came on horseback. We wish we could see them. Did the women ride side saddle? How many children rode on one horse? How long before they possessed riding horses? Did any come in ox wagons? We only know that they came, and that in the very early days there were men and women who were sensitive to the Voice Within and had messages of Grace for the worshippers. The museum occupies approximately the site of the first meeting house which was used for about thirty years.

In 1805 a second house of worship was erected west of the first building. This was of frame construction, and as one would suspect innocent of paint inside and out. There were two entrances — one for men and the other for women. The house, according to the ancient custom, was divided into two by a partition, and men and women sat separately. The upper portion of the partition was removed during worship, but put into position for the business sessions. There were numerous "upping blocks" in the yard, but youngsters of today will not know the purpose of such structures.

The third meeting place was designed by John Carter, Jeremiah Piggott and Allen U. Tomlinson and was erected in 1858 at a cost of $1,114.67. This was one of the first brick churches built in the community. This building is now the museum. It is well it has been preserved so that future generations may know that it did not require multitudes of modern conveniences and gadgets to develop character. By general desire this place of worship was built as nearly as possible on the site of the first, built in 1773. The upping blocks were utilized as steps for the new meeting house.

As time changes all things, so the Quakers of Springfield became possessed of new ideas, and they were among the first in the yearly meeting to realize that the outward appurtenances of Quakerism were non-essential, so in 1927 a new, modern, beautiful and attractive sanctuary was constructed at a cost of $50,000. This building is one of the most artistic in the whole Quaker world, but there was love for the old place, and so it was preserved and connected with the new by a colonnade, this being appropriately dedicated to Francis T. King, Allen Jay and Joseph Moore. In the assembly room are many bronze plaques memorializing the worthy men and women who had a part in making Springfield a little bit of the Kingdom of God on earth. At the dedication services Samuel Haworth and Elbert Russell brought appropriate messages, and the venerable and aged John C. Thomas of Baltimore, who had been the secretary of the Baltimore Association gave an account of the activities of Francis T. King and the association which had done so much to restore Quakerism in North Carolina. The Springfield Memorial Meeting has its full quota of activities in the Bible School, Women's Missionary Society, Men of the

Church and Young People's activities. A substantial home for the minister stands close by built in 1941 at a cost of $9,000.

Among those who were able ministers before the adoption of the pastoral system in 1914 were William and Amanda Richardson, Nereus Barker and Walter White. The first pastor was George Walker, of Ingersoll, Oklahoma. Clara I. Cox rendered a conspicuous service from 1918 to 1940.* Others who followed include Milton H. Hadley, Elbert D. Newlin, Millard Jones and David Stanfield. There is a membership of 496 and a Bible School of 229.

SPRINGFIELD HISTORICAL MUSEUM. Not only is Springfield an historian's paradise, it is a mecca for an antiquarian. The third meeting house was converted into an historical museum when the new sanctuary was built in 1927. Not only was there an attachment to the old place, but there was a concern that future generations should have the opportunity to see the conditions under which their forebears lived and worshipped. So many of the first and second generations had possessed inventive and constructive genius that there was not a family of the old stock that did not treasure various articles which their ancestors had utilized. These things were now out-of-date and stored away.

It was John J. Blair who headed the movement to collect these curiosities and display them as an historical exhibit. The suggestion met with unanimous approval, and so in 1927 repairs were effected to the structure built in 1858. So far as was possible the interior was restored to its original form, the oldest inhabitants being consulted. Then the community set to work, and from closets, attics, cellars, storerooms, barns, stables and garages articles which had done service between one and two centuries were produced. And what a collection there now is! Arranged in order one may see and handle the tools of the smith and the wagon maker, the carpenter and the weaver. There are the heavy iron pots that great-grandma hefted and the farm implements over which some saint sweated generations ago. There are all sorts of house furnishings, besides harrows, plows, knives, cobbler's tools, school equipment and many hand-made quilts. The old-time Quaker bonnets of grandma and great-great grandma always delight the children. Visitors come from all parts of the world to inspect this almost unique exhibit. It is not a conglomeration of

---

* See the story of Clara I. Cox in a later section in this chapter.

odds and ends gathered promiscuously, but it is a tangible memorial of the saints whose names the antiques bear. So much material has been accumulated that the Association faces the question of expansion.

A GENEALOGIST'S DELIGHT.   Not only is there an historical museum at Springfield but a storehouse of information for the genealogist. Friends from the beginning were meticulous in keeping records of births, deaths, marriages and removals.   Concerning burials they bore an ancient testimony against excessive grief and display and expense at funerals.   Elaborate monuments were not allowed in burial grounds, and many congregations insisted upon uniform and simple markers.   If the family of the deceased could not afford a marker, it was placed in position by the meeting.   The first graves at Springfield were near the old meeting house and had been neglected.   William D. Mendenhall, then living in Greensboro, but who loved to visit the scenes of his boyhood, became distressed at the sign of neglect.   On more than one occasion he would clean a particular area, but the job was too great for one person, so he called a few Friends together and laid before them his concern that some systematic and proper care should be taken of the graveyard.   One idea suggested another, and out of discussion arose the Springfield Memorial Association, in 1906.   A constitution was drawn up, members enrolled, with a small annual fee for the purpose of improving the grounds.   Then it was suggested that an annual gathering should include a memoir to one of the departed Friends and to attend to related business.   From this concern of William D. Mendenhall has developed one of the most beautiful fellowships.   John J. Blair was elected the first president and filled the office for a quarter of a century.   He was succeeded by Oscar E. Wilson, who served till his death in 1941.   Nereus C. English followed; John Fries Blair is now president; Byron Haworth the first vice-president; Dovie Hayworth is secretary; Amanda Mattocks, treasurer.   The annual gathering begins with a period of worship, followed by a picnic lunch, and then a memorial is read concerning some worthy member of the community.

THESE ALL DIED IN FAITH.   In sequence those who have been so memorialized are Nathan Hunt, John Carter, Mahlon Hockett, William Hill, Allen Unthank Tomlinson, Nancy Holton, Joash Reynolds, Annie Blair Reynolds, Allen Jay, William Richardson, Amanda Buffington Richardson, Jeremiah Pickett, B. Franklin Blair, George Fox, Dr. J. Milton Tomlinson, Martha Hunt Tomlinson, Yardley Warner, Mary Carter Millikan, Harrison Frazier, Gracette Pickett Frazier, Francis T. King, George Haworth, Henry Haworth, Micajah Haworth, George Haworth II, Eli Haworth, Nereus C. English, Duncan White, William Sidney Tomlinson, William D. Mendenhall, Abigail Hunt Blair, Sara English Blair, William Clinton Petty, Victoria Haworth Petty, John Jay Blair, Moses Hammond, Nancy Petty Hammond, Clara I. Cox, Cyrus P. Frazier, Charles F. Tomlinson, David H. Blair, Dora E. Richardson, Martha E. Blair, Susie M. Millikan, J. Edward Millikan, S. Halstead Tomlinson, William A. Blair, Richard R. Hollowell, Estelle Tomlinson Smith. Not many little communities have produced such a galaxy of worthy citizens.

The Springfield Memorial Association thus performs five valuable services: first, it provides an occasion when relatives and friends come from many parts, and often long distances, to renew the fellowships of former years; second: it brings to mind in the memorial a worthy Friend whose work on earth has been completed; third: it keeps alive the memory of the laborers of the past as the visitors inspect the graves; fourth: it includes a visit to the museum and as likely as not some contribution to the quaint and interesting collection; five: the uniting in worship deepens the spiritual life of the whole community.

During the dark days of the Reconstruction Period Governor Worth said that Springfield was the only green spot in the state. No Quaker visitor to North Carolina can afford to omit visits to Springfield and the neighboring Archdale and High Point. There one can see what the Faith of our Fathers has accomplished.

In 1942 on Sunday morning the meeting house caught fire. It was saved by heroic work, and not one thing was lost although the fire damage was extensive. Complete restoration was effected. In 1950 a beautiful chapel was added, and the Allen Jay House was restored at a cost of about $60,000. Eight acres were added to the cemetery at a cost of $10,000. The Memorial Association now has an endowment of $30,000.[9]

CLARA I. COX. No one more completely exemplified the ideal Quaker lady than did Clara I. Cox. She might have been a society belle, enjoying luxury, privilege and pleasure, but the Spirit of the Inward Christ led her to a life of loving sacrificial service. Her simplicity, naturalness and neighborliness were the fruit of the Holy Spirit. She was the daughter of J. Elwood and Bertha E. Snow Cox, and was born December 18, 1879, and passed away

January 31, 1940.   She was educated at Guilford College, White's
Bible School in New York and Columbia University.   Early in life
she decided that she could best express her personality by devoting
herself to the ministry.   She was an ideal pastor, for it was in
visiting in the homes that she exercised her choicest gifts.

For some years she was the pastor at Archdale and then for
more than twenty-one years at Springfield.   She merited the confidence and affection of all who knew her.   She was active in the
cause of temperance, peace and missions.   For several sessions she
was the recording clerk of the yearly meeting, and on one occasion
she performed this service for the Five Years meeting.   At her
memorial service tributes were paid by Murray C. Johnson, Joseph
H. Peele and Cecil Haworth.[10]

The Springfield Friends celebrated their 185th Anniversary
on May 4, 1958.   Mildred E. White, who had spent many years as
a missionary and teacher in Palestine and who later became the
Educational Secretary of the Board of Missions, was the guest
minister.

THE BLAIR FAMILY is a fine example of the North Carolina Quakers.
A knowledge of the characteristics and contributions of the Blairs
is an insight into the integrity, dignity and essential qualities of
members of the Society of Friends.   Not only did they possess
distinguished ancestors but they had the great privilege of associating through many years with a galaxy of God-fearing, intellectual and progressive neighbors and none could have desired a
more inspiring and wholesome environment.

For purposes of clarity the family tree will be presented first,
and some particulars of the individual members will follow.   The
patriarch Nathan Hunt* (1758-1835) had a son named Samuel
(1788-1877) who married Elizabeth Tomlinson.   Their daughter
Abigail Prudence Hunt (1829-1906) married in 1858 Solomon I.
Blair (1827-1896) who was a son of John and Elizabeth Blair.
Solomon and Abigail became the parents of eight children, one of
whom died in infancy.   The survivors were William Allen Blair
(1859-1948); John J. (1860-1937); Emma (1864-1949); Ada (1864-
1958); David (1868-1944); Martha (1868-1947) and Elva (1870-
1956).

WILLIAM A. BLAIR was a person of distinction, a graduate of
Haverford and Harvard Colleges, and a student at Johns Hopkins

---

* See chap. ix.

University. He became a well-known educator, lecturer, banker and served in many public capacities. He was for half a century a member and chairman of the State Board of Public Welfare and received a citation from the Governor and was honored by the University of North Carolina with the degree of Doctor of Laws.

JOHN J. BLAIR studied at Guilford and was graduated from Haverford. He made exceptional contributions to education in his native State, teaching at several public schools, being principal and superintendent in Winston. His ability attracted attention and he became Director of the State Schoolhouse Planning Board; President of the Teachers' Assembly; President of the State Association of City School Superintendents; President of the National Association of Supervisors of School Buildings. Thus for many years he was one of the leaders in the advancement of public education, and did much to revive the school system which had been almost completely destroyed during the War and Reconstruction Period. In common with his family connections he was deeply interested in all the concerns of the yearly meeting and was a prime mover in the establishment of the Springfield Memorial Association and the Historical Museum.

EMMA BLAIR received her education at Springfield, New Garden Boarding School, Westtown Academy, Pennsylvania, and Greensboro College for Women. She devoted herself to education, at a time when teachers received meager remuneration, and filled many appointments for more than half a century. Her activities were not limited to her school duties, for she was interested in all civic affairs and was devoted to the Springfield meeting.

ADA BLAIR (twin sister of Emma) also devoted her life to public education, and after attending Springfield, New Garden and Westtown taught at various centers, including Guilford College. Eventually she settled at the home place at High Point and taught there for thirty-three years. In recognition of her ability and devotion one of the public schools was named for her.

DAVID BLAIR attended the local schools and New Garden and was awarded the A.B. degree from Haverford; he also attended the State University to study law. For a while he practiced teaching in Winston-Salem and in Washington, D.C. This led him to become a commissioner of Public Revenue and to be identified with the National Republican Party. He was of much assistance in the financing of the reconstruction of the Springfield Meeting House.

MARTHA BLAIR (twin sister to David) in common with the family attended the local schools, New Garden and the Women's College in Greensboro, and had some experience in teaching, but the management of the large dairy farm and residence required her attention.   Much could be written of this household, for it was a typical Quaker home, and was the rendezvous of visiting Friends, famous for its hospitality and high level of conversation and fellow-ship.   The writer treasures the memory of gracious hospitality therein.   Martha was active in public affairs and shared fully in the activities of the yearly meeting, and the Springfield Memorial Association.   After the passing of her brother David she became the curator of the Museum.

ELVA BLAIR followed the family pattern in regard to education and teaching.   She cared for her mother in her last illness and was a leader for many years of her long life of over 86 years in the affairs of the Society, serving as clerk of the monthly meeting, teaching in the Bible School; especially interested in the young people's activities, possessing ability to coach them in plays and pageants. All members of the family excelled in intellectuality, leadership and integrity.   It it fitting that the homestead has been bequeathed to the Society of Friends for permanent use as a regional office of the American Friends' Service Committee.[11]

CHAPTER TWENTY-FIVE

IN JOURNEYINGS OFT

YADKIN VALLEY QUARTERLY MEETING — THE FRONTIER. In common with several other areas of Quakerism this quarterly meeting arose upon the frontier and until quite recently possessed the usual frontier characteristics. The writer relates the story at this stage because it was his privilege to visit many of the meetings in this quarter in 1918 and 1919 soon after he went to teach at Guilford College. He had known the conditions under which the Friends meetings existed in Canada ten years before. There he often walked fourteen miles on Sunday and preached three times. He lived two miles from the Pelham meeting (twelve miles from Niagara Falls); he would conduct Sunday School, teach a class; preach at morning meeting; have lunch nearby; walk four miles to Effingham, climbing a mountain between Lakes Ontario and Erie; conduct the afternoon services; recross the mountains; return to Pelham for the evening service; then walk home afterwards. There were few automobiles in those days; although there was rain and in winter much snow — sometimes six feet on the level and twelve feet in the drifts, and away below zero!

It is because the writer has had this experience that he can enter into fellowship with the pioneer Quaker preachers and can write this story to enable Friends who have been privileged to live in comfort and inherit the accumulated products of generations of ancestors to understand that the hireling ministry was no travesty of Quakerism, but a sacrificial service essential to the preservation of the Society in those days.

The writer was asked to visit some of the meetings in Yadkin Quarter. It was less than fifty miles from Guilford College, yet it took nearly all day to get there. First there was a walk of two miles to the railroad station; then a waiting period; then a train to Winston-Salem, 20 miles away; then a short walk to the Court House Square; then a long wait for a bus to Yadkinville; then a wait of hours for some one to take me several miles by horse and buggy to another place; then a transfer to another Friend who "carried me" to another Friend, who "carried me" to meeting.

Conditions have marvellously changed in the past forty years, but the writer is glad that he knew Yadkin before hard surface roads, automobiles, consolidated schools, telephones, plumbing and drive-in movies invaded the county.

A youngster could not write this book; he could not possibly conceive conditions existing at the beginning of this century. Yadkin County was hewn out of the wilderness along the river which gives the county its name.   Then there were a few one room school houses, with sessions of from four to six months; the teachers were dependent upon "subscriptions" which they might collect.   Conditions were primitive; life was hard; parents stinted themselves to send their children to Guilford College; from this frontier county came hundreds of the leading citizens of Winston-Salem; the writer knows many of these families and it is a perennial source of wonder that such people could originate from such untoward circumstances.   It is not trifling with truth when speakers frequently describe Winston-Salem as "a suburb of Yadkin County."

And the secret?   The churches and the Bible Schools and the parents who established their children in the faith.   What is true of Yadkin is equally true of other centers of Quakerism in the Old North State.   It is because it is the privilege of the writer to know well so many Yadkinites that some of the Quaker ministers will be portrayed here in order that distant readers may understand how Quakerism survived all the miseries and misfortunes that befell the Society in the Slave States.

This Quarterly Meeting embraces members in Yadkin and Iredale counties and although some meetings were established much earlier (for instance Deep Creek in 1793) the Quarterly Meeting was not set up till 1889.   The impact of Friends upon this area has been incalculable.   The Quakers are widely known and probably thousands who are active workers in other religious bodies confess with appreciation that they had Quaker ancestors, but the pity is that many were disowned for marrying out, or some other violation of the Discipline.   This meeting also suffered from the westward migration, and a few meetings were laid down, including gatherings at Westfield, War Gap, Bush Ford, Maple Spring, Mount Pleasant and Rood Creek.   For many years a mission was conducted in the Blue Ridge Mountains.   There are now the following congregations: Brannon established 1910; Deep Creek, 1793; East Bend, 1882; Forbush, 1845; Harmony Grove, 1894; Hunting Creek, 1801; Mount Carmel, Pilot View, Union

Cross, Winthrop, 1908.[1] There is a membership of 2,000 and a
Bible School attendance of about 850. In recent years Yadkin
County has made phenomenal progress. There are more young
people there than in any other quarterly meeting relative to population, and there is optimism as to the future of the Society. In
each monthly meeting the Women's Missionary Society is active.

Among the ministers who witnessed for the Truth in Yadkin
a quarter of a century ago were: David E. Sampson, Lucy Vestal,
G. Whitford Edgerton, Franklin Warden, James Ring, F. M. Welborn, W. Harvey Norman, Alice Spainhour, Ann Mendenhall
Benbow, William Patterson, Franklin Williams, Harold Sharpe,
Irving Cox, Worth W. Mackey. More recently there were Talmadge
T. Knight, Zeno H. Dixon, Milner Cox, Wade H. Adams, Emanuel
and Perchie Key. These persons endured hardship because of their
love for Christ and their devotion to the Society of Friends. They
travelled bad roads; preached at several places; maintained themselves with their own labors; expected little compensation — often
not even travelling expenses; went long distances to comfort the
bereaved; were truly shepherds of the flock.

A Quaker Woman Circuit Rider. Everyone has heard of the
Methodist circuit riders — those fearless, tireless itinerant preachers who in colonial days traversed the trackless forests, crossed
turbulent streams, climbed mountain ranges, braved encounters
with Indians, searched out isolated individuals and communities
and stirred them to the depths by the annual revivals.

But whoever heard of a Quaker woman circuit rider?

Listen to the story told by John Benbow, a lawyer of Winston-
Salem. The Benbows were originally Welsh. In all probability
they acquired the name by the prowess of remote ancestors with
the bow. Perhaps they were among the Cymri who opposed the
encroachments of the English and resisted until their chieftains
David and Llewellyn had been slain and then were by trickery led
to yield to the English.

It happened this way. Edward I (1272-1307) said to the
leaders: "If you will not acknowledge me as your liege lord will
you accept as your prince one who has never been out of Wales
and one who cannot speak a word of English?" They agreed, and
then Edward presented his new-born son (Edward II) who thus
became the first Prince of Wales.

John Benbow says that his great-grandfather, Thomas Benbow,
was among the first wave of British and Welsh Friends who came

to Eastern Carolina. He disembarked at Elizabethtown and settled in Bladen County. Some time later scores of these Friends
migrated *en masse* to New Garden Quarter. Among them was
Thomas, Jr., who married Ann Mendenhall about the time of the
conclusion of the Civil War.

The yearly meeting was greatly concerned over the mass
migration to the West, and laid before Ann, who was an able
minister and in short, a missionary and an evangelist, the duty of
going to Yadkin and attempting to revive Quakerism in that
Quarter.

She accepted the burden, and Thomas concurred and settled
down as a farmer, for there was no pay for Quaker ministers in
those days. In addition to being a persuasive and convincing
minister Ann was a physician and travelled the length and breadth
of Yadkin caring for the sick, comforting the sorrowing and preaching to the people at First Day Morning Meeting. She usually
travelled alone. Sometimes she used a vehicle, sometimes she rode
horseback, following the ancient buffalo trails, and preaching
several times on First Day.

John Benbow says his grandmother possessed a missionary
fervor which is not manifest among Quakers today. She was the
means of bringing hundreds into the Society and of establishing
or reviving the meetings at Deep Creek, Hunting Creek, Forbush,
East Bend and Shady Grove. Thomas was in full sympathy with
his wife's frequent journeys and absences from home and was
satisfied that she was Divinely led. She became the mother of
several children and lived to a great age.

John loves to tell this story concerning his parents. His
father, Evan Benbow, was a teacher and was rooming at the house
of a man named Hall, who had a daughter named Betty. Evan
was in love with Betty. One day he said to her: "Betty, my
father and my brothers and sisters decided to go west, to Iowa,
and I have agreed to go with them." Betty answered: "Well,
Evan, if that is what thee should do, thee must do it; but I intend
to stay here with my people." John was born in Yadkin County,
went to New Garden Boarding School and was graduated in the
second class of Guilford College in 1890. So it would appear
that Evan did not go west with the rest of his family, who were
afflicted with the "Western fever."

John Benbow says that his father, Evan Benbow, William
Patterson and Franklin Williams established the meeting at East
Bend, and that before that congregation was authorized the local

Quakers went considerable distances to worship at Forbush, Hunting Creek or Deep River.[2] John Benbow died March 20, 1959, at the age of 72.

BRANNON MEETING. This meeting in Yadkin Quarter was established in 1910, and the meeting house was provided about that time. This is one of the many Quaker centers in Yadkin County, which are making contributions to the betterment of the community. The county as a whole had a bad reputation for the illicit manufacture of liquor, and the various churches including the Friends have done much to set a higher moral standard. For many years the county was without good roads, and it was difficult to get produce to market. It was argued that liquor was the only available money crop, so the custom developed of slinging a couple of liquor jugs across the back of a mule and riding to town. Yadkin was no worse than other neighboring counties. This is not to cast aspersions upon the fine citizens of Yadkin, but rather to state that the many Quaker churches, though of a distinctly rural character were bastions of righteousness and vital factors in preserving many of the youth from dabbling with the liquor.

Yadkin Quakers are great folks to visit neighboring churches. There is a fine community spirit, and the annual revivals at the various churches are always inspirational. Those who have assisted in the ministry at Brannon include: Lucy Vestal, J. T. Chappell, Simeon Mixon, J. G. White, G. W. Edgerton, Benjamin Millikan, Charles Hutchens, Emanuel and Perchie Key. Several of these ministers receive little financial remuneration, but are self supporting, and frequently travel considerable distances on Sundays and serve more than one meeting. The whole of the Society is indebted to these devoted workers. Those who have served as clerks include: M. H. Brannon, Berta White, Martha Garner, C. G. Vestal, Dinah Steelman, Cora Wooten, Blanche B. Simcox and Williard Wooten. Members number 115; the Bible School has 91.[3]

EMANUEL AND PERCHIE KEY. It is partly because there are such stories as this to be told that this book is written. Here is a record of domestic union, joint dedication and mutual accomplishment that is worthy of the annals of any religious organization. It is the story of a man now past eighty-six who with his wife is still active in the ministry and who has a record of service probably without parallel in the Society of Friends. He was recorded a minister in 1921. In common with most farmers Emanuel was an expert carpenter and soon after the Brannon meeting house was built he did his share in ceiling the premises. Since then he has done much to improve the property. After the death of his first wife he married Perchie who developed a gift in the ministry and who has been his fellow laborer for many years. She commenced her ministry in 1918 and was recorded by Yadkin Quarter in 1922. They have worked together and she has served by herself as pastor.

Here is the record — a record of arduous, self-sacrificing services. Together they have labored at Pine Hill, Union Hill, Westfield, White Plains, Center Valley, Reavistown, Ararat and Mount Airy in Surry Quarter; and at East Bend, Brannon, Harmony Grove, Hunting Creek, Pilot View, Union Cross and Winthrop in Yadkin Valley Quarter. He has preached at Brannon over 40 years; they served Brannon and Union Cross for 20 years; Hunting Creek, 11 years; Winthrop, 13 years. Perchie was pastor at Galax, Hunting Creek and other rural churches.

They have served in all the Quaker settlements in Surry Quarter except two; in all the meetings in Yadkin except three; they have preached in 39 of the meetings; conducted revivals in 34; and have served as pastors in 19. Other instances of devotion will be found in this chapter. Yadkin Valley Quarterly Meeting stands high in Quaker annals.

DEEP CREEK MONTHLY MEETING. Soon after the settlement at New Garden Friends began to assemble at Deep Creek. By 1775-1780 there was a considerable gathering, and meetings were held at various dwellings. The monthly meeting was established in 1793 probably by the authority of Westfield Quarterly Meeting. About 1832 there set in a general exodus from the Quaker districts. The dark cloud of slavery descended. Friends began to realize that a free labor economy could not compete with the "mud-sill" economy based upon forced labor. Many were fearful of Negro uprisings; others were lured by the prospect of better land in the west. Addison Coffin (born in 1822) went throughout these Quaker communities urging Friends to leave "a God-forsaken land and go to God's country out west where there was better land and they could raise their children without the curse of slavery and the blight of tobacco." There was over the years such a departure from Yadkin, Guilford, Stokes and Surry Counties that eventually Westfield Quarterly Meeting was laid down. Till 1850 this area was part of Surry County. The first meeting house was naturally a log structure; later a place of worship quite large for a rural community was built in a beautiful grove. The graveyard bears markers dated 1802. Bascom Rollins was the evangelist for some time; Benjamin Millikan and Leslie Winslow gave part time; Francis Garner and Larry Emerson followed in 1957. Nora Shore is clerk; the membership is 212; Bible School 128. The Summer Daily Vacation Bible School is a decided success. Extensive additions and alterations were made to the premises in 1956.[4]

EAST BEND MONTHLY MEETING appears to have been established in 1882. David Sampson, of English birth, who later became blind, was one who preached the Gospel in this area. David made a conspicuous contribution to this yearly meeting. For several years he visited rural meetings, and when in California experienced a Divine call to return to this yearly meeting and labor to establish a meeting in Winston-Salem. This he did, and that congregation is now growing so fast that it bids fair to become within a short time the largest monthly meeting in this yearly meeting. East Bend has produced many Friends of distinction, among whom may be mentioned Dr. John D. Williams, who for many years was a practicing physician to the Guilford College community. He married Annie Edgerton, who spent many years in India as a Friends' missionary. Another who made his mark in the world was Sinclair Williams, a prominent attorney of Concord; William Welch, of Mount Airy is also a Friend, whose career bore testimony to the validity of a Quaker inheritance. Many of the residents of East Bend have been worthy students of Guilford College and later in life made meritorious records.

Among those who helped establish the Kingdom of God in East Bend were families bearing the names of Felt, Head, Hinsdale, Hunt, Kirkham, Needham, Spillman, Ring and Williams. Among the ministers were Annie Edgerton (Williams), Elizabeth Moon, Zeno Dixon, Perchie Key, Wade H. Adams, J. Waldo Woody, Charles Hutchens, Harrison Hinshaw and Luther McPherson. Edward Adams is clerk; the membership is about one hundred; the Bible School about twice as many.

On June 26, 1955 the Friends celebrated their seventy-third anniversary, with special services and fellowship lunch. Francis C. Anscombe gave an historical sketch of Quakerism in North Carolina, with special reference to Yadkin Quarterly Meeting. Friends are in the process of adding additional classrooms, of remodelling the basement and of installing water within the building. Luther McPherson is pastor of East Bend and of Hunting Creek.

FORBUSH MEETING was set up by Deep Creek Monthly meeting as a preparative meeting probably in 1898. A preparative meeting was one which met with another larger meeting for matters of business and was not self-governing. A former meeting house was built on the west side of the burying ground, but this was removed. The present sanctuary was erected in 1946. Some worthy Friends have labored and worshipped here in the past, including families named Patterson, Vestal, Hutchens, Hobson, Wooten, Jester, Jessup, Taylor, Norman, Williams, Prim, Leonard, Byron, Brannon. Those who have served as pastor include Wade Adams, Lucy Vestal, Benjamin H. Millikan, Claude H. Hobson, Frank Warden, Harvey Norman, Charles H. Hutchens (for many years), and Mark Hodgin. The clerks have included: Grant Wooten, Myrtle Wooten, Barbara Gentry and Jamie Hobson. The membership is 395; the Bible School numbers 300. The Young Friends and the Women's Missionary Society are active.[5]

HARMONY GROVE is located about one mile west of Yadkinville. The meeting is of service to the community. Its monthly meeting was authorized in 1894. Among those who have exercised the gift in the ministry are Charles H. Hutchens, Emanuel and Perchie Key, Benjamin H. Millikan, Harrison Hinshaw and Clifton C. Pearson. Harvey Hinshaw is clerk. The membership is 233; Bible School, 147. Among the families who have labored and worshipped here are those bearing the names of Belling, Driver, Hall, Hauser, Mackie, Queens, Reavis, Vestal and Wilson.

HUNTING CREEK was established in 1799 or 1801. It was discontinued about 1828 and revived in 1843, according to Alpheus Briggs' valuable paper preserved in the archives. The earliest meeting houses were of the colonial log type. About 1875 a frame house was constructed, the present meeting house which is brick veneered was built in 1941. In common with many rural areas preaching service is held once or twice a month in the smaller church buildings and churchgoers attend whatever center holds worship and Bible School. Most of the little rural communities are unable to maintain full-time pastors. The church intervisitation creates a fine neighborly spirit but it does not tend to produce deep religious convictions. Some of the part time pastors are engaged in farming or some other remunerative occupation and give generously of their time and energy to the spiritual needs of the community. Some of them have had no college or seminary training. However, they meet the needs of their neighbors, and are greatly appreciated. Among those who have served this community are F. M. Welborn, G. W. Edgerton, Isaac Harris, Norman Osborne, Emanuel G. and Perchie Key (for many years), and Luther McPherson. The clerks have included: J. G. Nicholson, Ross Edgerton, J. F. Barron, Maggie Sloan, Hattie Barron, C. F. Mullins. The membership is 72; the Bible School membership is 55. Luther McPherson became pastor after the 1955 Yearly Meeting.[6]

MOUNT CARMEL MONTHLY MEETING. This gathering was established in 1886, but a monthly meeting was not allowed until 1922. The meeting house was constructed about 1886 and renovated in 1930 and again in 1954. This group of Friends enjoyed for many years the able ministrations of "Aunt Lucy Vestal" and G. Whitford Edgerton. Other preachers were Nell V. Brady, Luther Williams, Claude Hobson, Perchie Key, James Marion and Guy Warden. The clerks have included Eunice Groce, Effie Hobson, Lucy Carter, Dorothy Carter, and Pearl Carter. The membership is over seventy, but although the attendance is small it is one of the many worthwhile centers of religious activity in the county. The spiritual condition is reported to quarterly meeting as good; the midweek prayer meeting is maintained; the attendance at monthly meeting is satisfactory and the Bible School under the superintendency of Harold Carter is doing a good work; the Young Friends are participating intelligently.[7]

PILOT VIEW AND A BRUSH ARBOR. The story of this Quaker meeting calls to mind the Frontier days. The first place of assembly was a "Brush Arbor." Southerners will understand this term, but Quakers of oldtime families in England and birthright members of Philadelphia will need enlightenment. According to well established records in the minds of Friends now living the first Quaker gatherings at Pilot View were reminiscent of the "booths" of the Israelites which they commemorated at the annual Feast of Tabernacles. A site would be selected in a forest where there was a natural avenue of trees. Some upper branches would be fastened together overhead, and the open spaces filled with "brush," (boughs and branches). Saplings would be cut and the sides and one end would be fitted where necessary with uprights. Brush would be piled around the outside in order to enclose the arbor to some extent. Sometimes a leafy canopy was erected over "the ministers' gallery," which was the enclosed end of the arbor. Seats were nondescript. During meeting the men folk leaned against the tree trunks either standing or sitting; women sat upon stumps or upon blankets or cushions brought from home. The children would squat upon the ground close to the "gallery." The pulpit or desk would be rustic. The writer has used more than one of them. An expert woodsman with his axe could hew a log, fix a slab at the top and nail some struts at the base in short order.

Such was the beginning of the Friends' work at Pilot View, and such was the manner in which many congregations upon the frontier gathered in fellowship and worship.

Having heard several of these "early ministers of the Word" hold forth, and having been stirred as he listened to their congregational singing accompanied by the birds in which it is still the custom to slur syllables several times, especially in their favorite hymn, "There is a Fountain filled with Blood," the writer can visualize these early services. Buzzards would circle overhead, or perhaps congregate within sight to gorge upon carrion; cattle and razorback hogs would come on the run when they heard the stentorian voice of the preacher; squirrels, chipmunks and rabbits would hop unmolested not far from the worshippers, and the horses tethered close by would whinny to each other. In 1959 the Pilot View Friends will gather in their Jubilee celebration, and it is quite likely that some patriarchal member will tell the youngsters of the days when their grandparents worshipped at a "Brush Arbor."

A school house was the next place where meetings were held. In other centers a tent became the second sanctuary, but there is no record of that at Pilot View. Meetings were well established by 1909, and a monthly meeting was authorized two years later. By 1929 a brick veneer building was erected and some time later a minister's home was built at a cost of $5,500.00.

Those who have labored in the ministry include James R. Jones, Lucy Vestal, Charles Hutchens, Wade Adams, G. Whitford Edgerton, Perchie Key, Bascom Rollins, Toby Presnell, Benjamin Millikan, Leslie Winslow and Larry Emerson. The clerks have been Bertha Holcomb, Ila Williams, Della Williams Hobson, Blanche Williams, Daisy Williams. The membership totals 226; the Bible School, 150. These rural meetings are not to be despised; yet there are many discouragements. Such congregations are essential to the preservation of civilization. On March 3, 1957, David Martin and his wife, members of this meeting, celebrated their Golden Wedding anniversary.[8]

UNION CROSS. B. M. Bovender appears responsible for the establishment of this meeting. He secured a large store building, and Friends and others were invited to come and worship. A Bible School was started, and the attendance soon justified the removal from the old store to a more commodious place of worship. "A cheap church building was put up." Still later a more substantial house of worship was built in a well situated spot. Among the early supporters of the community were families by the name of Adams, Anderson, Bovender, Brannon, Brown, Caudle, Groat, Hobson, Norman, Rockett, Vestal and Williams. Among the ministers the long services of G. Whitford Edgerton is lovingly remembered; others have been Benjamin H. Millikan and Perchie Key. Thad Wiseman and Sally W. Ryan have been recent clerks. The membership is 310; Bible School, 122. The various activities of the meeting are well maintained.

WINTHROP MEETING is one of our newest congregations. The first monthly meeting was held October 25, 1890. When the gathering was first organized, it met alternately at Winthrop and Hunting Creek. The minutes for the first month, 25, 1908, contain the sentence: "the committee to divide the congregations of Hunting Creek and Winthrop agrees the waters of South Hunting Creek be the line between the congregations." The first meeting place was in an old log school house near the present church site. The name "Winthrop" was given by Hannah Bailey, of England. There were approximately twenty charter members. After worshipping for a few years in the school house plans were made for a meeting house. That building was used till 1923 when the present building was erected.

Some of the ministers who visited this meeting before a pastor was called were David Sampson, Nathan Perry, Perron Reynolds, Sophronia Reynolds, Emily Drake, James Jones, Daniel Martin, Julia Martin, and John Folger. Pastors who have served this meeting are: Wade Adams, L. S. Mixon, Thomas Chappell, James White, F. M. Welborn, Lucy Vestal, Charles Hutchens, G. W. Edgerton, Milner A. Cox, Talmadge Knight, Perchie Key, and Harrison Hinshaw. Clifton C. Pearson is the resident minister at this time. Those who have acted as clerk include: Amos B. Templeton, W. P. Sharp, Jr., Edgar Templeton, Carl W. Sharpe, Mary Lee Sharp Watkins, Sadie Lowe. The charter members were: Sallie Baity, Mary Carolina York, James York, Catherine York, Isaiah York, Nancy Carolina York, Wilkins Lowe, Sophia Lowe,

Alfred York, Margaret York, Franklin York, Rebecca York, Nancy York, Ellen Lowe, Martin Templeton, Jane Templeton, Joe Dobson, Dorcas Dobson, James Mullis, Mary Ann Mullis. In 1950 the building erected in 1923 was brick veneered, and with an addition in front for two rooms for Bible School and entrance. Earlier remodelling had provided four rooms for Bible classes, and improvements effected in the basement.[9] The Young Friends Fellowship is active and gives promise of future leadership.

G. Whitford Edgerton is typical of the Frontier; it is of such persons that Southern Quakerism subsists. He passed away at the age of eighty-six. Born in Wayne County in 1869, of old-time Quaker stock, at a time when the South was "prostrate" due to the war and the abominations of the so-called "reconstruction era," there was little opportunity of education, for the war had wrecked the schoolhouses, scattered the teachers and rendered worthless the "Literary Fund" (public school funds) which had been converted into Confederate currency.

Whitford was converted early in life, dedicated himself at nineteen to the ministry, and spent half a century in building up the Society of Friends in this Quarter. He first served his home meeting at Nahunta and was active in the establishment of the meetings at Harmony Grove, Winthrop and Pilot View. He was the principal minister at Bethesda, in Sampson County, for seventeen years. Later he was active at White Plains, Pine Hill, Westfield and Union Hill, all in Surry County. In 1917 he returned to Yadkin and labored in the ministry at Harmony Grove, Deep Creek and Union Cross.

Without such devoted persons the Society could not have survived. He lived to see his beloved quarterly meeting provided with good roads, schools, modern homes and meeting houses. His funeral at Harmony Grove on September 13, 1956, was an occasion when Friends gathered from far and near to honor a beloved member.[10]

Charles Henry Hutchens is another typical example of a rural Quaker pastor in North Carolina. The story is told in order that readers in comfortable conservative meetings might understand what is sometimes derisively styled "the hireling ministry." Elsewhere Friends have not known the impact of Negro slavery, the horrors of armed invasion, the denial of all civil rights during the long period of so-called "Reconstruction," the ravaging of their properties, the destruction of their school system, the almost wholesale abandonment of plantations and mass migration of their friends to distant portions of a vast continent. Blessed be those who never endured the privations of "the prostrate South."

Charlie, as he is affectionately called, was born in 1893 of parents who had experienced the deprivations of the Civil War. His grandparents shared his boyhood home, and from them he learned the details of the Emancipation era. Charles as a boy found the chores exacting for there was no farm machinery at that time. Plowing was done by a single share; the grain was harvested with scythe and cradle; hay was mown by hand. Tobacco sold at ten cents per pound (it is now $53.82 per hundred pounds). The staple diet was corn bread and milk; occasionally on Sunday there was an egg apiece for breakfast. Most of the clothing was homemade, for a spinning outfit was necessary in every household. Charlie sometimes had a stick of candy — if he could catch a rabbit, skin it and sell the hide for a penny.

ENDURE HARDSHIPS. The first school to which Charlie went was a log house; the benches were slab like planks with peg legs and no backs; there were no desks. Later he went to another schoolhouse known as King Knob School; still later he entered the seventh grade at East Bend. In order to get further education he walked six miles on Monday morning and back home on Friday afternoon. He completed the eighth grade at Mountain Park in Surry County, and obtained a teacher's certificate. In Yadkin there were no roads worthy of the name, and Charlie was a grown man before the family had a buggy and a set of harness. For thirteen years he taught at Stoney Knoll, Smithtown, Forbush, Union Grove, Union Cross or Flint Hill. The school session extended four months, and Hutchens received one dollar a day. These conditions were common throughout the devastated South. Occasionally Charlie taught adults at night time. In 1917 he married Era Bessie Matthews and built his home in large part with his own labor. During a revival conducted by Wade Adams in 1910 Hutchens became converted and joy and purpose came into his life. In 1915 his local meeting authorized him to conduct evangelistic missions. Three years later he was recorded a minister. Since then he has preached the gospel in seventy different churches and in several funeral homes and has found an open door of service with many denominations.

He has served as pastor of Friends meetings at Winthrop, Hunting Creek, Brannon, Harmony Grove, Pilot View, Deep Creek,

Forbush, East Bend, Friends Union and Pine Hill — and has been a farmer all the time! For thirty-three years he was clerk of the quarterly meeting, and for many years secretary of the County Sunday School convention.

Charles Hutchens was one of the most widely known and best beloved of all the preachers in Yadkin County. It is believed he conducted more marriages than any other minister. On one occasion in a triple ceremony he married a father, his son and the father's brother to three sisters — all the girls in one family. He is also believed to have conducted more funerals than any other local minister. He was the means of bringing hundreds to a saving knowledge of the Lord Jesus Christ and many into membership with the Society.

This story is typical; there are many such ministers in North Carolina Yearly Meeting; some have little education; all are to a great degree self-supporting; all have several charges; all give themselves to the community in many forms of service. They have dedicated their time and talents to the service of the church. It is because there are such devoted souls that Quakerism in the Old North State survived the assaults of Negro slavery, the Civil War, the horrors of the Reconstruction Era, "the western fever," and the resultant impoverishment.[11] Charles became ill and was incapacitated for some years and passed away late in the summer of 1958. His obsequies brought together one of the largest concourses of recent times.

LUCY ROBERTSON VESTAL was a fine example of a Quaker woman upon the frontier. She was a daughter of Dr. William and Mary Hamlin Robertson and was born at Lynchburg, Virginia, in 1857. After receiving some private instruction there she attended Salem Academy and New Garden Boarding School. She was possessed of great natural ability, but the war and the Reconstruction Days which followed did not permit many Southern girls to acquire an advanced education. Her parents moved to Yadkin County when Lucy was quite young and she became converted at a brush arbor meeting* at the age of seventeen. She joined Friends and married Jarvis Vestal, of an old Quaker family, when twenty years of age. To this union were born three children, but the breadwinner was taken by death in 1892.

Lucy triumphed above her sorrow and difficulties by faith and testified in meeting of the sustaining grace of the Lord Jesus.

---

* For description of a "Brush Arbor" see Pilot View.

The Society of Friends afforded such a person a full field of service and it was manifest to the whole community that she had a gift in the ministry. She was recorded a minister in 1911. For over half a century this consecrated woman became a pioneer preacher in rural areas. In brush arbors, in tents, in primitive school-houses she preached the Gospel and won many for Christ, and was a mighty power for good in the county. Only those who know what the frontier was like half a century ago can appreciate her accomplishments. Until quite recently there were no good roads or modern conveniences in the county; even today there is no railroad line. She usually travelled alone and it involved the care of a horse and vehicle. She accepted graciously whatever accommodation could be afforded wherever she went, and she travelled from one end of the quarterly meeting to the other. She did much to establish or strengthen Friends meetings at Union Cross, Winthrop, Hunting Creek, Pilot View, Forbush and Mount Carmel. She was a welcome preacher at numerous other Protestant churches and her presence was a consolation at countless funerals. Perhaps her chiefest contributions were at Pilot View and Mount Carmel, but she was beloved throughout the whole yearly meeting. She passed away at Yadkinville at the home of a son on May 18, 1939, at the age of eighty-one years and seven months. Her memorial service brought together a vast concourse to pay tribute to a courageous, self-sacrificing Servant of God.[12]

THE WIDOWS' CHOPPING. All the oldsters near Yadkinville know the story of "the Widows' Chopping." During the Civil War labor was scarce, and as season after season passed and the woodpiles became depleted it was increasingly difficult to find the only fuel available. The women were not physically able to fell the trees, draw the logs to the dooryard and pile up the cords. The woods were scoured for dead and down timber, but inevitably the time came when the settlers suffered from the cold and also for kindling to cook the scanty food.

Then someone remembered "the Widows' Chopping." The news was spread and women and children gathered in an old schoolhouse near Yadkinville to call upon the Father of the Father-less and the Husband of the Widow for Divine deliverance. It was noted afterwards that not one of the many who voiced peti-tions made any suggestions as to how the Almighty might meet the crisis. The need was too great for any human mind to formu-late a solution.

A few days after the historic prayer meeting Yadkin county experienced a great drop in the temperature and there occurred a sleet storm which coated everything outside with thick ice. The dilemma appeared intensified. Before a thaw could set in there came a rushing, mighty wind, almost a hurricane. Weighted with ice hundreds of trees could not stand before the blast. Over a large area down came the giants; great limbs were broken off and women and children laughed and wept and prayed as they gathered "the Widows' Choppings." The term was based upon the universal custom for neighbors to form a "bee" and do the heavy chores for widows and disabled persons. The Mosaic Code champions the cause of Widows and orphans. In this case it was the Lord who did the Widows' Chopping.[13]

CHAPTER TWENTY-SIX

OUR FATHERS WORSHIPPED IN THIS MOUNTAIN

Surry Quarter in Surry and Stokes Counties in North Carolina and Carroll in Virginia was established in 1898. Being a comparatively young center it has not suffered the painful experiences of some of the other Quarters, but it is handicapped because of the distance from the other Quarterly meetings. There are now twelve meetings and only two in North Carolina — at Ivy Hill and Elk Creek — have been laid down. This area in the mountains is letting the Light of the Gospel shine. The Monthly Meetings are as follows: Ararat, Center Valley, Friends Union, Galax, Mount Airy, Mountain View, Pilot Mountain, Pine Hill, Reavistown, Siloam, Union Hill, Westfield and White Plains. The following meetings which were in Virginia under the care of Surry Quarter have been discontinued chiefly owing to the natural difficulties of remoteness: Blue Ridge Mission, Burke Fork, Chestnut Creek, Fruit Hill, Maple Spring, Mount Pleasant, North Providence and Road Creek.

Ararat Monthly Meeting was established in 1924; the meeting house was built the same year at a cost of about $1,500; the membership is about 90; with a small Bible School. Among the ministers who have labored there have been Lottie Marshall Robertson, a person of rare capacity and of whom there is special mention in the account of the White Plains meeting. Others include Perchie Key, Harvey Norman, Whitford Edgerton, Thomas Hendrix, Luther McPherson, Claude Hobson, Robert P. Miller, J. Waldo Smith, Milton Jordan. Among the clerks have been Savanna Norman, C. W. Chilton, Vilena M. Chilton. Among the charter members were W. L. Chilton, Martha Chilton, W. H. Norman, A. J. Jackson and E. W. Mills.

Center Valley Monthly Meeting was set up August 26, 1905. It is a small rural meeting, but is serving a useful purpose and acting as a light in a dark place. The membership is only 27, yet the people there have the same spiritual needs as persons living in larger communities, and the attenders find satisfaction and encouragement in worship. Among those who have served in the ministry are Samuel R. Pickett, L. P. Holmes, W. J. Reid, Frank J.

Long, Albert Peele, James R. Jones, J. M. Cain, J. E. Bartlett, Philip Moon, Murray Johnson, Herman Dotson, Emanuel and Perchie Key, David Moxley, Billy Brit, Luther Paine, James Crabtree, Wayne Dehart, Claude Hobson, Harold Ritze, Homer Barker, Benjamin H. Millikan and Robert Miller. The following have served as clerk: S. R. Pickett, J. E. Bartlett, Granville Lineberry, Birdie Davis, Sallie Kyle, U. D. Kyle, Birdie Kyle, Brida Mitchell, Mable K. Linesay, Mary Farmer.

FRIENDS' UNION. This meeting in Surry Quarter was set up in 1904, and a place of worship provided at that time. In 1936 a more commodious meeting house was provided. Those who have labored in the ministry include Wesley Wooten, Lucy Vestal, Wade Adams, Harvey Norman, James Ring, Sidney Butner, John Presnell, Herman Dobson, Cleta Briles, John C. Trivette, Charles H. Hutchens, Claude Hobson and James Reinhardt. The following have served as clerks: O. Brown, Sidney Butner, Cora Lee Norman, Edith Waller, Laurey Kirby, Holt Stone, Benson Jennings, Evelyn Jessup, and Ralph Waller. The premises were remodelled in 1938 and 1943. Membership 111; Sunday School attendance 91.

GALAX. This meeting is located just across the Virginia line. The premises were acquired from another denomination in 1927 and are out-of-date. The yearly meeting should render practical assistance in modernizing the structure. It is difficult for progress to be made under the circumstances. Galax is a busy center in the beautiful Virginia hills and the place is likely to grow. Those who have functioned as pastor include Elizabeth Moon, Lola Simpson Scott, Perchie Key, Murray C. Johnson, Benjamin H. Millikan, Edmund Bloom, and Robert H. Miller. Leslie Bartlett is clerk; there is a membership of 75; with a Bible School of 123.

MOUNT AIRY MONTHLY MEETING. This group, located in the famous granite center, is a comparatively new work in a State where Quakerism dates back to 1672, but it is in the western mountainous section which was late in being settled. The meeting was established in 1898, and the present substantial meeting house constructed of granite which contains no iron and therefore shows no rust, was erected in 1904. The work is well established, and there is now a membership of 391 with a Bible School attendance of 151. The members heartily cooperate in all the concerns of the Yearly Meeting and of the Five Years Meeting. Those who have assisted in the ministry and leadership include: Joseph Potts,

James R. Jones, Leverett J. Rugg, Alder Larzalere, Samuel Pickett, Franklin and Mary Moon Meredith, Miles Reece, Leannah Hobson, Wesley Wooten, Herbert Reynolds, David Brannon, G. Raymond Booth, Calvin Gregory, Benjamin Millikan, Emanuel and Perchie Key, John Permar, Clifton C. Pearson, Seth B. Hinshaw, Milo S. Hinkle, Reuben J. Payne and Howard B. Yow. The clerks include: W. Lee Dunman, Lela W. Welch, Virginia S. Hauser. This meeting is located in one of the finest apple lands in the whole world, and there is every prospect that the city will experience rapid growth.[1]

TRAGEDY AND HEROISM. The whole community was stirred in February 1955, when the alarming news was spread that the Flat Rock schoolhouse was afire, and that the school was in session. For a while it was supposed that all had gotten outside in safety but it became noticed that one badly handicapped boy who could not hurry was missing. Apparently (no one is certain) Cora Fulk Beasley, one of the teachers, tarried too long in her endeavor to assist the boy. She was overcome by smoke and heat and collapsed in a hallway. The Principal, a Friend named Phillips, crawled in, found her and pulled her out. She was so badly burned that she died within four days. The boy perished in the building. Cora Beasley, aged 53, the mother of two daughters, had been a teacher for 33 years and was greatly beloved in the community. She was a valued member of the meeting, a leader in the Bible School, an Elder, a member of the choir, and active in the women's work. It is understood that a suitable memorial will be established.[2]

DR. ROY COLONEL MITCHELL is another Friend who has made a worthy contribution to society. His grandfather was Colonel Mitchell of English stock (1834-1871); his father was Caleb Francis Mitchell, a merchant and substantial citizen of Mount Airy. Roy was born in 1894 and attended the local schools and then had two years at Guilford College; he received the degree of B.S. in 1917 from the University of North Carolina; served in the Medical Corps in World War I; and was awarded the degree of M.D. from the University of Pennsylvania in 1919. After medical experience in the Quaker State he returned to North Carolina, and became connected with the State Board of Health with headquarters at Raleigh. He later returned to his home place and practiced internal medicine. In 1941 he established the Mitchell Clinic in Mount Airy and the institution has been of inestimable benefit to the community. Dr. Mitchell has received many honors from various medical organizations. His father played a conspicuous part in the development of the Friends Meeting; was an elder and superintendent of the Bible School. The doctor is a member of the meeting and is prominent in other local organizations.

MOUNTAIN VIEW is a small meeting within Surry Quarter. There are only eighteen active members although there are many persons of Quaker descent in the community. A meeting has existed since 1906, but the present meeting house dates from 1941. Among those who have striven to establish the faith are J. E. Bartlett, David Moxley, G. W. Edgerton, James Crabtree, Wayne Dehart, Edmund Bloom, Harold Ritze, Guy Warden. The clerks are Guida Patton and Nannie Mae Bartlett.

OLD SILOAM is the most recent meeting to be established in the yearly meeting and is an encouraging evidence of growth and expansion. The meeting was authorized by Surry Quarterly Meeting, and Howard Yow, C. Gurney Robertson and Marvin Shore were appointed to attend and read the official minute. An inspiring service was held on April 13, 1958 and report was presented to the Quarterly Meeting held at Union Hill on the 26th of the same month. Cleta and Orah Evans are pastors.

PILOT MOUNTAIN MEETING was established January 16, 1915, and a meeting house acquired the next year. The ministers have included Eli Reece, Albert Peele, Clarence Macon, J. Thomas Chappell, Thomas F. Andrew, William C. Presnell, Lewis McFarland, Isaac Harris, Theodore Perkins, John C. Trivette, Luther McPherson, Robert O. Crow. The clerks have included Alice L. Waters, Andy B. Harrell, James T. Henley, Oscar J. Johnson, D. C. Fulk, Edith C. Hill. The membership totals 74; the Bible School, 48. During recent years there has been increased interest, and after consecrated efforts a new meeting house was built and with great rejoicing was dedicated September 22, 1957. Representatives of local churches and several meetings of Surry Quarter attended. Revival services were conducted by Leslie Winslow, and there were many professions, renewals and additions to membership.

PINE HILL is another meeting within Surry Quarter. This was set up as a monthly meeting in 1899, and a place for worship secured the same year. In 1939 a new meeting house was constructed. There is no dwelling provided for the pastor as yet. The following have served as resident ministers: Wesley Wooten, W. P. Presnell,

Emanuel and Perchie Key, Robert P. Miller, Robert O. Crow is now pastor. The clerks include Nereus Barker, and Emma E. Patterson. The membership is 195, with 155 attending Bible School.

REAVISTOWN is a picturesque but out of the way settlement among the Virginia hills not far from Galax. A few Friends live nearby and Bertie Matthews conducts services once a month. The writer attended a service there some years ago and is reminded of the Negro spiritual "Listen to the Lambs — all a'crying," for all night long a shepherd was laboring to get his flock across an adjacent bridgeless stream.

UNION HILL MEETING was established in 1907 and the first building served as meeting house and Bible School class rooms. In 1934 more suitable premises were obtained. These became outgrown and in 1956 Friends decided that an entirely new building should be provided. Funds were collected with enthusiasm, and the work of building was commenced in September, 1957, and completed in May the next year. The meeting room has been equipped with new pews and pulpit furniture, carpeting and new piano. The premises are provided with nine class rooms, nursery, study and other necessities including a well planned large basement. The grounds have been landscaped and about $26,000 has been expended upon the project. The long service of Lottie M. Robertson is a treasured memory, and among the other ministers were Wesley Wooten, G. Whitford Edgerton, Malphas Robertson, James Bartlett, Cora Marshall, Barney Pierce, Emanuel and Perchie Key, Warren Allen Pierce, Winfred Crouse. Among the clerks have been Pauline Coin Atkins, Gray Eads, Gussie Riggs, and Randolph Younger. The membership is 138 and about 100 attend the Bible School. The work is well maintained and the church exercises a spiritual influence in the community.

WESTFIELD MONTHLY MEETING is said to be the oldest religious organization in Surry County. The meeting dates from 1760, and the first meeting house was constructed twelve years later. A more modern meeting place was erected in 1883. The location was originally known as Tom's Creek, but Tom's claim was repudiated, and the name Westfield was adopted. The meeting boasts that it was within the limits of that meeting that alfalfa was first grown in this country, and that the seed was brought there from England by a Friends' missionary named Jessup. It is also of interest that Ellen Minthorn, a maiden aunt of the former Quaker President, Herbert Hoover, came to Westfield many years ago from Iowa. She conducted a school here, and old inhabitants still speak of her sterling character and her wonderful influence for good. Her remains were interred in the White Plains Friends burying ground. It is also a local belief that "Quaker Gap" received its name because the Quakers who lived across the Sauratown Mountains came through a trail in the mountains to attend meeting.

Among those who have assisted in the ministry are: Lottie Robertson, Thomas Andrew, Perchie Key, Lewis McFarland, James Crabtree, John C. Trivette, Luther McPherson, Orah and Cleta Evans. The clerks include Bertie Dix, Mandy Pell, Annie Marshall, Nannie Johnson, Stella Pell, Raynor Pell Wilson. The membership numbers 176; the attendance at Bible School is 101.

WHITE PLAINS is a relatively new meeting. The meeting house dates from 1885, and the monthly meeting from 1890. One of the early leaders among this group of Quakers was Jenny Ellen Minthorn, an aunt of Herbert Hoover, and a beloved teacher in the local Friends' School. The first clerk of the meeting was William D. Bunker, a son of one of the famous Siamese twins, who were born in North Carolina. The membership is rather large, being 449, but quite a number are non-resident. The attendance at Sunday School is 239. Recently a minister's home has been provided at a cost of $10,000. Those who have been resident ministers include Ellen Minthorn Marshall, David Sampson, Lottie M. Robertson, T. Wesley Wooten, J. Waldo Woody, Herbert Reynolds, Lewis McFarland, Perchie Key, John Permar, Lela Silla Garner, Luther McPherson, Willie R. Frye and Fred Morgan. The clerks include William D. Bunker, Lottie Robertson, Gurney Robertson, Christina Christian, Hobart Siske, Nelle Paterson, Bessie M. Simpson. The members greatly appreciated a visit from the clerk of the yearly meeting, Algie I. Newlin in recent months.[3] At the time of writing satisfactory progress is being made with a new building fund, and the Young Friends, the Women's and the Men's organizations are doing well.

LOTTIE MARSHALL ROBERTSON. No record of Quakerism in North Carolina would be complete without special reference to Lottie Marshall Robertson, of White Plains. Possessed of great natural endowments, a born leader, striking and handsome in appearance, she possessed authority tempered by Christlike grace. Such a person would be an adornment to any community.

She was born in 1867, went to school at White Plains and later at the Friends Mission School at Westfield, and then settled in her native county of Surry. She married Charles L. Robertson, a pioneer buggy manufacturer at the age of 23. He died in 1913 leaving her with seven children. By her energy, determination and devotion she enabled each of them to secure a college education at Guilford. She was enthusiastic concerning all phases of the work of the Society of Friends and about fifty of her family connections attended the Quaker institution.

She became a school teacher at the age of 18, and was one of the foremost advocates of the restoration of the public school system. She was a leader in a group which raised funds to establish the first graded school at White Plains. Later she had much to do in the securing of a high school. She lived to see the day when Surry County passed from an uncertain four months of elementary schooling, with the teacher receiving a dollar a day — if she could collect it from the patrons — to the time when all the counties of North Carolina had a State controlled system of consolidated grade and high schools equal to any in the Southland.

She received a call to the ministry and preached at White Plains, Mount Airy and Westfield, and helped in the setting up of meetings at Ivy Hill, Union Hill and Ararat. It is believed that she was the first woman preacher in the county. For more than sixty years her ministry extended to many places in the yearly meeting.

At the age of 22 she was appointed postmistress at White Plains, and she performed this public service efficiently until she retired at the age of 70. Throughout her life she was a recognized leader in all civic undertakings. In August, 1955, she celebrated her 88th birthday, and the occasion was suitably marked by the community, and received wide-spread notice in the press. Soon afterwards she became incapacitated and passed away five days before Christmas that same year. A vast concourse assembled at her funeral service. Few communities have produced a person of greater integrity and civic leadership.[4]

SAMUEL AND MIRIAM LEVERING are Friends of distinction and occupy a unique place in the Society of Friends. Samuel had the unusual experience of being instructed by his mother at home until he entered the sophomore year in Western High School in Washington, D. C., from which he was graduated in 1925. He spent a year in working in an apple orchard with his father, who was a man of marked individuality and convictions, and who developed a famous orchard upon a mountainside at Ararat in Virginia. Samuel graduated in Agriculture from Cornell University in 1930 and pursued graduate studies in his chosen field, B.S., Ph.D., Cornell. Later he became associated for five years with the Farm Credit Administration in the Capitol.

He married Miriam Lindsay and took over his father's business and became nationally known as a producer of the choicest apples, but he did not permit the demands of an ever increasing business to occupy all his time and interests, for he has made many outstanding contributions to national righteousness. He has been Chairman of the Peace Board of the Five Years Meeting, Chairman of the Executive Council of the Friends Committee on National Legislation; has done pioneer work in the development of World Law and enforceable disarmament; he was a founder of the United World Federalists, Inc., a national organization, and also of the North Carolina branch. He is also the founder and present chairman of the American Freedom Association, an educational association in this same field, and has also assisted in the founding of the High School World Peace Study and Speaking program, which is participated in annually by two hundred schools chiefly in North Carolina. Another unusual activity is that most years he takes and guides a group of about eighty teachers and students to the United Nations Organization.

Samuel is a tireless advocate of peace and national righteousness, and is one of the most active and forceful leaders of Quakerism in this generation.

His wife Miriam is a worthy helpmate. Born in the Quaker Commonwealth of Pennsylvania, she was graduated from Cornell University with a major in History and Government in 1934, and celebrated her graduation with marriage to Samuel. She has fully shared his labors in the vast orchards and also entered into his public services, as well as becoming the mother of six children. For five years she was Secretary of Peace and Christian Social Relations for the United Society of Friends Women; was Dean of the Carolina Institute of International Relations in 1953; was a State official of the United Church Women of North Carolina, and she made a memorable address at the Five Years Meeting at Richmond, Indiana, in 1950. The couple are distinguished scholars, and Miriam sums up their philosophy in the words: "We believe strongly in the three principles of the Bible — Law, (the Pentateuch); Justice (the Prophets); Love (the Gospels) — all are essential for peace and world order."[5]

CHAPTER TWENTY-SEVEN

OTHER SHEEP I HAVE

THE NICHOLITES. Students of colonial history are likely to find occasional references to the "Nicholites" or "New Quakers," but until recently there was no comprehensive account of these somewhat elusive people. Kenneth L. Carroll has just concluded extensive investigations and an article entitled "The Nicholites Become Quakers: an Example of Unity in Disunion" was published in the *Bulletin of the Friends Historical Association.*

During the famous walking and preaching tour of John Woolman along the Eastern Shore of the Chesapeake in Maryland, probably in 1766, a man named Joseph Nichols attended some Quaker meetings. He was profoundly impressed by the messages of John Woolman, and in 1782 about ten years after the death of Woolman he organized a Society very similar to that of the Friends. They worshipped as do Friends; held monthly business meetings; used Advices and Queries; issued Epistles; protested against the "hireling ministry" or "priests' wages"; decried slavery; conducted marriages in a similar manner. They referred to the days and months by number instead of using "the heathen names". Their outstanding characteristic was their extreme plainness and strictness. One of their peculiarities was the avoidance of colors or mixtures in their clothing, perhaps based upon Lev. xix: 19; Deut. xxii, 11. They wore headgear of natural wool — the men hats and the women caps.* Janet Whitney believes it is likely that Nichols was influenced by Woolman in regard to slavery, for the Nicholites made it a disownable offence for a member to hold slaves.

The sect attained considerable membership in Delaware, and especially along the Eastern Shore of Maryland. Woolman had

---

* Janet Whitney says "It would be far fetched to suppose that this had any connection with Woolman's undyed clothing," but Woolman was an unforgettable spectacle with "a white hat, a course raw linen shirt, without anything about his neck; his coat, waistcoat and breeches of white course woolen cloth with wool buttons on; his coat without cuffs; white yarn stockings and shoes of uncured leather with bands instead of buckles — so that he was all white." — Whitney, Janet: *John Woolman,* pp. 350; 393-394.

some contacts with Nichols and the sect was visited by such well-known Quaker ministers as Job Scott, Joshua Evans, John Wigham and Stephen Grellet. These Friends were appalled at their extreme conservatism and enforcement of discipline.

Elsewhere attention has been directed to the mass migration of the Quakers from the northeastern colonies just prior to the War of Independence. Carroll does not offer any explanation, but he produces evidence that in this same period there was a great removal of the Nicholites from the Eastern Shore to North Carolina, and it is a fair assumption that these Pietists were prompted by the same considerations as the Quakers in seeking betterment and security.*

One of the leaders of this movment was Paris Chipman, who settled near Deep River and who became possessed of 640 acres of land. Carroll says "there exists the old tradition handed down in the Marine family that Jonathan Marine, the great-grandfather of John Whitcomb Riley, was a leader of a "Quaker" migration of some seventy-five people from the Eastern Shore to North Carolina about 1774 or 1775." Joseph Standley became another well-known land owner.

These migrants were followed by others and for some time there existed a community of Nicholites at Gum Tree Swamp, near the Little Pee Dee just across the border in South Carolina. The outbreak of hostilities put an end to the mass migrations. They realized their close resemblance to the Quakers, for in a petition to the General Assembly of North Carolina in 1778 they averred "We do profess and confess the same principles the Quakers doth, but for some reasons which we could render if required we have not thought it best to joyn Membership with them."

A number, however, joined Friends because of the rigid discipline of their former body. At one time the Eastern Shore Nicholites were prepared by action of the Monthly Meeting to unite as a body with Friends, but were restrained by "several new ministers".

The writer has found no indication that Deep River Nicholites ever formally united with Friends.** Times were disturbed; a war-

---

* See chap. vi.
** The above particulars are culled from a very scholarly and exhaustive paper by Kenneth L. Carroll, who is the highest authority on the Nicholites. The paper is entitled "The Nicholites Become Quakers: An Example of Unity in Disunion" and is published in the *Bulletin of the Friends Historical Association*, Spring number 1958.

like spirit prevailed almost everywhere; roads were non-existent; travelling was dangerous; life was arduous. It is almost certain that some of the "New Quakers" became merged into the larger Quaker body without any recorded transfer of membership and the others died.

It is typical of the period that the only reference to theology in Carroll's scholarly paper is a reference to belief in "the Inner Light".[1] The Nicholites in North Carolina maintained correspondence with the remnant in Maryland, and had an organization here until the close of the century, for it is in evidence that Stephen Grellet visited them at Deep River in 1800, but there is no record of them after that date.

NORTH CAROLINA CONSERVATIVE FRIENDS. The Great Revival movement which began among Friends in New York and spread to Philadelphia and Indiana Yearly Meetings in the years just before the Civil War, eventually reached North Carolina, especially through the ministry of Mary Moon, who in 1878-1882 travelled extensively throughout this yearly meeting. Contemporary newspaper reports of her meetings indicate that extraordinary enthusiasm prevailed; sometimes she had an audience of five thousand,[2] and hundreds were converted almost everywhere she went. It was a novelty for a woman to preach, and Mary Moon was an unusual person and a powerful preacher. Her ministry, and that of other evangelists almost completely changed the character of Quaker meetings. It brought into membership hundreds who had no Quaker background, but who wanted to hear "the Old, Old Story" of the Gospel. The style of preaching became changed; the unprogrammed, silent meeting gradually disappeared, and singing became common. Naturally many Friends resented these innovations, and preferred to worship according to the traditional manner. In North Carolina the matter came to a head at the Rich Square Monthly Meeting in 1903, after the yearly meeting had adopted "the Uniform Discipline," which had been accepted by the Five Years Meeting held at Richmond, Indiana, in 1902. A goodly number of Friends at Rich Square withdrew from the North Carolina Yearly Meeting which was held at Guilford College, in tenth month. They met with others sharing the same objections to revivalism and a "creed" as they regarded the Declaration of Faith, and organized a separate yearly meeting in affiliation with Conservative Friends elsewhere. The old meeting house at Cedar Grove, Woodland, in Northampton County became the chief center. The clerk, David H. Brown, has supplied most of the following history of that meeting.

RICH SQUARE MONTHLY MEETING. This Quaker settlement dates from about 1750; there was a more or less regular meeting from 1753, and a meeting house was built in 1760, and that same year Eastern Quarterly Meeting authorized the setting up of Rich Square Monthly Meeting. Janet Whitney records that John Woolman visited this area in one of his visits to the South and that he held meetings at Wells, Simons Creek, Newbegun Creek, Little River and Old Neck, and that between six and seven hundred persons attended.* Many historians note that there was everywhere a yearning to meet visitors in order to relieve the oppressive loneliness experienced by the scattered frontiersmen, and to afford a chance to learn the news, especially concerning the frontier wars and the relations with England.

Beside the larger body of Friends in and near Rich Square the monthly meeting had members in Edgecombe and Hertford Counties. In 1782 the Tar River Friends in Edgecombe County were transferred to Contentnea Monthly Meeting and Fishing Creek was made the dividing line between the two monthly meetings.

In 1775 a meeting house was built at Jack Swamp, also in Northampton County. This became a considerable settlement and in 1794 was granted the right to hold a monthly meeting. It was short lived, however, as the membership began moving to the Piedmont in 1800 and to Ohio in 1805. The meeting was laid down in 1812 and the remaining members were transferred to Rich Square Meeting. Because of its short existence its records have been combined with those of Rich Square in the following extract:

"Rich Square Monthly Meeting was not affected by the tide of westward migration to the same degree as some other meetings in North Carolina. . . . They seem to have been better satisfied with their surroundings than other Friends, and hence there were few who tried their fortunes in the west."

Among the early settlers who became substantial Friends were Josiah Brown, Elizabeth Bryant, Anna Copeland, Henry Copeland, John Copeland, Mary Copeland, Beersheba Daughtry, Rachel

---

* Whitney, Janet: *John Woolman;* also *Records* by David H. Brown, the Clerk of the N.C. Conservative Yearly Meeting; also paper by Peele, Juliana: Founders of the Rich Square Monthly Meeting in Trinity College *Historical Papers,* 1906.

Daughtry, Sarah Duke, Sarah Fletcher, Sarah Hall, Sarah Hill, Absolam Hollowell, Silas Hollowell, Thomas Hollowell, Sarah Hollowell, Morening Hollowell, William Horn, Clariba Knox, Lydia Knox, Ann Lancaster, Charity Peele, Mary Peele, Robert Peele, Joseph Pittman, Esther Rose, Lydia Thomas and Phariba White. There were also families by the names of Baughm, Elliott, Griffin, Jacobs, Outland, Page and Parker. Among the records is the cryptic entry: "Moses Hall, Sr. much used in the early days of this meeting." Another frequent notation is: "No business that required entry."[3]

Dr. Stephen B. Weeks says: "The members in Eastern Quarterly Meeting introduced principles of faith and practice contrary to those of the early Friends." As a result Rich Square Meeting was divided in 1903, the majority withdrawing from their affiliation with North Carolina Yearly Meeting held at New Garden (Guilford College). In tenth month, 1904, they met with like-minded members of other meetings and organized a new yearly meeting at Cedar Grove in Woodland. This meeting has been held here since its organization. It has a membership of about 350 distributed throughout six monthly meetings. Of this total 135 members of Rich Square Monthly Meeting which is held alternately at Rich Square and Cedar Grove. The other five monthly meetings are Piney Woods, held at Snow Hill, near Belvidere; Oak Grove, near Goldsboro; Holly Spring at Friendsville near Ramseur; Marlboro, held at New Hope near Edgar; West Grove, near Saxapahaw.

These Friends preserve the traditional manner of worship without pre-arrangement and without singing. A few still wear the ancient garb and use the "plain speech". Among those who have exercised a gift in the ministry must be mentioned Benjamin P. Brown, familiarly known as Bennie Brown. He was noted as being steadfast in principle, successful in business, sincere in friendship, and unusually effective as a minister, "stirred by the simple spirit of Jesus." Others include Henry T. Outland, Cyrus Harvey, Guiliana Peele Harvey, Alfred E. Copeland in the past and at a later date Walter J. Brown, Henry T. Outland.

Edwin P. Brown, a grandson of Benjamin P. Brown, is a stalwart supporter of the faith of his illustrious Quaker ancestors. He is a graduate and a trustee of Guilford College, the President of the successful Riverside Manufacturing Company, is prominent in many civic affairs and is a member of the Board of Banks in North Carolina.

At a recent meeting Louisa Brown Wilson (a granddaughter of Benjamin P. Brown and also of John Gurney Frazier) was recorded a minister. She resides at Virginia Beach, Virginia, where a monthly meeting was set up due to her influence and that of her husband, Robert D. Wilson, who is clerk of that meeting. These Friends have started a school.

The Woodland meeting house was repaired and somewhat modernized in 1950. The time of holding yearly meeting was recently changed from eleventh month to eighth month so as to give opportunity for those of school age to attend. The Young Friends are active, and participate in summer conferences with those of other yearly meetings. The Friends are vigorous in maintaining Friends' testimonies concerning Peace, Temperance, Oaths and Public Righteousness. David H. Brown is clerk of the yearly meeting and Edwin P. Brown, clerk of monthly meeting.

RALEIGH AND DURHAM FRIENDS have in the past few years established monthly meetings and are holding unprogrammed services. Now that the Philadelphia Friends who led the separations in 1827-28 have re-united, the present is a suitable occasion for Friends in North Carolina to exchange greetings and intervisitations. *

DURHAM MONTHLY MEETING promises to become a permanent memorial to Elbert Russell who became Professor of Biblical Interpretation at the Divinity School at Duke University in 1926, and after 1928 the Dean of that branch of the University. Elbert came to Durham ripe with experience of teaching at Earlham, Johns Hopkins, Woolman and Haverford. He measured up to a great challenge and helped to make the new theological seminary one of the leading institutions in the country. It was inevitable that such a teacher, preacher, and great leader would gather about him a group who desired to worship after the manner of Friends, so in 1937 a group began to meet first in private homes, then later in a room at the Divinity School. The meeting took root, and there are about forty persons who may be regarded as members. The meeting has no need of a pastor as several of those attending are teachers or advanced students and are able to bring suitable messages. The group meets on the basis of silence, without programming. So far there has been no singing, though there is no objection to music as such. They have not established a Bible

---

* See also Raleigh Meeting in chap. xxiii.

School. For some years the meeting was unaffiliated with any larger group, but in 1943 it united with the American Friends Fellowship Council in Philadelphia. At first the group met twice a month, and then weekly assemblies were instituted. At the time of the organization the following were chosen as officers. Edward K. Kraybill, clerk; Willard Berry, treasurer; Elbert Russell, presiding elder; Susan Gower Smith, elder. During World War II many Civilian Public Service men and women attended the meetings. After the retirement and removal to Florida of Elbert Russell the meeting experienced weakness, but there were enough who had convictions to continue. At the time of this writing the group is meeting in the basement of the Duke University Chapel on Sunday evenings.

After much consideration the Durham Friends decided to unite with the Conservative Yearly meeting which convenes at Woodland, in Northampton County in this state. The Durham Friends participate in the usual activities of the Society. They regularly contribute clothing, supplies and money to the American Friends Service Committee, and discussions are held concerning Race Relations; the Penal system; Condition of the Aged; Displaced Persons; Deepening of Spiritual Life.

Plans have already been drawn for a suitable meeting house which is to be erected as a memorial to Elbert Russell, and considerable money has been collected for that purpose. The lot has been selected and is paid for. It is hoped to commence building in the near future. This is the sort of memorial Elbert would desire.

The following have served as clerks: Edward K. Kraybill, William Van Hoy, John de J. Pemberton, Harry R. Stevens, John Barlow, and Susan Gower Smith at present. Other officers are Stanley Guise, treasurer; Donald K. Adams, Katherine Banham, Willard Berry and Frances Jeffers, elders.[4]

NORTH CAROLINA INDEPENDENT FRIENDS. The Hicksite Separation[*] greatly disturbed the Friends in Ohio, and for nine successive years the matter was discussed at Yearly Meeting, and in 1854 a considerable number of Friends withdrew and united with an Independent body which had been "set off from Baltimore Yearly Meeting in 1813." One of the leading figures was Walter Malone

---

[*] For particulars of the Separations see chap. viii; also Thomas: *History of Friends in America,* chap. v.; also Mott, Edward: *The Friends Church in the Light of Recent History,* in toto. Also works by Edward Grubb and Elbert B. Russell.

who established a Bible Institute and was an ardent Fundamentalist. A few Friends in North Carolina who had become disturbed by the Wilbur-Gurney Separation withdrew from the parent body and united with the "Independent Friends of Ohio." At the present time these Friends hold meetings for worship at Immanuel, New Hope, Pomona, Pine Mountain, Pleasant Garden, Pleasant View, Putnam, Reidsville, Rock Hill and Saxapahaw. The membership in North Carolina is 574; in the Independent Yearly meeting, 6,821.

The separate Women's Business Meeting was discontinued in 1887. For many years the Yearly Meeting was held at Mount Pleasant until 1917, it was then transferred to Damascus. There is now a prospect that it will be transferred to Canton, Ohio, where there is a substantial Bible School — now known as the Malone Bible College.

These "Independent" Friends regard Hickism, Modernism, Evolution and "Liberalism" as heresies; they preach "holiness" and are careful not to admit into membership any who are not soundly orthodox. Their meetings engage pastors; they have singing in Meeting; none wear the traditional Quaker garb.[5]

THEY SHALL BECOME ONE. It cannot be out of place to refer once more to the healing of the wound which has recently taken place in Philadelphia. The first great Separation occurred there in 1827-28, and spread to several other yearly meetings. In March, 1955, the two main bodies of Friends — the Orthodox and the General Conference group — first held separate meetings and recorded minutes expressing the willingness to unite; then the two bodies met in joint session at the old Arch Street Meeting House. Love and unity prevailed, and the members joined in breaking down the "middle wall of partition between them"; goodwill produced a new bond of affection, and the Spirit of Christ found new expression. The writer expresses his own joy that the Friends of Chapel Hill, Durham and Raleigh are affiliated with both groups within North Carolina, and that invitations to the liberal branch to attend meetings of the Friends at Woodland are greeted with delight. Now that the parent meeting in Philadelphia has led the way, there is no reason why fraternal delegates should not be received from the branches in North Carolina. As a further indication that actual unity has been achieved *The Friend* and *The Friends' Intelligencer* have been merged into a new paper known as the *Friends' Journal*, and the first issue appeared in July,

1955.[6] Three branches of Friends in Canada have recently effected organic unity. If we can all have the grace to distinguish between unity and uniformity, then a new day can dawn for Quakerism in North Carolina.

It is not without significance that the 1956 North Carolina Yearly Meeting Minutes (p. 40), state that Epistles were received from a dozen or more Friends' bodies in America outside the Five Years Meeting, beside twelve from foreign countries. The meeting responded with messages of goodwill. Is it not time that definite steps be taken to have closer fellowship with our Friends at Woodland?

Two bodies of Friends have also united in New York, and in Baltimore there is the warmest co-operation between the two meetings. Who will champion the restoration of fellowship in this Yearly Meeting?

CHAPTER TWENTY-EIGHT

THE BOOK OF NUMBERS

SHEPHERDS OF THE FLOCK. The Society of Friends came into existence as the outcome of a great Revival; it was revitalized in a great Revival. George Fox and William Edmundson and a score of the other Founding Fathers of Quakerism were men who were filled with the Holy Spirit — men whose lives had been transformed by the power of the Indwelling Christ. What more sublime or significant expression could be found than that of Fox: "All nature gave forth a new smell . . . and I was brought into that condition in which Adam was before his fall." They did not go forth with the intention of founding a new denomination; they went out to preach Christ and the power of a victorious life. Quakerism was established because Fox and his companions had a living message. The movement spread to the Barbadoes and thence to the American continent because men everywhere needed that New Life. As people were "convinced" they passed into "Newness of Life." They became possessed of a Spirit of Righteousness which empowered them to witness to the transformation they had experienced. That Quakerism should crystallize into some formality, even when the members intended to avoid all forms, is according to human experience. That the first enthusiasm should subside and a less spiritual institution should appear is true of many movements in human society. That Quietism was not wholly due to the frontier is evidenced in the fact that Friends in England passed through a somewhat similar, though not identical, period of quiescence. It was the Adult School movement which revivified Quakerism there.

Some account has been given of the re-awakening that came to Friends in America. One who experienced it said "it was as though a hurricane had struck us."

The Great Revival came as do all revivals. A few persons surrendered themselves completely to Christ and were filled with the Holy Spirit. There is no substitute for the Spirit of Christ — education, intention, earnestness, enthusiasm, organization, money, advertisement will never suffice. The power must be of God. Saint Peter on the Day of Pentecost said: "This is that which was promised . . . God would pour forth His Spirit" and men and women would testify of the transforming power. Some of the leaders in this movement have been named, yet other thousands of persons in many communities were awakened. The membership was probably doubled within a decade and continued to increase.[1]

Without any planning the character of the Quaker meetings became greatly changed. Instead of long periods of silence and messages by a few who had "the gift and the tone" there were joyous testimonies of those who had experienced conversion; young people spoke in meeting freely; some would sing and others would spontaneously join; some would offer vocal prayer; others would publicly confess their sins and plead for forgiveness; evening meetings were requested. The old order gave way and there came vigorous and earnest preaching and "altar calls" and "mourner's benches." These practices had been common among some other denominations, and that they should sweep over established Quaker meetings for worship is evidence that Friends possessed vitality and had yet a mission to fulfill.

So overwhelming and irresistible was the revitalization that it became evident that some shepherding was necessary, and in many instances the person who had conducted the revival was requested to remain and continue the work. Provision had to be made for his maintenance, and thus the former testimony against "hireling ministry" became a dead issue. The revivalist became a leader; the function of the elders declined. The preaching became forceful, natural, direct. The old style of garb was discarded — except by elderly Friends who had never worn "worldly clothing." Young women adopted ordinary attire. Gradually many attenders spoke of the "Quaker church;" singing became common and annual revivals were expected.

A MIXED MULTITUDE. These changes brought into the Society many hundreds who had no Quaker background, and who cared little for Quaker doctrine or history. What they wanted was a church home and Christian fellowship. Some of the early pastors were young men who had been converted and who had ability in preaching. In Western Indiana, Ohio, Iowa, Kansas and Nebraska it was still the frontier seventy years ago; there were few schools and it would have been out of place for special educational qualifications to be required of ministers. It is not surprising, therefore, that practices and doctrines at variance with original Friends' views appeared temporarily in some meetings. In a few places Friends did not acknowledge that they engaged a pastor, but realizing that they had no satisfactory ministry would invite some Friend with a gift in the ministry to reside among them and "encourage him to bring a message at morning meeting if the Lord gave him one." He would be regarded as a visiting minister and some other remunerative occupation would be provided for him, and Friends would privately add to his income.

There has never been any official adoption of a pastoral system. Gradually the meeting on ministry and oversight became a pastoral committee, and it is this body which extends a call to a minister. Gradually the meetings became programmed, and in many places the morning meeting is not very dissimilar from a service of some other denomination; the only apparent difference is that Friends do not observe the forms of the Sacraments.

The meeting houses have been modernized; the ministry of women has regretfully declined; business meetings have become more important; the Bible School has become vitalized. For several decades the Christian Endeavor movement flourished; similar and appropriate activities are now carried on under the name of Young Friends Fellowship.

The writer has not found that North Carolina Yearly Meeting experienced such spectacular revivalism as some other yearly meetings. However, through visiting Friends (especially Mary Moon), through personal letters and religious periodicals the revival became known here, and gradually a new spirit came into the Quaker centers in this State. The Gurneyite dispute had not been conspicuous here, and so there was not the ready soil upon which the movement could take quick root. Naturally some very conservatively minded Friends were shocked at these "creaturely activities" and withdrew and united with the Conservative Friends of Ohio.

North Carolina had a common experience with others in this transition period. Pastors were insufficiently paid and several able persons who would gladly have given themselves to this service were compelled to seek livelihood otherwise. The revivalists deserve commendation; it cannot be questioned that they strengthened the Society of Friends. Wherever the pastoral system was adopted the membership increased.

Nowhere in America has the Society of Friends established a theological seminary; but Bible instruction and some allied subjects have been taught in the several Friends colleges. The statement of Fox "that Greek and Latin did not make a minister" was twisted by some to imply that a preacher did not need education; "he should say what the Lord gave him to say." These early pastors suited the age; they met frequently with the cold shoulder, and the woman Friend who prayed for the minister: "Lord keep him humble; we'll keep him poor" expressed the feeling of some.

At times there was opposition in some parts of the yearly meeting to Guilford College. Well meaning, but uninformed persons, who were in a position to have opened doors of service for members of the faculty and students failed to do so, and furthermore dissuaded would-be students from attending the institution. It was, of course, an attitude too common throughout the South, familiarly known as "the Bible Belt," against any scientific learning and interpretation of the Holy Scriptures along historical lines. We are grateful that that day has passed.

STUDY TO SHOW THYSELF APPROVED. Unless one has an actual experience of "Christ speaking to one's condition" and an awareness of the Light Within an extensive education is inadequate. What Fox said was true, but it is commonly overlooked that for about six years he made a practice of going from place to place to listen carefully to distinguished preachers in the hope that he might cease to be a Seeker and become a Finder. He had long and earnest discussions and disputes with these divines, and he knew the Scriptures so well that it became a proverb that "if the Scriptures were lost they could be made up again out of George's head." During his life he accumulated a considerable and varied library. He was by no means "an unlearned and ignorant man."

MYSTICISM. The preaching of early Friends was largely mystical and subjective; it was based upon the experience of the Voice Within; occasionally, (yet rarely as compared with contemporaries) the emotions were expressed in groanings. The messages were not marked by rationality, and the conscious process of thinking had little place in the message. The minister believed in "speaking as the Spirit gave him utterance." We do not question Divine leading, but some knowledge of psychology and psychical sciences enables us today to understand historic Quakerism. That sort of preaching did not require preparation.

There was little attempt to explain the Christian faith; few passages of Scripture were critically examined; there was no attempt to discuss Hebrew or Jewish history or to interpret Hebrew poetry or oriental symbolism; there was hardly any presentation of the historic Jesus of Nazareth; little attempt to account for the

Infinite, Universal, Creative Mystery we call Heavenly Father. The preaching usually had reference to "the Seed," "the Inward Light," "the Word," the "Universal Light." Personal experiences of Divine leading were often the basis of the sermons. The writer attended such meetings for thirty years. He wonders whether that manner of worship without the Bible Classes in connection with the Adult School and Sunday evening mission meetings would have brought him into the Truth. Although Friends stressed the Holy Spirit as that of God which we might experience there was little systematic presentation of the Person and work of the Spirit. The leading members would at one time have "eldered" a minister who attempted to be doctrinal; he would have been told to "avoid creaturely activity." In colonial days when schools were few and life upon the plantations very rigorous it is not surprising that some preachers became repetitious and uninspiring.

An Historic Development. This yearly meeting became conscious of this situation and some years ago a committee was appointed to consider the suitability of persons recommended by monthly meetings for recording as ministers. The committee consists of six persons whose terms overlap and who are appointed triennially. In previous times a monthly meeting could act without consulting a superior body; now recommendations have to be approved by the quarterly meeting, and then forwarded to the yearly meeting. If that body approves, then the matter is sent back to the monthly meeting for final action. An historic step was taken in 1957 to establish at Guilford College in connection with the Department of Biblical Literature a course definitely designed to provide future leaders with some of the essential studies — a graduate course leading to the degree of Master of Arts. One weighty Friend is satisfied that some advice should be given in pastoral care. To show that some guidance is necessary the writer will state that he has been hospitalized several times and from his own experience only one denomination has trained its ministers to visit the sick in an effective manner. The bedside visit of most ministers is just another call and no attempt is made to furnish spiritual sustenance. At Guilford College we have now the equipment, and additional instructors can be secured — in fact there are three teachers with advanced degrees in the Department at this time — and there is no valid reason why the Society of Friends should not require its future leaders to prepare themselves adequately for their important responsibilities. No longer are the

Quakers a selective group of only birthright members; we are a mixed multitude. Now that many members of the congregation have advanced education it is incumbent upon the minister to be well informed. This then is a call to the Society as a whole actively and enthusiastically to support Guilford College and advance the cause of ministerial education. A start has been made, and definite action should be taken by the whole body.

Times have changed; we are a new generation — and in many respects a different one. The researches of modern science have given us a new world. The argument that Fox did not have a theological education and therefore preachers do not need training is now recognized as fallacious. The scholarship of recent years has shed as much new light upon the Holy Scriptures, comparative religions, the history of Bible lands and peoples and the development of theological doctrines as upon any other field of knowledge.

The nation faces a crisis. We have no systematic religious or Bible instruction in our elementary schools; the teaching in our Bible schools is at best scrappy; few parents have the inclination or the ability to give their children worthwhile religious instruction; the old-time family worship has almost entirely disappeared; family counselling by the elders generally has been discontinued; pastoral calls seldom lead to worship with the families. The pitiful truth is that America has become too much a nation of Biblical and theological illiterates.

The writer had the great privilege of teaching Biblical Literature in colleges for over thirty years and it is the dreadful truth that not five percent of college students know anything worth while of the Scriptures. Very few can repeat the Books of the Bible in right order or quote the Ten Commandments. If these do not know then the lesser educated do not. In view of this appalling ignorance it behooves a minister to be well informed. Primitive Quakerism set the highest standards of Puritanism; it virtually expected all its members to be mystics, at all times responsive to "the leading of the Spirit." They claimed they did not need special sacramental observances, because all life was a sacrament, and as they were at all times in the Presence of Heavenly Father there was no need to call any special building "the House of God." They did not take oaths because they always spoke the truth; no minister should be styled "reverend" because all should be equally reverent. It was a high calling, and folks upon the frontier found it difficult to attain. A careful perusal of the official minutes is evidence that not all Quakers were saints — but they were far above the average in morals and manners.

A word of caution. It is not denied that thousands of worshippers do experience spiritual uplifts at Baptisms and the Holy Communion. Friends claim that "Christ is the Bread of Life," but if that be not a real experience and they miss the comfort of the Sacraments could it be that Friends are worse off than those who partake of the symbols. It is only as we actually experience the Baptism of the Holy Spirit and the sustaining Presence of the Bread of Life that the Quaker non-observance is tenable.

THE FUTURE OF THE SOCIETY OF FRIENDS. In consideration of the very marked departure of the Orthodox (Five Years Meeting Group) from much of traditional Quakerism it may well be asked whether there is any justification for its continuance as a separate body. It must freely be admitted that the morning service has in many places become almost indistinguishable from that of other denominations. The writer believes the Society will be preserved to the degree that our pastors and leaders are aware of the real implications of the Quaker manner of life and worship. The Society cannot survive permanently if our preachers strive to be like other ministers and copy other church programs. If our pastors do not know the essentials of Quakerism then they cannot inform the congregations. Friends do have a distinct message. In the opinion of this writer the outstanding feature of Quakerism is our concept of the Kingdom of Heaven or Kingdom of God. There are thousands of preachers who preach the need of forgiveness in order that the believer may go to heaven when he is dead. Quakers emphatically believe in the possibility of a redeemed human society. Christ taught us to pray "Thy Kingdom Come . . . Thy Will be done on Earth." He asserted "the Kingdom of Heaven is within you" . . . "is come near unto you" . . . "is in the midst of you."[2] Quakers believe that when an individual rejoices in following the will of God "the Kingdom of Heaven" is experienced.

The next great truth the Society emphasizes is concerning the Holy Spirit. God is Spirit; God is Holy; the Holy Spirit is that of God within that each believer may experience. Friends hold that every person may be consciously guided by the Spirit of God. He need not be told by others what to believe. The individual may be enlightened by the Spirit. "He will lead you into all Truth." . . . "If any man willeth to do his will he shall know of the doctrine." Friends consider that the Holy Spirit is the greatest need of mankind. That is all that is necessary to remedy every wrong; to prevent family disruptions; to adjust all differences in business or between capital and labor; to end corruption in politics; to settle all international disputes. If the parties concerned would meet together in the Spirit of Christ satisfactory and permanent adjustments could soon be found. We have in North Carolina sufficient materials, enough money and all the necessary skills and resources to make this "the State Beautiful." All we lack is enough of the spirit of goodwill which is the essence of the Gospel. Apart from the Holy Spirit faith in an Eternal, Incomprehensible Creator is a mere abstraction; and belief in Jesus of Nazareth is mere history; it is the peculiar office of the Society of Friends to stress that the same Divine Vitality which was manifested in Jesus Christ may be known by any individual as "a River of Life from within."

Friends have a special calling in regard to worship, which the pastoral system must not destroy. Worship has many elements, and no religious service is effective unless the worshipper becomes conscious of the Presence of God, and for himself offers the sacrifice of wonder, adoration and praise for the eternal mystery of Creation, Preservation and Redemption. Meditation, prayer, confession, penitence, adjustment to the Divine Will and dependence upon Divine Guidance are attributes of worship. Attendance at some religious service, and listening to a sermon or a choir are not necessarily worship. Attendance at a religious service is not the essential. There must be conscious fellowship.

Quakers are optimists. They believe that ultimately one can "overcome evil with good." Might does not make right. As Jesus taught the Holy Spirit (or goodwill) can work in human society as yeast permeates dough "till the whole is leavened."[3] Quakers believe that hatred, fear, revenge, suspicion, war and retaliation are foreign to the Spirit of Christ. Therefore the American Friends Service Committee has sponsored relief in warring areas, believing that the only alternative to hate is love, and the only remedy for war is peace. The teaching of Jesus is realistic and is truly the only proper manner of behavior.

Perhaps the attitude of the Quakers towards war has been the most widely known of their views. Friends hold that war is fundamentally opposed to the Spirit of Christ; therefore it can never be justified. In the Civil War Friends took a conspicuous stand.

Since then modern life has become so complex that it is far more difficult for individuals to act contrary to public opinion.

Since the Franco-German War of 1870-71 Friends have rendered non-combatant and reconstruction service as an alternative to fighting. In the first World War the distinguished Quaker, Herbert Hoover, headed up the Belgian Relief Commission, and afterwards served as Food Commissioner under President Wilson, and was also director of the American Relief Administration and of the European Children's Fund following the war.[4] The pressures exerted by the militarists in England during World War I almost destroyed the Adult School movement — a wide-spread movement of Bible classes for men and youths on Sunday morning. Friends in America were not overly conspicuous as Conscientious Objectors in World War II, although a number maintained their convictions. If our leaders do not revive this essential feature of Quakerism in the immediate future there is little chance that there will be any effective peace testimony against war in the dread event of another holocaust. It needs no foresight to perceive that if the present arms rivalry should result in conflict the jingoistic passions which would be unleashed would render it extremely difficult if not impossible for anyone to express convictions contrary to the nationalistic spirit.

Therefore all who occupy positions of leadership must become "convinced" so that they experience the Baptism of the Holy Spirit and know Christ as the Bread of Life and "live in that Spirit which makes wars impossible." Only under such circumstances can Quakerism survive. If another war should overtake humanity political and economic conditions will become such that individualism will almost certainly disappear, and any deviation from authoritative ideology will be regarded as treason. Caesar will become God, and there will be no freedom of choice. Quakers therefore hold the key to the future. We must afresh commit ourselves to the Guidance of the Spirit, and proclaim the paramount importance of following the Truth as revealed in the teaching of the Christ and the Word Within. We are in a unique way the guardians of public and private liberties. That has been our testimony in the past; it is now our heritage and obligation.

In regard to education, a new day has dawned for Friends. We have deliberately put away the false notion of some colonial Quakers that education was unnecessary. Friends in England early established boarding schools corresponding to our academies, but they established no colleges comparable to Haverford, Swarthmore, Earlham or Guilford;* neither have they supported any theological seminaries.** In regard to the ministry they adhered to the inspirational and mystic type, which did not require special education or preparation. As popular education spread in the United States the manner of Quaker preaching changed; it became somewhat expository, more natural in delivery and more evangelical.

As mentioned earlier some understanding of the psychical sciences enables us to appreciate Pietism and Quietism. Mysticism cannot be disregarded — there is too much of it recorded in the history of religion to be gainsaid — but for the writer it seems proper to take into consideration whatever can be learned from history, science, nature and experience as well as the Bible and the leading of the Spirit in forming one's concept (which is ever expanding) of the Eternal Creative Spirit we call Heavenly Father.

The Society of Friends has been foremost among religious groups to regard the promotion of social justice, probity in business, and national righteousness as essentials of Christianity. They have manifested their sympathy with the poor, the afflicted, the mentally defective, prisoners, and slaves. They pioneered in the emancipation of females; in advocating a fixed price and in temperance reform; they promoted humanitarianism by abstaining from cruel sports. They probably did more than any other body to free worshippers from priestcraft and to interpret religion as a quest for the Abundant Life rather than recitals of creeds and participation in ancient ceremonials.

It is not necessary that the Society of Friends should continue to exist as a small group which holds peculiar views; what is important is that the great truths for which the Quakers stand become the guiding principles of all mankind.[5]

---

* Friends were largely responsible for the establishment of Johns Hopkins University and Bryn Mawr College. They also had a part in the founding of Duke University.

** Half a century ago the British Friends realized the need of a broader education for Friends workers. They did not believe one could be educated to become a minister, but they were convinced that those who showed that they had a call to the ministry or some other form of Christian service should have opportunity of special training. George Cadbury gave his estate at Woodbrooke as a training center, and in the course of time quite a group of colleges were established for the training of preachers, home and foreign missionaries, social and Sunday School workers. So distinctive did this service become that several denominations, including high church Episcopalians desired to share it. The writer had the privilege of studying there in 1906-07, when the great and learned Dr. J. Rendel Harris was president. It was a common experience for ten or a dozen nationalities to be represented. The American Friends of both branches have for many years sponsored a similar seminary at Pendle Hill, Pennsylvania.

STATISTICS OF NORTH CAROLINA YEARLY MEETING
(Orthodox)

CONTENTNEA QUARTER
Established 1788

Monthly Meetings	Monthly Meetings Set Up	Mempership of Meeting	Attend Bible School
Bethany	1868	35	
Bethesda	1880	144	86
Goldsboro	1906	317	153
Hoods Swamp		62	50
Nahunta	1772	191	125
Neuse	1785	37	
New Hope	1878	92	83
Oakland	1880	165	
Rhodes	1890	56	55
Woodland	1870	56	70
		1,155	624

DEEP RIVER QUARTER
Established 1818

Monthly Meetings	Monthly Meetings Set Up	Mempership of Meeting	Attend Bible School
Archdale	1924	393	173
Deep River	1753	285	113
Hickory Creek		32	
High Point	1884	824	291
Oakhill	1908	246	118
Springfield	1773	496	229
		2,276	924

EASTERN QUARTER
Established 1680

Monthly Meetings	Monthly Meetings Set Up	Mempership of Meeting	Attend Bible School
Piney Woods	1794	211	79
Up River	1867	300	148
Rich Square (dissolved)		15	
		526	227

NEW GARDEN QUARTER
Established 1787

Monthly Meetings	Monthly Meetings Set Up	Mempership of Meeting	Attend Bible School
Chapel Hill	1937	32	
Glenwood	1930	203	201
Greensboro	1891	546	125
Kernersville	1907	110	129
New Garden	1751	511	161
Raleigh	1925	26	50
Spring Gardens	1909	359	128
Winston-Salem	1912	436	212
		2,223	1,006

SOUTHERN QUARTER
Established 1819

Monthly Meetings	Monthly Meetings Set Up	Mempership of Meeting	Attend Bible School
Asheboro	1915	368	251
Back Creek	1785	77	42
Bethel	1821	123	69
Cedar Square	1873	70	82
High Falls	?1902	32	27
Holly Spring	?1769	113	78
Hopewell	1885	69	57
Marlboro	1797	217	106
Poplar Ridge	1857	150	145
Prosperity	1880	53	40
Randleman	1945	57	103
Science Hill	1894	128	84
South Plainfield	1886	122	94
		1,579	1,178

SURRY QUARTER
Established 1898

Monthly Meetings	Monthly Meetings Set Up	Mempership of Meeting	Attend Bible School
Ararat		83	35
Center Valley	1905	37	
Friends Union	1904	110	65
Galax	1927	75	45
Mount Airy	1896	387	121
Mountain View	1906	42	
Pilot Mountain		77	48
Pine Hill	1899	295	
Revistown		43	
Union Hill	1771	138	
West Field	1780	176	55
White Plains	1886	434	107
		1,889	476

WESTERN QUARTER
Established 1759

Monthly Meetings	Monthly Meetings Set Up	Mempership of Meeting	Attend Bible School
Cane Creek	1751	356	150
Center	1757	364	130
Chatham	1824	86	57
Concord	?1880	93	74
Edward Hill		96	47
Graham		272	145
Liberty	1943	107	64
Plainfield		132	72
Providence	1792	155	46
Rocky River	1754	231	97
South Fork	1818	273	149
Spring	1773	56	34
		2,221	1,065

YADKIN VALLEY QUARTER
Established 1889

Monthly Meetings	Monthly Meetings Set Up	Mempership of Meeting	Attend Bible School
Brannon	1910	140	
Deep Creek	1793	212	128
East Bend	1882	98	80
Forbush	1845	389	195
Harmony Grove	1894	233	147
Hunting Creek	1801	75	
Mount Carmel		72	60
Pilot View	?1909	226	118
Union Cross	?	310	122
Winthrop*	1908	222	
		1,977	850

* Many sources have been consulted concerning these dates; and differences exist and some dates are uncertain.

SUMMARY OF STATISTICS OF NORTH CAROLINA YEARLY MEETING
(Orthodox)

	Members	Sunday School Attenders
CONTENTNEA QUARTER	1,155	624
DEEP RIVER QUARTER	2,276	924
EASTERN QUARTER	526	227
NEW GARDEN QUARTER	2,223	1,006
SOUTHERN QUARTER	1,579	1,178
SURRY QUARTER	1,889	476
WESTERN QUARTER	2,221	1,065
YADKIN VALLEY QUARTER	1,977	850
	13,846	6,350

STATISTICS OF NORTH CAROLINA YEARLY MEETING
(Conservative)

Quarterly Meetings, 2; Southern Quarter and Eastern Quarter.
Monthly Meetings, 6; 3 in each quarter.
Particular Meetings, 6.
Total membership is 200; with 40 attending the Bible School.
Later addition — Durham Meeting.

At the close of the XVIIth century there was one Quarterly Meeting consisting of two Monthly Meetings; at the close of the XVIIIth there were five Quarterly Meetings; and at the end of the XIXth century it had transferred a large Quarterly Meeting to Wilmington, and had lost a few score by separation in the Eastern Quarter. By 1908 there were 8 Quarterly Meetings; 22 Monthly Meetings and 68 recorded ministers, with 6,728 members.[6] By the middle of the XXth century there were eight Quarterly Meetings; seventy-three Monthly Meetings; seventy acting pastors and in addition fifty recorded ministers. The membership totalled 13,846 according to the Yearly Meeting minutes of 1954. It is frequently asserted that the North Carolina Yearly Meeting has a larger percentage of young people and a higher birthrate than any other Yearly Meeting.

BIBLIOGRAPHY

SOURCE MATERIAL

I. OFFICIAL RECORDS — mostly manuscript

1. NORTH CAROLINA YEARLY MEETING RECORDS.
   Yearly Meeting Minutes, 1708-93; 1794-1837; 1835-46; 1846-present. Minutes of
      1805-12 have been lost; those since 1845 have been printed.
   Minutes of the Meeting for Sufferings, 1757-1803; 1820-25; 1824-56
   Minutes of Standing Committee, 1757-1814; 1817-23
   Quarterly Meeting Minutes:
      Contentnea (Great Contentnay) 1793-1823; 1823-30; 1838-40; Women, 1851-75
      Deep River, 1819-70; 1870-present; Women 1819-89
      Eastern Quarter (variously labelled) date from 1680; Perquimans 1708-1866;
         1867-present; also Wells and Piney Woods
      New Garden, 1788-1830; 1830-88; 1839-present
      Perquimans (Eastern) 1708-1866; 1867-present
      Southern, 1819-present
      Surry, 1804-present
      Western, 1759-1866; 1867-present
      Westfield, 1803-32; Women, 1804-32
      Yadkin, 1793-present
   Monthly Meeting Minutes:
      Cane Creek, 1751-97; 1797-1837; 1838-present
      Contentnea (Falling Creek 1772); 1774-1817; 1790-95; 1814-43; Women, 1817-33
      Core Sound, 1733-91; 1791-1840; Women, 1774-1810; 1784-1804
      Deep River, 1778-1808; 1808-37; 1837-71; 1871-present; Women 1778-1843;
         1843-92
      Dover, Women, 1815-77
      Hopewell, 1824-49; Women, 1824-48
      Jack Swamp, 1794-1812
      Mount Pleasant, Women, 1802-25
      New Garden, 1754-75; 1775-82; 1783-1800; 1801-20; 1820-31; 1831-46; 1847-
         70; 1870-present; Women, 1790-1823; 1823-67
      Pasquotank, Women, 1715-68; 1768-1841
      Perquimans, 1681-1764 included Register of Marriages and Births — continued
         under Wells
      Piney Woods, 1794-1802; 1802-30; 1830-present
      Rich Square, 1760-99; 1799-1830; 1832-1873
      Spring, 1831-39
      Springfield, 1791-1820; 1820-59; 1860-85; 1865-present; Women, 1790-1850;
         1850-1886
      Sutton's Creek, 1794-1807; 1807-1835; Women, 1794-1835 (continued as Piney
         Woods)
      Symonds Creek, 1803-1837; 1837-1854; Women, 1768-1841; 1841-1853
         (continued as Piney Woods)
      Wells, 1764-1794 (grew out of Perquimans Meeting) was divided in 1794; a
         new meeting being set up at Simon's Creek and the former meeting continued
         at Piney Woods)
      Westfield, 1787-1823
      Many Meeting Records have been lost through war and fire.

2. RECORDS OF THE BALTIMORE ASSOCIATION.

The President's Letter Books (two).
The Secretary's Book.
The Treasurer's Book.
Superintendent's Annual Reports.
Minutes of the Baltimore Yearly Meeting; 1865-1891
Minutes of the North Carolina Yearly Meeting, 1865-1891
Minutes of the Board of Trustees of Guilford College, 1886
Earlham College *Bulletin,* Joseph Moore Memorial, August 1, 1905, Richmond, Indiana
Springfield Memorial Association *Records* — Emma Blair, Secretary
Souvenir of the Friends Boarding School Fiftieth Anniversary (Earlham College), 1897

3. OFFICIAL PUBLICATIONS:

Ashley, S.S.: *Reports of the State Superintendent of Education of North Carolina,* 1869
American Friend, Philadelphia, 1894-1912; Richmond, Indiana, 1913-present
Calendar of Yearly Meetings, London, 1956
Faith and Practice (Book of Discipline), 1956 ed.
Friends' Intelligencer, Philadelphia, 1844-1955, then combined with *The Friend,* Philadelphia, 1827-1955, with the *Friends Journal,* the first issue of which appeared July, 1955
Friends Review, Philadelphia, 1847-1894. An indispensable source many articles by Elijah Coffin concerning N.C.
Guilford College — very great number of *Bulletins* and *Reports*
Guilford College Bulletin, Alumni Directory, (various issues)
Handbooks of the Religious Society of Friends, ed 1935 and 1952, Philadelphia.
Minutes of North Carolina Manumission Society, 1815-1835, MSS
North Carolina Colonial and State Records, 26 vols. plus 4 vol. index, Raleigh
Society of Friends in North Carolina — Some Important Dates and Events, Guilford College, 1953
Trends in American and Canadian Quakerism, 1925-1950

4. NEWSPAPERS AND PERIODICALS:

Baltimore American, 8/26/1883; Friend, (Philadelphia) vol. xxxviii, 263, 345, 393; xxxix, 284; xcvii, nos. 7, 8, 9, 10, 12, 14, 16, 18
Friends Messenger, vols. xxix, nos. 11 and 12; 343
Guilfordian, 2/27/1918
Greensboro Patriot and Times, 11/26/1868; 2/25/1869
New North State, Greensboro, 4/30/1873; 5/14/1873

II. SECONDARY SOURCES

1. TYPESCRIPT:

Anscombe, Francis C.: *Contributions of the Quakers to the Reconstruction of the Southern States,* Univ. N.C., 1926
Binford, Helen: *Deep River Meeting*
Briggs, Alpheus: *History of North Carolina Yearly Meeting*
Collins, John: MSS *Among the Friends in North Carolina,* 3 vols., water color illustrations, 1869
Dix, B.E.: *Westfield Origins*
Frazier, Robert H.: Many papers in his possession
Haworth, Sara R.: *Springfield*
Springfield Memorial Association: numerous *Memoirs*
Wilson, W.M.: *Archdale*

III. GENERAL WORKS

1. RELIGIOUS:

Bell, J. Pinckney: *Our Quaker Friends of Ye Olden Times,* Lynchburg, Va., 1905
Besse, Joseph: *The Sufferings of the People Called Quakers* from 1650 to 1689, 2 vols., London, 1753
Bowden, J.S.: *History of the Society of Friends* in America, 2 vols., London, 1850, 1854
Braithwaite, W.C.: *Beginnings of Quakerism,* London, 1912
Brinton, Howard: *Friends For Three Hundred Years,* N.Y., 1952
Carroll, Kenneth L.: The Nicholites Become Quakers: an Example of Unity in Disunion, an article in *Bulletin of Friends' Historical Association,* Spring number, 1958
Cartland, Fernando: *Southern Heroes,* Cambridge, 1895
Cleveland, C.C.: *The Great Revival in the West,* 1797-1805; 1916
Coffin, Addison:
   Life and Travels, Cleveland, 1897
   "Emigration from North Carolina", *Guilford Collegian,* vol. iv, 1891-1892
   "Pioneer Days in Guilford County", *ibid, vol.* iii, 1890-91
Coffin, Elijah: Friends in North America — many articles in *Friends' Review,* vol. x, 1890-91
Coffin, Levi: *Reminiscences,* Cincinnati, 1880
Comfort, W.W.: *Quaker Way of Life,* Philadelphia, 1945
Cox, James: *Yearly Meetings in America,* a very comprehensive chart showing the various Separations and Affiliations, based on 1950 statistics.
Drake, T.E.: *Quakers and Slavery in America,* Yale, 1950
Edmundson, William: *Journal,* Dublin, 1715 and London, 1774
Emmott, E. Braithwaite: *Short History of Quakerism,* New York, 1923
Fosdick, H. Emerson (editor): *Rufus Jones Speaks to Our Time,* New York, 1951
Fox, George: *Journal* (undated old copy)
Grellet, Stephen, *Journal*
Grubb, Edward: *Separations, Their Causes and Effects,* London, 1914
Guest, William: *Stephen Grellet,* London, 1853
Harvey, Edmund: *The Rise of the Quakers,* London, 1905
Hobbs, Lewis Lyndon:
   "Francis T. King and Guilford College", *American Friend,* vol. xix, 1912
   "Jeremiah S. Cox" in *Guilfordian,* vol. xii, 1926
Hobbs, Mary M.:
   "Baltimore Association" in *The Friend,* vol. xcvii, 1923
   "Nereus Mendenhall", in *Guilford Collegian,* vol. vi, Nov.-Dec., 1893
   "Conditions in Carolina at the Close of the War" — in *Autobiography of Allen Jay*
   "Elihu Mendenhall", *Collegian,* vol. xix, 1906-7
   "Francis T. King", *Collegian,* vol. xx, 1907-8
   "Julia S. White, an Appreciation", *The Friend,* vol. cxix, 1926
Hodgkin, Henry T.: *Friends Beyond the Seas,* London, 1916
Janney, S.M.: *Causes Which Led to the Separation of the Society of Friends,* Philadelphia, 1868
Jay, Allen: *Autobiography,* Philadelphia, 1910
Jay, Edwin, Isaac and William: *Tribute to Allen Jay,* Indiana, 1910
Jones, Rufus M.:
   Quakers in the American Colonies, London, 1910
   Faith and Practice of the Quakers, London, 1911
   George Fox, Seeker and Finder, Philadelphia, 1903
   Service of Love in War Time, New York, 1920
Kavanaugh, John: *The Quaker Approach,* New York, 1953

King, Emma: *Friends and the Education of the Negro in North Carolina* (Records of the Springfield Memorial Association), 1893

Klain, Zora: *Quaker Contribution to Education in N.C.*, Philadelphia, 1924

Lazenby, M.E.: *Herman Husband, a Story of his Life*, Washington, 1940

Lindley, Harlow: Thomas Beals, *The First Friends Minister in Ohio* — from the *Ohio State Archaeological and Historical Quarterly*, vol. no. 1, Jan.-Mar., 1944

Mendenhall, Nereus:
Biographical Sketch of Dougan Clark, in *Collegian*, vol. 1, 1888-9
Francis T. King, *Collegian*, vol. iv, 1891-2
History of New Garden Boarding School, *Collegian*, vol. ii, 1889-90

Mode, P.G.: *The Frontier Spirit in Christianity*, 1923

Moore, Joseph:
"Building the College", *Collegian*, vol. i, 1888-9
"Education in North Carolina", *Friends Review*, vol. xxxvii, 1884

Mott, Edward: *The Friends Church in the Light of its Recent History*, Portland, Oregon, 1935

Nicholson, Timothy, Testimony in Honor of, Richmond, Indiana, 1908

Peele, Joseph H.: "Quakers of North Carolina", *Friends Messenger*, vol. xxxviii, no. 9, 1929

Pickett, Clarence: *For More Than Bread*, Boston, 1953

Pumphrey, Stanley: *Memoirs*, New York, 1895

Quaker Biographies, 10 vols., Philadelphia, 1909

Raper, C. Lee: *Church and Private Schools in North Carolina*, Greensboro, 1898

Russell, Elbert:
History of Quakerism, New York, 1942
Friends at Mid-Century, Richmond, 1950
Elbert Russell, Quaker — An Autobiography, Jackson, Tennessee
The Separations After a Century, reprints from the *Friends Intelligencer*, 1928

Sewell, William: *History of the Rise, Increase and Progress of the Christian People Called Quakers*, 2 vols., London, 1725

Sherrill, Paul McLoud: *The Quakers and the North Carolina Manumission Society*, Trinity College Hist. Soc. series x, p 32ff

Shillitoe, Thomas: *Journal*, London, 1839, 2 vols.

Slavery and the Slave Trade, Rise and Progress of the Testimony of the Religious Society of Friends against Slavery and the Slave Trade, Philadelphia, 1843

Sweet, W.W.:
The Story of Religion in America, New York, 1939
The American Churches, an Interpretation, New York, 1948
Religion in Colonial America, New York, 1951

Thomas, Allen C. and Richard H.: *History of Friends in America*, Philadelphia, 1930

Thorne, D.G.:
Guilford, a Quaker College, Guilford College, 1937
First Friends at New Garden — reprint from *Bulletin of the Friends' Historical Association*, Autumn, 1945
Planting of Quakerism in Piedmont Carolina — *Guilford College Bulletin*, Jan. 1950
Significance of Nov. 12th in Guilford's History — in *Guilford College Alumni Journal*, Jan. 1949
Quaker Migration to the Western Waters — reprint from *East Tennessee Historical Society Papers*, Nov. 1946
Early Settlements of Friends in North Carolina — typed for *North Carolina Friends Historical Society*, 1952

Tomlinson, C.F.: North Carolina Manumission Society, in *U.N.C. Magazine*, vol. xiv, 1894-5

Trueblood, Elton and Pauline: *Recovery of Family Life*, Harper, 1953

Trueblood, D. Elton: *The Career of Elias Hicks* (in *Byways* of Quaker History),
Pendle Hill, 1944
Vining, Elizabeth Gray: *Women in the Society of Friends,* being the Ward Lecture
at Guilford College, 1955
Warner, Stafford Allen: *Yardley Warner, the Freedman's Friend,* being a
Biography of his father. Wessex Press, Didcot, Berkshire, England, 1957
Weeks, Stephen B.:
The Religious Development in the Province of North Carolina, *J.H.U. Studies,*
vol. x., 1892
Church and State in North Carolina, *J.H.U. Studies,* series xi, nos. 5 and 6
Southern Quakers and Slavery, *J.H.U. Studies,* extra volume, xv, 1896
White, Julia: History of the North Carolina Yearly Meeting in *Bulletin of the
Friends Historical Society of Philadelphia,* vol. iii, 1909
Woodman, Charles M.: *Quakers Find a Way,* Indianapolis, 1950
Woodward, Walter: *Timothy Nicholson, Master Quaker,* Richmond, Indiana, 1927
Woody, John W.: *Memoir,* in Friends Messenger, vol. xxvii, 1920
Woolman, John: *Journal,* undated copy, Philadelphia
Wright, Luella M.: *Literary Life of the Early Friends, 1650 to 1725,* New York,
1952

2. HISTORICAL:

Adams, J.T.: *Provincial Society,* 1690-1763, New York, 1927
Andrews, C.M.: *The Colonial Period of American History,* 4 vols., Yale, 1934-8
Ashe, S. A'Court:
Biographical History of North Carolina from Colonial Times to the Present,
Greensboro, 1905
History of North Carolina, Greensboro, 1905
Bassett, J.S.:
Constitutional Beginnings of North Carolina, J.H.U. series xii, no. 3, Baltimore
Anti-Slavery Leaders of North Carolina, Baltimore, J.H.U. series, 1898
"The Regulators in North Carolina," (*Amer. Hist. Ass'n Report,* 1894)
Slavery and Servitude in the Colony of North Carolina, J.H.U. series xiv,
nos. 4 and 5, Baltimore
The Federal System, New York, 1907
Land Holding in Colonial North Carolina, (Trinity Coll. Hist. Soc. series ii,
Durham, N.C. 1898)
Slavery in the State of North Carolina, J.H.U. Press, 1899
North Carolina Methodism and Slavery (Trinity Coll. Hist. soc. series iv,
pp 1-11)
Bowers, C.G.: *The Tragic Era,* Cambridge, 1929
Boyd, W.K.:
History of North Carolina — the Federal Period, Chicago, 1919
North Carolina on the Eve of Secession, (Amer. Hist. Ass'n. Report, 1910,
published D.C., 1912)
Bridenbough, *Cities in the Wilderness,* 1625-1742, New York, 1938
Bruce, P.A.: *The Plantation Negro as a Freedman*
Caruthers, Rev. Eli, W.: *Life of Dr. Caldwell,* Greensboro, 1842, (lacking
contents table, chapters, index)
Connor, R.D.W:
History of North Carolina — Colonial Period, New York, 1919
Rebuilding an Ancient Commonwealth (N.C.), 4 vols. (Amer. Hist. Soc.),
1929. Refers to Quakers, vol. 1, pp 144-9, 121, 168, 174, 390, 450
Studies in the History of North Carolina, Chapel Hill, 1923
Crane, V.W.: *The Southern Frontier, 1670-1732,* (1929)
DeMond, P.O.: *Loyalists in North Carolina During the Revolution*

Draper, J.W.: *Intellectual Development of Europe*, New York, 1868
Dunning, W.A.:
  Essays on the Civil War and Reconstruction, New York, 1931
  Reconstruction, Political and Economic, New York, 1907
Fitch, W.E.: *The Regulator Insurrection — Some Neglected History of North Carolina*, New York, 1914
Fleming, W.L.:
  Sequel of Appomattox, Yale, 1919
  The South in the Building of the Nation, Richmond. Va., (Southern Hist. Soc.) 1909-13
Green, J.R.: *History of the English People*. London, 1878
Hamilton, J.G. DeR.:
  Reconstruction in North Carolina, Columbia, 1914
  History of North Carolina, New York, 1919
Hawk, E.Q.: *Economic History of the South*. New York. 1934
Hawks, F.L.: *History of North Carolina*. New York, 1857
Henderson, Archibald: *Winning of the Old Southwest*, New York. 1930
Hobbs, S.H.: *North Carolina, Political and Economic*, Chapel Hill, 1930
Knight, Edgar: *Public School Education in North Carolina*, Cambridge, 1916
Lefler, H.T. and Newsome, A.R.: *North Carolina*, Chapel Hill, 1954
Oberholtzer, Ellis P.: *American History Since the Civil War*, New York, 1917
Oliver, David: *The Society for the Propagation of the Gospel in the Province of North Carolina*, (N.C. Hist. Soc.) Raleigh, 1910
Phillips, U.B.:
  Life and Labor in the Old South, New York, 1929
  American Negro Slavery, New York, 1918
  The Course of the South to Secession, New York, 1939
Pike, J.S.: *The Prostrate State* (South Carolina), New York, 1935
Randall, J.G.: *The Civil War and Reconstruction*, New York, 1937
Raper, C. Lee: *Church and Private Schools in North Carolina*, Greensboro, N.C., 1898
Turner, F. J.: *The Frontier in American History*, New York, 1929

FOOTNOTE REFERENCES

The Numbers Refer to the Superior Figures in the Text

CHAPTER ONE

ON THIS ROCK I WILL BUILD MY CHURCH

1. Fox, Geo.: *Journal* (old copy undated), pp 67ff
2. I Cor. x 4
3. Russell, Elbert: *History of Quakerism,* pp 25ff
4. Jeremiah xxxi, 31
5. Lewis, Georgiana King: *George Fox* (in series), Friends Ancient and Modern

CHAPTER TWO

GREET THE FRIENDS BY NAME

1. Genesis i, 2
2. John vi, 63
3. John iv, 24
4. John iii, 5-6
5. Acts ii, 17ff
6. Luke xi, 11ff
7. Psalm xxxiii, 6
8. Romans x, 6
9. John i, 14
10. Rev. xix, 13
11. Matt. xxi, 14; xxii, 29; xxvi, 54; Luke xxiv, 27, 32, 45
12. 2 Peter i, 21
13. John vi, 52-59
14. Matt. xxvi, 1ff; Luke xxii, 19
15. 1 Peter i, 19
16. Isa. liii, 6
17. Rev. i, 6
18. Eph. iii, 6

CHAPTER THREE

LET ALL THINGS BE DONE DECENTLY AND IN ORDER

1. *Minutes of the Five Years Meeting of Friends,* 1915, pp 1-15
2. Russell, *op. cit.* p 215
3. Connor, R.D.W.: *History of North Carolina,* vol. i, pp 199-200
4. John i, 9
5. Russell, *op. cit.* pp 411-412
6. Weeks, Stephen B.: *Southern Quakers and Slavery,* 1896, *in toto*

CHAPTER FOUR

GREAT MULTITUDES FOLLOWED HIM

1. Connor, *op. cit.* chap. vi, pp 80-85

2. Connor, *ibid;* Bridenbaugh, C.: *Cities in the Wilderness,* p 105; Johnson, C.A.: *The Frontier Camp Meeting*

3. Edmundson, W.: *Journal,* pp 97-98

4. Ibid, pp 58ff; 97ff; Jones, Rufus M.: *Quakers in the American Colonies,* bk. iii, chap. 1; Weeks, S.: *Religious Development in the Province of North Carolina* (Johns Hopkins University studies), 1892; *Bulletin,* Friends Historical Society, vol. 3, no. 1, 1909

5. North Carolina *Colonial Records,* vol. 1, p 571; 708ff; Fox, G.: *Journal,* 458ff

6. Fox, *Journal,* p 458

7. *Colonial Records of North Carolina,* 1, pp 571, 708ff

8. Connor, *op. cit.* chap. vi

9. Jones, *op. cit.* p 288 (refers particularly to Maryland, but generally characteristic); Bowden, S.: *Journal,* i, p 356 (quoted by Jones)

10. Weeks, S.B.: *Religious Development in the Province of North Carolina,* (J.H.U. Studies, 1892.)

11. Bancroft, Geo.: *History of the United States,* quoted by White, Julia in *Bulletin,* Friends' Historical Society, vol. 3, no. 1, 1909

CHAPTER FIVE

AN ENEMY HATH DONE THIS

1. Connor, R.D.W.: *History of North Carolina,* pp 86ff

2. Weeks, S.B.: *Religious Development in the Province of North Carolina* (Johns Hopkins Series x, nos. v-vi, pp 246-303)

3. Connor, *op. cit.* p 87

4. Jones, Rufus M.: *Quakers in the American Colonies,* bk. iii, chap. 1; Russell, Elbert: *History of Quakerism,* chap. 10; Connor, *op. cit.* chap. vi

5. Connor, *op. cit.* pp 85ff

6. *Ibid,* p 88

7. Comfort, W.W.: *The Quaker Way of Life,* p 14

8. Connor, *op. cit.:* pp 118-120; Weeks, S.B.: *Church and State in North Carolina,* (J.H.U. series xi) chaps. v-vi, esp. p 224

9. Weeks, *op. cit.* (J.H.U. series xi, pp 224ff); *Ibid,* series xi, chaps. v-vi; Connor, *op. cit.* chaps. vi, vii, viii

10. Weeks, *Ibid*

11. Fosdick, H.E. (editor): *Rufus Jones Speaks to Our Time,* p ix Introduction

12. Thomas, Allen and others: *A History of Friends in America* quoted by Russell, E.: *History of Quakerism,* p 216

13. *Queries* of London Yearly Meeting, about 1890

14. Russell, E.: quotes Bownas, Samuel: p 194; footnote

15. A saying of John T. Dorland, a Canadian minister at the turn of the century

16. Woodman, Charles: *Quakers Find a Way,* p 89

17. Fosdick, H.E. (editor): *Rufus Jones Speaks to Our Time,* p 190

CHAPTER SIX

WHITHER THE TRIBES WENT UP

1. Crevecoeur, J. Hector St. John: *Letters From an American Farmer,* quoted by Thorne, D.G.: *Guilford, a Quaker College,* p 21

2. Thorne, D.G.: *Planting of Quakerism in Piedmont Carolina,* in toto in Guilford College Alumni *Bulletin,* Jan. 1950; Thorne: *First Friends at New Garden* (reprint of *Bulletin* of Friends Historical Association, 1945)

3. Weeks, S.B.: *Southern Quakers and Slavery,* pp 105ff

4. *Ibid;* Frazier, R.H.: *Nantucket and North Carolina* in Guilford College *Bulletin,* Oct. 1949

5. Thorne: *Planting of Quakerism, in toto*

CHAPTER SEVEN

THE TRIBES OF THE LORD

1. Russell, E.: *History of Quakerism,* p 77

2. *Ibid:* p 131

3. *Ibid:* pp 138-139

4. Information from many sources, especially paper by Alpheus Briggs

5. *Handbook of the Religious Society of Friends,* 1952; *Trends in American and Canadian Quakerism,* 1925-1950; *Friends Directory,* 1957-1958

6. Warner, Stafford Allen: *Yardley Warner, the Freedman's Friend,* p 100

7. Russell, Elbert: *Autobiography,* pp 44-45

8. Hunt, David: *Reminiscences of Nathan Hunt,* quoted by Thorne in *First Friends at New Garden*

9. *Friends Review:* vol. xiv; pp 420, 453, 470, 484, 500, 517, 531, 554, 565, 580, 613; Thorne, D. G.: *Guilford, a Quaker College,* pp 116-118, 143-144; Collins confirms this in his *Among the Friends in North Carolina,* by drawing and description

10. Information supplied by Seth Hinshaw, the Exec. Sec. of N.C.Y.M.

11. *Minutes* of North Carolina Yearly Meeting, 1956

CHAPTER EIGHT

THE LORD WILL BE GRACIOUS UNTO THE REMNANT

1. Lefler and Newsome: *North Carolina,* pp 395ff

2. *Ibid,* p 397

3. *Ibid,* pp 304ff

4. Russell, Elbert: *The History of Quakerism,* pp 53-54, 331, 345-357; Woodman, Charles: *Quakers Find a Way,* chap. xi

5. Lefler and Newsome, *op. cit.* p 304 and chap. xx

6. Woodman, *op. cit.* p 88

7. Grubb, Edward: *Separations, Their Causes and Effects:* Russell, E.: *The Separations After a Century;* Russell, E.: *History of Quakerism,* chaps. xxiii-xxvi

8. Jay, Allen: *Autobiography,* chap. xiv

9. *Handbook of the Religious Society of Friends,* 1952; *Trends in American and Canadian Quakerism 1925-1950*

10. Coffin, Charles F.: *Quaker Pioneers,* pp 115ff

11. Jones, L.T.: *Quakers of Iowa,* pp 164ff
12. Russell: *Quakerism,* chap. xxxi
13. Information culled from a scrapbook in the possession of Mrs. Nellie M. Taylor, a daughter of Mary Moon, who is well known for her devotion to church work and social improvements. In her book are clippings relating to Mary Moon's revivals in North Carolina from the *Danville Times,* Nov. 14, 1879; the *Tobacco Plant,* Feb. 8, 1879; *Reidsville Star,* Dec. 11, 1879; *Goldsboro Messenger,* Apr. 7, 1879; *Raleigh Christian Advocate,* July 23, 1879; *Marlboro Planter,* S.C., Feb. 27, 1880; *Southern Christian Advocate,* Mar. 6, 1880; *Western Sentinel,* Nov. 28, 1878; also from an obituary read by a nephew.
14. Jay, Allen: *Autobiography,* chap. xxii, pp 213ff

CHAPTER NINE

SITTING AMONG THE TEACHERS

1. Coffin, Addison: MSS *Friends and the Yearly Meeting* (at the Archives); Thorne, D.G.: *Guilford, a Quaker College,* p 24
2. Knight, E.W.: *Public School Education in North Carolina,* pp 32ff
3. N.C. *Colonial Records,* I, p 721; N.C. *Booklet,* IX, p 183
4. N.C. *Colonial Records,* I, pp 708-715
5. Grellet, Stephen: *Memoirs,* p 57
6. Klain, Zora: *Quaker Education in North Carolina,* pp 199, 289-292, 315. (A very valuable study)
7. N.C.Y.M. *Minutes,* 1911
8. Marlborough Monthly Meeting *Minutes,* 1834, 1835
9. Westfield Quarterly Meeting *Minutes,* 20/XI/1831
10. The writer acknowledges his obligations to Zora Klain for many particulars of the Monthly Meetings.
11. Thorne, D.G.: *op. cit.* chaps. iii & iv
12. *Ibid,* pp 11-15, 21ff; various papers at the archives
13. Craven, Bruce: The Early History of Trinity (College) in *Greensboro Daily News,* Nov. 24, 1927; *Winston-Salem Journal,* May 23, 1955; Thorne, *op. cit.* pp 54-58
14. Thorne, D.G.: *op. cit.* pp 63ff
15. Hobbs, Mary Mendenhall: Historical Society of Pennsylvania *Bulletin,* vol. I, no. 3, 1907; *Quaker Biographies,* series 2, vol. 1; Thorne, *op. cit.* numerous references; many other papers concerning Nathan Hunt in the Archives.
16. Cox, Isham: *Autobiography* (typed) in Archives; 44pp
17. Thorne, D.G.: *op cit.:* pp 99ff. Much material in the Archives
18. Springfield Memorial Association *Memorabilia* concerning Nereus Mendenhall; also letters and much material in the Archives
19. Information concerning Jeremiah Piggott obtained from Robert H. Frazier
20. Information from Margaret Davis Winslow

CHAPTER TEN

YE ARE MY FRIENDS

1. *Baltimore American,* Aug. 6, 1883
2. *Friends Review,* xviii, p 521
3. *Ibid,* vol. xviii, pp 522, 249, 633-635; Scott, Jn.: *Diary in extenso;* Jay, Allen: *Autobiography,* p 178; *The Friend* (London), xxxviii, p 303
4. *Ibid,* vol. xviii, pp 265, 343, 633ff; xix, 202, 488
5. *Ibid,* xix, 375

6. *Ibid*, xxiii, pp 219, 266, 348, 394, 492, 572; xx, 202; xviii, 824

7. Moore, Joseph: *Journal*, 1865-1868; Cadbury, Anna Moore: Article, Joseph Moore in *Quaker Biographies*, series 2, vol. 4

8. Knight, E.W.: *Public School Education in North Carolina*, p 242

9. *Ibid*, pp 244ff

10. *Friends Review*, xxi, pp 613, 201ff

11. Collected by the writer from numerous sources

12. Jones, Rufus M.: *Later Periods of Quakerism*, p 695

13. *Minutes* of Baltimore Yearly Meeting, 1892

14. The writer for his work on *The Contributions of the Quakers to the Reconstruction of the Southern States* made an exhaustive examination of the original records of the Baltimore Association and also of the Friends Freedmen's Association. Only a very small portion is reproduced here.

15. *Minutes* of the Baltimore Association

CHAPTER ELEVEN

PUT THEM IN MIND TO OBEY MAGISTRATES

1. Connor, R.D.W: *History of North Carolina*, vol. I, pp 74ff; Bassett, J.S.: *The Constitutional Beginning of North Carolina* in J.H.U. studies, series xii, no. 3, 1894; Article, "Archdale" in *Harper's Ency. Amer. Hist.*

2. Connor, *op. cit.* chap. vi

3. North Carolina *Colonial Records*, vol. 1, pp 250-253

4. Connor, *op. cit.* pp 90ff

5. North Carolina Yearly Meeting *Minutes*, 1711 and 1712; Weeks, S.B.: *Southern Quakers and Slavery*, p 166

6. Weeks, *op. cit.* pp 174ff

7. Bassett, J.S.: The Regulators of North Carolina in *Annual Report of the American Historical Association*, 1894; Caruthers, Rev. Eli W.: *Life of Dr. David Caldwell*, pp 100ff; Lefler and Newsome: *North Carolina*, pp 174ff; Weeks, S.B.: *Southern Quakers and Slavery*, pp 170-183; Lazenby, M.E.: *Herman Husband — Story of His Life;* Cane Creek Monthly Meeting *Minutes*, 12/8/1775, 1/7/1784

8. Brinton, Howard (editor); *Children of Light*, chap. x by Charles Francis Jenkins

9. N.C.Y.M. *Minutes*, 1772, pp 117ff

10. *Ibid*, 1776, pp 147ff

11. N.C. *Colonial Records*, vol. x, pp 476ff; Mar. 5, 1776

12. N.C.Y.M. *Minutes*, 1777, pp 156-159

13. Weeks, S.B.: *op. cit.* p 184

14. Caruthers, Rev. Eli.: *Life of Dr. David Caldwell*, p 239

15. Cartland, Fernando: *Southern Heroes, in toto*

16. Weeks, *op. cit.* p 190; Lefler and Newsome: *op. cit.* chap. xvi

17. *Ibid*

18. Weeks, *op. cit.* p 133; N.C.Y.M. *Minutes*, 1848, 1849, 1872, 1878

CHAPTER TWELVE

LET MY PEOPLE GO

1. *A Brief Statement of the Rise and Progress of the Testimony of Friends Against Slavery and the Slave Trade*, by Philadelphia Yearly Meeting, 1843; *Index of the Archives of Arch Street Meeting House*, prepared by Max L. Reich

2. Lefler and Newsome: *North Carolina*, p 397; Boyd: *North Carolina History*, pp 210ff; Coffin, Levi: *Reminiscences* (in extenso), especially pp 200ff; Wagstaff,

H.M. (editor): *Minutes of the North Carolina Manumission Society, 1816-1834.*
At the Quaker Archives

3. Weeks, S.B.: *op. cit.* pp 201ff
4. Woolman, John: *Journal,* chap. iv
5. Griffith, John: *Journal,* pp 372ff; *Friends Miscellany,* vol. xii, pp 253-256
6. N.C.Y.M. *Minutes,* 1771, p 117
7. *Ibid*
8. *Ibid,* 1771, p 119
9. *Ibid,* 1771, pp 117-118
10. *Ibid,* 1771, p 152
11. *Ibid,* 1780, pp 181ff
12. *Ibid,* 1780, pp 181ff. Extensive and well written *Minutes* largely devoted to the slavery issue
13. *Ibid,* 1786; Weeks, op. cit. p 219
14. *Ibid,* 1780, pp 180-185; 1781, pp 196-197; 1784, p 214; 1786, pp 229ff; 1788, p 253
15. *Ibid,* 1788, p 256
16. Weeks, *op. cit.* p 219
17. N.C.Y.M. *Minutes,* 1796, pp 31ff; also Evans, *Journal;* extracts printed in *Friends Miscellany,* vol. x, pp 144-146
18. Weeks, S.B.: *op. cit.* p 223
19. *Ibid,* pp 222ff
20. *Ibid,* pp 225ff
21. N.C.Y.M. *Minutes,* 1824, pp 219-221
22. *Ibid,* Book 1794-1888; 1797, pp 40-42
23. *Ibid,* 1780, p 181
24. Weeks, *op. cit.* pp 224-225
25. N.C.Y.M. *Minutes* (concerning the Sixth Query) 1851; 1852, p 8; 1853, p 9; 1854, p 9; 1855, p 6; 1858, p 6; 1859, p 5; 1860, p 5; 1861, p 3; 1862, p 4; 1863, p 3; 1864, p 3; 1865, p 6; and 1866, 1867, 1868, 1873 are all identical wording.
26. *Ibid,* 1862, pp 2-4
27. *Ibid,* 1864, p 3
28. *Ibid,* 1874, p 7
29. Lefler and Newsome: *North Carolina; op. cit.* esp. chap. xxvii; Hamilton, J.G. deR.: *Reconstruction in North Carolina* (in extenso)
30. Coffin, Levi: *Reminiscences* (in extenso)
31. Thomas, Allen C. and Thomas, Richard Henry: *A History of Friends in America,* p 115
32. Russell, Elbert: *History of Quakerism,* pp 249ff
33. N.C.Y.M. *Minutes,* 1871, p 25
34. Cartland, Stephen B.: *Southern Heroes,* (in extenso)
35. Records of the *Friends' Freemen's Association,* Philadelphia, — all examined at length by the writer at Arch Street Book Store in 1925; Anscombe, F.C.: *The Contribution of the Quakers to the Reconstruction of the Southern States;* Brawley, B.: *Short History of the American Negro,* chap. x; Fleming, W.L.: *The Sequel of Appomattox,* pp 34ff; *Negro Year Book,* 1816-1819, pp 261ff; Peirce, P.S.: *The Negro Church,* pp 206ff
36. Warner, Stafford Allen: *Yardley Warner, the Freedman's Friend,* Biography by his son. Didcot, Berkshire, England
37. Hood, J.W.: *Report to the State Superintendent of Public Instruction of North Carolina,* 1870, pp 272ff; Francis T. King: *Letter Book,* nos. 361, 368; *Minutes* Indiana Yearly Meeting, 1872; Lefler and Newsome: *op. cit.* chap. xxxiv; Hamilton, *op. cit.* chap. vi

CHAPTER THIRTEEN

GET THEE OUT OF THY COUNTRY

1. Information supplied by Robert H. Frazier
2. Russell, Elbert: *History of Quakerism,* pp 273ff: Lindley, Harlow: Thomas Beals (reprint from *Ohio State Archaeological and Historical Quarterly,* vol. iii, no. 1); Thorne, D.G.: *First Friends at New Garden*
3. Weeks, S.B.: *Southern Quakers and Slavery,* chap. x; quotes Coffin, Addison: *Reminiscences* in Guilford Collegian, vol. iv, 1891-1892
4. Russell, *op. cit.* pp 362, 365ff; Weeks, *op. cit.* pp 236ff, 254
5. Speed: *The Wilderness Road;* Coffin, Levi: *Reminiscences,* p 34ff; Coffin, Addison: *Reminiscences,* supra
6. Weeks, *op. cit.* p 252
7. *Ibid,* pp 257ff
8. Jay, Allen: *Autobiography,* p 161
9. Weeks, *op, cit.* p 271ff
10. *Ibid,* p 269
11. Coffin, Addison: *Life and Travels,* part one
12. Baltimore Association *Report,* 1867
13. *Baltimore American,* August 6, 1883
14. Moore, Lavonne: in *Winston-Salem Journal,* Feb. 12, 1947

CHAPTER FOURTEEN

SEE WHAT BUILDINGS ARE HERE

1. *Guilford College Bulletins* and *Alumni Directory,* various issues; also information from Robert H. Frazier
2. *Ibid*
3. Thorne, Dorothy G.: *Guilford, a Quaker College,* pp 32-33, 42-43, 227-228
4. *Ibid,* pp 145-151
5. *Ibid,* pp 201-204, 227, 267; also personal knowledge
6. *Ibid,* pp 157-160; later College Bulletins; personal knowledge
7. *Ibid,* pp 229-232, 257; also from Robert H. Frazier
8. *Ibid,* pp 200-230, 257; personal knowledge; college *Bulletins*
9. *Ibid,* pp 224-226, 288-290; many recent President's Reports; personal knowledge
10. Doak, Frances: *Mary Mendenhall Hobbs,* lecture at Guilford College on Founders Day, 1955; Thorne, *op. cit.* pp 239ff; numerous articles in the Archives
11. Information from President Clyde A. Milner
12. Guilford College *Bulletins* (many); personal knowledge
13. *Ibid*
14. Guilford College *Bulletins* and information from President Milner
15. Information from Robert H. Frazier

CHAPTER FIFTEEN

A TEACHER COME FROM GOD

1. Memoirs gathered from the abundant material at the Quaker Archives; personal knowledge
2. *American Friend,* vol. xii, p 47; extract from *Memoir* by this writer
3. Personal acquaintance
4. Information from J. Waldo Woody
5. Information from Joseph D. Cox
6. Guilford College *Bulletin — Alumni Directory,* 1937

CHAPTER SIXTEEN

LOOK HOW THY BRETHREN FARE

1. Journal in *Friends' Library,* vol. xii, pp 168-172
2. *Ibid*
3. *Ibid,* pp 370-380
4. *Ibid; Journal of John Griffith* in Archives
5. Wilson, Elmina: *Reminiscences;* typed paper at the Archives
6. Woodman, Charles: *Quakers Find a Way,* p 139
7. Thorne, D.G.: *First Friends at New Garden*
8. Vining, Elizabeth Gray: *Women in the Society of Friends* (Ward Lecture, Guilford College, 1955); Comfort, W.W.: *The Quaker Way of Life,* esp. chap. iii
9. Briggs, Alpheus: *Short History of Beard's Hat Shop,* MSS in Quaker Archives; Binford, Helen: MSS *Deep River,* p 1
10. Contributed by Margaret Davis Winslow

CHAPTER SEVENTEEN

WHAT THOU SEEST WRITE IN A BOOK

1. Hinshaw, W.W.: *Quaker Genealogies,* vol. i, p 6
2. *American Friend,* May 28, 1936
3. New Garden Monthly Meeting *Minutes,* 1754-1755
4. North Carolina Yearly Meeting *Minutes,* 1704, pp 3-4
5. *Ibid,* 1848, 1849, 1851, 1854, 1855, 1863, 1865, 1868, 1872
6. *Ibid,* 1849, 1852, 1879
7. *Ibid,* 1858, 1860, 1867, 1868, 1869, 1870, 1873: especially 1864
8. *Ibid,* 1876
9. *Ibid,* 1861, 1865
10. *Ibid,* 1867
11. *Ibid,* 1864, 1872
12. *Ibid,* 1871, 1876, 1878, 1879, 1883
13. *Ibid,* 1867, 1871, 1891, 1853
14. *Ibid,* 1871, 1874; See also references to Joseph John Gurney
15. *Ibid,* 1863, 1873, 1878
16. *Ibid,* 1880, 1883, 1897
17. *Ibid,* 1831, 1850, 1880
18. Collins, John: *Among the Friends in North Carolina,* MSS and water color illustrations, 3 vols.
19. Bell, James Pinckney: *Our Quaker Friends of Ye Olden Time,* esp. pp 145-146

CHAPTER EIGHTEEN

A CITIZEN OF NO MEAN CITY

1. Hamilton, J.G. de R.: (editor) *Correspondence of Governor Jonathan Worth,* Introduction
2. Blanche Dixon, Elkin, N.C.
3. Supplied by Robert H. Frazier
4. Supplied by Francis Nicholson
5. Supplied by Robert H. Frazier

CHAPTER NINETEEN

THE BODY HATH MANY MEMBERS

1. Information concerning each meeting obtained upon request from each monthly, quarterly and yearly meeting clerks; also from each pastor and especially from the *Minute* Books at the Quaker Archives at Guilford College; also many particulars from a MSS believed to be the work of Alpheus M. Briggs, but the title page is missing and there is no date or signature. The paper gives a long list of meetings which had been discontinued at the time the paper was prepared.

2. Albertson, Catherine: *History of Belvidere; History of Piney Woods Meeting,* loaned to the writer by Edwin White

3. Received from the family of Elizabeth White

4. Woodward, W.C.: *Testimonial in Honor of Timothy Nicholson,* Richmond, Indiana

5. From Mable Ward Wolff and the old record books re-typed by Marshall

CHAPTER TWENTY

YET BEING MANY ARE ONE BODY

1. North Carolina Yearly Meeting *Directory, 1956*

2. Marshall: typed *Minutes* of Great Contenay, Neuse and Woodland Meetings, pp 17-18

3. Cartland, Fernando: *Southern Heroes,* esp. chaps. xx and xxi

4. *Minutes* of Great Contenay, Neuse and Woodland Meetings typed by Marshall, pp 14-15

5. Information received from the clerks, pastors and members of the several meetings; also old *Minute* Books

6. Information supplied by Eunice Massey

CHAPTER TWENTY-ONE

ALL MEMBERS HAVE NOT THE SAME OFFICE

1. Briggs, Alpheus: *Extracts From a History of North Carolina Yearly Meeting* (some in handwriting, some pages typed — a valuable source)

2. *Ibid*

3. See account of Herman Husband in this work, chap. xi; also Lazenby, M.R.: *Herman Husband, Story of His Life;* Deep River Monthly Meeting *Minutes,* 1755, 1784; Lefler and Newsome: *History of North Carolina,* pp 174-177

4. *Memorial for Eula Dixon,* anonymous and undated

5. History of Centre Friends Meeting, 1757-1954, prepared by a Committee headed by Beatrice Hockett, 1954

6. Thorne, Dorothy G.: *Two Hundred Years of Rocky River Friends Meeting,* 1953 — a valuable source

7. Weeks, S.B.: *Southern Quakers and Slavery,* pp 279ff

CHAPTER TWENTY-TWO

WORKERS TOGETHER WITH GOD

1. Information received from the clerks and pastors of the several meetings and from many *Minute* books

2. Back Creek Monthly Meeting *Minute* Books at the Archives, esp. *Women's Meeting Record Book,* no. 1

3. *Poplar Ridge Minute Book,* no. 1, 1906-1939, pp 87-98
4. *Historical Sketch of Southern Quarterly Meeting and its Constituent Monthly Meetings,* prepared by Seth Hinshaw and Allie R. Kemp at the request of the quarterly meeting, 1931; Prosperity and High Falls *Minute* Book, vol. 1, 1921-1938; (very meagre entries 1935-1936)

CHAPTER TWENTY-THREE

AN HABITATION OF GOD THROUGH THE SPIRIT

1. Information supplied by Dudley D. Carroll
2. From Ray Walker and Harold Mesimore
3. From Philip W. Furnas
4. From Robert H. Frazier
5. From Herbert Petty
6. From Dosky Nelson and Myrtle Nelson
7. Thorne, D.G.: *Planting of Quakerism in Piedmont Carolina and First Friends at New Garden;* Reports from Algie I. Newlin; also Jay, Allen: *Autobiography,* pp 154ff
8. Hobbs, L.L.: *Concerning the New Garden Graveyard*
9. From Ellen Rayford Glenn
10. From Mollie Cooper
11. Personal knowledge and *Record Books;* Robert H. Frazier contributed much to this chapter by revision and addition.

CHAPTER TWENTY-FOUR

BRETHREN DWELL TOGETHER IN UNITY

1. Information concerning each meeting obtained upon request from the clerks of each monthly and quarterly meeting; also from the Executive Secretary of the Yearly Meeting; much information from a MSS in the Archives believed to be the work of Alpheus M. Briggs (the first page is missing and no signature appears); much information from numerous monthly meeting books in the vault.
2. Archdale Monthly Meeting *Minute Books* in the Archives; Wilson, Winship McBride: *Archdale,* an illustrated booklet, 1912; Mary M. Petty collaborated; very informing; also several Memoirs read at the Springfield Memorial Association from time to time.
3. Deep River Friends Meeting — Bi-Centennial History prepared in 1954 by a committee; Valuable illustrated pamphlet; Various Memoirs from the Springfield Memorial Association
4. High Point Friends *History* and *Directory,* 1950; *Minute* Books
5. *Memorial* of Alpheus M. Briggs in records of the Permanent Board
6. Memoir of Dr. Frederick Taylor in *High Point Enterprise,* Nov. 2, 1955
7. Information from Cecil Haworth
8. Information from Wade Russell
9. Richardson, Sara; Springfield, 1773-1940; a most valuable illustrated pamphlet of 36 pages; also Memoirs from the *Records of the Memorial Association;* also information from Herbert Petty, Joseph D. Cox, and many old *Minute* Books
10. Information from Joseph D. Cox
11. Information from Marian Hunt Blair; also Blair, John W.: *Chronicles of Randolph County*

CHAPTER TWENTY-FIVE

IN JOURNEYINGS OFT

1. Weeks, S.B.: *Southern Quakers and Slavery,* pp 331ff; Briggs, Alpheus, *History of N.C.Y.M.*
2. Information received from John Benbow, Attorney, Winston-Salem
3. Information from Williard Wooten, clerk
4. From Nora Shore, clerk
5. From Barbara W. Gentry, clerk
6. From C.F. Mullins and Sadie Oritz, clerks
7. From Lucy Carter, clerk
8. From Della W. Hobson and Daisy Williams, clerks
9. From Mary S. Watkins, clerk
10. *Yadkin Ripple,* Sept. 13, 1956
11. Hutchens, Charles H.: *Birth and Boyhood;* much use made of the Yadkin Valley Quarterly Meeting *Minutes,* beautifully written by Lottie M. Marshall, clerk; see *Memorial* to Ellen M. Marshall
12. Information from the family
13. Information from Robert M. Allgood, Winston-Salem

CHAPTER TWENTY-SIX

OUR FATHERS WORSHIPPED IN THIS MOUNTAIN

1. Information from the clerks, pastors and *Minute* Books of the several meetings.
2. Information from Howard Yow
3. Information from Bessie M. Simpson
4. *Winston-Salem Journal and Sentinel,* Aug. 28, 1955
5. From Miriam Levering

CHAPTER TWENTY-SEVEN

OTHER SHEEP I HAVE

1. Carroll, Kenneth L.: *The Nicholites Become Quakers;* an Example of Unity in Disunity in *Bulletin of the Friends Historical Association,* vol. 47, no. 1, 1958
2. See references to Mary Moon in chap. viii
3. Information from David H. Brown, clerk; also *Record Books* esp. Men's Meeting, 1760-1926; four vols. of Women's Meeting, 1760-1928; two vols. of Births and Deaths; two vols. of Marriages — all of Rich Square Meeting; one vol. of the Men's Minutes and one of the Women's Meeting of Jack Swamp Monthly Meeting. These records are in the possession of the Conservative Friends at Woodland, N.C. William Marshall copied and bound five vols. which are at the Quaker Archives at New Garden. The Births and Deaths retyped cover 37 pages; the Marriages, 20 pages; the Genealogies occupy 60 pages. There are numerous entries of Disownment. In 1825 several were disowned for holding slaves. In 1847, Elizabeth Johnson was "put out of meeting for using the plural language and absenting herself from meeting;" others for drinking; in 1849 several "condemned their marriages out of meeting;" such offenders were sometimes re-instated, sometimes not.
4. From Gower Smith, clerk of Durham Meeting
5. Information from Paul T. Osborne, of the Reidsville Meeting; also Mott, Edward: *The Friends Church in the Light of Recent History*
6. *Friends Intelligencer,* June 11, 1955

CHAPTER TWENTY-EIGHT

THE BOOK OF NUMBERS

1. Russell, Elbert: *History of Quakerism*, pp 432ff

2. Matt. vi, 9; Lu. xvii, 21; Lu. xvii, 20; Mk. xii, 34; Matt. v, 10; Matt. xxi, 31

3. Matt. xiii, 33

4. Pickett, Clarence: *For More Than Bread;* Jones, Rufus M.: *Service of Love in War Time*

5. See also Clark, Elmer T.: *The Small Sects in America;* and Wright, L.M.: *The Literary Life of the Early Friends,* esp. chaps. xxviii-xxxi

6. Statistics gathered from numerous sources, especially: *N.C.Y.M. Minutes,* 1955; *Handbook of the Religious Society of Friends,* 1952; *Trends in American and Canadian Quakerism,* 1925-1950; (some disagreements)

INDEX

Date Due